Introduction to the Analysis of the Literary Text

ADVANCES IN SEMIOTICS
General Editor, Thomas A. Sebeok

Cesare Segre

with the collaboration
of Tomaso Kemeny

ès

Introduction to the Analysis of the Literary Text

TRANSLATED BY

John Meddemmen

ès

INDIANA UNIVERSITY PRESS
Bloomington & Indianapolis

Translated from *Avviamento all'analisi del testo letterario,* © 1985
by Giulio Einaudi editore s.p.a., Turin by arrangement
with the publisher.

© 1988 by Indiana University Press
All rights reserved

No part of this book may be reproduced or utilized in any form or by
any means, electronic or mechanical, including photocopying and
recording, or by any information storage and retrieval system, without
permission in writing from the publisher. The Association of American
University Presses' Resolution on Permissions constitutes the only
exception to this prohibition.

Manufactured in the United States of America

Library of Congress Cataloging-in-Publication Data

Segre, Cesare.
Introduction to the analysis of the literary text.

(Advances in semiotics)
Includes indexes.
Translation of: Avviamento all'analisi del testo
letterario.
1. Literature.   I. Title.   II. Series.
PN45.S34613   1987   809   86-34412
ISBN 0-253-33106-4
1 2 3 4 5 91 90 89 88 87

Contents

vii   *Foreword by Thomas A. Sebeok*
xi   *Preface: Introduction to the Analysis of the Literary Text*

Part I: The Analysis of the Literary Text

3   1. Communication
24   2. The Text
80   3. Text Contents
116   4. The Text Historicized

Part II: Themes of Literary Activity

141   Prologue: Experience, Culture, and Text
151   1. Discourse
183   2. Fiction
199   3. Genres
223   4. Narration/Narrativity
236   5. Poetics
258   6. Style
277   7. Theme/Motif
300   8. Text

327   *Subject Index*
331   *Name Index*

Foreword
by Thomas A. Sebeok

The International Association for Semiotic Studies was created at a meeting in Paris on January 21, 1969. The late Emile Beneveniste, of the Collège de France, was elected its first President. The initial organizational headquarters were established in France.

After the First Congress, brilliantly conceived and arranged by Umberto Eco in Milano, held in June 1974, IASS headquarters were removed to Italy, with Cesare Segre, of the University of Pavia, becoming its second President, and Eco, of the University of Bologna, succeeding Julia Kristeva as its second Secretary General. Segre served for two terms, ten years in all. Eco resigned in 1979 to become a Vice President of the IASS. He was then replaced by Gianfranco Bettetini (Milano), who resigned in 1984, to be replaced in turn by Antonino Buttitta (Palermo).

These bureaucratic housekeeping details are noteworthy if only for what they disclose about the extraordinary standing of Italy in the global flowering of the semiotic "landscape" (the precise banner term Eco insisted upon to characterize the goings-on at Milano).

Italy is the country where the European rinascimento of semiotics has its true roots and whence some of its best work continues to resonate worldwide, via some very fine translations. As Bettetini and Francesco Casetti put it, no doubt with undue modesty, in their authoritative survey (1986) of "Semiotics in Italy" (p. 293), the emergence of semiotics on the Italian scene "was fostered by traditional and modern influences from France and the United States and by quite original Italian contributions." Naples, after all, was where the most elaborate and orderly pioneering manual on nonverbal semiosis, or "the mimic art," the Canon Andrea de Iorio's grand edifice of 1832 (forty years antedating Darwin's classic treatise), was conceived and written, to be followed, just a century afterwards, by Giuseppe Cocchiara's radically different, fascinatingly Anglophile *Il linguaggio del gesto* (Torino, 1932). The thirty-one year old Peirce traversed Italy from Sicily to Pisa between July 1870 and February 1871, and it was in Florence, later, where his and William James' ideas—as became evident from their monthly, *Leonardo* (1903–1907), and as I noted in the April 1982 issue of *Alfabeta*—jolted such members of The Florence Pragmatism Club as Amendola, Calderoni, Papini, and Vailati.

In the interwar period, the historical idealism of Benedetto Croce became inimical to the unfolding of modern semiotics in Italy. Although he died in 1952, Croce's influence persisted into the 1960s, but the balance was eventually restored, mainly owing to the impact of structuralism and the rediscovery of the legacies of Charles Morris (about whom the late Ferruccio Rossi-Landi published an important book as early as 1953), and, eventually, of Peirce. Much of this is spelled out by Casetti, in Part II of his joint article, where he singles out the early role played in the semiotic revival by Segre (who was born in 1928): "In his important inquiry based on a questionnaire submitted to scholars of different disciplines," this Italian master "made clear the significance of the new categories proposed for the practice of literary criticism and pinpointed the problems to be dealt with, all while aiming at a thorough absorption of the structuralist approach. This inquiry not only provided a clear picture of the then [1965] current situation, but also strongly stimulated debate" (p. 297). Largely through the authority of Segre, and of such important linguists as Luigi Heilmann (Bologna), structuralism became a rallying cry among many Italian intellectuals in the late sixties, and the success of this widespread movement became in Italy, in Casetti's words, "the best foundation for the emergence of semiotics." The foundations of Segre's work in linguistic theory are echoed at the outset of this very book before the reader, while in the same sentence its borders are also clearly demarcated: "Semiotic criticism cannot be reduced to linguistics, but it is clear that in linguistics its bases are found."

In 1963, Segre published his first major work, *Lingua, stile e società*, followed, in 1965, by his *Strutturalismo e critica*, a collective work which he edited, and which is generally considered the first Italian text devoted to the semiotics of literature.

In 1969, there appeared Segre's detailed, state-of-the-art review, decidedly semiotic in orientation, *I segni e la critica*, with—significantly—the four words *Fra strutturalismo e semiologia* featured on the paperback cover. In his *Semiotica, storia e cultura* (1977; note the shift in terminology), Segre develops the then novel thesis that, if semiotics is capable of capturing, in texts, the mediating element between a society's economic infrastructure and its superstructural levels, it would enable an effective reconstruction of the history of a culture. He returns to this theme again, from a different angle, in *Le Strutture e il tempo* (1974), remarking in the Preface to the English version (1979: ix) that the problems treated "are directly suggested by the semiotic approach of the work . . . ."

Segre's authority is intensified, in Italy and beyond, by his varied editorial activities, especially through the celebrated journal *Strumenti critici* and the series *Critica e filologia*, as well as through critical impressions, which have become standard, of the *Chanson de Roland*, of Ariosto's *Orlando Furioso*, and of works by Richard de Fournival and Bono Giamboni. Like his friend Eco, he frequently contributes to periodicals and newspapers read by the general public. A bibliography, edited by F. Angeli, of approximately 600 of Segre's works is about to be published.

Advances in Semiotics, one of the premier series of the Indiana University

Press, is proud to have published no less than seven books thus far, in which some of Italy's leading contemporary semioticians focus on a surprising variety of topics. The series was, in fact, inaugurated in 1976, with Eco's landmark *A Theory of Semiotics*. Since then, we have brought to an English readership four further books by Eco (1979, 1983, 1984), one by a distinguished former collaborator of Segre's Maria Corti (1978), another by Paolo Valesio (1980), and now this remarkable rendition—more than simply a translation—of a major achievement by Segre. There are at least three other important Italian works being readied, in English, for press, and we confidently expect the series to be continued to be ornamented in the future with semiotics books representing this most fertile of lands.

References

Bettetini, G., and Casetti, F.
    1986. Semiotics in Italy. In T. A. Sebeok and J. Umiker-Sebeok, eds., *The Semiotic Sphere*. New York and London: Plenum Press. Pp. 293–321.
Mincu, M., ed.
    1982. *La semiotica letteraria italiana*. Milano: Feltrinelli.
Regn, G.
    1981. Tendenzen der Semiotik in Italien. *Zeitschrift für Semiotik*, 3, pp. 55–78.

Preface:
Introduction to the Analysis
of the Literary Text

Introduction is an unassuming word. The first part, the more didactic part, of this book tries to exercise the virtue of modesty, avoiding wide-ranging theoretical problems and remaining on the level of analytical techniques and strategies.[1] Rather than discuss principles and methods, I have attempted to put forward in an organized fashion what I judge to be the operations which can most profitably be applied to a text. Modesty has not reached the point of merely listing techniques for analysis, although these make up the material of the exposition, and a great deal of attention (something which still alarms the occasional timorous soul) is given to terminology (the technical terms are explained as simply as possible). Indeed, I have attempted to sketch a general program of the operations which can be applied to the literary text so as to face progressively the problems it poses (in its formal aspects and in the elaboration of its contents) or those which are posed by its relations with its cultural context and with history. Naturally enough, I have made choices, because at present analytical models abound and the techniques that have been elaborated are innumerable. If the program sketched out is valid, it should be possible to accommodate within it those techniques of which I make no mention, either because of my plan of exposition or because I doubt their utility or because they did not come to mind.

That this program might itself have theoretical implications, and that the presentation of techniques is anything but neutral, is something there is no point in denying. Without referring to the other books in which I have fully discussed these implications, I shall say no more than that the overall conception in this book is that of literature as communication, even over time, and that, where its relations with the cultural context are concerned, I have tried to make use of the culturological models of the Tartu School, although it is not my intention to deny other historiographical models to which I have recourse elsewhere. I must add that the theoretical model I have used has led me to check in continuation analytical techniques which derive from diversified experiences and theories, certainly not from the semiotic sphere exclusively (I would underline that one of the advantages of this approach is that it is able to absorb a considerable number of critical proposals). Techniques are thus discussed and redimensioned, and in particular they are related to the conceptions which are basic to our program. I have not hesitated to refer fairly frequently to possible or desirable developments. I hope the critical sense has not suffered from this didactic clarity.

The second part of this book is, on the contrary, made up of a series of monographs dedicated to fundamental problems of the text, to text typology, to literary activity and its relations with reality. The theoretical plan which these chapters, taken as a whole, strive to execute is expounded in the foreword. This makes it possible to present them in alphabetical order and not in any rationalized, and perhaps questionable, order. But this alphabetical order derives from another fact. The chapters were conceived as articles for the *Enciclopedia Einaudi,* where they represented a unified block within the survey of knowledge there attempted.[2] Since they were in fact written in alphabetical order, I had already organized their basic arguments in such a way that each article presupposed those that had gone before but not those still to come; alphabetical order thereby became the order of the demonstration itself.

In these chapters, partly because more space was available, there is a great deal more theoretical elaboration. Here, though, its conditioning is more likely to have been the fundamentally historical approach: theory thus takes the form of interpretation or necessary integration and often points to problems yet to be solved and to research worth undertaking. But the themes are dealt with in all the implications that their history has served to bring to light; the space available has often made it possible to give information concerning the principal developments of speculation.

In both parts, the undertaking was to expound in more detail than is usual the premises of the program and of the techniques discussed, and it entailed frequent, and closely argued, reference to linguistic theory—in particular, to Saussure and Hjelmslev for the foundations, to Jakobson and Benveniste for aspects of the language in action. Considerable incentive derived from text linguistics and discourse pragmatics, despite some polemical observations in their regard. Semiotic criticism cannot be reduced to linguistics, but it is clear that in linguistics its bases are to be found.

References to other works are dealt with differently in the two parts. In the first, given the functional distribution of the arguments dealt with or referred to, it seemed useful to include numbered notes, so that more developments could be indicated. In the second part, each chapter has a bibliography at its close, and references to the bibliographies have been incorporated into the texts of the chapter. With respect to the *Enciclopedia,* however, there has been an important change. There, the bibliography was no more than a list of the works quoted textually in the exposition; here, it is this and more, a summary bibliography of the whole subject. Hence, the considerable increase in the number of works quoted, which will, I hope, meet with the reader's approval.

The theoretical coherence of the book should be apparent from the subject index. It refers the reader to the pages in which a term is defined or where it is treated most systematically. The index makes it possible for the reader to go back to those parts of the volume which illustrate the conceptions on which each point is based. Naturally enough, since its aim is to be useful, the index is selective.

The English translation of this book is, in its first part, markedly different from the Italian text. I have, in fact, eliminated references to little-known Italian authors and removed the analyses I had dedicated to them. Instead, the volume contains a great many examples from ancient and modern authors in English, some of which are looked at in a new light. This is to be attributed to my colleague Tomaso Kemeny, who kindly consented to re-elaborate my examples for an English-speaking public. His breadth of knowledge and his critical acumen have resulted in whole pages which dovetail perfectly with my own discourse, while enriching it and constituting its better part. The pages in question are those devoted to Shakespeare, Donne, Milton, Pope, Keats, Stevenson, Joyce, E. M. Forster, Faulkner, T. S. Eliot, Yeats, Dylan Thomas, and E. E. Cummings. I thank Tomaso Kemeny most warmly for his generous collaboration, and I wish to thank, too, John Meddemmen, another of my colleagues, who has once again taken on the task of translation with the scrupulousness and stylistic inventiveness of which he has given proof in other translations of my books. He conducted the bibliographical research that located the English translations for the Russian and German extracts, which I quoted from Italian translations. Lastly, I wish to express my gratitude to Thomas A. Sebeok, who kindly agreed to publish my book in the present series.

Notes

1. "The Analysis of the Literary Text," part one of this book, appeared in *Letteratura italiana*, ed. A. Asor Rosa, vol. 4 (Turin: Einaudi, 1985), pp. 21–140.

2. See *Enciclopedia Einaudi*, vols. 4 (1978), pp. 1056–84; 6 (1979), pp. 208–22, 564–85; 9 (1980), pp. 690–701; 10 (1980), pp. 818–37; 12 (1981), pp. 559–65; 14 (1981), pp. 3–22, 269–91; 15 (1982), pp. 677–85.

Part I
The Analysis of the Literary Text

1.
Communication

1.1. Communication Schema

An axiom—that literature is a form of communication—underlies the discussion on the following pages. (In a broader sense, it might be said that art is a form of communication, but this is not relevant here). A communicative goal is implicit in the very act by which one's own written or oral composition is destined to a public whose limits are unforeseeable. The addresser is convinced that he will be understood, and he wishes to be understood. It should be remarked that communication has a much broader value than information. Information is purely factual; it can be translated into symbols, and *a fortiori* into another language, in such a way that nothing will be left over. Communication, however, further embraces noninformative levels which, by the very fact of their being communicated, take the form of notions.

Literary communication is effected in the same way as any other communication. Jakobson[1] writes:

> The ADDRESSER sends a MESSAGE to the ADDRESSEE. To be operative the message requires a CONTEXT referred to ("referent" in another, somewhat ambiguous, nomenclature), seizable by the addressee, and either verbal or capable of being verbalized; a CODE fully or at least partially, common to the addresser and addressee (or, in other words, to the encoder and decoder of the message); and, finally, a CONTACT, a physical channel and psychological connection between the addresser and the addressee, enabling both of them to enter and stay in communication. All these factors inalienably involved in verbal communication may be schematized as follows:
>
> CONTEXT
>
> ADDRESSER   MESSAGE   ADDRESSEE
> --
> CONTACT
>
> CODE

It is possible, with this schema as a starting point, to define the peculiarities of literary communication. This can be done by comparing it with ordinary day-today dialogic communication, because this represents the primary use of language for the purposes of communication.

A first and basic observation is that in literary communication the addresser and the addressee are not co-present; indeed, in general they belong to different periods of time. It is exactly as if literary communication worked not with the addresser-message-addressee triad but with two dyads instead: addresser-message and message-addressee. It follows that the communication is all one-way; there is no possibility, as there is in conversation, either of the addressee's checking his understanding (*feedback*[2]) or of any adjustment of the communication to accord with his reactions. In consequence, the contact itself is a fairly unstable one. To begin with, it involves only the message-addressee dyad; it is also entrusted entirely to the addressee's interest in the message. The addresser, absent or no longer alive, enjoys at most the possibility of concentrating within his message incentives toward its utilization. Further difficulties arise from the fact that the context to which the addresser refers may be unknown to the addressee or known only in part. The addresser foresees this fact and will seek to include in his message as many references to the context as he can. In short, he introjects the context into his message. Add to this the absence of paralinguistic expression devices such as intonation, gesture, etc. "Many of the features that differentiate written style from spoken style can be traced back to a need, in writing, to compensate for the loss of suprasegmental and individual elements of speech."[3] The difference in code between addresser and addressee is another cause of difficulty. The language code itself is shared only in part by both parties, and, as temporal distance increases, this difference, too, will increase. The codes in play are all the codes of culture, and here defects in the information of the addressee may prove to be quite serious.

These difficulties of communication are not without remedies, as we shall soon see, although advantages exist with respect to dialogic communication. Philological investigation is able to verify the authenticity of the message (and to compensate for lack of feedback). Furthermore, one may read (or listen) anew, and this makes possible more thorough understanding. Reiterated readings—normal for the critic—lead to total assimilation of the message. Gaps in attention are thereby bridged, as are distractions during fruition, etc. Verification of other sources of information, those of the addresser or of others, can also be effected. It thus becomes possible to reconstruct, at least in part, the "encyclopedia" of the message (i.e., the sum of its knowledge) and its implications as well.

We also should not underestimate the difference that exists between oral communication of the message (song or public recitation, reading aloud to a small circle) and fruition by way of private reading. Oral fruition is conditioned by the channel (the speaker): it takes place at such times as the speaker wishes, and the text it furnishes is already interpreted (through music, suprasegmental features, gestuality, etc.). Oral fruition allows no checking—there is no going back over earlier parts of the text—and it must bridge any break in attention.

This was the case, in the Middle Ages, for the greater part of folk production, and today it still holds true for stage plays, films, television plays, etc.

1.2. The Author

1.2.1. The sender of the message, its addresser, is usually called the author. There was a time when criticism oriented the fruition of literary texts toward a kind of empathy between reader and author. The message became the intermediary, however necessary, by whose means the addressee was enabled to arrive at the addresser's sentiments, and so to live them anew. This approach was based on a conception of literary activity that implied a hardly credible immediacy between inspiration and literary realization. It was as if the creation of literature served as a mere outlet for feeling, as if the personal reactions present in the work had for their expression no need of complicated filters, painstakingly employed.

In its early stages, psychoanalytical criticism seemed in some measure to be harking back to this earlier approach, even though it was looking not for feelings and passions in authors but for complexes and drives. The more able representatives of this line of thought, however, soon drew attention to the fact that complexes and drives were being studied, in the literary sphere, in terms of their formal emergence in the texts—put simply, as structural elements. Or, better still, the unconscious expressed itself as language, and no linguistic product was immune from the working of the unconscious. The terrain of this elaboration is the language rather than the author.

1.2.2. The author is nonetheless an indispensable element in literary communication, for the author is the addresser of the message. He is the artificer and the guarantor of the work's communicative function.[4] The literary text's nature as message is determined by the fact that the author, in order to become addresser, has had to place himself in a particular relation with the addressee(s). This relation is cultural with respect to contents and pragmatic in its aims (transmitting the message changes the state of things). Essential to this relation is the confluence of codes within a linguistic utterance (the work).

Understood in this sense, the word *author* comes to mean exactly what it did in the Middle Ages (I recall the *Derivationes* of Uguccione, which Dante reproduced to the letter in the *Convivio* [IV, vi, 3–5]). It means not so much a writer as a "promoter," a "guarantor"—in a word, an "authority" (to which it is, in fact, etymologically related). The author produces a new linguistic construction whose communicative potential (and meaningfulness) he underwrites.

1.2.3. In serious literature, although his prestige may vary, the author's name is as a rule handed down. Many authors indeed seek to ensure by means of a signature placed within the work that their names will be remembered. One thinks of Bono Giamboni who quoted himself at the end of his *Libro de' Vizî e delle Virtudi*, just as Dante named himself in the *Purgatorio* (XXX, 53) and at the beginning of his *Brut* Layamon described the genesis of his work and introduced himself as well. As a rule, it is the *incipit*, and it may be the *explicit*, of a manuscript which gives us the author's name; on the title page of printed books it usually precedes or follows the title of the work. It is only as a precautionary measure that certain works are published anonymously.

In literature of the oral tradition, anonymity is much more frequent. Folk song is an extreme case. It does indeed "thrive on variation," to the point that no one remembers the persons (generally not professionals) who first shaped the texts. But we should not lose sight of the fact that, even with much more outstanding works, the commitment of the first compilers was, as a rule, held, even by those directly concerned, to be beneath the notice of fame. Franco-Venetian *chansons de geste* (like their French forerunners) were anonymous, and the singers of fourteenth- and fifteenth- century ballads in *ottave*, the *cantari*, were anonymous as well. The connection between oral performance and anonymity is obvious enough: in the case of polite literature, it is the addressee who sets out to look for the work, not improbably because of the author's reputation; with oral literature it is the work which goes a-begging in the marketplaces, in search of addressees, in search of a public. It was in the marketplaces that the ballad singers (only occasionally were they the authors as well) offered their recitations or their songs for sale. A clear connection also exists between illiteracy (that of the majority of the audience) and anonymity; for those who lie beyond the pale of writing, it is difficult to grasp the concept of author.

Several literary works, from the *Divine Comedy* to the *Gerusalemme liberata*, were committed to memory as well and enjoyed a wide circulation at folk level, though only occasionally did this mean that they fell outside the realm of polite production. Franco Sacchetti tells a typical tale in *Il Trecentonovelle* (CXIV), which derives from Diogenes Laertius (and Don Juan Manuel had already told it of a troubador).[5] In Sacchetti's tale, the protagonist is Dante, annoyed because a blacksmith, as he struck his anvil, "sang Dante /i.e. the *Comedy*/ the way you sing a *cantare* /i.e. an oral composition, performed orally/, jumbling together his verses, lopping them and joining them." Dante sets to work in a fury hurling the blacksmith's tools—his hammer, tongs, and scales—into the street. When the man protests at this disordering of his effects, Dante is said to have replied, "Se tu non vuogli che io guasti le cose tue, non guastare le mie": "If you don't want me to spoil your things, don't spoil mine." He goes on, more explicitly, "You sing the book; you don't say it the way I made it. I have no other trade, and you are ruining it for me." With anonymous compositions there was no need for anyone to complain that they were not being sung as they had been written. The blacksmith, Sacchetti tells us, from that time forward, "when he wanted to sing, sang of Tristan and of Lancelot, and left Dante alone." In other words he made do with texts which were traditionally anonymous.

1.3. The Reader

1.3.1. The author often has an explicit dedicatee (perhaps the person who commissioned the work) and an ideal reader (a muse, real or imaginary). The addressee cannot be identified with either: certainly not with the former—given the subservient, opportunistic nature of the choice—nor with the latter, precisely because the author projects on him (or her) his own communicative aspirations. Nor is it possible, even with a historical approach to literature, to concentrate on ideal dedicatees, groups of persons close to an author who share his literary conceptions (the Italian *stilnovo*, for example, or the Pre-Raphaelites, etc.). Dedicatees are, in reality, situated in a sector of quasi-dialogic communication, which is still under the control of the addresser, where temporal and spatial co-presence takes the form of collaboration.

The reader to be referred to, because in statistical terms he corresponds to the infinite (or at any rate uncountable) readers a literary work will have over time, has no direct links with the author—only a feeling of curiosity, of affection, of attraction, without which he would not have approached the work in the first place. Such a reader finds himself between two poles: understanding and variation. He may attempt to understand the meanings which the work unfolds, or he may surrender himself to the associations of his own imagination and indulge in unbridled elaboration. If I speak of poles, it is because no reading can possibly leave aside liberty of the imagination (which may well be interpretive insight), nor can any reading totally repress the dictation of the text.

This dilemma was exacerbated by some critics in the sixties. They stressed reading and saw it as a continuation of writing (both the one and the other regarded as the expression of a single subject—language). They further stressed a proliferation of meanings, susceptible of neither delimitation nor arrangement, so that the critic at best could do no more than quote parts of a text, any other discourse whatsoever on his part merely drifting out to join the current of infinite discourse. Nowadays, going into such matters is perhaps superfluous; it suffices to say that the communications schema allows us to take stock of literary communication's potentialities and limits, while keeping a firm hold on the reality of both addresser and addressees.[6]

1.3.2. The reader who inclines toward the pole of comprehension behaves in much the same way that the critic does. The latter differs from the former only because his application is systematic and because he is alive to method and may, in his turn, be committed to communicating, by word of mouth or in writing, such operations as he has performed on the text. A totally "thoughtless" reading would only be possible for a reader who remained deaf to meanings; otherwise (i.e., always), what we inevitably deal with is comparison between two systems, the system of the text and that of the reader. Essentially this is what comprises the critical act.

The word *hermeneutics*, somewhat limited though its application has been, might well converge with criticism or even become synonymous with it. Hermeneutics was developed in the service of biblical and legal texts and has as its aim exactness in interpretation, of both the letter and the whole. The range of practices proper to criticism is certainly broader than that of hermeneutics; criticism is syntonized differently and differently motivated. The goal of both is, nonetheless, a common one: fuller understanding of the text. The substantial difference between them lies in their object: a literary text, when compared with a religious or a legal text, is richer or, to put it better, involves a greater number of codes.[7]

Hermeneutics of this kind would be very welcome and would unquestionably be a semiotic activity. The text offers itself to the reader as a set of graphic signs. These signs have a denotative meaning whose character is linguistic. At the same time, they constitute, in the variety of their combinations, complex signs, which also have a meaning of their own. Further meaningful potentialities arise from connotation (cf. §2.1.2). In any event, all meanings are entrusted to signs and, in particular, to signs which are reciprocally homogeneous linguistic signs. Hermeneutics may well become the semiotics of the literary text.

1.3.3. While the author is the guarantor of the text's semiotic constitution, it is the reader who guarantees its semiotic action. The signifiers, in fact, remain within the text, black marks on a white page, unless successive readings revive their sign function, i.e., their capacity to point the way to meaning. Textual meanings emerge from their potentiality and become actualized meanings only during reading, and as a result of reading alone (it is then that they become part of the cultural system). Any reading of a noncontemporary text is thus a multiple reading, because the reader is bringing meanings up to date—meanings that have already entered culture and have entered the reader's own culture, thanks to earlier readings.

In other words, the text constitutes a sign diaphragm: on one side of it lies the addresser's commitment to translating meanings into literary signs; on the other, the addressee's commitment to recovering meanings wrapped in signs. The second operation is the better known, for any reader can put it to the test. What is more, it gives rise to strategies which can be planned and improved, as against the addresser's procedures, which are asystematical and far from clear. These two ways of working may legitimately be regarded as mirror images of each other. A "simulation" of the individual reading would probably arrive at the same elements which were involved in production, although it would invert their order. Generally speaking, the textual models of literary criticism are models of reading.

1.4. Implied Author and Implied Reader

1.4.1. It is difficult, it would seem, to immobilize and define both author and reader. The author does not really interest the reader of the text. Often he is unknown, or information concerning him is slight. Hardly ever is what we know what we would like to know. The reader is not a specific person but an abstraction. A recently formulated hypothesis suggests that in narrative texts (though why stop here?) it is possible to individuate well-defined traits which are not those of the historical author but those of the author who reveals himself in the work, an author whose real features have been refined away and whose characteristics are those postulated by the work. In like manner, it is possible to characterize exactly the kind of reader who is envisaged by the work, even though real readers will, to a greater or lesser degree, prove to be different. The former has been called the implied author, the latter the implied reader.[8]

1.4.2. Thanks to this contrivance, the communication circuit (which in literary communication has two stages: addresser-message and message-addressee) is once more integrated with the work. The implied author may be called the addressee plane and that of the I (-YOU) character different from the author. which forged the message with the intention of communicating it; similarly, the implied reader may be defined as the real addressee, thanks to those very differences which mark him off from real readers.[9] We will then have:

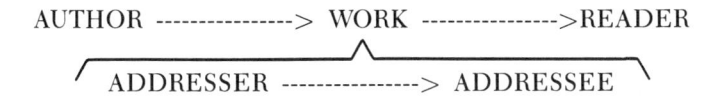

```
AUTHOR ----------------> WORK ---------------->READER
          ‾‾‾‾‾‾‾‾‾‾‾‾‾‾‾‾‾‾‾‾‾‾‾‾‾‾‾‾‾‾‾‾‾‾
          ADDRESSER ----------------> ADDRESSEE
```

Almost all of the statements made by traditional criticism about the author more properly apply to the implied author. Such traits as are definable on the basis of the text fit the implied author to perfection. Only temporally, if at all, could they ever have belonged to the real author. It is the implied author who persists within the coordinates that can be defined on the basis of the text. The real author will continue to evolve, and to transform.

The implied author, or addresser, is necessarily present in any literary text. But often the real author attempts to establish himself somehow or other within the text, in the guise of narrator, as a direct or indirect witness of events, as it were.[10] This narrator, too. who says *I* and who not infrequently gives evidence of moral character, of personal reactions and idiosyncrasies, has often been held to be the real author; he is, though, a deliberate stylization and, quite often, an intentionally unfaithful one. Even when we do find correspondences between the personal traits of the narrator and those of the real author, in so far as they can be reconstructed from more straightforward statements (letters, diaries, etc.), the two sets of traits must be kept absolutely separate, because of the stylization and perhaps idealization already mentioned and because the narrator is beyond the reach of temporal developments. Like any character he is confined to the pages of a book. In conclusion, we might call to mind that it is a common practice to invent a fictitious narrator, explicitly distinct from the author, in order to pretend that it is from him that the narration derives.

Light is thrown on this aspect of the matter by the utterance/utterance act formula (in French, *énoncé/énonciation*). Benveniste in particular has underlined this aspect.[11] An utterance act "is the act itself which produces an utterance and not the text of the utterance which is our object." In the utterance act a speaker undertakes to employ the language in relation to an "other" to whom the utterance act is directed. We are, then, dealing with "an accentuation of the discoursive relation with a partner," given that *I* stands for the subject of the utterance act and *you* for the addressee. Taken together, they actualize temporal perspectives (the present is the tense of the utterance act; the past and the future have become such by being related to this particular moment) and ostensive or deictic signs (*this, here,* etc.) as well.[12]

The literary text is an utterance (product), which bears the signs of the act of its uttering. The subject who speaks (the narrator) doubles for the subject of the utterance act (the author as locutor) and may act as his spokesman. It is he, then, who is *I*, and deictics and tenses are to be interpreted as they relate to him. In all other cases, utterances refer us to the utterance acts which are attributed to characters (if it is they who are speaking) or else to the person (the imaginary narrator) whose point of view and, it may be, whose person (when the narrator reveals himself) mediates narrative content.

1.5. Persons or Voices

1.5.1. A communications circuit constitutes a minimal social unit: two people communicate, thanks to their knowledge of the same code, while other people, outside the circuit (for the moment), may form the object of the communication itself. In terms of the persons of the verb, the addresser is I, the addressee is YOU, the object of communication is HE. In everyday communication, the two interlocutors take turns as I and YOU, depending on which of them is speaking and which listening; in literary communication, though, it is clear that the roles of addresser and addressee cannot be interchanged.

In designating HE as the object of his communication, I effects the realization of a *diegesis,* a narration. Narration is a semiotic phenomenon of some complexity. Man is able to make use of language to describe gestures and situations, and he may also state, in direct form, the content of speeches. It is clear that a narrative *competence*[13] exists by which the addressee understands, from the addresser's discourse, exactly which gestures and situations are being spoken of by him and which discourses are to be attributed to the person who forms the object of the communication.

The addresser, though, may make another choice; he may repeat the discourses of the character-object, and those of his interlocutors, and even, perhaps, reach the point of imitating their voices and inflections. He may go further and repeat their movements and gestures. In such a case, there will be no need for him to verbalize nonverbal events, unless they are put into the actors' mouths. What we will have is *mimesis,* an imitation. The terms *diegesis* and *mimesis* derive from Aristotle *(Poetics),*[14] and he used them to stand for the different modes of tragedy and epic poetry. In much more general terms, it might be said that mimesis equals theater and allied forms of representation, while diegesis equals narration. It must at once be added that Aristotle himself envisaged a mixed form, of both diegesis and mimesis, one in which narration would embrace first-person discourses directly pronounced by, or similar to those pronounced by, the characters. This is commonly the case, both in the private recounting of personal experience and in folk tales, short stories, and novels.

1.5.2. With this as a starting point, a whole theory of literary genres might be elaborated. This, however, is not our intention; rather, what seems to be called for is a typology of literary communication, one which would precede the specifications established by genres. It is natural enough at this point to have recourse to the persons of the verb, and there are precedents. Jakobson, for example, refers to E. S. Dallas and on the question of genres writes:

> To reduce the problem to a simple grammatical formulation, we might say that the first person of the present is at once the point of departure and the sustaining theme of lyric poetry, while this role is sustained in the epic by the third person of a past tense. Whatever the particular object of a lyric narration may be, it is no more than an appendix, an accessory, a back-drop for the first-person present tense; a lyric past tense itself presupposes a subject engaged in calling things to memory. On the contrary, the present in epic is decisively referred to the past, and when the I of the narrator finds expression, it is no more than one of the characters: this objective I appears as a variant of the third person, the poet observing himself, so to speak, out of the corner of his eye. It may well be, when all is said and done, that this I is thrown into relief as an exigency which records but which must never be confused with the object recorded; which comes down to saying that the author, insofar as he is "object of lyric poetry" and addresses the world in the first person, is radically extraneous to epic poetry.[15]

These observations illuminate the person-time relation. Allusion to the present is legitimate only for I, since HE, i.e., the object of the narration, by the very fact of being narrated, at once enters the past (and, in fact, the present of certain narrations is of necessity a "historic present": the events narrated have already taken place, even if they are narrated as though they were unfolding) (cf. §1.6.3).

But the few points touched on by Jakobson are not sufficient for our purpose. Each person of the verb is such only in relation to the other persons, and no weight is given to this fact. Face to face with whom does one say I? Or designate someone as HE? We will be well advised to have recourse to the communication circuit once more.

Inside the circuit, I can belong to such sentences as are directed by the addresser to the addressee or to other sentences attributed to third parties who are themselves the object of a narration mimetic in form. These character-objects operate inside a communication circuit which is analogous to an ordinary one (the voices of the two interlocutors alternate, although, of course, their exchanges have been prepared by the addresser), and the roles of addresser and addressee are not interchangeable.

1.5.3. Recourse to mimetic I and YOU serves at once to isolate a comprehensive subsystem of literary texts. Theatrical texts play a dominant role here, since they are entirely made up of speeches and gestures, while any other codes involved (costumes, scenery, music, etc.) can be neglected as belonging to a later phase of the text. To convince ourselves of this mimesis, we need only call to mind certain specific departures from it:

(a) stage directions. Originally concise and strictly limited to staging, they may at times become descriptive or even narrative. They may, on different occasions, mediate private reading, or their aim may be to influence production, at the level of atmospheric effect;

(b) use of an actor to recite the prologue. The prologue is generally expressed diegetically and may sometimes utter the author's own opinions. It is no accident that Ariosto, who makes frequent use of the device (in *Cassaria, Suppositi, Negromante, Lena*), preferred to recite his prologues himself. Wycherly makes use of the prologue in *The Country Wife* to declare a conciliatory and resigned attitude in the face of a Restoration public that only occasionally paid attention to the play and whose constant chatter competed with it;

(c) the Chorus. Originating in Greek tragedy, it is to be found in Milton's *Samson Agonistes*, in Shelley's *Prometheus Unbound*, and, among many modern examples, in T. S. Eliot's *Murder in the Cathedral*. It expresses an opinion, over and above the actors' opinions, which coincides more or less with that of the addresser;

(d) asides and monologues. In these the mimetic I communicates to the addressee things which are to remain hidden from the various mimetic YOU-characters. It is a device which unmasks a part of the fiction, and textual communication is made to shift from the mimetic level to the addresser-addressee level, although it is left to a person on the mimetic level (an actor) to effect such "leakage."[16]

We must be prepared to realize that communication of this kind may involve nontheatrical texts as well. The epistolary novel is the most obvious example: in its purest form, one or more interlocutors do not engage in direct oral exchange; they exchange letters, while any other kind of communication between addresser and addressee is never taken into account. The plot and meditation upon it are expounded only by those directly involved.

1.5.4. The field is widened even further if we include texts in which, while there is no alternation of speakers, a discourse is, nonetheless, attributed to an I which is quite distinct from the I of the addresser. With this I the addresser attempts to identify himself, exactly as he would with the characters of a play. All forms of monologue can be made to fall under this heading, for example:

(a) monologue-like theatrical texts: from Ruzzante's two *Orazioni* to Beckett's *Krapp's Last Tape;*

(b) poetic narrative compositions in the form of monologues. Superb examples are those of Robert Browning, who in the form of dramatic romances and lyrics, e.g., in *A Light Woman,* confers absolute communicative autonomy on an I who succinctly tells her own story to a YOU who acts as the text's silent addressee. The use of blank verse and of couplets lends an even more marked degree of theatricality to dramatic monologues like *My Last Duchess*, where the I narrator wears a well-defined historical mask, as does the YOU he addresses. Here the sequence of events involves a SHE as protagonist. The technique has been

carried forward in an individual form by T. S. Eliot, for example, in *The Love Song of J. Alfred Prufrock;*
(c) poetic compositions attributable not to any specific character but to a generic type which the tone of the composition itself defines. A list would be long indeed and would include almost the whole of "burlesque" poetry, from Rustico and Cecco Angiolieri in the thirteenth century to the nineteenth-century Roman poet Belli. A good example in English might be Matthew Prior's *The Orange*. At one time biographers found it difficult with texts of this kind to reconcile, or to keep apart, the character traits of the addresser and those of the person involved directly. They did not accord sufficient weight to a form of mimetic mediation which enables the addresser to pass himself off as another person (although overlapping may exist and needs to be determined case by case).

1.5.5. A dialogue exchange I-YOU is not possible in an unadulterated form, for it would exclude absent third persons, and it would exclude the past, when YOU and I were not as yet in converse, when indeed they were in quite different dialogue situations. Whole tracts devoted to HE will be found embedded in their discourses. This is the case when, for example, an actor in a play tells another what a third person (HE) did (in the past). We then have the following figure:

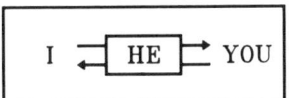

The mimetic nature of the dialogue, in a situation of this kind, will remain unchanged.

There are also structural reasons why diegetic parts and mimetic parts will either overlap or tie in with each other. In *Pamela*, for instance, the reader is addressed directly halfway through the work, and again at the end, by the editor of the letters, so that the moral values represented by the heroine can be pointed out and certain aspects of the plot clarified.

1.5.6. So far, we have been looking at cases of simulated dialogue communication (I-YOU) or at cases of zero dialogue, for which no more than one I exists inside a monologue whose forms may vary. Both techniques have in common the fact that the addresser brings a character to life and attributes to him or her speeches which are consistent with the personality endowed. Dialogues and monologues unfold, in the case of theater, in the presence of the real YOU, the work's addressee, and, in the case of the nontheatrical text, in his reading of it. What is important is that this YOU is located on a different plane. He cannot participate in the dialogue nor can he intervene in the monologue. He will be called upon to take part only when the fiction is suspended (e.g., with a request for applause at the end of the comedy); otherwise, he may intervene and interrupt the fiction, as Don Quixote does during the puppet plays (II, XXVI).

In fact, what characterizes diegesis is that it has an immediate addressee in a reader (or listener). No phase difference exists between the I-YOU addresser-addressee plane and that of the I (-YOU) character different from the author. Diegesis in its simplest forms (folk tales, popular narration, factual accounts) does not need to highlight the person of the narrator. The narrator is postulated by the narration itself; he may well remain impersonal. This is what happens in a great many novellas and short stories from the *Novellino* to Verga and D'Annunzio or Jack London, e.g., in *Build a Fire*.

1.5.7. Writers seem to have sensed something inhuman underlying the impersonality of this kind of narrator. What is certain is that they have often felt the need to reactivate the communication circuit at least symbolically, for it was no longer easy to grasp, when the addresser was so distant and the addressee a mere potentiality. The many and varied solutions available can all be brought down to a decision to make the voice of the narrator personal.

An initial solution to the problem might be to attribute to the narrator not merely command of diegesis but metacommunicative interventions as well, in short, comment on the diegesis itself. In other words, the narrator becomes a mediator between the world of fiction and its addressee. Stanzel, in this sense, speaks of *auktoriale Erzählsituation*[17] and Booth of *undramatized narrator*.[18] The narrator is rendered personal in terms of two polarizations: insistence on YOU, i.e., on allocutions directed to the addressee, and insistence on I, on the narrator's individual character, because he puts himself forward as judge and interpreter of events and behavior. Thackeray's *Vanity Fair* is a supreme example.

A second solution might be to have facts narrated by a secondary character who has been present at, or has become aware of, events which he then recounts to the addressee. Such a narrator will express himself in the first person (Stanzel speaks of *Ich Erzählsituation*, Friedman of *I as witness*,[19] Booth of *dramatized narrator*). This, though, need not necessarily be the case; the witness he bears may well be expressed in the third person.

The standpoint of a narrator who is not a secondary character at all but the protagonist of events is related only in part (Stanzel and Booth class this standpoint with the preceding category, though Friedman distinguishes it, calling it *I as protagonist*). The difference between the two solutions is that an *I as witness* may effect the same mediation between events and addressee as that encountered in the first solution, whereas an *I as protagonist* who identifies himself with events can distance himself no further than a temporal distance between the events and their narration will permit.

Types in which the narrator is a person distinct from the author come very close indeed to mimetic types: a narrator is imagined as being endowed with characteristics of his own which are distinct from those of the author, and the author must organize the narration attributed to him in such a way that it will harmonize with the traits in question. It is the differences, though, which will come to the fore: (1) the narrator unfolds events extraneous to himself or which have taken place some time earlier; he does not so much express himself in relation to an action as recollect and register memories; as a result, his function is diegetic, not mimetic; (2) the narrator does not address an interlocutor, however silent, situated on the same plane as himself, on the plane of fiction; it is the work's addressee to whom he turns.[20]

1.5.8. Diegesis pure and simple is obviously impossible; narration frequently relates speeches made by the characters. Fundamental, however, is the fact that in this group of texts the I-YOU of the characters is embedded in a diegetic HE, as distinct from mimetic types where the I-YOU framework may contain a series of HE. We have, in short, the following formula for mimetic literary communication:

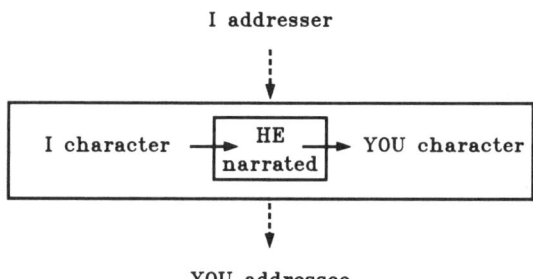

For all cases of mediated narration the general formula would be this:

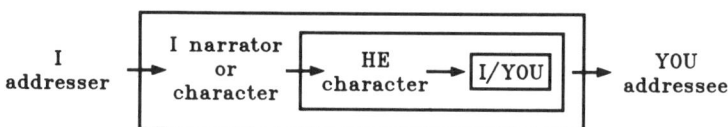

I should point out at once that, in my belief, HE can be used for a narrator protagonist as well, given that, at the moment of his narration, he is different from, and distanced from, the person he was at the time of the facts related. I will thus be his by right insofar as he is narrator, but he will be HE insofar as he is the object of the narration.

It is typical of the second formula that, whereas the author, as we have repeatedly affirmed, has no contact with the addressee, the narrator does maintain such contact. This is indicated by the arrow which, from within the outer frame, reaches a YOU addressee outside the frame. The first frame indicates a metanarrative and *phatic* space,[21] that of the narrator; the second frame, the space of events related; the third, the space of mimetically reproduced dialogue.

This formula is well able to multiply frames within itself. In fact, any given narrated character can, in his turn, become the narrator of other events; he may retail mimetically the dialogues of the characters of whom he himself tells; he may so arrange things that these characters of his narrate yet other events, and so on and on, to infinity. This is the technique that Ariosto put to excellent use in his *Orlando furioso*, and it has been imitated many times, by Cervantes, for example. Matthew J. Lewis, in *The Monk*, showed how striking it can be when, in his third chapter, he introduces, in the Marquis de las Cisternas, a narrator who is to put the case of one of the characters, Lorenzo. Thanks to this device, narrative space and time can be multiplied from within.

One final type of communication is that which Vygotskij calls "inward language" and Lotman "self-communication," or I-I communication. In communication of this type, the addresser "transmitting messages to himself . . . reorganizes from within his own essence, since the essence of his own personality can be treated as an individual selection of socially meaningful codes, and here, in the process of a communicative act, this selection itself changes."[22] The addressee, who is the addresser himself, knows the message already; in communicating it to himself, he attempts to move it on to a higher level by the introduction of new codes, thereby making it in some measure new. The codes employed are formal in character, and rhythm is first among them. "Between the original message and the secondary code a tension is set up which leads to the semantic elements of the text being interpreted as if they were included in a complementary syntactic construction and received from such interconnection new (relational) meanings."[23] The aim of Lotman's exposition is better definition of the poetic function. But, if we take into account that this poetic function is dominant in lyric poetry, and that it is from lyric poetry that Lotman deliberately takes many of his examples, we may regard I-I communication as proper to the lyric. With this corrective, however, in the case of the lyric, a communication I-I in type, self-communication, is inserted into an I-YOU addresser-addressee communication. Thus:

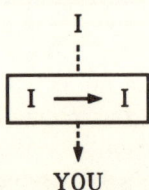

What we have here is, in a certain sense, a mimesis of I-I communication, where the communicated I, like the implied author of narration, is the addresser purified and sublimated. He is also the addresser who renders public what is private and who gives definition to the transient.

1.6. Point of View

1.6.1. Henry James established *point of view* as a technical expression in literary criticism,[24] when he remarked upon the novelist's need to create the illusion of a real process, to frame his events progressively in terms of the consciousness of one or the other of his characters, thereby avoiding the neutrality of the so-called omniscient narrator so typical of classical narration and of the epic in particular. James's statements sound, though, more like a personal poetic program than an interpretative schema, and those critics who have set out to apply them have often mixed heterogeneous data. They have, for example, ascribed to point-of-view phenomena like those of the previous paragraph which are really concerned with person. Genette rightly distinguishes between the two questions to which, by the very fact of studying point of view, an answer is implicitly sought.[25] First, "who is the character whose point of view orients the narrative perspective?" Second, "who is the narrator?" As we have seen, in reply to the second question, *persons* (or, as Genette calls them, *voices*) can be used with some accuracy.

It is not just that persons and voices do not coincide; what gives rise to a basic combinational pattern is the very fact of their alternating convergencies, which the following table sums up.[26]

	EVENTS ANALYZED FROM WITHIN	EVENTS OBSERVED FROM WITHOUT
Narrator is present as a character in the action	(1) The hero tells his own story	(2) A witness tells the hero's story
Narrator is absent as a character from the action	(4) The author analyst and omniscient tells the story	(3) The author tells the story from outside

We may speak of point of view with respect to opposition—(1), (4)/(2), (3). But in opposition—(1), (2)/(4), (3)—what we are dealing with is voice (or person). The table lends itself to the following internal specifications: (1) a narrator is present as a character in the story (*homodiegetic*) and analyses its events from within (*intradiegetic*); (2) a narrator is present as a character in the story (*homodiegetic*) and analyses its events from without (*extradiegetic*); (3) a narrator is absent as a character in the story (*heterodiegetic*) and analyses its events from within (*intradiegetic*); (4) a narrator is absent as a character in the story (*heterodiegetic*) and analyses its events from without (*extradiegetic*). An example of (1) might be *Adolphe;* of (2), Watson who tells the Sherlock Holmes stories; of (3), Agatha Christie who narrates Hercule Poirot; of (4), *Armance.*

"Who is the character whose point of view orients the narrative perspective?" Genette replies to this question by recourse to a figurative use of a category of the verb—*mood.* The verb, through the category of mood, expresses in assertive, interrogative, optative, and other such forms the thing it is dealing with and the different points of view from which its existence and action are considered; in like fashion, narrative mood indicates the wider or more restricted range (the quality and kind of detail) and the point of view from which a vicissitude is narrated. I shall quote the definition Genette himself gives, if only because of the two new categories he introduces, distance and perspective.

> Narrative "representation," or, more exactly, narrative information, has its degrees: the narrative can furnish the reader with more or fewer details, and in a more or less direct way, and can thus seem (to adopt a common and convenient spatial metaphor, which is not to be taken literally) to keep it at a greater or lesser **distance** from what it tells. The narrative can also choose to regulate the information it delivers, not with a sort of even screening, but according to the capacities of knowledge of one or another participant in the story (a character or group of characters), with the narrative adopting or seeming to adopt what we ordinarily call the participant's "vision" or "point of view"; the narrative seems in that case (continuing the spatial metaphor) to take on, with regard to the story, one or another **perspective.** "Distance" and "perspective," thus provisionally designated and defined, are the two chief modalities of that **regulation of narrative information** that is mood.[27]

The persistence, indeed the multiplication, in Genette's analysis of metaphors derived from optics (*focusing*, as we shall see, remains to be added), is a good indication of how difficult it is to delimit these phenomena, important though they are. As we move forward (§3.12–13), we shall see how stylistic analysis makes possible a closer grasp of the argument. For the moment our approach may remain general.

1.6.2. Distance may in part be located along a line which leads from mimesis to diegesis, from full particulars to their absence. At one extreme lies direct discourse, given in mimetic form; at the other, *narrativized discourse,* i.e., a summarized discourse, introduced by a *verbum dicendi* or, it may be, quite without any reference to the discoursive nature of its content. Midway between them lies indirect speech or discourse, preceded by a *verbum dicendi* or by *that*. Both the diegetic type (the second we have mentioned) and the indirect type (the third) entail, as an invariable consequence, a greater degree of compression (unnecessary though this may seem in theory), and this may give rise to the most synthetic statement.

That the range is conditioned not so much by the exigencies of syntax as by stylistic practice and convention seems to be made clear by the important anomaly of *free indirect discourse,* that is, when discourse content and thought content are not preceded by explicit signs because the narrator has taken them into his own hands. When he does so, he will make it perfectly clear that what we encounter are not his own thoughts but those of the character being dealt with.[28]

It is even more difficult to define the concept of narrative perspective. What is certain is that it concerns the relation between the quantity of information attributed to single characters and that which the narrator keeps to himself.

With a sweeping simplification, Todorov provides three basic formulas: narrator > character (when the narrator shows that he knows, and tells, more than what is told or known by each of his characters); narrator = character (when the narrator knows and tells at each stage no more than what his characters know); narrator < character (when the narrator knows less, and tells less, than his characters know).[29] Genette's figure, which follows, is a more flexible one.[30]

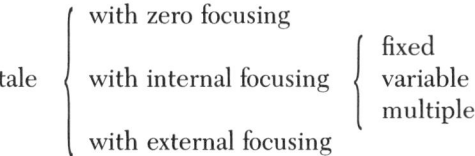

By the term *focusing* (Brooks and Warren[31] had spoken of *focus of narration*), Genette indicates the place (or the person) within whose perspective (or within whose field of vision) the narration is conducted. Zero focusing will be that of narration which (like a classical epic) never takes up the standpoint of its characters at all; narratives where the phenomenon is to be met with have *internal focusing*. Internal focusing may be fixed, and, when it is, everything is looked at through the eyes of one single character (for example in Henry James's *The Ambassadors* and *What Maisie Knew*). Internal focusing may be variable, when from one episode to another different characters take turns being "focal" (an example is Flaubert's *Madame Bovary*); it may be multiple, when the same event is seen successively through the eyes of a number of characters (Wilkie Collins's *The Moonstone*, Robert Browning's *The Ring and the Book*, and epistolary novels like Smollett's *Humphry Clinker*). We may speak of external focusing when the characters act in the sight of the narrator but he gives no sign whatsoever that he is aware of their thoughts and feelings (the short stories of Hemingway, Dashiell Hammett's novels). It should also be noted that focusing may be progressive; narrators often present their characters from outside, and, as the tale goes forward, narrators move progressively closer to the individuality of the characters, whose thoughts and feelings they penetrate.

1.6.3. Of considerable importance for the study of these problems is the use made of verb tenses.[32] Weinrich, for example, distinguishes narrative tenses (imperfect, past, pluperfect, and conditional) from commentative tenses (present, present perfect, and future). It is their alternation throughout the text which serves to mark off more strictly diegetic parts from those devoted to comment (or metacommunication) or to description. Another connection exists with the persons of the verb, given that, as a rule, I (or YOU) governs tenses which comment, whereas HE is predominant in narrative tenses (cf. §1.5.2). Of the many critical applications of the verb opposition under consideration, two deserve mention: (1) in the text, the distribution of its verbs obeys fairly constant norms, and this contributes both to the text's coherence and to definition of its beginning and end;[33] (2) alternation of verb types plays a part in establishing narrative planes (e.g., *close ups* and *background*); as a result, it is a constituent element of the story's perspective; the different attitudes of the writer toward the material he narrates finds one of its main expressions in his choice of tenses.

Notes

*In these pages I make free use of two works of mine: "Segni, sistemi e modelli culturali nell'interpretazione del testo letterario," in M. Dufrenne and D. Formaggio, eds., *Trattato di estetica*, 2 vols. (Milan: Mondadori, 1981), 2: 157-79, and *Teatro e romanzo* (Turin: Einaudi, 1984). In certain paragraphs I touch on problems already dealt with in other, earlier studies, though here the perspective and mode of presentation are different.

1. R. Jakobson, "Linguistics and Poetics," in *Style in Language*, ed. T. Sebeok (Cambridge, Mass.: M.I.T. Press, 1960), pp. 350–377 (p. 353), now in *Essais de linguistique générale* (Paris: Editions de Minuit, 1963). There are a number of analyses of communication which distinguish the various constituent elements of the context (time, place), of the message (among them, presuppositions as to the addressee's knowledge and capacity), etc., from pragmatic elements like the situation of the addresser and his social relations with the addressee. See D. Wunderlich, "Pragmatik, Sprechsituation, Deixis," in *Zeitschrift für Literaturwissenschaft und Linguistik*, 1 (1971) 1–2, pp. 153–90. But the analysis into six elements is the most functional. One should also consult the exposition of the communication diagram/schema in U. Eco, *Trattato di semiotica generale* (Milan: Bompiani, 1975), pp. 49–53. For the English translation, see *A Theory of Semiotics* (London: Basingstoke, 1977), pp. 32–36. There is an interesting, conflictive approach to the addresser-addressee relation in J. Fetterley, *The Resisting Reader: A Feminist Approach to American Fiction* (Bloomington: Indiana University Press, 1978). See in addition, E. Guhlich and W. Raible, *Linguistische Textmodelle* (Munich: Fink, 1977), pp. 21–26; and R. Escarpit, *Théorie générale de l'information et de la communication* (Paris: Hachette, 1976).

2. The term in information theory, indicates the possibility for the addressee to send information in the direction of the addresser with the aim of focusing the message more clearly.

3. A Martinet, *A Functional View of Language* (Oxford: Clarendon Press, 1962), p. 123. Supersegmental, or prosodic, features are types of intonation, length, etc., in short, all the phonic characteristics which involve segments longer than a phoneme.

4. See C. Segre, *I segni e la critica* (Turin: Einaudi, 1969). For the English translation, see *Semiotics and Literary Criticism* (The Hague-Paris: Mouton, 1973), pp. 74–77.

5. See L. Di Francia, *Franco Sacchetti novelliere* (Pisa: Nistri, 1902), p. 103.

6. For more detailed discussion, see C. Segre, *Semiotica filologica* (Turin: Einaudi, 1979), pp. 18–21.

7. For the definition and diffusion of literary hermeneutics, especially in Germany but in the United States as well, see P. Szondi, *Einführung in die literarische Hermeneutik* (Frankfurt am Main: Suhrkamp, 1975). See also H. G. Gadamer, *Wahrheit und Methode: Grundzuge einer philosophischen Hermeneutik*, 5th ed. (Tübingen: Niemeyer, 1965); P. Ricoeur, *Le conflit des interprétations: Essai d'herméneutique* (Paris: Seuil, 1969); E. D. Hirsch, Jr., *Validity in Interpretation* (New Haven: Yale University Press, 1967), and *The Aims of Interpretation* (Chicago: University of Chicago Press, 1976); S. J. Schmidt, ed., *Interpretation*, monographic issue of *Poetics*, 12 (1983): 1–2; E. Holenstein, *Linguistik, Semiotik, Hermeneutik* (Frankfurt am Main: Suhrkamp, 1967); and H. R. Jauss, *Ästhetische Erfahrung und literarische Hermeneutik I*, 3d ed. (Frankfurt am Main: Fink, 1984).

8. The theory of the implied author has been formulated by W. C. Booth, *The*

Rhetoric of Fiction, rev. ed. (Chicago: University of Chicago Press, 1983). See also B. Romberg, *Studies in the Narrative Technique of the First-Person Novel* (Stockholm: Almqvist and Wiksell, 1962); J. Rousset, "La prima persona nel romanzo: Abbozzo di una tipologia," in *Strumenti critici*, 6 (1972): 19, pp. 259-74; N. Tamir, "Personal Narrative and Its Linguistic Foundation," in *PTL: A Journal for Descriptive Poetics and Theory of Literature*, 1 (1976): 3, pp. 403-29; W. Krysinski, "The Narrator as a Sayer of the Author," in *Strumenti critici*, 11 (1977): 32-33, pp. 44-89; S. Chatman, *Story and Discourse: Narrative Structure in Fiction and Film* (Ithaca: Cornell University Press, 1978); and M. Pagnini, *Pragmatica della letteratura* (Palermo: Sellerio, 1980), pp. 20-22. See also the considerations of U. Eco, *Lector in fabula: La cooperazione interpretativa nei testi narrativi* (Milan: Bompiani, 1979), pp. 50-66. On the implied reader, see W. Iser, *Der implizite Leser* (1972). For the English translation, see *The Implied Reader* (Baltimore: Johns Hopkins Press, 1974). Also see Iser, *Der Akt des Lesens: Theorie ästhetischer Wirkung* (1976). For the English translation, see *The Act of Reading: A Theory of Aesthetic Response* (Baltimore: Johns Hopkins Press, 1978); S. R. Suleiman and I. Crosman, eds., *The Reader in the Text: Essays on Audience and Interpretation* (Princeton: Princeton University Press, 1980).

9. A wider-ranging exposition is in W. Mignolo, *Elementos para una teoría del texto literario* (Barcelona: Editorial Crítica, 1978), pp. 146-50.

10. In symmetry with the narrator, criticism has indicated a narratee, or addressee of the narration. Prince, "Introduction à l'étude du narrataire," *Poétique*, 14 (1973): 178-96. The narratee is not the generic reader but the type of reader implied by the narrator's figure and attitude. For the necessity, or near necessity, of the mediation of a narrator, see Mignolo, *Elementos*, pp. 230-31.

11. See E. Benveniste, *L'appareil formel de l'énonciation* (1970), in *Problèmes de linguistique générale*, vol. 2 (Paris: Gallimard, 1974), pp. 79-88. See also O. Ducrot, "Enunciazione I" in *Enciclopedia*, vol. 5 (Turin: Einaudi, 1978), pp. 495-522.

12. The term *deictics* is used for those linguistic elements which are referred to the situation, to the moment, or to the subject of the utterance act, principally personal pronouns, demonstratives, adverbs of place and time.

13. In generative linguistics, competence is the system of grammatical rules used by the speaker; it enables him to understand, and to formulate, an infinite number of sentences in the language he uses.

14. See Aristotle *Poetica* 1460b-1462b.

15. R. Jakobson, *Randbemerkungen zur Prosa des Dichters Pasternak* (1935), now in *Selected Writings*, vol. 5 (The Hague: Mouton), pp. 416-32.

16. See C. Segre, *Teatro e romanzo*, p. 11.

17. See F. K. Stanzel, *Die typischen Erzählsituationen im Roman* (Vienna-Stuttgart: Braumüller, 1955), *Typische Formen des Romans* (Göttingen: Vandenhoek und Ruprecht, 1964), and *Theorie des Erzählens* (Göttingen: Vandenhoek und Ruprecht, 1979).

18. See Booth, *Rhetoric of Fiction*.

19. See N. Friedman, *Point of View in Fiction: The Development of a Critical Concept*, in *PMLA*, 70 (1965): 1160-84.

20. An extremely clear description of novel types has been made by R. Bourneuf and R. Ouellet, *L'univers du roman* (Paris: PUF, 1972).

21. Those techniques whose scope is to maintain contact between addresser and addressee are defined as *phatic*. Jakobson speaks of a phatic function (cf. §2.5).

22. Ju. M. Lotman, *O dvuch modeljach kommunicacii v sisteme kul'tury* (1973). For the Italian translation, see "I due modelli della comunicazione nel sistema della cultura," in Ju. M. Lotman and B. A. Uspenskij, *Tipologia della cultura*, ed. R. Faccani and M. Marzaduri (Milan: Bompiani, 1975), p. 114.

23. Ibid., p. 123. This approach is developed and integrated by J. I. Levin, *Lirika s.*

kommunikativnoj točki zrenija (1973). For the Italian translation, see "La poesia lirica sotto il profilo della comunicazione," in C. Prevignano, ed., *La semiotica nei Paesi slavi* (Milan: Feltrinelli, 1979), pp. 426–42. He points to the presence, in filigrana behind the author's I-I communication, of a "participating" addressee and classifies the various types of I and of YOU which are in play in poetry. Levin prefers to speak of "intra-textual communication," rather than of self-communication.

24. See H. James, *The Art of the Novel* (New York: Charles Scribner's Sons, 1934). This work contains prefaces written between 1907 and 1909. For an elementary exposition, see R. Scholes and R. Kellogg, *The Nature of Narrative* (New York: Oxford University Press, 1966), chap. 7.

25. See G. Genette, *Figures III* (Paris: Seuil, 1972), p. 203. For the English translation, see *Narrative Discourse* (Oxford: Blackwell, 1980), p. 186. On point of view in general, see Friedman, *Point of View;* J. Lintvelt, *Essai de typologie narrative: Le "point de vue"; Théorie et analyse* (Paris: Corti, 1981); S. Volpe, *L'occhio del narratore: Problemi di punto di vista* (Palermo: Circolo Semiologico Siciliano, 1984); and Segre, *Teatro e romanzo*, pp. 85–101.

26. G. Genette, *Figures III*, p. 204, and in the English translation, p. 186.

27. Ibid., pp. 183–84, and in the English translation, p. 162. In the sphere of discourse pragmatics, distance and perspective may be identified with restrictions—factual, cognitive, communicative, etc.—which are imposed upon formulation of the discourses by subjects and by situations. See T. A. van Dijk, *Text and Context: Explorations in the Semantics and Pragmatics of Discourse* (London: Longman, 1977), p. 2, chap. 8.

28. For a general description, see A. Neubert, *Die Stilformen der "erlebten Rede" im neueren englischen Roman* (Halle-Salle: Niemeyer, 1957); D. Cohn, *Transparent Minds: Narrative Modes for Presenting Consciousness in Fiction* (Princeton: Princeton University Press, 1978); A. Banfield, "Narrative Style and the Grammar of Direct and Indirect Speech," in *Foundations of Language*, 10 (1973): 1–39, and "The Formal Coherence of Represented Speech and Thought," in *PTL: A Journal for Descriptive Poetics and Theory of Literature*, 3 (1978): 2, pp. 289–314, and *Unspeakable Sentences: Narration and Representation in the Language of Fiction* (Boston: Routledge and Kegan Paul, 1982); and B. Mc. Hale, "Free Indirect Discourse: A Survey of Recent Accounts," in *PTL: A Journal for Descriptive Poetics and Theory of Literature*, 3 (1978): 2, pp. 249–87. The best semiotic description of direct style, free direct style, free indirect style, and mixed style is that of L. Doležel, "Vers la stylistique structurale," in *Travaux linguistiques de Prague*, 1 (1966): 257–66. The most complete work is now that of B. Garavelli Mortara, *La parola d'altri: Prospettive di analisi del discorso* (Palermo: Sellerio 1985).

29. See T. Todorov, "Les catégories du récit littéraire," in *Communications*, 8 (1966): 125–51; in particular, pp. 141–42.

30. See Genette, *Figures III*, and in the English translation, pp. 206, 189. An interesting development is in J. Lintvelt, "Pour une typologie de l'énonciation écrite," in *Cahiers roumains d'études littéraires*, 1 (1977): 62–80.

31. See C. Brooks and R. P. Warren, *Understanding Fiction*, 2d ed. (New York: Rinehart, Holt, and Winston, 1967). See, for distancing, M. Bal, "Narration and Focalisation," in *Poétique*, 8 (1977): 29, pp. 107–27, and *Narratologie (Essai sur la signification narrative dans quatre romans modernes)* (Utrecht: Hes Publishers, 1984). One should observe the way the whole matter is discussed in G. Genette, *Nouveau discours du récit* (Paris: Seuil, 1983).

32. See, for example, G. Müller, "Die Bedeutung der Zeit in der Erzählkunst" (1947), in *Morphologische Poetik: Gesammelte Aufsätze* (Tübingen: Niemeyer, 1968), pp. 247–68; E. Lämmert, *Bauformen des Erzählens*, 4th ed. (Stuttgart: Metzlersche Verlagsbuchhandlung, 1970); H. Stammerjohann, "Strukturen der Rede: Beobachtungen an der Umgangssprache von Florenz," in *Studi di filologia italiana*, 28 (1970): 295–397; H. Weinrich, *Tempus: Besprochene und erzählte Welt* (Stuttgart: Kohlhammer, 1964);

and W. J. M. Bronzwaer, *Tense in the Novel: An Investigation of Some Potentialities of Linguistic Criticism* (Groningen: Wolters-Noordhoff, 1970). See, in addition, E. Benveniste, *Problèmes de linguistique générale*, vol. 1 (Paris: Gallimard, 1966), chap. 19.

33. See, for example, the analysis of short stories of Boccaccio, Pirandello, Buzzati, etc., in Weinrich, *Tempus*, chap. 5. See also §2.6.

2.
The Text

2.1. Introductory Remarks

Used widely but vaguely, the word *text* takes on a particular value in literary analysis. In ordinary usage, *text*, which derives from the Latin *textus* ("Texture," "tissue"), develops a metaphor that sees the words, which because of their interconnection constitute the work, as a woven cloth.[1] This metaphor precedes other investigations of textual coherence and alludes in particular to text content, to what is actually written in a work. When applied, as it was in the Middle Ages, to texts endowed with particular authority (the Bible, the Gospel, or legal texts), the metaphor stressed the authenticity of the letter of the text as opposed, on the one hand, to inexact transcriptions (thus, the text is a complete and trustworthy transcription) and, on the other, to any annotations and glosses which illustrated it. In all these meanings the text is being thought of as a written text, even though its transmission may be oral. This explains why the word also comes to stand for the written material by means of which it is handed down. Text now comes to mean the manuscript or a printed volume which contains a given work.

If graphic signs (letters, punctuation, etc.) are looked at as signifiers for sounds, pauses, etc., and if we reflect on the fact that such signs can be transcribed over and over and in different ways (for example, with different scripts and characters) without the value changing, we will be led to conclude that it is the text which is the invariant, the succession of values, with respect to variables like characters, script, etc. We may also speak of *signifiés*, if we make it clear that the allusion is to what is signified graphically by the series of letters and punctuation marks which constitute the text.[2] The text, then, is a fixed succession of graphic meanings. These graphic meanings are carriers of semantic meanings as well, as we shall soon see. But it is the original constitution of the text which must be insisted upon from the outset.

Such insistence is necessary because it is the practically infinite implications of a text which attract readers, often for hundreds and thousands of years. These implications are entirely contained in the literalness of the graphic signs—hence, the importance of philology, which engages in the most accurate possible conservation of these graphic meanings. That the survival of texts may involve damage during transmission makes an effort to safeguard their authenticity all the more necessary.

2.2. Textual Linguistics

A recent current of linguistics, text linguistics, has put forward a different definition of text.[3] The text is seen as a large utterance (or complex utterance), oral or written.[4] What interests text linguists is the fact that our syntactic knowledge, which is sufficient to explain the conformation of single propositions or periods, cannot tell us why it is that a certain succession of utterances will constitute one coherent utterance, while another will not. Text linguistics attempts to determine the rules (which, taken as a whole, constitute our "textual competence"), for it is on the basis of the rules that we are able to construct coherent utterances and to judge the coherence of the utterances that others offer us.[5]

A history of these investigations is not necessary here. Their starting point is Hjelmslev's statement that the language system can be individuated only on the basis of processes, i.e., of the texts wherein it has found or finds its realization. Another source is Z. Harris's attempts at *discourse analysis*, i.e., individuation of regular characteristics; these are trans-sentential insofar as they are operative beyond the confines of the sentence. It may, however, prove useful to indicate the kind of linguistic techniques upon which text linguistics is based.[6]

Many linguists make use of descriptive concepts, sometimes deriving them from rhetoric. It was rhetoric which first attempted to investigate the way sentences are linked. Anaphora is a prime example. For text linguistics it means not just repetition of a given word but the use of pronouns to indicate a given person or object: "*The countess* arrived at five; *she* came in like a whirlwind. The maid took *her* fur, and showed *her* into the drawing room. The other guests came to meet *her*." Recurrence is akin: "I saw a *car*; it was a blue *car*." A broader concept is coreference, i.e., a common referent for a number of words; it embraces not just anaphora but cataphora as well, i.e., anticipation of substitution forms with respect to a proper noun ("When George met *him*, he seemed in good health. *Charles*, though, was already ailing") and the use of synonyms ("Peter saw a *motor scooter*. The *machine* was gleaming in the sunlight") and paraphrase ("He lives *with me, at home*. Under *my roof*").

These phenomena can also be defined on a logical, rather than linguistic, plane as cases of inclusion and implication. When we do so, we seize upon new intersentential techniques, such as recourse to classes and their members: "Frank saw a great many vehicles. *One* was a motorcycle, *another* a bicycle. All the *others* were cars."

Within this frame of analysis, the ideas of the Czech Mathesius, his "functional analyses," have found fertile soil.[7] In Mathesius's opinion, any utterance will, in general, contain a *theme* (*topic* in English), i.e., a part which will refer to entities and facts previously dealt with in the text, and a *rheme* (in English, *comment*), which will contain such new information as the utterance is designed to furnish. The discourse or text can then be looked at, in accord with present-day exponents of the Prague School, as a phenomenology of the possible alternatives between topic and comment. For example, we find a linear progression when the comment of one sentence becomes the topic of the one that follows ("I met a colleague. He spoke to me"); or persistence of the topic ("My colleague is called John. He is a good scholar. His works are full of humor"); or block progression, when the comment is divided among a number of topics ("We met two soldiers. The first . . . The second . . .").

Much more common, though more difficult to represent schematically, is the phenomenon of lexical or semantic contiguity; this is to be found when the same words recur, or when words belonging to the same lexical field recur, or when the same semantic features are recurrent in the terms employed by an utterance. In the first case, an immediate, autonomous analysis of the text is possible; in the second, recourse to a metalanguage, which will reduce synonyms, homonyms, and equivalent constructions to a common level, is necessary; the third case requires the mediation of semantic assessment. Here is an example: "I was *driving* along the *motorway* when quite suddenly the *engine* began to make an odd noise. I stopped the *car* and unscrewed the cap and saw that the *radiator* was overheated." Even before the car is named, the word *motorway* has already introduced us to the semantic sphere of the automobile, a sphere to which words like *driving, engine, radiator,* etc., belong as well.

2.3 Isotopy

The concept of *isotopy* was introduced into linguistics by Greimas, and it may well prove helpful here. It stands for "iteration along the syntagmatic sequence of classemes /= minimal contextual units of meaning/ which guarantee for the discourse-utterance its homogeneity."[8] Greimas lists various types of isotopy. Isotopy may be grammatical, with recurrence of categories, or semantic, and this "makes possible uniform reading of the discourse as it results from partial readings of the utterances which constitute it." Isotopy may be actorial, coinciding with anaphora, and so on. Greimas enlarges the concept to cover any recurrence of semic categories. In the first instance, though, we will do well to keep to the original meaning of the term, for it will serve to justify the weight isotopy may assume as a revealing element for reading: "From the point of view of the receiver of the utterance act, isotopy constitutes a grid for reading, one which renders the text surface homogeneous, given that it permits removal of its ambiguity."[9]

Some idea of isotopy can be given on the basis of a famous passage from Coleridge's *The Rime of the Ancient Mariner.*[10]

1 Around, around, flew each sweet sound,
2 Then darted to the sun;
3 Slowly the sounds came back again,
4 Now mixed, now one by one.
5 Sometimes a-dropping from the sky
6 I heard the sky-lark sing;
7 Sometimes all little birds that are,
8 How they seemed to fill the sea and air

    9 With their sweet jargoning!
10 And now 'twas like all instruments,
11 Now like a lonely flute;
12 And now it is an angel's song,
13 That makes the heavens be mute.

One isotopy is spatial in character. It presents a "circular" movement, which is "horizontal" at first and highlighted by the internal rhyme (*A*round, *a*round, . . . s*ound* in line 1) and, then (from line 2 onward), "vertical" as it follows the angelic spirits in their flight.

A supernatural isotopy appears at the close of the passage (*an angel's song* in line 12) as, in the silence, the transcendent beings fade, while their previous manifestations are made linear through an isotopy that is at once natural (*sound* in line 1; *sounds* in line 3; *sky-lark* in line 6; *little birds* in line 7) and cultural (*instruments* in line 10; *flute* in line 11).

The intersecting of supernatural, natural, and cultural isotopies is mediated and encompassed by the diffused musical isotopy which permits the "euphoric" contact between the deserted sea, to which the lone mariner is confined, and the silent skies.

Obviously those we have indicated are only a few of the isotopies to be found in a text of this kind. What needs stressing is that this wealth of isotopies, with all the complexity of their interlacings, is a consequence of the conceptual concentration proper to poetry. What we are verifying is the especially compact nature of the poetic text. With techniques such as these, and with others more complex but akin, text linguistics seeks to individuate the properties which make a text *coherent*. It should be noted that a text, especially if oral (conversation is a favored field for text linguistics), is isolated from the *continuum* of those utterances of which social life consists. Every dialogue has been preceded, and will be followed, by others. It may be interrupted for motives external to it, or it may change its argument, etc. Coherence, in short, is an internal fact with respect to the elements included in the text; it is, however, external with respect to everything which, in the continuum of utterance acts, constitutes other texts.

I might also remark that oral texts are closely tied to their situation: anything that clearly belongs to the situation can be taken for granted by the speakers, who can allude without naming, who can integrate their discourse with gestures (a pointing finger can replace a pronoun), or who can have recourse to superseg-mental features (intonation, etc.), and so on. In a word, the text-context connection is indissoluble, and this means that close attention must be paid to pragmatic factors.

2.4. The Literary Text

The above observations enable us to characterize the properties of the literary text. There is, for example, its more clear-cut delimitation, suggested or explicitly indicated when it is transcribed or printed, or the indeterminacy of its context, for the addresser will, for the most part, ignore the conditions under which his text will be read. Supersegmental features are also absent; how they are to be integrated is for the reader to decide (especially if he is to read aloud). And he will act on his own initiative.

The investigations of modern text linguistics have defined the problems and have gone some way toward solving them. It should, though, be added that, because the term *text* has been extended and made to embrace all utterances, oral and written, it is obligatory to redefine what, in ordinary usage, was quite clear enough in itself. There may be advantages in the extension of meaning; nonetheless, the word *text* will in this book be used from now on to refer exclusively to the literary text.

The literary text is characterized by the fact that it establishes a communication *sui generis*. Addresser and addressee are not "face to face," not even in a figurative sense, and it can be said (cf. §1.1) that communication is effected in two segments: addresser-message (there is no knowledge of who the real addressee is to be); message-receiver (one is ignorant of the precise context of emission and even, with anonymous works, of the addresser himself). Cases of works whose dedicatee was their addressee, or which were written expressly for a particular person or group of persons, do not modify the overall phenomenology, for a work can always go on being read, beyond such use as was initially foreseen and intended.

The main consequences of a communication so constructed are that:
(a) The addresser must introject the context into the message and order things in such a way that the message, embracing such references to the situation of its sending as are necessary, will be rendered practically autonomous. If it is the genesis of the work we wish to describe, it will be useful, when feasible, to reconstruct its context, but the work itself is now well able to do without such a context, except insofar as it retains it within itself;
(b) There is no possible feedback, i.e., the addressee cannot turn to the addresser for clarification, nor can he influence the way the message will proceed. The addresser himself, once he is faced with the message now fully fashioned, will find himself in exactly the same position as any other addressee;
(c) The text persists in a kind of potentiality after its sending and before its reception. It has been reduced to the series of graphic signs which constitute the support for its meanings. Such meanings, which in conversation unfold almost contemporaneously with the emission and reception of the message, here will become operative only in the course of subsequent readings. The addressee is now in a position to check, and to investigate further, what he has understood of the message. He may break off his reading in order to meditate on it; he may reread and compare different parts of the text, etc. (Although this is less true for oral execution, there is always the possibility that the addressee will be present at a number of performances and so receive the message, in whole or in part, twice or even many times over.)

2.5. Linguistic Functions

These three characteristics strongly motivate the particular linguistic elaboration of literary texts. From this point of view, there can be no question about the existence and effective operation of what Jakobson calls the "poetic function" (which characterizes the literary text without being limited to it alone). The poetic function, as we know, consists in orientation of the language toward the message in itself, instead of, let us suppose, toward the addresser (upon whom the *emotive function* is centered) or toward the addressee *(conative function).*[11] It is important to observe, as against any idealistic approach, that in the literary text the poetic function prevails over the emotive function. It is by concentrating on the message that the addresser safeguards a communication which, as we have seen, is sectioned and which otherwise might risk becoming impossible.

The engagement of the addresser with his message further entails the unity and coherence of the message itself. As distinct from ordinary discourse, the addresser is not subject to coexistence and succession of stimuli toward expression; on the contrary, he elaborates an inner discourse of his own, within limits that, to a large extent, he has chosen for himself. The result is that both reader and critic can verify for themselves whether the message is endowed with artistic coherence. The point they will start from will be, though, the notion they initially have of the text's individuality.

2.6. Types of Text

The reader is placed in a position to gauge the text's autonomy and range, thanks to a combined use of material elements and formal elements. (There are material elements such as the existence of one or more numbered volumes; in the case of publications in periodicals, we find titles, texts, and signatures, blank spaces, changes of typeface.) Formal elements belong to well-established and, as a rule, easily recognizable traditions, and they will for the most part fall within the theory of genres and subgenres. In a given society, any educated person is able to foresee the type of text he will be offered as novel, short story, tale of chivalry, collection of lyrics, etc. He will also recognize at first sight—running an eye over it will suffice—whether he is dealing with a novel, a short story, a tale of chivalry, or a collection of lyrics. Anomalies, too, are such only with respect to dominant usage. This is why they can be isolated and then catalogued.

So much for a first approximation. But choice of a genre or subgenre was, from the very moment the message was sent, already determinant for its form and thus for its coherence as well. As writers have always known, but as literary criticism is just beginning to realize, connections between choice of argument, of genre, and of the stylistic and linguistic means involved are very close indeed.[12] The coherence of the text is the form itself of this connection. What must be borne in mind, though, is that not all genres are closed to the same degree. The sonnet is mathematical in its exactitude, but, in the schema of the *canzone*, stanzas are variable in number and type, while the *ottave* in narrative poems are arranged with great freedom. It is perfectly clear that what is open or closed is the content level itself. Traditionally a sonnet will exhaust a single situation ("sonnet sequences" are a different matter); on the other hand, a narrative poem or, even better, a novel will embrace an infinity of situations. This explains why more demarcation signs are called for. A short composition needs no *explicit;* there is no need for the word *end*. Such devices are adopted when compositions are on a vaster scale and when their limits are not obvious.

There have been investigations into the ways the beginnings and endings of compositions are handled, in both poetic and narrative compositions. In fact, in all periods, they will be found to be substantially codified. Taken all in all, they serve to show how much care is devoted to putting forward and bringing to a close the imaginary world which is set up by the text. One is told from the outset what kind of development one is authorized to expect; the text in closing gives us the key in which the whole of its development is to be remeditated. In narrative works, for example, a clear and immediate definition of spatial-temporal coordinates is provided, even in a descriptive sense (and in this perspective the tenses of the verb play an important role: cf. §1.6.3), and the characters and setting are introduced to us. Equally familiar is the conceptual concentration at the end of a poem; it will sometimes be enhanced by a *mise en relief* imposed by a diversified concatenation of rhymes. Such techniques are not really very far removed from the raising and lowering of a curtain.[13]

2.7. Coherence of the Text

This all serves to show that coherence exigencies, obvious in ordinary discourse, are different, more subtle and less rigid, in the literary text. I might point out, on the one hand, that, although the literary text may in appearance seem to be incoherent (futurist prose, surrealist poetry, stream-of-consciousness prose),[14] its unity, apart from the external characteristics already mentioned, is sustained by a *performative utterance*[15] of the following type: "These disconnected phrases are to be interpreted as the thoughts of x in situation y." On the other hand, a literary text is often the coherent sum of different coherences. Take, for example, the criterion of coreference (§2.2). In an episode from a novel, this requirement is undoubtedly respected: any new character will immediately be "placed" with respect to those we already know, so that persons and things will all be brought into relation by means of pronominalization, anaphora, and so on. It is true that successive episodes may set up different areas of coreference, but, at a certain point, these will be unified by the revelation of relations between the characters of the various areas, relations which were not necessarily indicated from the outset or which did not then exist.

The most typical case of this coherent sum of various coherences is the theater text. For each scene a discourse situation is simulated, analogous to real situations; what the whole text effects, however, is the realization of a programmed whole (coherent on another level), made up of diverse situations. One need only remark, to show this more clearly, that between one scene and the next a change of context may intervene (with a difference of characters, settings, and time), with a clear-cut difference in the use of deictics: *these, this, those, that,* etc., will now refer us to a different system of referents.[16] One last example: in a narrative text it may easily happen that some isotopies are present only in certain sections (motifs come to mind) alongside large-scale isotopies and that these knit the sections together in their entirety.

It may prove useful taxonomically to indicate the main types of coherence which coexist in the literary text. (Often they will integrate each other, those of formal character being at times less evident, though as a rule sense coherence will persist. Sense coherence can, however, always be recovered so long as we place ourselves on an adequately encompassing level.) Doležel,[17] for example, indicates four levels of coherence, two of them semantic (i.e., pertinent to overall meaning) and two relative to texture (i.e., to the surface of the discourse):

(a) long-range semantic coherence;
(b) short-range semantic coherence;
(c) long-range discourse coherence;
(d) short-range discourse coherence.

The expressions *long-range* and *short-range* refer here to connections over distance which serve for structuring or else to immediate connections between the text's single parts.

The conclusion must, I think, be that the types of coherence that text criticism shows us have, in the literary text, no merely connective and distinctive function. They are stratified to form hierarchies, and, in the case of the text, it is these which constitute its structure. A problem of structure thus comes to replace any problem of unity and coherence, and it prepares the materials for our discovery of artistic coherence, a different and more complex coherence.

2.8. Macrotext

The unity of a text derives from the act of its sending. A correspondence between the addresser's intention and the addressee's recognition is made possible by the literary conventions they share. Cases of texts, totally or partially autonomous, which have been grouped together to form a more ample text, a macrotext, do, though, exist. This theoretical problem finds correspondence in practice, for example in the three following cases (and this exemplification might be considerably extended):

(1) Lyrical compositions subsequently inserted by their author into prose works or brought together in accord with an overall pattern to form a "canzoniere," or

a sonnet sequence. A typical example of the former case is Dante's *Vita nuova*. It comments literally on, and illustrates in narrative form, the genesis of the poetic compositions it contains. As an example of the latter, Petrarch's *Canzoniere* soon became paradigmatic. In English examples are Sir Phillip Sidney's sonnet-sequence *Astrophel and Stella* and George Meredith's *Modern Love*, a sequence of fifty poems, each of sixteen lines, which documents the decline of passion and the consequent dissolution of a marriage. But we might add to these all of the collections in book form of poems written and circulated one by one and then brought together by the poet, either in terms of a pattern in some sense biographical (Ungaretti's *Vita d'un uomo* would be an example) or else in obedience to affinities of content, theme, etc;

(2) Tales published piecemeal and then brought together by their author in accord with some specific design, perhaps even placed within a specific framework,[18] as in the ancient collections of India (*Pañcatantra, The Book of the Seven Sages,* or in the *Decameron*, where the narrative frame, with its fictional device of the young people who seek refuge in the countryside from the plague, also serves to classify thematically—each of the ten nights being devoted to a group of ten tales—the hundred tales which make up the work);

(3) Private letters, brought together by their author in the form of collected correspondence and arranged in terms of periods, addressees, topics, and so on. Petrarch's or Cicero's letters, variously collected, come to mind.

The way authors behave with regard to works whose status has shifted (once autonomous, they have become part of more ample compositions) can help us to seize upon the forces which unify texts and macrotexts. On the one hand, we find a tendency to make the texts more homogeneous in the light of their new employment (by eliminating from each such peculiarities as might compromise balance and sound a false note within the whole and by actively effecting a formal unification or harmonization); on the other hand, the overall structure of their forces of cohesion is reinforced (by use of headings and other means of classification, which underline the unity conferred; weight is accorded to the opening and closing texts, while, within the whole, the arrangement follows a calculated parabola). The most interesting effect is perhaps elimination of repetition (realized to the full in cases where some of the texts included are seen as anticipations of, or comments on, themes which other texts will develop), with all the reciprocal clarification such thinning out entails. In other words, it is the authors themselves who have already considered (1) the coordination of the texts they include,[19] (2) the establishment of relations with the whole, and (3) the establishment of relations among single texts inside the order of succession now actuated.[20]

Text coherence must be considered in terms of a progression whose later phase assimilates the earlier. Every text will, in general, maintain an internal autonomy and coherence of its own, but this will subsequently be absorbed into a broader autonomy and cohesion. Proportional relations between these types of cohesion may vary, for they will depend on how rigidly the macrotext is structured. This hierarchy of autonomies exists for conventional texts as well, given that a single dialogue may embrace any number of duly delimited texts, while any number of dialogues may in their continuity constitute one single macrotext. It only remains to add that, as in the case of the isolated text, it is the author's commitment to elaboration which will highlight and calculate conjunctive and separative elements alike.

2.9. Structure

2.9.1. Structure has always been discussed; it is the application of an obvious metaphor derived from the art of building. We might make a dictionary definition our own: structure, in the *Oxford English Dictionary,* is "the mutual relation of the constitutent parts or elements of a whole as determining its peculiar nature or character." In literature, a metrical or stanzaic pattern, or the distribution of material into books or chapters, etc., might be described as structure. Such structures are often the work of the authors themselves. We might recall the *Divine Comedy* with its three books, or *cantiche,* each made up of thirty-three cantos, and an opening canto brings the total to a hundred. There is the *Decameron,* whose tales—there are a hundred of them, too—are divided into *decadi* (like the Decades of Livy). Many long poems will come to mind. Wherever possible they are made to fall into twelve books on the pattern of the *Aeneid* (this is true of Boccaccio's *Teseida* and of *Paradise Lost*), or importance is attributed to the number 9 (the chapters of *Fiammetta*) or to 5 and 10 and their multiples (there are five books in Boccaccio's *Filocolo* and fifty in his *Amorosa visione,* twenty in Tasso's *Gerusalemme liberata,* etc.). The division of comedies and tragedies into acts and scenes whose number is nearly always fixed in advance is itself a fact of structure. Another example is the distribution of parts in prose and parts in poetry (or lyric compositions) in works like *De consolatione Philosophiae* of Boethius or in Dante's *Vita nuova,* Boccaccio's *Commedia delle ninfe fiorentine,* Sannazzaro's *Arcadia,* etc. Through structures of this kind, which are immediately evident, the author expresses his desire for order and communicates it to the reader.

Metrical patterns are structure as well: the more complex the pattern the greater the wealth of symmetry, parallelism, and opposition. If we take sonnet form, we find ourselves faced with a complex of abstract possibilities. These are proper to its structure, but the authors of sonnets will make use of them in a variety of ways:

> The sonnet has the same number of strophes as a tetrad of quatrains; in both cases three binary oppositions underlie the *coniugatio stantiarum* and enable us to look for three similar types of correspondences in the internal, particularly grammatical, structure of the four strophes. Both odd strophes (I, III) may differ from the two even strophes (II, IV), and each of these pairs is apt to display inner grammatical correspondences. Both outer strophes (I, IV) are expected to show common traits different from those grammatical features which unify both inner strophes (II, III). Finally, both anterior strophes (I, II) are likely to differ in their

grammatical texture from both posterior strophes (III, IV), in turn united by distinct similarities. Thus a tetrastrophic poem exhibits three virtual sets of correspondences between its distinct strophes: 1) odd (I, III), 2) even (II, IV), 3) outer (I, IV); and in turn three sets of correspondences between the adjacent strophes: 1) anterior (I, II), 2) posterior (III, IV), 3) inner (II, III).

On the other hand, the sonnet displays substantial differences from a four-quatrain poem. All the strophes of the latter exhibit a mutual symmetry, and the three types of correspondences mentioned may be extended to the microcosmic interrelationships of the four lines within each strophe. The sonnet, however, combines an identical number of lines within the pairs of its anterior and posterior strophes with a numerical difference between these two pairs. An ingenious union of symmetry with asymmetry, and particularly of binary with ternary structures in the interconnection of strophes, secured the enduring career and expansion of the Italian-born sonnet model.[21]

2.9.2. Today, as a rule, something less evident and more important is intended by structure. The following very broad definition might prove acceptable: "structure is the set of latent relations among the parts of an object." In a literary work, where all our attention is directed toward the message, we might well hold that no elements exist which do not enter into this set of relations. It is the critic's task to find these relations and such elements as are determinant for the text's characterization.

The difference between the two conceptions of structure, internal and external, has today been understood thanks to the elaboration of structuralist conceptions. It had, of course, been sensed intuitively long before. Here, for example, is Foscolo (it is Orelli who draws attention to the passage):

> This observation of Galileo regarding inlaying *(intarsiature)*, I admire much more than a great many rhetorical treatises. It caused an idea to germinate in my mind which, though not new perchance, will now stand newly forth, I believe, clearly unfolded. It is this: in prose, no less than in verse, the writer must exactly observe the *design* of his thought. I do not mean the overall design of the work, what others call its architecture, its economy, or, with a French borrowing, its *piano* or plan. What I have in mind is the design of each thought separated out, one word being first weighed against another, then each idea arising from each word, and then each grouping of minimal ideas in relation to their neighbors; subsequently, the whole thought produced by the ideas when brought together; and then, the period, and one period with another. This will be effected in such a way that what results will be a progression of members and sounds, where each member is endowed with ideas neither too many nor too few and where there are neither more nor fewer . . . ideas than are needed, the whole exhibiting a variety of sounds, of shades, of shifts in light and in chiaroscuro, which is, after all, nothing less than the enchantment summoned up by harmony, by that art which is so difficult in architecture, which is the predilection of painting and of the other fine arts, and which Nature, with its power divine, has diffused over all things in the universe.[22]

Good use can be made of the system-structure pair: where structure is one of a number of possible realizations and where the structure actually realized is realized in terms of the possibilities offered by a given system. In effect, when other sciences speak of structure, the conception is always a dynamic one, as Piaget's definition shows:

> As a first approximation, we may say that a structure is a system of transformations. Inasmuch as it is a system and not a mere collection of elements and their properties, these transformations involve laws: the structure is preserved or enriched by the interplay of its transformational laws, which never yield results external to the system nor employ elements that are external to it. In short, the notion of structure is comprised of three key ideas: the idea of wholeness, the idea of transformation, the idea of self-regulation.
>
> The discovery of structure may, either immediately or at a much later stage, give rise to formalization. Such formalization is, however, always the creature of the theoretician, whereas structure itself exists apart from him. Formalization sometimes proceeds by direct translation into logical or mathematical equations, sometimes passes through the intermediate stage of constructing a cybernetic model, the level of formalization depending upon the choice of the theoretician.[23]

With respect to the literary work, such dynamism preexists, and it is intrinsic to the work's elaboration. Dynamism may come after in cases of reworking, new versions, etc. Inside the text, though, dynamics are immobilized: what remains is the totality; inside it, transformations and self-regulation are immobilized. The system-structure pair embraces both the dynamic moment and the static and (provisionally) definitive moment as well. If the work is considered as a whole, we consider the sum of its elements and their relations as a system distinct from the particular use which is made of them within the text; the same whole, when considered in the latent relations conferred upon its elements by their arrangement in the text, is seen as a system.

2.10. Levels

2.10.1. When we speak of the elements of a text, we may be alluding as much to elements of the signifier as to those of the signified. It should be stressed that the latter are implied, developed as it were, by the former. Any analysis of the text must therefore take as its starting point the fact that the text is made up of a succession of graphic signifiers, or *monemes,* and that these are made up of groups of *graphemes.*[24] It is this succession, immutable unless there is damage in transmission, which, in the act of reading, will then unfold meanings.

But if, like Saussure, we are led to treat the text (like the signs of the *langue*) as a two-level signifier-signified construction, it may prove useful to envisage further stratifications for each of the levels and to take into account the varieties of analysis which can be effected either on the signifier level (of phonological, morphological, or lexical analysis) or on the level of the signified (of meanings—verbal, sentential or trans-sentential, etc.). One of the advocates of this arrangement is Ingarden, who sees the literary work as a many-tiered structure:

> The essential structure of the literary work inheres, in our opinion, in the fact that it is *a formation constructed of several heterogeneous strata*. The individual strata differ from one another 1) by their characteristic material, from the peculiarity of which stem the particular qualities of each stratum, and 2) by the role which each stratum plays with respect to both the other strata and the structure of the whole work. Despite the diversity of the material of the individual strata, the literary work is not a loose bundle of fortuitously juxtaposed elements but an *organic structure* whose uniformity is grounded precisely in the unique character of the individual strata. There exists among them a distinct stratum, namely, the stratum of meaning units, which provides the structural framework for the whole work. By its very essence it requires all the other strata and determines them in such a way that they have their ontic basis in it and are dependent in their content on its qualities. As elements of the literary work they are thus inseparable from this central stratum.[25]

The whole of Ingarden's main book is organized to accord with these strata, for in his opinion they make up the literary work—strata of verbalized language formations, of meaning units, of figurative objectivity, of aspects schematized. Ingarden's framework is clearly based on Husserl, and, as a result, it deals principally with modalities of perception and representation, with mental activities which precede textual activity. Of the strata he brings to light, only the first two would fall within an analysis of the kind we are describing. What ought rather to be underlined is (1) that the four strata succeed one another in inverse order with respect to the production of the literary object, which means that they start from the literary object itself, and (2) that Ingarden attributes a structuring function to the second stratum; as a consequence, the others must be considered in their relation to this function. In other words, order in strata is not accidental in the least; it corresponds to stages in the activity of representing. Only when perception intervenes will the strata stand revealed in polyphonic form.

The special role conferred upon the stratum of meaning units fits into a rational (not rationalistic) conception of the literary work. As distinct from other works of art, it "can never be a *totally* irrational formation, as is quite possible in other types of artistic works, especially in music. This moment of *reason*, even if it resonates only vaguely, is always contained in even those literary works of art that are oriented entirely on mood and feeling."[26]

2.10.2. This ideal subdivision of the literary work into strata or, as they have usually been called, levels, has proved acceptable to the exponents of a variety of approaches. The levels which have been, and are, indicated are those of "phonology, morphology, lexis, syntax, the utterance, semantics, the symbol,"[27] but the list remains open. There has also been talk of metrical and prosodic levels, etc. Such division into levels does not, as a rule, appeal to any particular doctrine. If it is Saussure's or Hjelmslev's terminology we adopt, then the phonological, morphological, lexical, and syntactical levels will pertain to discourse, while those of the utterance, semantics, and symbol will belong to discourse content. The image of levels is not an easy one to project in spatial terms. Take discourse, for example. Morphemes do not exist independently; they exist only when united with lexemes. Both morphemes and lexemes are made up of phonemes, exclusively so, and it is their union which constitutes syntagms. These so-called levels, in short, constitute one single plane, that of the signifier. The image of levels, though it is somewhat inappropriate, finds some justification with content levels (those of the utterance, of semantics, of the symbol), given the hierarchization of meanings within a connotative perspective.

The term *level* ought, then, to be desemanticized, though a useful pigeon-holing role may be accorded to it in an initial taxonomy. Unfortunately, isotopy, the other image we have discussed, cannot replace it. Isotopy is itself the result of sorting anew material initially pigeon-holed, on the basis of homogeneity of semic character.[28] Levels, on the contrary, are classes whose character remains grammatical (phonemes, morphemes, etc.) or semic. Inside such classes, isotopies which already reflect the forces of conceptual organization can be individuated.

2.10.3. The convergence of the two terms, level and isotopy, is not without its lessons. Classification of materials by levels ought to precede interpretation (whereas the individuation of isotopies is already a distinct act of interpretation). But the most neutral observer, even by the barest glance, cannot free himself from a hypothesis of interpretation, however unconscious. Reading itself, in its most ingenuous or hedonistic forms, is already an interpretive undertaking. The transformation of signifiers into signs which it effects is the outcome of a conflict between codes of transmission and codes of reception, of a choice among possible values for the signs which cannot confine itself to strict denotation.

The danger that besets operations of classification is the exact opposite. From the start, one's material has been collected in function of a working hypothesis, before any examination had been undertaken thorough enough to authorize its formulation. One of the lessons of structuralism, and of early structuralist analyses, might well be that care should be exercised to ensure that no element of a whole is allowed to escape attention because it is perhaps regarded as secondary or not pertinent to global understanding. It may well be that only at the end will its pertinence appear.

In the passage quoted earlier from Coleridge's *The Rime of the Ancient Mariner* (cf. §2.3), the syntactic level unfolds in synchrony with the stanza structure. When, however, the rhythmical phrase exceeds the measure of "common meter," so that the rhythmical period is extended (vv. 5–9), the same thing happens on the level of the syntactic period. The three stanza-sentences are articulated, homologously, as main sentences which are determined principally by subordinates (*Then* in line 2, *Now . . . now* in line 4, *Sometimes . . . sometimes* in lines 5–7, *now* in line 11) or by temporal coordinates (*And now*

... *And now* in lines 10–12). In the last lines, the narrative past is replaced by the present. But the warning against too hasty a presumption of pertinence in terms of interpretation for such an arrangement needs little justification. We will remind ourselves that the literary text is built up on the basis of connotation, i.e., on the use of denotative semiotics, and that these, subordinate to, and functionalized in terms of, other semiotics, become connotative (cf. §2.12).

In this text, the evident syntactic parallelism delineated by the temporal determinations brings into focus the chiastic alternation of the "orchestra" (*sounds . . . mixed* in lines 3–4, *all little birds* in line 7, *all instruments* in line 10) and of the "soloists" (*sounds . . . one by one* in lines 3–4, *sky-lark* in line 6, *lonely flute* in line 11, *an angel* in line 12), in homology with a musical composition.

In conflict with the overall negative denotation of the "narrative" (the mariner is abandoned, however reluctantly, by the angelic hosts), the syntactically coordinated and subordinated alternation of "natural" sound manifestations—of solos (*sky-lark* in line 6), of choir (*all the little birds* in line 7)—and of "cultural" sound manifestations—choral (*all instruments* in line 10) and solo (*lonely flute* in line 11)—finds its integration on the meaning plane which is instituted by the "supernatural" isotopy. Here, the same "music" asserts itself as "vehicle" whose "tenor" is metaphysical and establishes, between "heaven" and "sea," a fleeting link, markedly positive in connotation. The replacement of the narrative past tense by the present tense in lines 12 and 13 contributes to an additional connotation of the cyclical reawakening of the cosmos with the coming of dawn.[29]

For *The Flea*, a poem of three four-line stanzas by John Donne, an assessment of deictics might prove a good starting point; there are an unusually large number of them from the outset, and due weight will be accorded to the demonstrative, argumentative, persuasive quality of *this*, iteratively linked to *flea* (lines 1 and 4 of the first stanza, line 3 of the second, lines 3 and 9 of the final stanza). Here is the poem's first stanza:

```
1 Mark but this flea, and mark in this,
2 How little that which thou deniest me is;
3 It suck'd me first, and now sucks thee,
4    And in this flea our two bloods mingled be:
5 Thou know'st that this cannot be said
6 A sin, nor shame, nor loss of maidenhead,
7    Yet this enjoys before it woo,
8 And pamper'd swells with one blood made of two,
9 And this alas, is more than we would do.
```

Here the following deictics should be noted: *this* (twice in line 1), *that, thou, me* (line 2), *me, now, thee* (line 3), *this* (line 7), while *this* in line 5 and line 9 takes on an anaphoric function. This dense initial distribution of deictics is functional with respect to the structuring of the internal "world" of the text. On the other hand, *this* (line 1) enters into rhythmical conjunction (eye rhyme) with *is* (line

2). In lines 3 and 4 of the second stanza—its corresponding position in the structure is no accident—this is the recurrence we find:

> This flea is you and I, and this
> Our marriage bed and marriage temple is.

Here, both terms, rhyme constrained, appear again, linearized, at the beginning of line 3 (*This . . . is*), where they frame *flea* (line 3), the manifest and understood subject of the two paratactic propositions. These are diversified structurally only by their different collocation of the double and composite nominal predicate *you* and *I* following the copula *is* (line 3), whereas *our marriage bed* and *marriage temple* precede it (line 4). The metaphorical identification of the deictics *you* and *I* with *flea*, and with *our marriage bed* and *marriage temple*, has the function of representing a sexual union, obviously an imaginary one, between the addresser and the female addressee of his discourse. Such a union is shown, paradoxically, to be "legitimate," in terms of such rituals as were at that time obligatory.

2.11. Expression and Content

For the signifier-signified relation in discourse, Hjelmslev's description is still a useful one.[30] He provides a four-tiered model:

$$\text{expression} \begin{cases} \text{form} \\ \text{substance} \end{cases}$$

$$\text{content} \begin{cases} \text{form} \\ \text{substance} \end{cases}$$

This bears the stamp of Saussure (expression = signifier; content = signified), especially in the stress on the inseparability of expression and content (no content can exist which precedes form, such that it can be decked out in various forms). It is, however, the nature of the linguistic sign that it most profitably illuminates.

Expression and content are functives of the sign function: "By virtue of the content form and the expression form, and only by virtue of them, exist respectively the content substance and the expression substance, which appear by the form's being projected on to the purport, just as an open net casts its shadow on an undivided surface."[31] Given a manifestation, form will constitute the constant, and content will be the variable; it is thus clear that the sign function is constituted by the solidarity between expression form and content form.

In order to illustrate, with Hjelmslev, this fourfold division, we might take the case of a color, red. Its content substance is constituted by a class of vibrations belonging to the continuum of the color spectrum. It is only by means of content form that a language like English can select from within such a continuum a class of vibrations which is to be designated by the word *red*. The word *red*, in its turn, is realized with variable phonic or graphic material (there may well be differences of accent and of stress, variety of typographical characters, etc.), and it constitutes a precise formal structure, a union of the phonemes /r/, /e/, /d/. In a text, the fourfold division appears as an overlapping of lines or of planes.

But if form and substance are indivisible, and if the signs that result really do segment reality differently for different languages, a point of convergence must exist which is prior to the formal activity that is language. A common factor must exist, definable "only by its having function to the structural principle of language and to all the factors that make languages different from one another."[32] For Hjelmslev this is *purport*, i.e., the sense, the thought. The sentences *Non so* (Italian), *je ne sais pas* (French), *jeg véd det ikke* (Danish), *en tiedä* (Finnish), *naluvara* (Eskimo), all more or less correspond to the concept "I don't know," but in their way of saying it they articulate their material differently. The subject and the object may or may not be expressed, and the order will vary, while the verb may show different aspects and moods (a literal translation of the Eskimo would give "not-knowing am I that"), etc. This concept of material, or purport, is fundamental when we come to account for the possibility of translation and transcodification. It is also worth pointing out that Hjelmslev's analysis deals with words or with syntagms, at most. Once we move beyond the limits of the sentence, this indissoluble connection between the expression plane and the content plane breaks down. On the contrary, ample blocks of discourse, even total discourse, can be made to fall within a phenomenology of connotation.

2.12. Connotation and Denotation

The term *connotation* is opposed to *denotation* because it designates a certain supplementary knowledge with respect to the purely informative and codified knowledge of denotation. Any word at all will denote more than an object, an action, etc.; it will give rise to further concepts relative to the use of the object or to the sphere within which, as a rule, the word will be used, and so forth. Many linguists have offered more stringent definitions, but they are in conflict with each other.[33] Hjelmslev's own definition is to the point: "a connotative semiotic is a semiotic that is not a language, and one whose expression plane is provided by the content plane and expression plane of a denotative semiotic. Thus it is a semiotic one plane of which (namely the expression plane) is a semiotic."[34] Without delving too deeply into the implications of this doctrine, two decisive facts must be pointed out:
(1) The connotative semiotic thus described seems to be absolutely identical with a description of the functioning of the literary text. Nobody believes that such a text limits its communication possibilities to denotative meanings, i.e., to

the literal value of the sentences of which it is constituted. There is a communication surplus, and it is brought about by the fact that the expression and content planes of syntagms are raised to an expression plane, of which, united as they are, they form the content plane;

(2) This interplay of planes, which may be rendered hierarchic to infinity by multiplication of the fourfold division described earlier, takes us far beyond any merely linguistic analysis of the text; it serves to show that the text, in the linearity of its aspect as a language product, compacts a density and a plurality of planes in the semiotic order. This explains why Hjelmslev does not speak of connotation but of connotative semiotics.

2.13. Expression and Content in Literature

It is difficult to resist the temptation to adopt Hjelmslev's quadripartition for analysis of the literary text. Its polyvalent complexity is evident to anyone, irrespective of its definition.[35] The first to succumb was Sørensen, a member of the Copenhagen School itself.[36] He suggested that language might be looked at as expression substance; style, as expression form; ideas, feelings, and inspirations, as content substance; themes, composition, and genres, as content form. This is an attractive way of making use of Hjelmslev's schema; it is, though, little more than a filing system which will accommodate findings from different spheres. What is lost here is the close interconnection and the bifrontalism postulated by Hjelmslev; all he intended to explain was the binomial signifier/signified.

A great deal more cogent in its functionalism is the schema put forward by Greimas.[37] Expression and content are bifurcated on the basis of their reference to single syntagms or to broader utterances. Thus we have:

		Language plane	
		Expression	Content
Dimensions	Syntagm	Phonematic schemata	Grammatical schemata
	Utterance	Grammatical schemata	Narrative schemata

Greimas himself is well aware of the limits of his diagram, for he adds: "It is evident that subdivisions within the levels described are possible and foreseeable and a more complex classification of poetic schemata, for they are based on well-known principles of linguistic analysis into immediate constituents." In other words, this is a filing cabinet, too, and nothing more.

This objection applies even more to Zumthor.[38] In dealing with Charles d'Orléans and the language of allegory, he posits: expression substance—personifications as subjects; expression form—metaphors as actions; content substance—the "ideological" universe; content form—the irradiation of the metaphors. And yet all the elements assessed by him are of the semantic order; it is rather risky to speak of substance and form.

A more coherent attempt at theorizing our quadripartition is that effected by Trabant,[39] who encompasses the whole semiotics of the literary work. For him, language is the expression substance of the aesthetic sign, while the text is its expression form. He deals at length with content substance and content form but offers no clear-cut concretization for them. It is a fact that contents are arranged on different connotative planes and that the sense, beyond any denotation, can be determined for text sections of different extension, which will then lend themselves to different paraphrases. In other words, Hjelmslev's quadripartition only functions for the language and for the denotation that it conveys. It does not work for a semiotic object of many meanings like the literary text.

If we consider text content, and leave aside language content in its inseparability from expression (the signified is similarly inseparable from the signifier), our object will be closer to what Hjelmslev calls *purport* than to what he calls *content* (cf. §2.11). A substantial heterogeneity exists (and heteronomy as well), and for some time attempts have been made to define it by contrasting the *signified* to *signification* and to *sense*. Literary criticism cannot leave aside signification and sense, for, were it to do so, it would hardly be able to move away from literal interpretation. It cannot, however, just ignore the difficulty and treat signification and sense in the same way as signifiers which can be ascertained in linguistic terms.[40] This is why, in the paragraphs that follow, only expression substance and expression form will be dealt with, for they can properly be referred to the signifier plane. The whole of paragraph 3 will be devoted to textual content and meanings which lie beyond the linguistic aspect of discourse, irreducibly so. Such an approach will not be modeled on Hjelmslev, for he gives no guidance when it comes to studying purport and sense.

2.14. Expression Substance

If Hjelmslev's quadripartition is to prove heuristically useful, we must refer back to the text in its immediate aspect of linguistic product. To the word *signified* (the equivalent of Hjelmslev's *content*) must be attributed the same value that it has in linguistics, one which will correspond to the linguistic function of the *signifiers* (which correspond to *expression*).

Let us begin with expression. The substance is involved in all those effects whose assessment depends upon reading aloud. Play with vowel colors, or with sound effects based on consonants and consonant clusters, are foreseen by certain texts, though their action is modest; undeniably they are less readily recognizable if the reading is silent. Or again, play may be made with form, or with typeface, or, even better, with a grouping of characters which takes advantage of another substance, graphic substance. Recent criticism has increasingly turned its attention to such techniques, hitherto the province of amateurs. Stress is laid not so much on the effects, or on the symbolism, of

THE TEXT 43

single sounds or groups as on their connection, in possible concomitance with significations expressed on another level.

A written text can thus be appreciated both in its visual aspect and in such acoustic aspects as can be achieved in reading. These (coexisting) possibilities fall into the categories of space and time respectively. The former finds one of its preferential realizations in icons,[41] which emphasize formal resemblances; the latter, in symbols, which suggest conceptual resemblances. This is one of Jakobson's observations,[42] and it might well serve as an initial classification for phenomena relative to the expression substance.

2.15. Iconic Use of Substance

The form of certain letters has often been used iconically. Observe the way in which the exclamation mark and the bracket taken from a poem by E. E. Cummings,[43] in the following text, suggested surprise and grief at the death of Paul Rosenfeld:

1 o

2 the round
3 little man we
4 loved so isn't

5 no!w

6 a gay of a
7 brave and
8 a true of a

9 who have

10 r
11 olle
12 di

13 nt

14 o
15 n
16 o

17 w(he)re

Here the *o* transfigures the exclamation of pain in such a way that it becomes regret visualized; it is, at the same time, an icon which depicts the tiny round figure of a departed friend. This is made explicit metadiscoursively with lines 2,

3, and 4 *(the rOund / little man we / lOved sO isn't)*. This *o* is then focalized dramatically in *no!w* (line 5). The exclamation mark inscribed in the word splits it and, at the same time, underlines the agonizingly temporal nature of pain and rebellion against the event itself *(no!)*: the impossibility of accepting it here and now. In lines 12–17, the agrammatical spacing of *into nowhere* stresses in modular fashion the iconic character of *o* (lines 14 and 16) contiguously and synchronically. It further highlights a reiterated *no* (lines 15–16).

In the last line, the atopic nature *(nowhere)* of the person lost is contradicted by the autonomous lexical fragment *w(he)re*. There is a place for feelings of affection, a place where the *he* thus put forward will not totally disappear. The iconic use of brackets has the function of drawing attention to mourning and to the fact that forgetting is not to be considered. Obviously it is the iconic value of *o* which makes it possible to metaphorize the death of *the rOund / little man* (lines 2–3), thanks to the cleverly segmented syntagm *whO have /r/Olle/d . . .* (lines 9–12).

When iconism involves more ample sectors of discourse (words and syntagms), statements like the following of Jakobson are an invitation to further investigation:

> The chain of verbs *veni, vidi, vici* informs us about the order of Caesar's deeds first and foremost because the sequence of co-ordinate preterits is used to reproduce the succession of reported occurrences. The temporal order of speech events tends to mirror the order of narrated events in time or in rank. Such a sequence as "the President and the Secretary of State attended the meeting" is far more usual than the reverse, because the initial position in the clause reflects the priority in official standing.[44]

We may also follow Peirce and speak of *diagrams*, i.e., of icons of intelligible relations (just as they do in diagrams, curves plot out statistically an increase or decrease with respect to given quantities). Jakobson cites a number of elementary examples: among them, degrees of comparison (a higher rank is often indicated with a longer word: *altus-altior-altissimus; high-higher-highest*) and the terminations of the verb (terminations are not infrequently longer in the plural than they are in the singular: *je finis–nous finissons; tu finis–vous finissez*).[45]

2.15.2. An immense field of possibilities is opened up by the physical nature of letters and blocks of writing on the one hand and, on the other, by the meanings these letters and blocks of writing convey. This is the case whether they are considered in their materiality or whether what is taken into account is the sign values conferred upon them. I shall mention only "calligrams" and *carmina figurata*,[46] because they are extreme cases of the kind of thing that may well be present in writing of any kind.

Calligrams were invented in the Alexandrian period, and since then they have been in vogue many times—from Francesco Colonna to Rabelais, from George Herbert to Apollinaire. What they play upon is the opposition based on what is to be found on the page: written / not written, dark against light. The idea is to obtain figures (silhouettes) which will, as a rule, allude to the dominant theme of the composition in much the same way as a title does. As an example, here is a description of Apollinaire's *La cravate et la montre:*

> Clusters of words represent the hours, at first with short formulae, which then lengthen progressively (and this too is a figurative way of representing a concept, the numerical increase of the hours; it may be an acoustic phenomenon as well, for the later the hour the more prolonged will be its striking). Around the clock face, on the right, a sentence has been arranged: it represents in rudimentary fashion, as would the tracing of a pencil, the watch-case in perspective. . . .[47]

Far more complex are *carmina figurata*, and here the unrivalled master was Rabanus Maurus (d. 856). Without going into excessive detail, we shall limit ourselves to the most striking features of the phenomenon. With *carmina figurata* we are still dealing with a use of writing to form overall designs (letters, crosses, human forms stand out from the page, thanks to different or more intense colors). The letters, however, are used in their sign function as well; this, though, is *multiplied*. Inside the overall discourse, other, easily definable discourses unfold. These carry further a potential geometrical linking of letters, whose best-known and simplest type is the acrostic (letters whose position is analogous in successive lines of poetry—the initial position is usually preferred—give rise to other words or verses, etc.).[48] Letters here are being used simultaneously (a) as features of a figurative design, (b) as signs of a discourse sequence, and (c) as signs of other discourse sequences which cut across, or embroider, the basic sequence.

2.15.3. It is always possible to use parts of a text iconically, and this is frequently done. In cases other than those listed, iconism is made visible exclusively because of its concomitance with meaning. There is an excellent example in Ennius, whose splitting of a brain is at the same time a linguistic splitting (*cere comminuit brum* in place of *cerebrum comminuit*), so that visual form is given to the fact narrated. A whole line of poetry, in the arrangement of its words or verbal symmetries or both, may imitate iconically what is being spoken about. Line 12 of the first section of T. S. Eliot's *Preludes* is a good example: *A lonely cab-horse steams and stamps*. The prosodic equivalence conferred upon the predicates *steams* and *stamps* by the regular iambic beat which informs the line, and which the iteration of *st* throws into relief, makes the whole content plane of the metrical syntagm converge upon the depiction of an acoustic image stamped out by the hooves of the steaming horse.

Literature in the English language boasts a specific form of poetic iconism, one which imitates the intonation of "the spoken voice."[49] Such iconism is virtually assured by the canonical iambic pentameter, as can be seen, for example, in the first quatrain of Shakespeare's Sonnet LXXIX:

> Whilst I alone did call upon thy aid,
> My verse alone had all thy gentle grace;

> But now my gracious numbers are decay'd,
> And my sick muse doth give another place.

Each line here shows a unity of tone which is integrated into the sentential intonation unity represented by the quatrain.

Or consider the way in which in the line *So all day the noise of battle rolled,* from Tennyson's *The Passing of Arthur*,[50] the word *rolled* can refer to a noise like the rumbling of distant thunder or to the sound of a far-off rolling of drums. It is an effect which the muted sonorousness of the line as a whole reinforces.

A particular use of the form of the letter is found when a word, present in the title of the work and reiterated within it, subsequently appears in an intertextual relation with a word differentiated from it by a single letter. The relation between the two words acts as a pun and serves to focus a particular kind of semantic ambiguity, which is dominant in the text. This phenomenon can be observed in Shakespeare's *Much Ado About Nothing*, where *nothing*, at the time a homophone of *noting*, is differentiated both in meaning and in spelling. Observe the following passages in which the two words are playfully linearized:

> *Balthasar:* **Note** this before my **notes**;
>   There's not a **note** of mine that's worth the **noting**.
> *Pedro:* Why, these are very crotchets that he speaks;
>   **Note notes**, forsooth, and **nothing**.
>
> (II, III, 54–57)

In a vertical reading, we then meet with another passage where the "difference" is rendered evident by a triple alliteration, followed by highlighting of the letter itself:

> *Beatrice:* . . . I am exceeding ill;
>   Heigh-ho!
> *Margaret:* For a Hawk, a horse, or a husband?
> *Beatrice:* For the letter that begins them all, **H**.
>
> (III, IV, 49–52)

The intertextual play on words and letters is also an indirect invitation to the audience to take "note" of "the nothing" on which the world of human passions is based, in a context wherein machinations "malevolent" and "beneficient" easily impede or provoke the union of two couples, whose relations in the plot are patterned as a mirror image.

Many rhetorical figures are iconic in nature. Repetition in the same environment of a word or a syntagm (anaphora, epiphora, *complexio*, etc.) serves to bring forth their persistence, their insistence in the discourse; antithesis contrasts in spatial terms two elements which are already contrasted conceptually, etc. These iconic aspects of rhetorical figures have an interpretive or reinforcing function with respect to their conceptual value. In other words, what we are dealing with is a multiplication, an overloading, of signs.

2.16 Anagrams and Paragrams

Another use of letters and of sounds, which sets aside any relation to monemes and thereby interrupts the links of double articulation,[51] has been described by Saussure under the heading *paragram*, or anagram.[52] These are verbal *themes*, to be met with in the verse or in prose passages of classical and modern authors. They arise out of the linking of such letters or phonemes as form part of an utterance, in such a way that the monemes to which they, in the first instance, belong are left out of account. An example is the word *hystérie* at the end of a line in Baudelaire's *Vieux saltimbanque*. It is anagrammatically foreshadowed earlier in the same line: "Je sentIs ma gorge Serrée par la main TERrIblE de l'hystérie." In like fashion, Saussure discovered the name Aphrodite inside the verbal texture of the opening lines of *De rerum natura* and the names Philippus, Leonora, and Politianus in Politian's epitaph for fra Filippo Lippi (whose lover was a certain Leonora Butti).

According to Saussure, the author on each occasion set out from a verbal theme and then went on to build up verses or phrases out of words which lent themselves to its representation in the succession of letters (or sounds) which constitute them. This was done in obedience to norms which can subsequently be disengaged. Saussure suspected that some, perhaps secret, tradition had handed down a technique similar in many ways to the cryptogram.

Recent research would link paragrams to unconscious obsessions and see in their realization the not improbable result of their author's mastery of language.[53] Such mastery would cause an interplay between utterance and language, reading and writing, linearity and tabulation (because paragrams violate the linearity of language and set up an intertextual network, one which cuts across denotative meanings and which may well reinforce or contradict them). What is created in this way is "either above or below the semantic plane, a sort of non-meaningful 'text,' dedicated to the realization, through sub-linguistic signification modes, of the form or forms of a trans-contextual communication."[54]

Look at the opening lines of *Sir John's Hill* (1949), a text that Dylan Thomas intended to integrate, together with *In Country Sleep* (1947) and *In the White Giant's Thigh* (1950), into a "long poem," which, however, he never finished. Here the grapheme *w* is activated in a statistically significant way (ha*w*k, line 2; cla*w*s, line 3; gallo*w*s, line 4; *w*ars, line 6; sparro*w*s, *w*ho, s*w*ansing, *w*rangling, line 7), one which serves to indicate the double anagrammatic inscription, in a singular/plural variation, of *war* (SpARroWs and WRAngling, line 7) within a single line, while the word itself is linearized explicitly in the plural (*wars*, line 6) in the line which immediately precedes. The semantic valence of the term is thereby obsessively iconized (*w*) and disseminated throughout a context which is dominated by reference both direct and oblique to the "threat of nuclear war." This theme is further underlined paratextually by the poet himself: "The earth has killed itself. It is black, petrified, wizened, poisoned, burst; insanity has blown it rotten. . . ."[55]

To assist a reading, here is the passage under analysis:

1 Over Sir John's Hill
2 The haWk on fire hangs still;
3 In a hoisted cloud, at the drop of dusk, he pulls to his claWs
4 And GalloWs up the rays of his eyes the small birds of the bay
5 And the shrill child's play
6 WARs
7 of the spaRroWs and such Who sWansing, dusk, in WRAngling hedges.

Perhaps it is not too arbitrary to observe that, parallel to the anagrammatizing of *war*, we are faced with an iconic value of *w* which not merely signals the dissemination under discussion but may also contain, in the context, a reference to the "figured sema" of "birds in flight."

What might make us feel uneasy when faced with a hypothesis of this kind is not so much doubt as to the voluntariness of the operation (it might well be attributed to the unconscious)[56] as a real difficulty in eliminating purely statistical combinatorial results when relatively few letters of the alphabet are involved. This should not lead us to abandon the hypothesis; rather, it should induce us to seek the widest possible range of counterdemonstrations to support our advance of it.

In this sense, we may find more attractive the (related) concept of dissemination, which points to the presence of phonic or graphematic fragments of a word that is explicitly present as well and which synthesizes the theme of some part of the text. In *The Fire Sermon*, the third section of T. S. Eliot's *The Waste Land*, we encounter in lines 187 and 195 the sign manifestation of the reiterated word *rat*. Normal linearization is followed by an anagrammatic inscription of the term into the context. Here are lines 266–68:

266 The RiveR sweATs
267 Oil And TAR
268 The bARges dRifT.

This dissemination is confirmed in the acrostic-anagrammatic presentation of lines 281–85:

281 *T*he stern was formed
282 *A* gilded shell
283 *R*ed and gold
284 *T*he brisk swell
285 *R*ippled both shores

What needs to be stressed particularly in the phenomenon is the way this particular anagram is integrated with TART. The hierarchically structured intersecting of the two lexical units, anagrammatized and extraordinarily focused by the device of the acrostic, may well prove to be relevant thematically when account is taken of line 279, *Elizabeth and Leicester*, a lexical coupling followed by the sexual (especially phallic) suggestion of *Beating oars* in line 280.[57]

Eliot was certainly aware of the imaginary equivalence of *rat* and vagina. The fact is reinforced by the metaphorical valence, of female sexual organ, attributed to *rat* by Tristan Corbière, certainly one of Eliot's poetical masters.

The anagrammatized thematization, carried by *rat*, is verifiable in the context in relation to the motif of the three Thames daughters, fallen women like Elizabeth, who, her rank apart, is *carried down the stream* (line 287). The encyclopedia reminds us of Elizabeth's reputation, fitting the epithet "Tartar" (in the definition of the *Oxford English Dictionary*, "a rough . . . or irritable and intractable person").

2.17. The Acoustic Substance

Textual phenomena of the acoustic order involve problems of phonic symbolism, of synesthesia, etc., which linguistics has on the whole neglected but which it is in the process of looking at anew.[58] Here we come up against the physical nature of sounds and of psychic reactions to them and are led to meditate, in agreement with Plato's *Cratylus*, on the naturalness of language *(physis)*, whose arbitrariness *(thesis)* it is more usual to consider. On the whole, findings in the acoustic order seem better motivated and are more readily perceived when some correspondence on the part of meanings exists. For example, *u* is frequently associated with an impression of darkness, and *i* with impressions of light. But their use will interest us and impress us in conjunction with the meanings they marshall. Here, for example, is what happens in the first five lines of Coleridge's *Kubla Khan*:

1 In Xanad*u* did K*u*bla Khan
2 A stately pleasure dome dec*ree:*
3 Where Alph, the sacred r*i*ver, ran
4 Through caverns measureless to man
5   Down to a sunless *sea.*

The idea of darkness is prevalent and linearized explicitly in "*sunless sea*" (line 5). It is reinforced by the paradigm in *u*, manifested in "Xanad*u*" and "K*u*bla," while *u* is framed chiastically by the *ae* pair, activated in "X*a*nad*u*" and "Kh*a*n" (line 1). It is thus counterpointed by the idea of luminosity conveyed by the sound paradigm in *i*. This is thrown into relief by rhyme in "dec*ree*" and "*sea*" and is re-echoed, however weakly, by the *i* of "r*i*ver" (line 3). This, in its turn, is linked to "sea" by the sema "liquidness."

Equally common is the connection between sibilants and anything that has to do with rustling, not excluding the soughing of the wind. A good example is the second line of Spenser's *Prothalamion*:

1 Calm was the day, and through the trembling air
2   *S*weet-breathing Zephyru*s* did *s*oftly play.

Here the sound-based icon is articulated as an alternation of *s* and *z*. The alternation of voiceless and voiced fricative palatals mimes the breeze which lightly plays around the natural obstacles to its invisible flow.

A tight-packed series of *s*'s in the third stanza of Poe's *The Raven* mimes the rustling of the (lexicalized) curtains in an atmosphere of melancholy veined with "fantastic terrors":

1 And the *s*ilken, *s*ad, un*c*ertain ru*s*tling of each purple curtain
2 Thrilled me–filled me with fanta*s*tic terror*s* never felt before.

Mention might also be made of the obvious phonic importance of alliteration,59 institutional in Anglo-Saxon poetry and in Middle English texts of the fourteenth-century Revival and which is still a striking feature of much contemporary English.

These techniques find their fullest realization in what is called onomatopoeia, imitative harmony, or articulatory metaphor (and which, in any event, is iconic in nature, insofar as it resembles the referent). And here reference may be made to a necessary correspondence, in discourse rather than in single words, between sound and sense:

> Grammont rightly observes that the fascination of sound would remain inoperative were there not sense fascination as well, if the referent of the word did not orient the semantic value given by the sound. From the *Cratylus* to Leibnitz, from Grammont to Jespersen it has been observed over and over again that /r/ is not unrelated to meaning, and that it serves particularly to underline movement. But this does not emerge in configurations other than literary (I quote, from innumerable examples, the following: "come una freccia, il prato ampio radea / radea bassa la rondine)."60

Among many examples (which might act as starting point for a literary history of these techniques, one which would indicate their frequency in relation to epochs and authors), we shall chose a passage from Book I of Keats's *Endymion*:

154 From his right hand there swung a vase, mi*l*k white,
155 Of ming*l*ed wine, out-spark*l*ing generous *l*ight;
156 And in his *l*eft he he*l*d a basket fu*ll*
157 Of a*ll* sweet herbs that searching eye could cu*ll*:
158 Wi*l*d thyme, and va*l*ley-*l*i*ll*ies whiter sti*ll*
159 Than Leda's *l*ove, and cresses from the ri*ll*.

Here the extraordinary sequence of *l*'s activates perceptions of tenderness (= compositive olfactive icon) and softness (= compositive tactile icon) to be referred to a "basket full / Of all sweet herbs" (lines 156–57), while chromatic nuances are lexicalized to the full.

The correspondence of sound and sense is a safeguard against amateurish and impressionistic generalization. But a systematic and exhaustive census of Italian authors such as Dante and Pascoli has shown that the employment of phonic structures which involve verses or groups of verses goes far beyond mere imitation.[61] It becomes possible to seize upon formal messages which are not mechanically related to denotation, voices which integrate, or in some particular way modulate, what the text "says":

> Linguistic inventivity, the artifice of a language composed of tensions capable of producing artificial harmonies not thanks to any mimetic appropriateness, to any direct reproduction of nature, but rather to the make up of an arbitrary whole, constitutes an equal number of tensions for facing the elusive, the indecipherable, the unconscious. It is, therefore, not reproduction of nature, nor language as communication, but formal messages which strive to escape from nature, to evade from appearances, from materiality.[62]

2.18. Alternative Discourses.

It is essential to point out that in almost all of the examples quoted elements have been extrapolated from the linearity of discourse and have then been linked together. In other words, we have moved beyond the so-called linearity of language (where phonemes in combination form monemes and follow each other in the temporal order of their pronunciation or in the physical space of their writing, with no overlapping). The discourses now set up are alternative discourses which link together elements derived from the original discourse. This operation is performed mentally, and often unwittingly, by the listener; but it is much easier for a reader to effect it, because he is able to go back over the same section of text any number of times in order to determine ever more closely which elements are connected and which discourses are alternative.[63] It should be noted that all these discourses are asyntactic in type, for only load-bearing discourse can be syntactic. The force which would render them syntactic is the operation by which we link things, our own metadiscourse.[64]

As a rule, alternative discourses reinforce and define load-bearing discourse, or they refer it to the sense discourse in which the message's dianoetic line stands revealed. But it is quite possible that another discourse will unfold, and it may even prove to be an antidiscourse (whose presence will call for convincing corroboration, as does any working hypothesis based on asserted contradiction). If this antidiscourse exists, it will depend not so much on the astute insinuations of an author who prudently limits himself to the less compromising letter as on exigencies of repression, on personal or collective exclusion; it may well be the outcome of a tension toward horizons as yet barely glimpsed.

2.19. Hypostases in Meter

Prosody, rhythm, and meter play an important role in this description of potentialities, given the complexity of their contribution to signification. Not decisive, though worth mentioning, is the fact that a rhythm or metrical form may take on an evocative function akin to that of word play on the phonic level. What needs underlining is the fact that, when they are examined autonomously, metrical-rhythmical patterns constitute strong codes, codes which are akin to those of music in that they lack any meaning that can be registered or transcribed. Technically, it is their hypostatic nature which should be stressed,[65] i.e., their use in appropriate ways of the properties of those monemes which constitute the discourse: accents, pauses, word length. In this lies their meaning value; they form an "empty schema" within which monemes will be arranged. This empty schema provides alternatives and offers constraints. Between alternatives and constraints the flow of discourse is emphasized and underlined, and there are effects of expectation and surprise, monotony and break in monotony. Thanks to such *reinforcement signs,* one has the sense of a strict form of dialectic between what is actually said and what is sayable.[66] This is a technique for highlighting the discourse's definitive choice of signs and its interdiscoursive relations, of recall or of opposition, among its noncontiguous parts.

Take, as an example, a text in terzinas of hendecasyllables. We know already that every line will have its final accent on the tenth syllable; what we do not know, however, each time the pattern introduces a new rhyme, is whether the corresponding line will have ten, eleven, or twelve syllables. We know, too, that the main accents will, by and large, fall on the fourth and sixth syllables, though we do not know in which lines we shall find them nor in which lines we shall find other, less common types of accent arrangement. Finally, we do not know whether we will find—to vary the density of the line—dieresis, syneresis, dialoepha, or synaloepha.

The same thing is true of the metrical schema. In an Italian sonnet, we know that we will find fourteen hendecasyllables (unless the sonnet has a *coda* or is *rinterzato*) and a division into two quatrains and two tercets. The way the rhymes will interlace is something that will become clear to us only after the third line, and it is only after the fifth line that we will be in a position to foresee those of the tercets. Oxytone or proparoxytone rhymes will be even rarer than they would be with other patterns, but their presence will remain unpredictable. Naturally, one never knows, until the end of the reading, how the lines are going to be organized syntactically, although we will expect a break, for the most part though not obligatorily, between quatrains and tercets.

Meters and their groupings thus constitute an abstract matrix, with internal options and specific constraints. The linguistic discourse is so formulated that it will conform to this matrix and satisfy its free valencies. Meter, in other words, constitutes a "conventional system for the organization of the sound system."[67] Within this system, rhythm is of enormous importance; it regulates the succession of free accents in combination with obligatory accents so that a particular all-encompassing character is guaranteed for the lines (and these, with allusion to classical patterns, are termed iambic, anapestic, etc.). As Brik so accurately puts it, "The rhythmical movement is anterior to the verse; it is not rhythm which is to be understood on the basis of the verse but, on the contrary, verse on the basis of rhythm."[68]

We should also note that rhythm can be perceived only when the execution is oral, or at least mentally so.[69] This brings us back yet again to the sphere of phonic phenomena, for such phenomena adapt themselves to rhythm, and it is in rhythm that they find their fullest realization.

2.20. Metrics and Discourse

Between metrical progression and discourse, particular collaborations are developed: metrical progression furnishes an actuation schema for verbal discourse, and thereby conditions it from the outset; on the other hand, the poet from this conditioning derives incentives toward rendering his verbal discourse more effective. In a sense, meter is employed by the poet as a repertoire of norms for a *mise en relief* different from those in normal use.[70]

In practice, meter must come to terms with syntax and with such intonation norms as exist. Whoever makes use of it may attempt, with infinite variations, to enhance syntax and intonation through the rhythms of meter, or he may realize, through alternation of their contrast and coincidence, an inexhaustible series of expressive possibilities.

A relation-creating force different from syntax and intonation, meter modifies the links forged by these two elements. It thus appears as a new constituent element of the semantics of the *parole*. Once it has oriented a choice of signs, it acts to accentuate or to modify the meaning of the signs themselves. We are all well aware, for example, of how important the principal accents of a line of poetry can be in highlighting vowels, consonants, and consonant clusters; of the diversified effect obtained when discourse is broken down into very short words which correspond to feet or to parts of feet (arsis and thesis), or of the use that can be made of long words which take in a number of feet; or of the effect of hiatus, sustained and reinforced by rhythm, and so forth. These are all facts which can be brought more or less satisfactorily under the heading of iconism.

Poets and readers recognized, even before literary critics, the possibilities offered by *enjambement* in its welding together of two different movements—the one metrical, the other, syntactical. Its effects are varied but always striking. Some authors make a characteristically frequent use of this device (Della Casa is proverbial), while others have, in the course of their activity, given much thought to the relation of syntax and verse and even reached quite different conclusions at different points in their career.[71]

With great clarity the 1929 *Thèses* formulated an expedient for the study of meter, namely, analysis of parallelism, which has since proved highly profitable (G. M. Hopkins, though, had already drawn attention to the phenomenon). The Prague School proposes:

> Parallelism of phonic structures, realized by the rhythm of the verse, rhyme, etc., constitutes one of the most effective devices for actualizing different lin-

guistic planes. Artistic confrontation of reciprocally similar phonic structures brings to the fore concordances and differences in their syntactic, morphological and semantic structures.[72]

Enhancing the parallelisms already present in the text, with their effects of similitude and dissimilitude (involving rhythmical, or rhythmically analogous, phonic or syntactic structures) and of correspondence and counterposition (involving rhythmical and phonic and syntactic structures) is a most revealing application of a contrastive type. This is all the more true because similitude and dissimilitude, correspondence and counterposition, are all present in terms of the possible, and more or less minute, segmentations which can be effected within a text.[73]

Rhyme, over a long period of time and in many cultures, has marked the barrier (and the slight pause) between one line of poetry and another; it is one of the principal points at which the phonic, the semantic, and the rhythmic converge. This is the result not merely of the alternation between one rhyme and another when these are diversely constituted but also of the seriality of identical rhymes, for, by means of phonetic equality, this serves to underline grammatical similarity or difference (so that, e.g., verb is set against verb or verb against noun). Rhyme can also underline affinity or lack of affinity in the semantic sphere or in stylistic tonality.[74] The kind of concentration of meanings and connotative effects which can be achieved through rhyme was long since pointed out by Parodi in the case of the *Divina Commedia*.[75]

There is no need to go back over what we already said (§2.14) about the overlaying of elements of expression substance and content substance, regarded as the most satisfactory outcome (connotative in nature) of technical excellence. What should be called to mind, though, is the existence of purely phono-rhythmical effects, the surfacing of structures which, though they are endowed with an autonomous constitution, can be enlisted in the cause of reinforcing sense.[76] The potentiality, in the co-text, of such abstractions as rhythm and timbre refer to, or anticipate, the sense, though they do not express it.

2.21. Expression Form: Style

2.21.1. There can be no doubt that the text's language discourse, made up as it is of monemes, i.e., of lexical and morphological units of the first articulation (cf. §2.16), constitutes its expression form in Hjelmslev's sense (cf. §2.11). Its expression substance is the physical (phonic or graphic) realization of the same discourse. Monemes are linguistic signs, i.e., they belong to that coherent set of signs used in articulated verbal discourse and whose norms and usage are studied by linguistics. It has always been evident, however, that any text, the literary text in particular, which applies itself seriously to the formal plane, will either adopt particular categories of language signs (literary language, or epic language, lyric language, etc.) or make use, at any rate, of language signs in its own particular way. Thus, although it is obvious that the monemes employed by the literary text belong to the language in every sense, the attempt has been made to define the particular nature of the choice and connections which, with a peremptoriness as a rule commensurate with the skill and mastery of its writer, characterize any literary text.

The word *style* has two basic values: (1) the set of formal traits which characterize (as a whole or at a particular moment) the way a person expresses himself, the way an author writes, or the way a work is written; and (2) the set of formal traits which characterize a group of works whose association is typological or historical. At this point, it is the first meaning which will engage our attention, while for the second the reader is referred to paragraph 2.25. It should be borne in mind, however, that the second meaning is, in historical terms, the earlier. In the classical world, one spoke of *stilus atticus, stilus asianus*, while individual style, hardly ever studied as such, either was the object of normative counsel or was seen as a repertoire of rhetorical techniques.

2.21.2. Style analysis, in the twentieth century, has tended to take one of two main routes. The names of Bally and Marouzeau sum up the first of them, those of Vossler and Spitzer the second. According to Bally, stylistics "studies the affective value of the facts of organized language, and the reciprocal action of the expressive facts which come together to form the system of a language's means of expression"; "stylistics thus studies the expression facts of organized language from the point of view of their affective content, i.e., the expression of facts of sensibility on the part of language and the action of the facts of language on sensibility."[77]

For Bally (who works within Saussure's framework), the *langue* possesses expression resources, options, which in the consciousness of the speaker are copresent; he, in accord with the situations of his sensibility, will on each occasion choose the variant which most closely corresponds to them. This greatly enriches, and perhaps even transforms, Saussure's concept of "associative relations" (and that of system as well).[78] The expression resources of the *langue*[79] are arranged by Bally along a scale which takes us from the "intellectual expression mode," whose terms may function as "identifiers," to synonyms, whose character is affective, linked to notions of value, of intensity, of beauty. Expressivity is based both on *natural effects* and on "evocation effects," i.e., on marked elements and on elements which, unmarked within the linguistic group from which they derive, become marked when they are introduced into a different context. The investigation which, in relation to his theorization, Bally conducted on French lexis and syntax took the form of a reasoned census of synonyms of different tonal value.

In Bally's research, which was strictly limited to the sphere of the *langue*, states of mind were examined as mere potentialities, open to arrangement as a system which would flank, and correspond to, the potentiality system of the language. Bally thus laid the foundations of a form of psychostylistics which (when the reactions of addressees were taken into account) could well lay claim to sociostylistic ramifications, centered upon "evocation effects" to be studied from the addressees' standpoint.

Jules Marouzeau devoted his research to literary texts and set out from the perspective of the practitioner and not from the perspective of the *langue*, which would determine repertoires of synonyms.[80] What interests him is choice between synonyms and its motivation. The best-informed and most able of all practitioners is unquestionably the writer, for it is he who constantly makes decisions of a stylistic order.

In literary analysis, though, it is the method of Leo Spitzer which has been most influential (it was foreshadowed, rather than put into effect, by Karl Vossler). In the few comments that follow, justice will hardly be done either to the breadth of Spitzer's horizons or to the series of revolutionary rearrangements and insights evidenced in the whole course of his activity as a historian of style. We can do no more than touch upon the techniques which are characteristic of him and which might be grouped together as "the method of Leo Spitzer." Spitzer set out from the proposition that "to any emotion, i.e., to any movement away from our normal psychic state, there corresponds in the field of expression, a movement away from the normal use of language; whereas . . . any movement away from ordinary language is symptomatic of an unusual psychic state."[81] It is a question of seeing these deviations from the usage or ordinary language as indicators of the writer's state of mind. (We might note parenthetically that the concept of deviation, in Greek and Latin *tropos*, already existed in classical rhetoric, where such "deviations" were not, however, linked to states of mind, nor were they adopted to characterize individual authors.)

As an example of Spitzer's way of working, we might refer to his essay on Ch.-L. Philippe, whose abundant use of causal expressions and conjunctions (*à cause de, parce que, car*), and their "improper" use, allows us to determine the presence of a "pseudo-objective motivation," the reflection of an ironical and fatalistic resignation which is to be found in Philippe's unfortunate characters and which he made his own.[82] Or there is the essay on Péguy, whose Bergsonian experience is seen as being betrayed by a preference for words like *mystique* and *politique*, for compounds in *dé-* and *in-*, by the parentheses which often open up infinite perspectives, by the decimation of commas, etc. Another essay individuates in the writings of the pacifist Barbusse an obsessive presence of blood images whose character is markedly sexual.

There is a great deal more than a mere foreshadowing of structuralism (stressed by Spitzer in his final years)[83] in a conception which sees details as only to be grasped in terms of the whole, and the whole only in terms of the details. Today it is somewhat dated to regard the mind of the author as "a kind of solar system into whose orbit all categories of things are attracted: /so that/ language, motivation, plot, are only satellites of this / . . . / entity,"[84] and above all to place at the center of such a system a spiritual etymon, i.e., "the psychological root of several individual 'traits of style' in a writer."[85] But it must be added that the description still holds good. Instead of "author," though, we should prefer to read "text," while references to psychology might more satisfactorily be applied to formal tension.

2.22. Choice and Stylistic Deviation

2.22.1. The stylistics of Bally and Spitzer are different and very nearly complementary. The former is stylistics of the language, the latter stylistics of the literary work. Bally speaks of the *choices* available to the speaker of the language, Spitzer of *deviations* from normal use activated in the work. The concept of choice is a simplification, but an acceptable one. It is a simplification because the language is not a unified system: it falls into subsystems which relate to the varieties of the language's social and cultural use. Choices are made either inside subsystems, when the speaker makes them his own, or above them, when (and here we are necessarily dealing with writers) the speaker (or writer) takes into account groups of choices offered by various subsystems; in other words, he obtains "natural effects" from "evocation effects."

The concept of *deviation* might lead us to formulate additional reservations. First and foremost, deviation from what? Spitzer seems to be alluding to the *langue*. What is certain is that he makes little reference to the mediation of literary language or indeed to its numerous subspecies. The same thing is true of the Prague Structuralists, who refer to "deviation from the standard" as one of their basic descriptive criteria (but then the Prague School has had little to do with style). But, even when language varieties have been recognized and assessed, how is one to know what range of choices really were available to the writer or what the "average" expression was from which he is supposed to have deviated?

There is, though, another, more serious reservation. If an author's style is to be determined on the basis of the system of his deviations, should the rest of his text be regarded as utterly devoid of stylistic features? If so, the text would become a kind of neutral backdrop for the highlighting of symptomatic elements, the only ones endowed with stylistic value.[86] Or are we the ones who have recourse to deviations, seeing them as particularly striking, indeed irrefutable, symptoms, while taking for granted that some striving after style, though in less marked a form, will be in operation throughout the work? This is more or less the sense of Terracini's rejoinder. He replaced the concept of *deviation* with that of *punto distinto*, or distinctive feature (a noncontrastive concept). Distinguishing features, within a work, are those explicit and direct traces of the symbolic value that the textual complex in its entirety bears; they are those privileged areas wherein is unfolded "that process by means of which the symbol takes the articulate form of words."[87]

2.22.2. This is not a problem that can be solved by stylometrics, whose development is the result of new possibilities of electronic elaboration. These make possible extremely important statistical investigations, concordances, and so forth. But few important deductions, for example, will derive from the chance thus offered of measuring a work's "richness index" (the relation between the number of vocables it employs and the total number of words the text contains). The formula, put forward by P. Guiraud,[88] follows:

$$R(\text{ichness}) = \frac{V(\text{ocables})}{\sqrt{N(\text{umber of Words})}}$$

It is also possible to measure the distance between the rank conferred upon the single words of a text and the rank which would normally fall to their lot in an "average lexis." But apart from the doubtful status of such a concept (the lexis, depending upon the corpus from which it is derived, may show different forms, and it does not bear any relation to an author's "average lexis"), what still remains doubtful—as the researchers themselves know only too well—is how one is to assess words of high frequency *(theme words)*, words of relatively high frequency *(key words)*, or words whose frequency index is low, when the basic axiom is that a message will be all the more informative the less it can be foreseen.

2.23. Language Varieties

The expressive possibilities of the language comprise a system which constitutes a historical and social stratification. The choices each writer makes will place him exactly in relation to the history of the language and to its sociological varieties.[89] Stylistics in Italy from the outset took this path. It individuated in the literary sphere those stratifications with which sociolinguistics would later deal, though their motivations would be different. An author's physiognomy was defined in terms of a dialectic between conservation and innovation, regarded as the very life of the language (Terracini) or as it related to *stylistic traditions* (Devoto). "Style," says Devoto, "offers us a relation. It is the outcome of a dialogue between ourselves and the linguistic institutions of which we make use: on them the writer leaves his mark, but he is also conditioned by them, in his work."[90]

From a theoretical point of view, the language in a given synchronic section ought to be regarded as a system of systems. At its center lies the structure of the *langue* (from phonetics to lexis); each semantic field will then be incremented, or differently structured, in relation to different groups of speakers. These groups will be representative of professions and of specialized fields. (Morpho-syntactic variability, though not negligible, will be of less weight, while phonetic variability will be minimal.) Around the perimeter of the system lie the *sociolects* (socially marked varieties), each with its own rigidity, its own attenuations, etc., with respect to the norms of the *langue* itself. Various polarizations can be individuated inside the language system. We shall here touch upon the most important of them.

2.24. Sociolects and Registers

What we are dealing with is a series of language varieties (linguistic diatypes) relative to the social environments to which speakers belong (sociolects) and to the conditions under which the utterance is realized (registers, which may go from the most sublime poetic diction, the most elegant of styles, to the informal and to folk styles). Sociolects are not strictly delimited because there is considerable circulation and contact among social strata; classification of registers is even more elusive. (Marked oscillations exist even within such categories as researchers have put forward.) The fact remains, however, that sociolects and registers break down the system of choices into subsystems which only in part overlap. What is more, words and expressions exist which are characteristic of one single language variety and which come to constitute "stylistic markers" for that particular variety, even with only partial recourse to it. For the ordinary speaker, whose social position is already defined and to whom the context will suggest the type of register he should adopt, stylistic choice is limited from the outset to the options offered by his sociolect and, inside this, to those which the register being employed will authorize. The behavior of the writer is different. Contamination is a possibility for him, and, though as a rule he will operate within the confines of one literary register, he will not infrequently feel authorized to ransack all of the other varieties, all of the other registers, of the language.[91]

2.25 Ideologemes, Ideological Conformations, "Écritures"

Every conception of the world, and each of the ideologies which in association set up conceptions of the world, involve particular uses of language and of "stylistic markers." Bachtin, within this perspective, speaks of *ideologemes*.[92] The semantic values of words are chosen not just because they are linked together to form utterances but also because the utterances themselves belong to a given "discourse pattern" which is itself a subspecies of "ideological patterns." For example, in the Middle Ages, a "religious ideological pattern" was the dominant ideological form. As discourse patterns linked to it, we might cite the sermons of country priests, those the higher clergy designed for the upper ranks of the nobility, and so forth. The ideological pattern, and hence the various discourse patterns, activated particular selections and orientations inside a basic conceptual system.[93] In an analogous discourse (though its aims were different), Barthes introduced the term *écriture* and contrasted it to style on the grounds that style belonged to the biological order and was instinctive, whereas *écriture* was the outcome of an intention, an act of historical solidarity. For Barthes, in short, *écriture* is "the relation between creation and society, . . . the literary language transformed by its social finality, form considered as a human intention and thus linked to the great crises of History."[94]

2.26. The Varieties of the Literary Language

Considerable attention has been devoted to these, partly because in antiquity they fell within a well-defined system of norms. Classical rhetoric had already remarked the existence of levels of style, some of which were more, others less, elevated. Indeed, it had sketched out a kind of sociological characterization for these levels, basing it on constant correspondences of argument, style, and the social rank of the characters. (The three principal works of Virgil—the *Bucolics*, the *Georgics*, and the *Aeneid*—served as paradigms for the three principal levels, namely, humble, middle, and sublime.)

Only with romanticism was any attempt made to withstand the linguistic and stylistic codification of literary genres which had been inherited from the Middle Ages and which had enjoyed its greatest vogue in the Renaissance. Each genre and subgenre not only entailed use of particular verse or stanza forms but also imposed restrictions on the use of lexis and might even involve phonetic choice. The lexical range which was legitimate for a romance of chivalry did not coincide with the much more restricted range set aside for the love lyric, while liberties were accorded to the playwright to which other writers might not aspire.

These efforts at codification were all the more hazardous in that the literary language developed in a problematical relation with the vicissitudes of the language and its dialects, of cultural levels and borrowed regionalisms. A writer whose realization was achieved in terms of a given style was not faced with a unified language; he was caught up in a dynamism of tensions and tendencies. This is why research into the history of the language and research devoted to stylistics have come to converge. The clear-cut choices envisaged by Spitzer have been replaced by blocks of choices, i.e., by words and expressions which, taken together, refer us to given linguistic levels.

The attempt has been made to use the word *register* in this field to mean "a network of pre-established relations among elements proper to different levels of formalization, as also among the levels themselves."[95] Inside the language of a given work, it is, in fact, possible to individuate different sublanguages which are codified in relation to the tonalities of the language of the work. Such registers are sufficiently traditional to be found in a certain number of works, which means that they can be linked together, but only in relation to contents.

2.27. Global Definition of Style

An all-embracing definition of the style of a work can hardly avoid referring to the famous Prague *Thèses* of 1929. They state: "The poetic work is a functional structure, and its various elements cannot be understood apart from their connection with the whole."[96] In short, the literary work is regarded, as Saussure would, as a structure wherein "tout se tient," one where everything fits. As regards the structuring element, the following statement contains *in nuce* Jakobson's definition of the "poetic function": "the organizing principle of art, in function of which it is distinguished from other semiological structures, is that the intention is directed not toward what is signified [le signifié] but toward the sign itself [sur le signe lui-meme]."[97]

This totally coherent approach is even more closely defined by Jakobson (who, in fact, had taken part in drafting the *Thèses*) when he states that "the poetic function projects the principle of equivalence from the axis of selection into the axis of combination."[98] In other words, while ordinary discourse will, for each linguistic element, effect a choice among the possible equivalents offered by the language (the axis of selection), the literary text, when it chooses, will take syntagmatic relations into account as well (the axis of combination). It will weigh effects of recurrence, correlation, contraposition, and the network of such effects will involve every element of the text, which will, for this very reason, constitute a "functional structure."[99]

Some doubt may remain over the rather nominalistic nature of this poetic function and over the difficulty of measuring the "quantity" of its presence in texts. (In fact, Jakobson maintains, and rightly so, that the effects of the poetic function may make themselves felt equally well in nonliterary texts, while their presence in literary texts may be secondary.) As a counter to such reservations, which further research will serve to attenuate, we should set the triumphant revindication of the all-inclusive character of style. Style is not limited to single elements or to isolated constructions; it is the result of an engagement on the formal plane which involved every part of the text.

The definitions just quoted are exact opposites of those based on choice or deviation, which stress single elements in relation to the *langue* or to specific language traditions. The single stylistic feature is characterized within tradition and in relation to it. The paradigm itself is regarded as a historical manifestation. In structuralist definitions, on the contrary, it is the syntagm (the axis of combination) which is important; the value of each element of the text depends on the way it relates to all of its other elements, while there is no part of the text which does not interact with all of its other parts. Only a more marked degree of prominence, the circumstantial character as it were, of certain elements and connections might lead the critic to stress them rather than others and rather than all of the others.

If the text's unity and individuality are to be preserved, a global definition is required, a definition which on each occasion will take concrete form and specify, for each text, the type of elements involved and the type of connections to be encountered. The different kinds of stylistics broke down or sectored this unity and individuality and went on to reimmerse its components in a historical flux, which should be seen as no more than a purveyor. With the advent of structuralism, it is obviously no longer possible to speak of stylistic criticism. One must speak rather of historical and descriptive stylistics seen as the premise for an overall study of the text, because the interpretation of the text is semiotic in character, as we shall soon see.

2.28. The "Avant-texte"

2.28.1. The text is the outcome of a development, many (at times all) of whose phases have been removed. The mental mechanisms, which presided over the linking together of concept and images, and then of words and rhythms, until the point of linguistic and metrical realization was reached, to a large extent escape us, just as in all probability they escape the writers themselves. Occasionally, though, writers have made an attempt to give us some account of them. What can be mastered, however, is the way the written phase developed in cases where we possess sketches and first drafts or when a work was published in a series of successive editions. The sum of the material which precedes the final draft has been termed by some critics the *avant-texte*.[100]

Some specification might be of help. Every sketch or early draft is, from a linguistic point of view, a text which has a coherence of its own. Even if all of the texts which precede a given work were to be lined up in chronological order, we would still not achieve diachrony; we would only arrive at a series of successive synchronies. When a manuscript has been retouched on many different occasions, the correct approach is to regard it as a stratification of synchronies and of texts. If the concept of *avant-texte* really does have the intention of showing us literary or poetic productivity at work, the only result will be disappointment. It is, though, quite certain that, when each text is considered as a system, successive texts can be regarded as the effect of driving forces present in preceding texts. These new texts, in their turn, contain driving forces which will result in texts to come. In this way, analysis of the history of compilation and of variants will provide at least partial knowledge of the dynamics which are at work in literary creation.

2.28.2. In Italy, variant criticism played a significant role in establishing structural criticism.[101] Variants oblige us to make combined use of two points of view: a synchronic point of view, which will determine the system of relations in terms of which each stage of the text has been organized; and a diachronic point of view, which, after it has defined the different successive stages assumed by each part of the text and by the text itself, will determine the driving forces which have favored such shifts. It quite soon became evident that only rarely do changes have local improvement of the text as their goal: much more frequently they are moves in an overall strategy, one which involves the structural relations of its connected elements.

In other words, we are witnessing, when we study variants, shifts internal to the text's system: displacements which progressively involve related sets of readings and variants. Variants make it possible to assess text materials on the basis not just of their reciprocal relations but in terms of slight changes of these relations as well. We are in a position to surprise the writer at work, to find out what effects he was seeking, where he put the accent, what stylistic ideas he was attempting to activate. In the study of the finished text, the language of its writer will be compared with the literary language of his epoch, his figurative code with the standard stereotypes of his time. Variants, however, lead us to more microscopic findings; phases of the same idiolect, actuations of a single stereotype, can be matched against each other.

If the poem *This bread I break* by Dylan Thomas[102] is compared with the original draft, dated December 24, 1933, in the *August 1933 Notebook*,[103] it will be observed that only one variant exists and that it involves the close of the poem, the fourth and fifth lines of its third stanza (each of the stanzas is made up of five lines). The definitive version is "Born of the sensual root and sap; / My wine you drink, my bread you snap." In correspondence, the first and second drafts give "Born of the same sweet soil and sap. / God's bread you break, you drain His cup" and "Born of the same sweet soil and sap. / My wine you drink, my break you break."

Even though in the hemistich "you drain His cup" (first version) the semantic feature -liquid corresponds to the final draft, the version determines a univocal reference to the Eucharist for a poem which has become "word of the word." This kind of univocal procedure was alien to the more mature Thomas.

The second variant, where obviously the first *break* is a *lapsus calami* for *bread,* provides for a formal circularity which is excessively obtrusive in terms of the poetics immanent to this poet's work and in terms of the period's poetic exigencies as well. The second hemistich of the last line, "my bread you break," is all too evidently the varied repetition of the first hemistich of the line which opens the poem, "This bread I break was once the oat."

It might be maintained that the rhyme-linked words of the final version *(sap, snap)* have been selected or combined by breaking down and reassembling the idiomatic syntagm "to drain the wood of sap." This kind of demechanization technique would be typical of Thomas's compositional modes. In the first version, *drain* is manifest, while *wood* is related paradigmatically, graphically, and semantically to *root (root* will, in fact, be present in the final version). The first version's *same sweet* is periodically equivalent to *sensual* in the final version, and the new term evidences a more resolute semantic solidarity with *snap* (by contraposition).

Chiasmus, which plays such a large part in organizing the syntagms and semic permutations of this poem, accounts for the linearization of the second version (first variant: . . . *bread* . . . *cup;* second variant: . . . *wine* . . . *bread);* where *cup,* which replaces *wine,* also involves a shift in meaning in terms of synecdoche. It is a chiasmus which, in the definitive context, will be realized relative to the first stanza, lines 1–2 (. . . *bread/* . . . *wine)* and to the third stanza, line 1 (. . . *flesh/* . . . *blood).* The double substitution, in accord with the figure of metaphor, should also be observed in the third stanza, line 1, and the conversion/return, mirrored and circular, in the final verse of the poem (. . . *wine* . . . *bread).*

The hypothesis is that *snap* was fixed upon, not just because a closing rhyme was needed but in order to provide a transgressive derivation from the current expression "the dog snapped at my leg," or some such. *Dog* would imply *snap* and vice versa, while *dog,* as W. Y. Tindall reminds us, "according to Joyce is opposite to God, according to Thomas, too."[104]

If we take into account the first version's *God,* then *dog* is the mirror image of a signifier present in the poem's substratum, while *snap* is merely its metonymic extension. The negative connotation, the destructive action conveyed by *drain* (first variant), is maintained, but the final draft impedes any merely univocal reading.

The circularity of such composition will be found to be subtle indeed, once we have observed the way Thomas projects his paradigms onto the page and transforms them into syntagms to accord with a backward and forward alternation of equivalences by contrast and similarity of one single semantic feature. The final version, in fact, shows the following proportion: *root* (-liquid): *sap* (+ liquid) + *wine* (+ liquid): *bread* (-liquid). The semantic chiasmus thus brought into focus reinforces the lexical chiasmus we earlier observed, for in the text it is the more evident.

We may give another example from the opening of the passage which ends the first section, *The Burial of the Dead*, of T. S. Eliot's *The Waste Land*. As a result of the remarkable cuts suggested by Ezra Pound, lines 60–61 of the definitive version, "Unreal City, / Under the brown fog of a winter dawn," are lines 114–15 in the version made public by Valerie Eliot: "Unreal City, I have sometimes seen and see / Under the brown fog of your winter dawn."[105] It is immediately evident that the notable cut made in line 60 (again at the suggestion of Pound) makes it possible to focus with greater immediacy, and at the same time to delocalize, the *City* evoked. Furthermore, the depiction has now been freed from its earlier narrator-monologue perspective. In line 61, the replacement of *your* by *a winter dawn* is a consequence of the cut made earlier, while it serves to distance the mythical subject of the utterance from his addressees; a visionary and prophetic weight is thereby conferred upon his voice.

Another interesting example is the second stanza of Yeats's *Sailing to Byzantium*. We give consecutively (enclosing in parentheses the words cancelled) its first and second versions, followed by the final version, in order to show the importance of rhyme in this specific compositional practice.[106] In the first fragmentary version, it is obvious that Yeats is in search of "good" rhymes, of what are, in effect, generative nuclei on the surface, around which the text is then to be woven. For example, in line 2, every word is cancelled except the single rhyme-bound word *unless*. This word will remain unchanged in the stanza's final version. *Dress* and *oar* are noted in the margin as sonorous-semantic motifs, though only the first of them will be accorded confirmation. Right from the first fragmentary draft, the first four rhyme words are firmly established. The second version, later subjected to considerable variation, already represents the definitive manifestation of the rhyme scheme:

First Fragmentary Version

1 (The) / An aged man is but a paltry thing
2 (A paltry business to be old), unless
3 (My) / Soul clap (hands) its hands and sing and then
4   (sing more) louder sing
5   dress
6   oars
7 For every tatter in its mortal dress

THE TEXT 65

Second Version

1 An aged man is but a paltry thing
2 Nature has cast him like a shoe unless
3 Soul clap its hands and sing, and louder sing
4 For every tatter in its mortal dress
5 And there's no singing school like studying
6 The monuments of (its old) / our magnificence
7 And therefore have I sailed the seas and come
8 To the holy city of Byzantium

Definitive Version

1 An aged man is but a paltry thing,
2 A tattered coat upon a stick, unless
3 Soul clap its hands and sing, and louder sing
4 For every tatter in its mortal dress
5 Nor is there singing school but studying
6 Monuments of its own magnificence;
7 And therefore I have sailed the seas and come
8 To the holy city of Byzantium.

This example would seem to confirm that the first line is indeed a "gift of the gods" and that the technique and the codified practice of composition are crutches upon which the poet is inclined to depend.

The study of variants is particularly illuminating when a text, already substantially achieved, is progressively reworked and repolished by its author. An analysis may start with the manuscripts, as in our examples, or it may base itself on printed copies, in cases where a number of editions (versions) were issued successively, each of them at the moment being seen as "definitive." The three versions of Ariosto's *Orlando furioso* are a famous example, and a critical edition of it provides in its apparatus the material for comparison,[107] while Manzoni's *Promessi sposi* has in a modern edition been rendered synchronic in visual terms.[108]

2.28.3. It is possible, though, to go back even further. We possess the complete autograph of an earlier, and quite different, draft of the *Promessi sposi*, called *Fermo e Lucia*. We also have the first drafts of the cantos Ariosto added to his last *Furioso*.[109] The complicated, indeed dramatic, history of the editions of Tasso's *Gerusalemme liberata*, which ends with a rewriting, *La Gerusalemme conquistata*, began with a quite different poem on the same argument, *Del Gierusalemme*. A much more detailed list might be given, but these examples are sufficient to show the diversified approaches this kind of material requires. Except occasionally, it is no longer a case of minute comparison of variations with respect to a substantially stable text. What we are dealing with are blocks of subject matter, with eliminations, displacements, and shifts of accent. Such variants involve broad units of content, inside which we may perhaps be able to seize upon some kind of verbal permanence (or refining).

Another example, *The Sisters,* the first story in Joyce's *Dubliners,* will help us move beyond any "evolutionary" preconception, which might lead us to see, in the various drafts of a text, the progressive definition and refinement of an initial idea. But the story in question, in the form in which it appeared in *The Irish Homestead* of August 13, 1904, under the heading "Our Weekly Story," is little more than the portrait of a dead priest, seen by a boy and by others who knew him in the last years of his life. Clearly the version set out to satisfy the magazine's desire for a piece at once "simple" and "rural," something which would prove agreeable to "the common understanding and liking."[110] Although the narration is filtered from the boy's point of view, its focusing is effected in a mechanical fashion, and no really meaningful relation is established between the observer and the object of his attention. This is so true that the text would not suffer if the point of view was exchanged for that of any other person. In the final draft, the one included in *Dubliners* (1914), we read, "Every night as I gazed up at the window I said softly 'paralysis.'"[111] In the first draft, the term *paralysis* was absent, as were the descriptive elements which derive from it. The linearization of the lexeme is, in our opinion, an essential intertextual signal, given that the connotative code of paralysis has become a dominant one in all the other tales, a phenomenon which contributes to the book's cohesion and to its condition of macrotext.

The oneiric-oriental motif, absent from the first draft, becomes pertinent in this perspective and links our tale to *Araby* and to *A Little Cloud* in particular. In his dream, the boy (once again in the final version) "remembers" that the priest "had died of paralysis and I felt that I too was smiling feebly as if to absolve the simoniac of his sin."[112] This passage inscribes the word *simony* in the text, and the term will take on considerable resonance in *Dubliners,* to the point of embracing any kind of action or choice dictated by interest to the detriment of "spiritual" values.

But, apart from the integration in the final version of elements of intertextual cohesion, note might be taken of the intratextual valence of a network of clues, which prepares the way for a retrospective and conclusive epiphany. A pointer to the extraordinary textual solidarity now attained is the fact that the priest's body is represented in the definitive version with his "hands loosely retaining a chalice"[113]; there is an obvious thematic connection with "that chalice he broke."[114] In the first version in *The Irish Homestead,* his hands clutched a rosary and, in an intermediate version, a cross.[115] If the first text was little more than an improvisation, the final draft manifests a well-known strategy in terms of which the narration is merely instrumental, adapted in such a way as to prepare the reader for the epiphanic "illumination" of the tale's denouement.

In some quite special cases we are able to survey the whole broad extension of an elaboration, from preliminary annotations, from the foulest of papers, to the cleanest and clearest of forms. For Alfieri's tragedies, we still possess the initial prose drafts; we have the short stories which Pirandello wrote and then rewrote for the stage. It is possible to start with a word or an idea, a rhyme or a stanza form. Pascoli's *Il gelsomino notturno* is one of the most striking cases we have of almost total documentation. From a first draft in prose or in verse, it is possible to trace out a diagram which is anything but uniform. The changes occur in conceptual systems and orientations, as well as in rhythms and lexical insight, and external models—Virgil, D'Annunzio, etc.—play a role in varying degrees dictatorial. Contacts and differences with respect to other poems of Pascoli, allied in argument, allow exact definition. In the case of D'Annunzio, the discovery of his notebooks, the *Taccuini*, has made it possible to reconstruct the iter of verses and of entire compositions, from sheer chance and impressionism of observations and feelings to poetical construction within the framework of the *Laudi*.

Although many moments of the text's elaboration escape us because they are mental moments, possessing the whole, or the greater part, of the phases of its elaboration in writing, from the first drafts to the most detailed retouching, places at our disposal a mass of material which may be described as the avant-texte. The concept is, though, not entirely free of a certain materialistic simple-mindedness. The maturing of any work will keep pace with the progressive maturing of the author himself, and this will transpire from the whole of his concurrent activity. There will exist interferences from one text to another or from different moments in the correction of texts spread out over time. We should describe all of the works of our author down to a given moment as *avant-texte*, not that this will be any great gain, terminologically speaking.

What is more, such fervid intertextuality (cf. §2.29) on the part of the author moves within the labyrinth of an all-embracing intertextuality, because influences may involve other authors, contemporary or not (we find projects in common or influences which act over time). To accord with the textual approach in these pages, the conclusion must be this: while a text will have its own specific delimitation—it will be this way, exist thus—its prehistory will mark it off, but will not cut it off, from the whole flux of text-producing activities.

2.29. Intertextuality

Bachtin holds that multivoiced discourse (cf. §3.12) is a phenomenon peculiar to the novel, and it is undoubtedly true that the novel affords more scope for its development. A partially related phenomenon exists, however, which is, in the refinement of its applications, particularly characteristic of the poetic text, though it might be met with in any literary text. This is *intertextuality*. The term, recently introduced, seems to be grouping together under a new label such well-known features as reminiscence, the use (explicit or disguised, ironical or allusive) of sources, and quotations.[116] The novelty of the term underlines the fact that the phenomenon is no longer being envisaged as a question of mere erudition.[117] Instead of accepting it in all its possible uses (the development of a literary language, in particular, may be regarded as a macroscopic case of continuous text interchange, hence as intertextuality), we would prefer to limit the term to clearly definable cases of the presence of earlier texts inside a given text. Intertextuality will then be seen to be the equivalent in the literary sphere of the many-voicedness proper to the language:

(a) just as elements which belong to a variety of sociolects and ideological orientations are to be found in many-voicedness, so in the case of intertextuality it is possible to perceive strands of those cultural affiliations which lie behind the text as it stands. They might almost be the characteristic traits of an intentional heredity. Whereas many-voicedness draws on registers, group languages, etc. (cf. §2.23–24), intertextuality draws on the varieties of the literary language and on individual styles;

(b) once intertextuality has been perceived, the text will no longer stand in the isolation of its message; it will take its place as part of a discourse which, as it were, unfolds by means of texts, a dialogical discourse where the exchanges are the texts, or parts of the texts, that writers utter;

(c) by means of intertextuality the language of a text will in part take unto itself, as one of its own components, the language of an earlier text; the same thing will happen for the semantic code and for the various subcodes of literariness. The way this is done, the co-text[118] of its employment, asserts the rights of the assimilating code, but it is noteworthy that the code assimilated will remain in some measure recognizable within the assimilating code. In short, an earlier historical phase has been absorbed into a later one.

"Orientation on the message," proper to the poetic function, becomes complex indeed in the spheres of intertextuality. This is because the derived elements effect a compromise between their initial orientation and that of their point of arrival.

Milton, who in terms of a Renaissance commonplace was the champion of the superiority of Christian as opposed to pagan epic themes (the former being held superior in point of "heroism"), obliquely communicates this conviction, which is that of the age, by having recourse to the quotation in English guise of forthright single lines from Dante, his greatest precursor in the epic field. The lines are decontextualized and recontextualized and, at times, repeated at a distance. In Milton's context, this intertextual calque functions as a metalinguistic sign as well, as the mark of a privileged genre.

The line "se voler fu o destino o fortuna" (Dante, *Inferno*, XXXII, 76) is, in its original context, proffered by the poet's persona depicted as he treads on the face of one of the damned, Bocca degli Abati. In Milton, it finds its textualization at the moment in which Satan challenges divine supremacy: "Whether upheld by Strength, or Chance, or Fate" (*Paradise Lost*, I, 133). Here fidelity to the model, which involves lexical structure and an iterated paratactic-disjunctive expression as well, is quite patent. The line "che sanza speranza vivemo in disio" (*Inferno*, IV, 42), which Virgil in the *Comedy* refers to the condition of the noble pagans, thematized as "senza speranza desideranti," is used by Milton in a passage in which Satan contrasts his own destiny with that of Adam and Eve:

508 . . . while I to Hell am thrust,
509 Where neither joy nor love, but fierce desire,

(Paradise Lost, IV)

And it is used again when Eve contemplates suicide, because the human condition is "with desire to languish without hope" *(Paradise Lost, X, 999).*

It is interesting to observe the way in which a line of John Webster—"But keepe the wolfe far thence, that's foe to men" *(The White Devil, V, 4)*—is restructured in T. S. Eliot's *The Waste Land* (I, 74). Eliot's variation is "O keep the Dog far hence, that's friend to men." The significant replacement of *wolfe* by *dog* involves the further replacement of *foe* by *friend*, its antonym. These lexical variations bring about changes in connotative codes and in isotopy as well. Whereas in Webster's work Cornelia fears that the *wolfe* will commit sacrilege by profaning the tomb of her son Marcello, in Eliot's poem the whole first section, *The Burial of the Dead*, unfolds on a meaning plane which is dominated by terror of a return to "life." (Of this, the well-known opening is sufficient indication: "April is the cruelest month, breeding / Lilacs out of the dead land. . . .") Here, disinterment of a symbolic corpse would do no more than reinforce the cyclical and natural reflowering of a biological existence which the dessication of the spiritual life of the epoch has made unendurable.

Webster's line, reelaborated but still recognizable, merely confirms, in the context, a rejection of natural and mythical rebirth under given social and cultural conditions. The potential intertextual dialogue tends to produce an ideologeme according to which, in modern "alienated" and "alienating" society, the concept of "rebirth" is paradoxically more terrifying than that of "sacrilege," since sacrilegious acts are involved in the system of rules which governs "civil" coexistence.

In Shakespeare, on the contrary, the faithful, widely disseminated calques of the classics may act as focal points for effects of universal truth. See, in this sense, *Romeo and Juliet* (II, ii):

92   At lovers' perjuries,
93 They say, Jove laughs.

The reference is to "Iuppiter ex alto periuria ridet amantum" (Ovid, *Ars Amatoria*, I, 633).

These are macroscopic cases. But, taken as a whole, the language and the style of every poetical composition are the result of close-knit intertextuality. This is differentiated from analogous features in spoken or in prose texts by virtue of the awareness, and often the allusiveness, with which it is put into effect. Every poet, as he writes, is conversing with a host of other poets, whose successor, in some sense, he is, even as he outdoes them. Pope will come to mind with his capacity for smoothing over breaks, for avoiding any unevenness in the interconnected and diverse materials he employed. The systematic utilization in his work of classical, primarily epic, material is overridingly determined by the mock-heroic genre, and, although the expression form of *The Rape of the Lock* achieves an irreproachable autonomy, references to classical sources make it possible to activate, in the reading, a polemical dialogue which favors the Enlightenment values of Augustan "polite society," tolerant and cynical as it was, at the expense of an axiology which extolled the exemplary character of such heroism as was inscribed in the temporal absolute of an aristocratic model, where values were understood as being self-sufficient and metahistorical. The promotion, however ironical, of the frivolous elegance of contemporary living, sublimated by the airy, ethereal refinement of the form, has as its end result an indirect devaluation of the deeds of old.

It is in this light that lines 117–20 of Canto II should be read:

117 To Fifty chosen Sylphs, of special Note,
118 We trust th' important Charge, the Petticoat;
119 Oft have we known that sev'nfold Fence to fail,
120 Tho' stiff with Hoops and arm'd with Ribs of Whale.

Here, instead of activating the arming system which the classics provided, the poet exhibits a differential feature of the fashion system of his period. In fact, *Petticoat* (line 118), when defined as *sev'nfold Fence* (line 119), is merely a calque of the shield of Ajax, the suicide. In Ovid's *Metamorphoses*, it is depicted as *septemplicis* (= sev'nfold), the complete syntagm being "clipei dominus septemplicis Aiax" (XIII, 2). It is taken for granted that lexical substitution will also entail a change at the level of isotopy, or of meaning plane.

This intertextual maze involves Shakespeare's *Antony and Cleopatra* as well (IV, 14):

38 Off, pluck off,
39 The seven-fold shield of Ajax cannot keep
40 The battery from my heart.

This passage was certainly more accessible to the English reader of the time. In this way, the titanic suicide of Ajax interacts with the heroic-melodramatic suicide of the Shakespearean Antony, who re-echoes his model's pathetically asserted invincibility (IV, 15):

16 So it should be, that none but Antony
17 Should conquer Antony.

This is an extremely obvious reference to Ovid's ". . . ne quisquam Aiacem possit superare nisi Aiax" (*Metamorphoses*, XIII, 390).

The battle between eighteenth-century beaux and belles did not provide for textualization of an extreme gesture like suicide, which persists interdiscoursively, in joyous contrast, in the substratum of the text, where it is conveyed by illustrious intertextual fragments. That Shakespeare, for his part, took his Ovidian passages from Arthur Golding's translation (which went through seven editions between 1567 and 1612) merely serves to show how adventurous are the ways of intertextuality.[119]

Intertextuality from work to work is commonly met with, especially in modern authors. (Its limit is parody or rewriting, but there is no need for us to dwell here on products whose interpretation is all too easy.) Everyone knows that Joyce's *Ulysses*—as its very title informs us—adapts contemporary characters and events to a Homeric pattern and that an increase in sense is achieved from such parallelism. More recently, Tom Stoppard's play *Rosencrantz and Guildenstern are Dead* has staged a history which is rendered absurd because its characters relive episodes from Shakespeare's *Hamlet*, while being unaware—as the audience is not—of the details of the plot and of the outcome. This is a good case of conceptual "parasitism," for the meaning of events can only be deduced by integrating the comedy with Shakespeare's drama.[120]

For the invention of a whale who swallows the hero and is found to contain in its stomach a whole, greatly diversified, infernal geography, a succession of examples can be given.[121] They will lead us from the *True History* of Lucianus to Ariosto's *Cinque canti* (IV) to Collodi's *Pinocchio* (XXXV). Both Italian authors, though, can only be interpreted satisfactorily if due weight is given to the biblical story of Jonah and to its inherent symbols (death and resurrection, sin and repentance). Calvino's *Le citta invisibili*, too, implies the existence of Marco Polo's *Milione*, where the relation between Marco and Kublai is unfolded in all its developments and in all its characteristics.

Notes

1. G. Gorni, "La metafora del testo," in *Strumenti critici*, 13 (1979): 38, pp. 18–32.
2. Most enlightening is M. M. Bachtin's *Problema teksta* (1976). For the Italian translation, see "Il problema del testo," in V. V. Ivanov et al., *Michail Bachtin: Semiotica, teoria della letteratur e marxismo* (Bari: Dedalo, 1977), pp. 197–229.
3. For a first approach, see W. U. Dressler, *Einführung in die Textlinguistik* (Tübingen: Niemeyer, 1972); M. E. Conte, ed., *La linguistica testuale* (Milan: Feltrinelli, 1977); and R.-A. De Beaugrande and W. U. Dressler, *Introduction to Text Linguistics* (London: Longmans, 1981). The work which devotes most attention to the literary implications of text linguistics is T. A. van Dijk, *Some Aspects of Text Grammars: A Study in Theoretical Linguistics and Poetics* (The Hague: Mouton, 1972). This work was subsequently reelaborated and recast with the title *Textwissenschaft: Eine interdisziplinäre Einführung* (Tübingen: Niemeyer, 1980). It should be compared with G. Genot, *Problèmes de calcul du récit* (Paris: Seuil, 1980). For a critical contribution (besides C. Segre, *Semiotica filologica*, pp. 23–37), see J. S. Petöfi, ed., *Text vs. Sentence: Basic Questions of Text Linguistics* (Hamburg: Buske, 1979). See also the following two collections: *Del testo: Seminario interdisciplinare sulla costituzione del testo* (Naples, 1979); and *Linguistica testuale: Atti del XV Congresso internazionale di studi; Genova-Santa Margherita Ligure 8–10 maggio 1981*, ed. L. Còveri (Rome: Bulzoni, 1984).
4. I have elsewhere (in *Semiotica filologica*, p. 23) expressed my doubts concerning the use, by now generalized, of *text* applied even to oral utterances; it might well have been better to have followed Harris and adopted the term *discourse*.
5. The values of the term *coherence* are defined in M.-E. Conte, "Coerenza testuale," in *Lingua e stile*, 15 (1980): 1, pp. 135–54.

6. The problems had already been clearly defined by R. Ingarden, *Das literarische Kunstwerk* (1931). For the English translation, see *The Literary Work of Art: Investigation on the Borderlines of Ontology, Logic, and Theory of Literature* (Evanston: Northwestern University Press, 1973), sect. 2, chap. 5, §23.

7. See V. Mathesius, "On Linguistic Characterology with Illustrations from Modern English," in J. Vachek, ed., *A Prague School Reader in Linguistics* (Bloomington: Indiana University Press, 1964), pp. 39–67.

8. The definition comes from A. J. Greimas and J. Courtés, *Sémiotique: Dictionnaire raisonné de la théorie du langage* (Paris: Hachette, 1979), pp. 197–99. For the English translation, see *Semiotics and Language: An Analytical Dictionary* (Bloomington: Indiana University Press, 1983). But, for earlier definitions, see A. J. Greimas, *Sémantique structurale* (Paris: Larousse, 1966). For the English translation, see *Structural Semantics: An Attempt at Method* (Lincoln: University of Nebraska Press, 1983), chap. 6. See also F. Rastier, "Systématique des isotopies," in A. J. Greimas, ed., *Essais de sémiotique poétique* (Paris: Larousse, 1972), pp. 80–105. More recent bibliography is discussed in P. Pugliatti and R. Zacchi, *Terribilia meditans: La coerenza del monologo interiore in "Ulysses"* (Bologna: Il Mulino, 1983).

9. Greimas and Courtés, *Sémiotique*, p. 199.

10. Coleridge, *The Rime of the Ancient Mariner*, pt. 5, lines 354–66.

11. There also exists a *referential* function (oriented toward the context), a *metalinguistic* function (oriented toward the code), and a *phatic* function (relative to the contact). See R. Jakobson, "Linguistics and Poetics," in *Style in Language*, ed. T. A. Sebeok (Cambridge, Mass.: M.I.T. Press, 1960), pp. 350–77, esp. 357. The attempt has been made to enlarge Jakobson's list of functions, but at the cost of obliterating the correspondence between functions and constitutents of the communication and with the added risk of confusing functions with the characteristics of literary genres (e.g., suggesting a lyric function, a dramatic function, and so forth) or with techniques (narrative, descriptive, stage production functions). See for example, M. Pagnini, *Pragmatica*, pp. 26–33.

12. See K. W. Hempfer, *Gattungstheorie* (Munich: Fink, 1973); and M. Corti, *Principi della comunicazione letteraria* (Milan: Bompiani, 1976). For the English translation of Corti's work, see *An Introduction to Literary Semiotics* (Bloomington: Indiana University Press, 1978), chap. 5. See also Part II, chap. 3, of this book, where I discuss this point. An example of homology between symbolic codes, formal codes, and the language is illustrated by M. Corti, "Il codice bucolico e l 'Arcadia' di Iacobo Sannazaro" (1968), in *Metodi e fantasmi* (Milan: Feltrinelli, 1969), pp. 281–304.

13. See N. Miller, ed., *Romananfänge: Versuch zu einer Poetik des Romans* (Berlin: Literarisches Colloquium, 1965); B. Herrnstein Smith, *Poetic Closure: A Study of How Poems End* (Chicago: University of Chicago Press, 1968), and *On the Margins of Discourse: The Relation of Literature to Language* (Chicago: University of Chicago Press, 1978); Ph. Hamon, *Clausules*, in *Poétique*, 6 (1975): 24, pp. 495–526; E. W. Said, *Beginnings: Intention and Method* (Baltimore: Johns Hopkins Press, 1975); V. Coletti, "Dall'inizio alla fine: percorso didattico attraverso il romanzo," in *Otto-Novecento*, 4 (1980): pp. 175–96; and W. Mignolo, *Elementos*, pp. 246–47. For the communicative analysis of titles, see, for example, L. H. Hoek, *Pour une sémiotique du titre* (Urbino, 1973); E. Casadei, "Contributi per una teoria del titolo: Le novelle di Federico Tozzi," in *Lingua e stile*, 15 (1980); I, pp. 3–25; and M. Di Fazio Alberti, *Il titolo e la funzione paraletteraria* (Turin: Eri, 1984).

14. Stream of consciousness is an attempt to represent the thematic incoherence and the free association of thought on the part of a character engaging in monologue; with its not altogether rational syntax, it imitates the workings of the unconscious. Typical is Molly Bloom's monologue in Joyce's *Ulysses*.

15. Performative utterance is the name given to an utterance which imposes (or proposes) a certain kind of behavior (in our case, of interpretation).

16. See for example, J. Honzl, "The Hierarchy of Dramatic Devices," in L. Matejka and I. R. Titunik, eds., *Semiotics of Art: Prague School Contributions* (Cambridge, Mass.: M.I.T. Press, 1976), pp. 118–27. See also the analyses brought together in A. Canziani *et al.*, *Come comunica il teatro: dal testo alla scena* (Milan: Il Formichiere, 1978).

17. See L. Doležel, "Narrative Semantics," in *PTL: A Journal for Descriptive Poetics and Theory of Literature*, 1 (1976): 1, pp. 129–51.

18. For a still-valuable discussion of the "frame" technique, see V. Šklovskij, *O teorii prozy* (Moscow: Federacija, 1925). See also J. Hambuechen Potter, *Five Frames for the "Decameron": Communication and Social Systems in the Cornice* (Princeton: Princeton University Press, 1982).

19. For example, *Gli idilli difficili* (1958) of Calvino evidences, in its ten tales of Marcovaldo, a combinative system of invariants arranged in terms of a well-defined progression at the level of content; this is not the case in *Marcovaldo ovvero Le stagioni in città* (1966), where the ten stories have become twenty but where there is a loss of unity and of thematic economy. See M. Corti, "Testi o macrotesto? I racconti di I. Calvino (1975)," in *Il viaggio testuale: Le ideologie e le strutture semiotiche* (Turin: Einaudi, 1978), pp. 185–200.

20. See C. Segre, "Sistema e struttura nelle 'Soledades' di A. Machado," in *I segni e la critica*, pp. 95–134. For the English translation, see *System and Structures in the "Soledades" of A. Machado*, in *Semiotics and Literary Criticism*, pp. 81–116. See also Segre, *I sonetti dell'aura*, in the collective *Lectura Petrarce*, III, 1983. (Florence: Olschki, 1984). G. Genot, "Strutture narrative della poesia lirica," in *Paragone: Letteratura*, 18 (1967): 212, pp. 35–52, stresses the narrative sequence. J. Geninasca, *Les Chimères de Nerval* (Paris: Larousse, 1973), regards a *canzoniere* as a sentence whose single components are words. M. Santagata, *Dal sonetto al canzoniere: Ricerche sulla preistoria e la costituzione di un genere* (Padua: Liviana, 1979), carries out a systematic comparison of the poems in Petrarch's *canzoniere*, in search of (a) transformation connections and (b) equivalence connections, and he takes account of relations pertaining both to the expression sphere and to the content sphere. S. Longhi, "Il tutto e le parti nel sistema di un canzoniere," in *Strumenti critici*, 13 (1979): 39–40, pp. 265–300, follows the "narrative" developments of three dominant thematic lines in the *Rime* of Giovanni della Casa. See also Z. C. Minc, *Struttura compositiva del ciclo di A. Blok "Snežnaja maska,"* in Ju. M. Lotman and B. A. Uspenskij, eds., *Ricerche semiotiche: Nuove tendenze delle scienze umane nell'Urss*, ed. C. Strada Janovic (Turin: Einaudi, 1973), pp. 251–317. It individuates the unity of the cycle in the spheres of "landscape," of "personal state," of love-passion, of "world picture," and in references to biography.

21. R. Jakobson and P. Valesio, 'Vocabulorum constructio in Dante's Sonnet 'Se vedi li occhi miei'" in Roman Jakobson, *Selected Writings*, vol. 3, *Poetry of Grammar and Grammar of Poetry*, ed. S. Rudy (The Hague, 1981), pp. 177–78. All the analyses Jakobson dedicated to sonnets follow this pattern. See, in the volume cited, the chapters on Dante (pp. 176–92), Du Bellay (pp. 239–74), Shakespeare (pp. 284–303), Baudelaire (pp. 447–64 and 465–81), Martin Codax (pp. 169–75), Pessoa (pp. 639–59), etc. The following refer in varying degree to Jakobson's previous work: F. Orlando, "Baudelaire e la sera," in *Paragone: Letteratura*, 17 (1966): 196, pp. 44–73; S. Agosti, *Il cigno di Mallarmé* (Rome: Silva, 1969), and *Il testo poetico: Teoria e pratiche d'analisi* (Milan: Rizzoli 1972); M. Pagnini, *Critica della funzionalità* (Turin: Einaudi, 1970); J. Geninasca, *Analyse Structurale des "Chimères" de Nerval* (Neuchâtel: A la Baconnière, 1971); and A. Serpieri, *I sonetti dell'immortalità: Il problema dell'arte e della nominazione in Shakespeare* (Milan: Bompiani, 1975).

22. U. Foscolo, *Opere*, edizione nazionale, vol. 3, *Esperimenti di traduzione dell'Iliade*, ed. G. Barbarisi (Florence: Le Monnier, 1961), t.I, pp. 232–33.

23. J. Piaget, *Le structuralisme*, 3d ed. (Paris: PUF, 1968). For the English translation, see *Structuralism* (London: Routledge and Kegan Paul, 1971), p. 5. But all the

above considerations are based on chapter 3 of my *Semiotica, storia e cultura* (Padua: Liviana, 1977).

24. The *grapheme* is a minimal graphic unit, corresponding to a letter of the alphabet; it does not entirely correspond to the *phoneme*, or minimal phonic unit, because the phoneme may be represented by a number of graphemes (in *ciò*, the phoneme *č* is represented by *ci*; in *che*, the phoneme *K* is represented by *ch*; this for Italian); or graphemes may represent a number of phonemes (*i* tonic in English represents the phonemes *a* plus *i*). The *moneme* is the minimal meaningful unit: root, prefix or suffix, case ending, etc.

25. R. Ingarden, *Das literarische Kunstwerk* (English translation, p. 29).

26. Ibid., p. 211.

27. See M. Pagnini, "La critica letteraria come integrazione dei livelli dell'opera," in the collective volume *Critica e storia letteraria: Studi offerti a Mario Fubini* (Padua: Liviana, 1970), 1, pp. 87-102.

28. The term was introduced by Buyssens and subsequently accepted in a slightly different sense by Greimas; *sèma* stands for the minimal unit of meaning.

29. The lark's song connotes the dawn. See, for example, Shakespeare, *Romeo and Juliet*, III, v, 6: "It was the lark, the herald of the morn."

30. See L. Hjelmslev, *Prolegomena to a Theory of Literature*, 2d ed. (Madison: The University of Wisconsin Press, 1961), pp. 47–60; the first, Danish edition appeared in 1943.

31. Ibid., p. 57.

32. Ibid., p. 50.

33. For the concept of connotation in linguistics, from Bloomfield and Hjelmslev to today, see C. Kerbrat-Orecchioni, *La connotation* (Lyon: Presses Universitaires de Lyon, 1977); and B. Garza Cuarón, *La connotación: problemas del significado* (Mexico City: El Colegio de México, 1978).

34. Hjelmslev, *Prolegomena*, p. 119.

35. One of the first to appreciate the potential of Hjelmslev's figure when applied to the literary sphere was R. Barthes, *Eléments de sémiologie* (Paris: Seuil, 1964).

36. See H. Sorensen, *Studier i Baudelaires poesi* (Copenhagen: Munksgaard, 1955), pp. 18–21. Much closer to Hjemslev is S. Johansen, "La notion de signe dans la glossématique et dans l'esthétique," in *Travaux du Cercle linguistique de Copenhague*, 5 (1949): pp. 288–303. He attributed rhyme, for example, to the expression substance; rhythm to expression form; denotation to content substance; the use of tenses, syntatic choices (asyndeton, parataxis, etc.) to content form. But the *peculiarity* of literary invention was relegated among "the author's material and intellectual idiosyncrasies," his "preference for certain arguments or for certain intellectual problems"; the same is true of Trabant, quoted below (cf., for example, chap. 3).

37. See A. J. Greimas, *Modelli semiologici* (Urbino: Argalia, 1967), pp. 122–23.

38. See P. Zumthor, "Charles d'Orléans et le langage de l'allégorie" (1969), in *Langue, texte, énigme* (Paris: Seuil, 1975), p. 198.

39. See J. Trabant, *Zur Semiologie des literarischen Kunstwerks: Glossematik und Literaturtheorie* (Munich: Fink, 1970).

40. For a polemical contraposition of a semiology of communication (which bears the stamp of Saussure) and a semiology of signification, see G. Mounin, *Introduction à la sémiologie* (Paris: Minuit, 1970), pp. 11–15 and 189–97; L. J. Prieto, *Etudes de linguistique et de sémiologie générales* (Geneva: Droz, 1975), pp. 125–41; and J. M. Klinkenberg, "Communication et signification: L'unité de la sémiologie," in the collective volume *A Semiotic Landscape: Proceedings of the First Congress of the IASS, Milan, June 1974*, ed. S. Chatman, U. Eco, and J.-M. Klinkenberg (The Hague: Mouton, 1979), pp. 288–94. Here both sides are in error: those whose aim it was to deal with signification problems in terms of ordinary linguistic formulae and those who wished to exclude signification from the field of semiotics.

41. Peirce describes as *iconic* a sign which shows some formal resemblance or affinity with the object it is to denote.

42. See R. Jakobson, "Le langage en relation avec les autres systèmes de communication" (1968), in *Essais de linguistique générale*, vol. 2, *Rapports internes et externes du langage* (Paris: Minuit, 1973), p. 96 (cf. *Selected Writings*, vol. 2, *Words and Language*, pp. 697–708).

43. The extract of the poem by E. E. Cummings is from the collection *XAIPE* (1950).

44. R. Jakobson, "Quest for the Essence of Language" (1966), in *Selected Writings*, vol. 2, *Words and Language* (The Hague: Mouton, 1971), pp. 345–59.

45. Ibid., p. 352.

46. See P. Zumthor, "Carmina figurata" (1969), in *Langue, texte, énigme*, pp. 25–35; and G. Pozzi, "Gli artifici figurali del linguaggio poetico e l'iconismo," in *Strumenti critici*, 10 (1976): 31, pp. 349–83; 1 *La parola dipinta* (Milan: Adelphi, 1981), and *Poesia per gioco: Prontuario di figure artificiose* (Bologna: Il Mulino, 1984).

47. Pozzi, *Gli artifici figurali*, p. 364.

48. One of the most impressive acrostics of Italian literature is Boccaccio's *Amorosa visione*: all the initial letters of the poem's tercets make up three sonnets, two are tailed and one is *rinterzato* and tailed, with "signature."

49. See, in this regard, Anthony Easthope, *Poetry as Discourse* (London: Methuen, 1983), p. 105.

50. See Geoffrey N. Leech, *A Linguistic Guide to English Poetry* (London: Longman, 1969), p. 99.

51. In the medieval doctrine *de modis significandi*, a distinction was made between *articulatio prima* and *secunda*; Martinet has since spoken by analogy of a *double articulation*. Linguistic utterance acts are articulated into meaningful units, endowed with sense, whose minimal units are monemes (cf. §2.10.1). But this primary articulation is realized by means of another, made up of *phonemes* deprived of meaning but having a distinctive function, in the sense that any change in a phoneme changes the meaning of a moneme (*bit* vs. *bite* vs. *bait* vs. *boat*, and so on).

52. See J. Starobinski, *Les mots sous les mots: Les anagrammes de Ferdinand de Saussure* (Paris: Gallimard, 1971). For the English translation, see *Words upon Words: The Anagrams of Ferdinand de Saussure* (New Haven: Yale University Press, 1979). Cf. P. Wunderli, *Ferdinand de Saussure und die Anagramme: Linguistik und Literatur* (Tübingen: Niemeyer, 1927); A. L. Johnson, "L'anagrammatismo in poesia: Premesse teoriche," in *Annali della Scuola Normale Superiore di Pisa*, 3d ser., 6 (1976): 2, pp. 679–717. The widest-ranging application of the method, which has recourse to permutation calculus, is G. Sasso, *Le strutture anagrammatiche della poesia* (Milan: Feltrinelli, 1982).

53. See J. Kristeva, Σημειωτική: *Recherches pour une sémanalyse* (Paris: Seuil, 1978). For the English translation, see *Desire in Language: A Semiotic Approach to Literature and Art* (Oxford: Blackwell, 1980); and Agosti, *Il testo poetico*.

54. Agosti, *Il testo poetico*, p. 197.

55. Dylan Thomas, *Quite Early One Morning* (London: Dent, 1954) pp. 156–57.

56. A well-balanced position is that of R. Jakobson, "Subliminal Verbal Patterning in Poetry," in *Selected Writings*, vol. 3, pp. 136–47.

57. For the systematic treatment of the anagrammatization of *rat*, see "The Domain of the Rat" and "The Anagrammatic Presence of the Rat," in Anthony L. Johnson, *Sign and Structure in the Poetry of T. S. Eliot* (Pisa: ETS, 1976), pp. 259–378 and 379–82. We have made interdiscoursive use of this text.

58. See, for example, S. Ullmann, *The Principles of Semantics* (Oxford: Blackwell and Mott, 1957); and R. Jakobson and L. R. Waugh, *The Sound Shape of Language* (Bloomington: Indiana University Press, 1979), chap. 4. See also P. Dombi Erzsébet, "Synaestesia and Poetry," in *Poetics*, 11 (1974): pp. 23–44 (with bibliography). There is an elegant application in G. Genette, *Figures II*, *Essais* (Paris: Seuil, 1969).

59. For relations with rhetoric and metrics as well, see P. Valesio, *Struttura dell'allitterrazione: Grammatica, retorica e folklore verbale* (Bologna: Zanichelli, 1967).
60. G. L. Beccaria, *L'autonomia del significante: Figure del ritmo e della sintassi; Dante, Pascoli, D'Annunzio* (Turin: Einaudi, 1975), p. 75. (The verse quoted is from G. Camerana, "Rammento il borgo sulla via montana," in *Bozzetti*, vv. 4–5).
61. Ibid., p. 203. On the musicality, in the strictest sense of the word, of Pascoli's poetry, see M. Pagnini, "Il testo poetico e la musicalità," in *Linguistica e letteratura*, 2 (1977): 2, pp. 203–21.
62. Beccaria, *L'autonomia del significante*, p. 202. The most systematic analysis of the phonic functions of a single poet is perhaps that of M. Picchio Simonelli, *Figure foniche dal Petrarca ai petrarchisti* (Florence: Licosa, 1978).
63. The reader may take further advantage of a phonic reactivity akin to that of the listener by reading aloud or by articulating mentally.
64. See Segre, *Semiotica filologica*, p. 42, where it is shown that there is a kinship between these connections and all of the operations of "mental restructuring" of which the criticism of the literary text consists (individuation of isotopies, themes, and motifs, rearrangement of the plot as *fabula* and classification of functions, etc.).
65. See P. Guiraud, "Les fonctions secondaires du langage," in A. Martinet, ed., *Le langage* (Paris: Gallimard, 1968), p. 469. He states, "Poetry is an hypostasis of the signifying form which needs to be rescued from selectivity and transitoriness."
66. See Segre, *Semiotica filologica*, p. 43.
67. B. V. Tomashevsky, "Sur le vers/O stiche" (Leningrad, 1929), partly in T. Todorov, ed., *Théorie de la littérature* (Paris: Seuil, 1965), pp. 154–69, esp. p. 155. See also the systematic treatment in B. V. Tomaševski, *Teorija literatury: Poetika* (1928). For the English translation, see *Literary Genres*, in *Formalism: History, Comparison, Genre; Russian Poetics in Translation* (Oxford: Colchester, 1978), pp. 52–93.
68. O. Brik, "Ritm i sintaksis (Materialy k izučeniju stichotvornoj reči" [Rhythm and syntax (materials for the study of verse discourse)], in T. Todorov, ed., *Théorie de la littérature*. A modern and well-informed presentation of the terms of the problem is P. M. Bertinetto, *Ritmo e modelli ritmici: Analisi computazionale delle funzioni periodiche nella versificazione dantesca* (Turin: Rosenberg e Sellier, 1973). See also C. Di Girolamo, *Teoria e prassi della versificazione* (Bologna: Il Mulino, 1976); P. G. Bertrami, *Prospettive della metrica*, in *Lingua e stile*, 15 (1980), and *Metrica, poetica, metrica dantesca* (Pisa: Pacini, 1981). And, for all metrical problems, see R. Cremante and M. Pazzaglia, eds., *La metrica* (Bologna: Il Mulino, 1972).
69. See Tomashevsky, *Sur le vers/O stiche*.
70. Fundamental for meter, alongside the works mentioned in the previous note, is Ju. N. Tynjanov, *Problema stichotvornogo jazyka* (1924). For the Italian translation, see *Il problema del linguaggio poetico* (Milan: Il Saggiatore, 1968). See also V. Žirmunskij, *Vvedenie v metriku: Teorija sticha* (1925). For the English translation, see *Introduction to Metrics* (The Hague: Mouton, 1966); and S. Chatman, *A Theory of Meter* (The Hague: Mouton, 1965).
71. I am alluding to Ariosto, who forced the syntax into continual conflict with the meter in the first version of his *Furioso*, while in the final version his aim was to bring them into harmony. See C. Segre, *Esperienze ariostesche* (Pisa: Nistri-Lischi, 1966), pp. 38–39. For the contrast between syntactical and metrical discourse in Ungaretti, see G. Genot, *Sémantique du discontinu dans L'Allegria d'Ungaretti* (Paris: Klincksieck, 1972), pp. 103–44 and 183–200. The main theoretical work on *enjambement* is A. Quilis, *Estructura del encabalgamiento en la métrica española* (Madrid: Consejo Superior de Investigaciones Científicas, 1964). But see also G. Tavani, "Verso e frase nella poesia di Cernuda," in *Studi di letteratura spagnola* (Rome, 1966), pp. 71–126.
72. See *A Prague School Reader in Linguistics*, ed. J. Vachek (Bloomington: Indiana University Press, 1964), pp. 33–58. The *Théses* are in French.
73. See for example, S. R. Levin, *Linguistic Structures in Poetry* (The Hague:

Mouton, 1962); R. Jakobson, "Grammatical Parallelism and Its Russian Facet" (1966), in *Selected Writings*, vol. 3, *Poetry of Grammar and Grammar of Poetry*, pp. 89–135; and Ju. M. Lotman, *Struktura chudožestvennogo teksta* (1970). For the English translation of Lotman's work, see *The Structure of the Artistic Text* (Ann Arbor: University of Michigan Press, 1977), pp. 119–36. See also G. Genot, *Sémantique du discontinu*. For the use of parallelism, even in the study of prose, see S. Agosti, "Tecniche della rappresentazione verbale in Flaubert," in *Strumenti critici*, 12 (1978): 35, pp. 31–58, and in a more elaborated version, in the volume *Tecniche della rappresentazione verbale in Flaubert* (Milan: Il Saggiatore, 1981), chaps. 1–2.

74. For its bibliographical references as well, see Beccaria, *L'autonomia del significante*, pp. 27ff.; and P. M. Bertinetto, "Echi del suono ed echi del senso," in *Parole e metodi*, 1 (1972): 3, pp. 47–57.

75. See E. G. Parodi, *La rima e i vocaboli in rima nella Divina Commedia* (1896), in *Lingua e letteratura*, ed. G. Folena (Venice: Neri Pozza, 1957), vol. 2, pp. 203–84.

76. See G. Contini, "Un'interpretazione di Dante" (1965), in *Varianti e altra linguistica: Una raccolta di saggi (1938–1968)* (Turin: Einaudi, 1970), pp. 369–405.

77. Ch. Bally, *Traité de stylistique francaise* (1909), 2d ed. (Heidelberg: Winter, 1921), pp. 1 and 16.

78. F. de Saussure, *Cours de linguistique générale* (1916). For the English translation, see *Course in General Linguistics* (London: Duckworth, 1983), p. 123. Saussure distinguishes between syntagmatic relations, which link words together in the linearity of the discourse, and associative relations, which, outside discourse, link each word with all the other words which have something in common with it (etymology, meaning, case ending, etc.). After Saussure, relations of the second type have increasingly been called paradigmatic rather than associative.

79. For Saussure, the distinction between *langue* (language, the language) and *parole* (speech) marks off "what is social from what is individual" and "what is essential from what is ancillary and more or less accidental." Ibid., pp. 13–14.

80. See J. Marouzeau, *Traité de stylistique latine*, 2d ed. (Paris: Les Belles Lettres, 1946), and *Précis de stylistique française*, 2d ed. (Paris: Masson, 1946).

81. L. Spitzer, *Zur sprachlichen "Interpretation von Wortkunstwerken"* (1928), in *Romanische Stil- und Literaturstudien I* (Marburg a. Lahn: Elwert, 1931), p. 4.

82. L. Spitzer, "Pseudoobjektive Motivierung bei Charles-Louis Philippe," in *Stilstudien*, vol. 2, *Stilsprachen* (Munich: Hueber, 1928), pp. 166–207, *Zur Charles Péguy's Stil*, in *Stilstudien* (1927), pp. 301–64, and *Studien zu Henri Barbusse* (Bonn: Cohen, 1920).

83. See for example, L. Spitzer, "L'Aspasia di Leopardi" (1963), in *Studi italiani* (Milan: Vita e pensiero, 1976), pp. 251–92, and, for theoretical statements, L. Spitzer, "Les études de style et les différents pays," in the collective *Langue et littératures: Actes du VIII Congrès de la Fédération Internationale des Langues et Littératures Modernes* (Paris: Les Belles Letters, 1961), pp. 23–39.

84. L. Spitzer, *Linguistics and Literary History* (Princeton: Princeton University Press, 1948), p. 14.

85. Ibid., p. 11.

86. This seems to be the opinion of M. Riffaterre, *Essais de stylistique structurale* (Paris: Flammarion, 1971).

87. B. A. Terracini, *Analisi stilistica: Teoria, storia, problemi*, 2d ed. (Milan: Feltrinelli, 1975), chap. 1.

88. See P. Guiraud, *Les caractères statistiques du vocabulaire* (Paris: PUF, 1954), pp. 52–55; and L. Rosiello, *Analisi statistica della funzione poetica nella poesia montaliana*, in *Struttura, uso e funzione della lingua* (Florence: Vallecchi, 1965), chap. 4.

89. The best synthesis of the theoretical problems of stylistics is N. E. Enkvist, *Linguistic Stylistics* (The Hague: Mouton, 1973).

90. G. Devoto, *Nuovi studi di stilistica* (Florence: Le Monnier, 1962), p. 185, *Studi di*

stilistica (Florence: Le Monnier, 1950), and *Itinerario stilistico* (Florence: Le Monnier, 1975) The last work rearranges the earlier writings. G. A. Papini's preface to this latter volume should be referred to.

91. I have attempted to apply sociolinguistic models in the chapter "La tradizione macaronica da Folengo a Gadda (e oltre)" in *Semiotica filologica*, pp. 169–83 (with bibliography). One must now add R. A. Hudson, *Sociolinguistics* (Cambridge: Cambridge University Press, 1980).

92. See M. M. Bachtin, *Voprosy literatury i estetiki*. For the Italian translation, see *Estetica e romanzo* (Turin: Einaudi, 1975). The concept of *ideologeme* has been developed further by P. N. Medvedev, *Formal'nyj metod v literaturovedenii: Kritičeskoe vvedenie v sociologičeskuju poetiku* (1928). For the Italian translation, see *Il metodo formale nella scienza della letteratura, introduzione critica al metodo sociologico* (Bari: Dedalo, 1978). See also Kristeva, Σημειωτική, and *Le texte du roman* (The Hague: Mouton, 1970). For Bachtin's thought in relation to that of Medvedev and Vološinov, see T. Todorov, *Mikhaïl Bakhtine: Le principe dialogique, suivi de Écrits du Cercle de Bakhtine* (Paris: Seuil, 1981).

93. See M. Pêcheux, "Analyse du discours, langue et idéologies," in *Language*, 37 (1975): 7–20.

94. R. Barthes, *Le degré zéro de l'écriture* (Paris: Seuil, 1953), p. 14 (English translation, p. 20).

95. P. Zumthor, *Langue et techniques poétiques à l'époque romane (XI-XIII siècles* (Paris: Klincksieck, 1963). For an overall view, and further attempts at definition, see Segre, *Le strutture e il tempo*, pp. 32–33 and 109–15 (English translation, pp. 23–24 and 86–92).

96. *Thèses*, p. 46.

97. Ibid., p. 49.

98. Jakobson, *Linguistics and Poetics*, p. 358.

99. See, for example, Lotman, *Struktura*, chaps. 5–7.

100. See J. Bellemin-Noël, *Le texte et l'avant-texte* (Paris: Larousse, 1972). See also Corti, *Principi*, pp. 98–106 (English translation, pp. 70–77); and B. Basile, "Verso una dinamica letteraria: Testo e avantesto," in *Lingua e stile*, 14 (1979): 2–3, pp. 395–410.

101. See D'A. S. Avalle, *L'analisi letteraria in Italia: Formalismo, strutturalismo, semiologia* (Milan: Ricciardi, 1970); M. Corti and C. Segre, eds., *I metodi attuali della critica in Italia* (Turin: ERI, 1970), pp. 332–33; and Segre, *Semiotica, storia e cultura*, pp. 69–70, and "Du structuralisme à la sémiologie en Italie," in A. Helbo, ed., *Le champ sémiologique: Perspectives internationales* (Brussels: Complexe, 1979). For a different, though convergent, framework see J. Levy, "Generi e ricezione dell'opera d'arte," in *Strumenti critici*, 5 (1971): 14, pp. 39–66.

102. Dylan Thomas, *Collected Poems* (London: Dent, 1952), p. 39. The experience has been a fundamental one for the development of Italian literary criticism. See G. Contini, "Implicazioni leopardiane" (1947), in *Varianti e altra linguistica*, p. 44. The volume brings together Contini's main studies of variants (Petrarch, Manzoni, Leopardi, Mallarmé, Proust). Contini's contribution takes the form of a discussion with another, and no less remarkable, critical approach: G. De Robertis, "Sull'autografo del canto 'A Silvia'" (1946), in *Primi studi manzoniani e altre cose,* (Florence: Le Monnier, 1949), pp. 105–68.

103. *The Notebooks of Dylan Thomas*, ed. R. Maud (New York: New Directions, 1965), pp. 260–62.

104. W. Y. Tindall, *A Reader's Guide to Dylan Thomas* (Letchworth: Thames and Hudson, 1962), p. 97.

105. T. S. Eliot, *The Waste Land: A Facsimile and Transcription of the Original Drafts Including the Annotations of Ezra Pound*, ed. Valerie Eliot (New York: Harcourt Brace Jovanovich, 1971).

106. See M. Perloff, *Rhymes and Meaning in the Poetry of Yeats* (The Hague: Mouton, 1970), pp. 126–27.

107. See L. Ariosto, *Orlando furioso*, ed. S. Debenedetti and C. Segre (Bologna: Commissione per i testi di lingua, 1960). For examples of investigations of variants in the three *Furiosi*, see C. Segre, "Storia interna dell'Orlando furioso" (1961), in *Esperienze ariostesche*, pp. 29–41: E. Bigi, "Appunti sulla lingua e sulla metrica del 'Furioso,'" in *Giornale storico della letteratura italiana*, 138 (1961): pp. 249–63; and E. Turolla, "Dialettologia e enjambement nell'elaborazione dell' 'Orlando Furioso,'" in *Convivium*, 31 (1963): pp. 19–34.

108. See A. Manzoni, *I promessi sposi*, ed. R. Folli (Milan: Briola and Bocconi, 1877–79); and, with the same criterion, *I promessi sposi*, ed. L. Caretti (Turin: Einaudi, 1971).

109. For an analysis, see S. Debenedetti, ed., *I frammenti autografi dell'Orlando Furioso* (Turin: Chiantore, 1937), introduction; and G. Contini, "Come lavorava l'Ariosto" (1937), in *Esercizi di lettura* (Turin: Einaudi, 1974), pp. 234–41.

110. See M. Magalaner, *Time of Apprenticeship: The Fiction of Young James Joyce* (London: Abelard-Schuman, 1959), p. 73.

111. J. Joyce, *The Sisters*, in *Dubliners* (New York: Viking Press, 1967), p. 9.

112. Ibid., p. 11.

113. Ibid., p. 14.

114. Ibid., p. 17.

115. See M. Magalaner, *Time of Apprenticeship*, pp. 174–80.

116. See, for these problems, H. Meyer, *Das Zitat in der Erzählkunst: Zur Geschichte und Poetik des europäische Romans* (1961). For the English translation, see *The Poetics of Quotation in the European Novel* (Princeton: Princeton University Press, 1968). See also Z. Ben Porat, "The Poetics of Literary Allusion," in *PTL: A Journal for Descriptive Poetics and Theory of Literature*, 1 (1977): pp. 46–54; G. Wienold, "Das Konzept der Textverarbeitung und die Semiotik der Literatur," in *Zeitschrift für Literaturwissenschaft und Linguistik*, 7 (1977): pp. 46–54; and A. Compagnon, *La seconde main, ou le travail de la citation* (Paris: Seuil, 1979). In any case, any text is already, to some extent, the parody of earlier texts, as the Russian formalists well understood. For a history and typology of parody, see G. Genette, *Palimpsestes: La littérature au sécond degré* (Paris: Seuil, 1982).

117. In Kristeva, who gave currency to the term, its values are still wider: it would involve all the code "interchanges" present in the text. See Kristeva, Σημειωτική, setting out from the index (English translation, p. 299). For observations concerning the term's inexactitude and excessive breadth of meaning, see Greimas and Courtés, *Semiotique*, p. 194. For a methodological framework, see A. Popovič, *Text a metatext*. For the Italian translation, see Prevignano, *La semiotica nei paesi slavi*, pp. 521–45. See also Segre, *Teatro e romanzo*, chap. 7.

118. Coined by J. S. Petöfi, the word *co-text* indicates the verbal context to which a word or utterance belongs. The neologism is an attempt to avoid confusion with the situational *context*.

119. In the judgment of J. A. K. Thompson, "If he [Shakespeare] kept a Latin Ovid before him, he troubled very little to consult it." P. Simpson, *Studies in Elizabethan Drama* (Oxford: Clarendon Press, 1955), p. 4.

120. See P. Gullí Pugliatti, "Per un'indagine sulla convenzione nel testo drammatico," in *Strumenti critici*, 13 (1979): 39–40, pp. 428–47.

121. See A. H. Gilbert, "The Sea-Monster in Ariosto's 'Cinque Canti,'" in *Italica*, 33 (1956): pp. 260–63.

3.
Text Contents

3.1. Levels of Meaning

3.1.1. We have seen (§2.11–13) that Hjelmslev's quadripartition—expression form and expression substance, content form and content substance—can be applied, strictly speaking, to linguistic utterances alone. It lends itself to literary analysis only as regards expression, because expression is fully realized at the level of the discourse, i.e., at the level of the verbal texture. It cannot be applied to contents, because Hjelmslev's theory deals only with such contents as are proper to the language. Text contents, i.e., the contents communicated by the text (which of its nature is not a linguistic product but a semiotic product which makes use of a linguistic vehicle), call for different analytical methods and more sensitive focusing, given that meanings in this case are not those denoted by the linguistic signifiers; they all result either from the intervention of connotative effects or from the integrations and generalizations which arise out of any global deciphering of the message.

Something might be said here about the various analyses which have been put forward for text meanings. I shall deal with the two cases which can be situated, first, at a minimal and, second, at a maximum distance from the denotative semiotics of explicit discourse level: semantic meaning and dianoetic meaning.[1]

Semantic meaning is the meaning of single terms or syntagms. The best commentaries have always attempted to define the value of words open to doubt by relating them to (1) the sentence and (2) the author's idiolect.[2] Contextual elucidation has been investigated by modern linguistics, and the selections and the refocusing to which the potential meanings of any single word may be subject have been illustrated. A word is a bundle of meanings (potentialities) in the dictionary; it will take on one single meaning and one only (cases of ambiguity apart) once it has been linked to the other words of a text. From the beginning, philologists have normally had recourse to idiolect *(usus scribendi)*.

But reference to idiolect is not enough, because, behind denotative meanings, connotative meanings exist as well, and in poetry connotative meanings are the most important. The word *volo* ("flight"), for example, as denotation is quite clear, but its connotations unfold once they are brought into relation with a figurative system like that of Montale. This becomes possible once a lexical inventory is compared with that of the corresponding semantic field. Words like *penna, ali, piume* ("pinion," "wings," "feathers") integrate the area of *volare* ("to fly"). This is the primary basis for any thematic interpretation.[3] The semantic field is, in fact, inscribed within a thematic field which prepares the symbolic links attributable to meanings. Movements from the lexical to the semantic field are more clear-cut, because continuous control of the utterances accompanies them. More hazardous, and thus more fascinating, are movements toward the thematic field, because they are already linked to an imaginative and interpretative conception of the whole and because, as distinct from the former kind of movement, they are not susceptible to falsification. In fact, two or more thematic representations of a work are possible and may even at times prove compatible.

Here is the first strophe of John Keats's *Ode to a Nightingale:*

1 My heart aches, and a drowsy numbness pains
2   My sense, as though of hemlock I had drunk,
3 Or emptied some dull opiate to the drains
4   One minute past, and Lethe-wards had sunk:
5 'Tis not through envy of thy happy lot,
6 But being too happy in thine happiness,
7   That thou, light-winged Dryad of the trees,
8   In some melodious plot
9 Of beechen green, and shadows numberless,
10   Singest of summer in full-throated ease.

It is possible to determine chains of meaning in opposition: one of them refers to the human world of the "poet" ("My heart aches . . . ," line 1); another to the animal world of the nightingale (". . . thou, light-winged Dryad of the trees . . . ," line 7); a third to the vegetable world (". . . some melodious plot / Of beechen green, and shadows numberless," lines 8–9). The dominant noological isotopy is introjected into the perceived animal and vegetable world, to the point at which it comes to depict the interior world of the "poet" as it is subjected to the exhausting dynamics of metamorphosis.

The initial suffering ("My heart aches . . . ," line 1) is transformed to torpor ("drowsy numbness," line 1; "hemlock," line 2; "opiate," line 3) and then turns to oblivion ("Lethe-wards," line 4). The exaltation of Keats's fantasy finds its "objective correlative" in the world of the nightingale (". . . melodious plot / Of beechen green, and shadows numberless," lines 8–9), which achieves depiction of the poetic ecstacy attained through fancy and through the poetic labor which derives from it ("Singest of summer in full-throated ease," line 10).

The normal limits of experience, with the semantic categories of its representation, are dexterously surpassed, and, as we have observed, the animal and vegetable worlds, and the meaning chains which convey them, blend in the dynamic order of the interior world of the "poet's" soul, which thereby attains its own depiction.

3.1.2. A task no less arduous is individuation of the determinant fundamental concepts—that is, dianoetic nuclei. It is easier, and more convincing, when these surface at discourse level and furnish *stylistic vectors*.4 In Day VII of the *Decameron*,5 two conceptual triangles are in action, and their vertexes precisely correspond to, and counter, each other: parsimony—marriage rights—prayers; pleasures of the table—pleasures of the flesh—false or burlesque "prayers." Boccaccio himself points to the existence of this second triangle when he writes (VII, 1, 9) "A grande agio e con molto piacere cenò e albergò con la donna; ed ella, standogli in braccio, la notte gl'insegnò da sei delle laude di suo marito" (he "did most comfortably, and to his no small satisfaction, sup and sleep with the lady, who lying in his arms taught him that night some six of her husband's lauds"). The opposition between the elements of the two triangles is made manifest not just by the double meaning attributed in the passage to "lauds" but also in paragraphs 12 and 13, where the "great capons," the "many fresh eggs," and the "good flagon of wine" prepared for Federigo contrast with the "little salted meat" boiled for the husband, Gianni. And, although there are many passages which keep alive this amusing shifting from real prayers to a jocular or metaphorically obscene use of them, correlation between the pleasures of the table and those of the flesh is underlined by the curious commutative exercise of an alternative ending: (a) Federigo loses his night of love but is consoled by supping "to his no small satisfaction" (30); (b) Federico "andotosene, senza albergo e senza cena era la notte rimaso," that is, "was fain to take himself off, having neither slept nor supped" (32). By multiplying observations of this kind, it would be possible to illustrate Boccaccio's naturalism and his hedonism in detail.

In Thackeray's *Vanity Fair*, two similarly corresponding and counterpoised triangles also exist: interest—cold enjoyment—femininity; disinterest—happiness—motherhood. The opposition of these triangles is activated within the narrative discourse and articulated by way of systematic parallelisms which alternately depict the vicissitudes of Becky Sharp, a cold-blooded but ingenious social climber, and those of Amelia Sedley. Many aspects of Amelia derive from the heroines of the "sentimental" novel. She can love disinterestedly, and her marriage with George Osborne allows her to experience brief but intense happiness. After the birth of Georgy, which follows her husband's death at Waterloo, she finds in motherhood a refuge, by no means precarious, for the insecure world of her affections.

Many of the aspects of Becky Sharp derive from a Biedermeier deformation of the heroines of the "picaresque" novel. She is a governess who manages to get herself married to Captain Rawdon Pitt, the son of a land-owning family, for whose person she feels no affection whatsoever. On the birth of her son Rawdy, she rejects the role of mother and reaches the point of abandoning her son as well when her husband repudiates her. The stark contrast of the contraposition of motherhood and femininity, the latter depicted as insidious, serves to illustrate an ethical tension in the author which is specifically Victorian. That there are strands of the Puritan tradition in all of this is clear from the novel's title, for it refers us intertextually to Bunyan's *The Pilgrim's Progress*.

The attempt has even been made to formalize the operations by which the reader moves from the system of expression techniques, i.e., from motifs, to the higher system of semantic (or dianoetic) oppositions, until he reaches the point of individuating the author's "poetic world."[6] This is a question of generalization and unification, and it is easy enough to define and order its specific stages.

Some have attempted to fly even higher, toward a "fundamental semantics— different from the semantics of the linguistic manifestation"[7]—and toward elementary signification structures, capable of providing a pertinent semiotic model, one able to deal with primary sense articulations inside a semantic microuniverse. Each of these structures

> must be conceived of as the logical development of a binary semic category, of the type *white* versus *black*, whose terms, among themselves, are in a relation of contradiction /*dans une relation de contrariété*/, each of them being capable as well of projecting a new term which will be its contrary, while the contradictory terms may, in their turn, contract a presupposition relation with respect to its opposing and contrary terms.[8]

In short, there exist structures which can be represented by the square of Psellus or Apuleius, a square revived by Greimas and by him denominated "semiological square." (Contraries are placed at the top, and contradictories, their positions interchanged, at the bottom.) The facility with which these squares have increased and multiplied in the works of followers and epigones serves increasingly to prove how feeble are the links between an impregnable but abstract logical schema and the semantic world which finds its realization in a given work. Agglomerations and intertwinings, disequilibrium and hypertrophy, will always be present in a work and will serve to ensure its incompatibility with any aprioristically reasoned classification.

As an example of facility (all too often what we are offered is the obvious underlined), it is worth considering the way in which the requisite square has been made to derive from the opening sentence of Maupassant's *Deux amis:* ("Paris était bloqué, affamé et ralant" ("Paris was besieged, famished, at its last gasp"). Greimas wrote, "Saying that someone is moribund is the equivalent of recognizing that his state is to be defined as /not death/, just as the state of the living is that of /life/, precarious states, it is true, given that they tend toward their contradictories, stages of /death/ and of /not life/."[9] That this issue is a forced one, and that it is irreparably so, is all too evident from yet another "square," which on *life* versus *death*, and on *not death* versus *not life*, superimposes respectively the sun and Mont-Valérien, water and the sky. This is done on the basis of a precarious symbolism which only with great difficulty can be made to derive from the opening sentence, and it is then expanded and made to embrace all that remains of this particular short story.[10]

We might further remark that, if what we really want to achieve is a universal logic, then the square of Apuleius has been improved in Blanché's hexagon: pairs of contraries and contradictories are replaced with triads which contain a middle term as well:

The importance of Blanché's operation is worth remarking, not just because of the greater versatility of the logical hexagon with respect to the square of Apuleius, in that it allows a larger number of operations, but in particular because a structure of this kind, once it is disengaged from any truth function, will lend itself, in practice, to the structuring of a conceptual field of any kind, in such a way that it will assume considerable operational utility for semiotics.[11]

What we must face (and no one, so far, has done so) is the important question of the possibly, though not obligatorily, logical structuring of the "poetic world." Key ideas are prone to realize a binary conformation, a yes or no situation, one based on contraries or even more complex conformations, groups of four, for example. On the other hand, it is easy enough to verify the existence of an hexagonal schema. Acceptance of a univocal thesis may all too easily lead one to do violence to elements arrived at as a result of a schema fixed in advance. Respect for the semantic organization of the text should suggest the greatest possible disposability toward whatever results are there to be found. A semiotic operator has the right to attribute authority, and invariability, to schemata in the logical order, but the semiologically oriented literary critic will always prefer findings whose confirmation is derived from analysis of his text. He will accept the existence not only of "poetic worlds" but of different kinds of "poetic logic" as well.

3.2. Event Contents

When the contents of narrative texts are analyzed, what immediately becomes clear is the very particular nature of events and actions. It is events and actions which to a considerable extent constitute the coherence of a narrative text. This is not just because they stand out in high relief from the continuum of the text; it is because we are able to individuate them (after the pattern of reality) on the basis of the concepts of our experience, such concepts as relation, succession, cause and effect. This explains why analysis of narration (where the principal objects are events and actions) has played such a fundamental role in the study of text content.

But even with analysis of events (and actions), two points should be immediately clear: (1) events may be hypodenotated; in other words, they may be communicated either by way of inferences (deductions based not on events themselves but on clues scattered throughout the text) or by way of implications and presuppositions, and these may even involve literary conventions themselves; and (2) events may be hyperdenotated; in other words, they may be communicated as a cluster of events which only a rationalizing, and simplifying, operation will be able to reduce to a single denotative term. (Thus, a murder may be denoted without any direct use of the term itself or of any of its synonyms, because the event may be broken down into its constituent acts.) This is the moment at which paraphrase, with all its inevitable approximation, becomes the main tool by which we reveal our individuation of hypodenotative or hyperdenotative contents.

3.3. Paraphrase

We have seen (§ 2.11) that, in Hjelmslev's terminology, the content of a sentence is its meaning, i.e., the meaning which results from the word sequence of which it is composed. We have also seen that the sentences themselves, insofar as they belong to a wider co-text, may often mean something else, or something more, than might seem to be entailed by their literal evaluation. Specifications, deviations, and augmentations may result from causes whose character is co-textual or is derived outside the co-text.

When we recall that, for literary texts, co-text replaces the explicative and syntonizing framework which context provides for spoken texts, it is clear that, in a text, any sentence whatsoever can take advantage of the sum of the information which the text itself had earlier provided. It is this network of references which makes it possible to remove ambiguity from anything in a sentence to which two or more meanings might be attributed. The logic, from outside the co-text, of presuppositions and implications in the co-text will take the concrete form of well-defined areas of presupposition and implication.[12]

All explanations or, at any rate, all delimitation of alternative possibilities which are derivable from general knowledge, or from specific knowledge of an epoch, and which may prove applicable to the text, are overtly drawn from outside the co-text. (These in their totality are now metaphorically called the "encyclopedia." Such explanations may also derive from more specific information of a literary kind, information whose pooling will constitute internal rules for the texts, and especially for the literary genres, of a given epoch. In some sense what they give rise to is a "horizon of expectation."

In E. M. Forster's *Where Angels Fear to Tread* (1905), Lilia escapes from Sawston in order to marry her earthy Italian lover, Gino. The novel contrasts the constricting, imaginatively poverty-stricken, middle-class life of Sawston with the "natural," liberating life of Monteriano. The plot is thickened by the fact that Philip Herriton, a rather pathetically middle-class English boy, falls in love with Gino. Discourse conventions, shared by the author, make it unthinkable for this element, vital to the unfolding of the narration though it is, to be brought into the open. The fact is, though, that Philip's attraction to Gino is unequivocally communicated by the text. We learn that Gino in some measure responds to Philip's "love" from sentences like the following: "As for Gino, he would remember some time that Philip liked vermouth."[13] The seemingly innocent statement that "so the two young men parted with a good deal of genuine affection" takes on a definite sense, "forbidden" at the time, when we read the sentence that follows: "For the barrier of language is sometimes a blessed barrier, which only lets pass what is good."[14] This sentence, metatextually, also connotes the barrier of "right-thinking" language which delimits the work of composition itself.

Another famous example, from the same point of view, is the opening paragraph of Faulkner's *The Sound and the Fury* (1929). In this case, it is not so much reticence which renders the communication oblique as the narrator himself—Benjy, a character who is mentally retarded. Here is how he describes a game of golf:

> Through the fence, between the curling flower-spaces I could see them hitting. They were coming toward where the flag was and I went along the fence. Luster was hunting in the grass by the flower tree. Then they put the flag back and they went to the table, and he hit and the other hit. Then they went along the fence. Luster came away from the flower tree and we went along the fence and they stopped and we stopped and I looked through the fence while Luster was hunting in the grass.
> "Here, caddie." He hit. They went away across the pasture. I held to the fence and watched them going away.

The overriding function of this passage is depiction of the narrator's alienated mental state. This, though, does not stop the reader from grasping the content of his "perceptions," a content which might be manifested in a statement like "they putted and teed off at the next hole."[15] The content is made transparent by the telegraphic paraphrase which the six sentences articulated by Benjy break down and deprive of causal connections. The intention, indeed, is to depict how impossible it is for him to effect an interpretive synthesis of his disseminated perceptions. We might also note, in the passage quoted, that the narrator fails to mention the ball, an object which is essential to any cognitive description of the scene, although there is no difficulty in designating Luster as the caddie named.

These observations will suffice to show that paraphrase, though not admissible for the linguistic content of a sentence, particularly if it forms part of a literary text (where any substitution of words, any shift, will create a disturbance in meaning values), may well prove a useful tool when what we aim to describe is text contents. As a tool it may well prove to be absolutely indispensable. In the two examples we have given, paraphrase was the only way of indicating content, for only paraphrase could give expression to what reticence had left unspoken. The story otherwise might easily prove incomprehensible.

It is far from pointless to state that a paraphrase is not the content of its corresponding textual segment. It is the verbalization of a nonverbal semic content. In fact, many different paraphrases are possible, but they will need to be assessed in terms of their approximation, never in terms of equivalence. The same thing is true of translation. It may be faithful to a greater or to a lesser degree, even though no translation will ever be able to take the place of the text it translates.

3.4. The Scale of Generalization

Contents may be paraphrased using different scales of magnitude. The broadest paraphrase is one which will correspond to the contents of a sentence; the most concise paraphrase is one which will correspond to the contents of a whole work. In all cases relative to extensions greater than the sentence, a paraphrase will also be a summary. Paraphrases whose scale is intermediate are not possible for any section at all of the work; they are possible only for such unified sections as segmentation of the text will bring to light.

Tolstoy, as Sklovsky reminds us, stated that any attempt to explain what he had intended to say with War and Peace would have involved him in rewriting *War and Peace* just as it stands.[16] Any summary will of necessity eliminate parts, perhaps quite consistent parts, of the content. The elements entrusted to the summary will be those which are pertinent to a certain program of analysis. It is as well to be aware of this unavoidable limitation. For our demonstration it is a providential one, and there is no call for amazement. Any critic in the field of the visual arts indulges in analogous, and even more serious, pertinence operations; he not only points out in his description the elements and connections on which he has based it but goes even further and translates figurative language into verbal language. His ambition is perhaps to find an equivalent, uncertain though it be.

In the literary text, summaries individuate isotopies and structures. There has been some talk of deep structures in the text.[17] The expression would be acceptable, and even fascinating, if it did not give rise to a series of equivocations: (a) it appears to be going back to the deep structures of generative syntax, which on every occasion are unique and bi-unique; (b) it appears to entail rules for the generation of surface structures which set out from deep structures, and for literary texts this cannot be the case; and (c) it appears to exclude, or certainly does not render explicit, the plurality of the connections to be found inside a text; it thus excludes any possibility of individuating its structures in many concurrent ways, even for the same segments.[18]

Although the paraphrase problem has not yet been investigated in sufficient depth, an attempt has been made to formulate the safeguards which would help to ensure that a paraphrase is as "honest" as possible.[19] But such operations only make clear that, come what may, paraphrase is already an act of interpretation, if only because, as we have stated, it will always involve the comprehension and assimilation of a prior co-text.

Some have sought to synthesize contents (narrative contents, at least) in nonverbal fashion.[20] But, although formulae at first sight seem less compromising than words (for words are always accompanied by a halo of connotation), what they tend to do is to force realities, which remain composite and complex and are falsified by the seeming impassibility of formulae, into the strait jacket of given meaning.

If these are regarded as mere difficulties, this would be tantamount to considering univocal definition of textual contents as, in the last resort, possible. If, instead, we realize that these contents are the result of a meeting between different code systems, the system of the text and those of the addressees, then any serious attempt at a maximum understanding, hedged about with precautions though it be, must be referred to as a striving after decodification. Such decodification will be constant, but it will never be definitive, because text structures will continue to transmit meanings as collective semiotic systems change.

3.5. Motifs

The set of contents can be divided into various subgroups: factual contents (events and actions), descriptions, psychological analyses, etc. It is fairly clear why it is the first of these subgroups which has been the object of the most intense and profitable investigation.[21] As Machado says, a fact *"es algo / perfectamente serio."* Among the facts, those that stand out in the narrative text are the ones which constitute actions and whose succession and interconnection constitute the plot. As distinct from descriptions of psychology or environment, events follow each other (a) in terms of temporality (whereas a description may set out from any point) and (b) in terms, often, of clear-cut cause and effect; this is temporality that has become necessity and been made irreversible. It is no accident that narrated actions can even be described in terms of the logic of *the theory of action* (§3.10).

From the continuum of experience—and a text expounds an experience too—actions stand out distinctly and offer themselves for ready assessment. Nineteenth-century scholars, ethnographers in particular, used the word *motif* to stand for a minimal unit of narration. Veselovsky writes:

> by the term *motif* I mean the simplest narrative unit which, in the form of an image, met the most various requirements of the primitive intellect and of everyday observation. Given the resemblance, the outright equality even, of life forms and psychological processes in the early stages of social evolution, motifs of this kind may have been formed autonomously and, at the same time, show similar traits.[22]

Of necessity, any action will have an agent, a patient, a scope, etc. These do no more than duplicate the structure of the sentence (or, better, it is the sentence which duplicates the pattern of action). This explains why various authors have used terminology more or less uncompromisingly grammatical to represent the indispensable constituents of a motif: Burke speaks of *act* and *agent* in addition to *scene*, to say nothing of *coagent, counter agent, purpose,* and *agency* (and *attitude*). Pike speaks of *actor, goal, action, causer, place, instrument, enabler, time, beneficiary,* and Meletinsky proposes an analysis of motif in terms of Fillmore's sentence model *(agent, object, place, time, instrument, source, goal, experiencer).*[23]

The reason why motifs present this basic syntactic structure is that they are what remains of an atavistic experience. They represent, in fact, the activation of "representability patterns,"[24] in other words, of those forms by whose means man, an animal endowed with speech, learned to translate facts into words, to organize events to accord with syntactic organization. Thus, he can choose from his perceptions those that are pertinent to the event in which he is involved.

These patterns set up stereotypes on the signifier plane. Taken as a whole, they constitute what is semiotically available to a writer who is engaged in giving form to his inventions.

Some of these patterns of representability reflect most distinctly elaborations of the collective unconscious. Patterns of typical situations are used by speakers to evoke or to designate representation of these situations. In the hands of writers, they enclose symbolical values, to be further accentuated or transformed.

Archetypal motifs, and many others of perhaps less venerable consistency—which may be recurrent in discourse production because typical or because they give concrete form to shared desires and fears—constitute a thematic inventory. To this all narrators have recourse, from the anonymous and polyphonic narrators of folk tale and myth to the more clearly defined and ambitious exponents of literature.

Archetypal motifs, traditional motifs, motifs of common experience (which in any case can be traced back to patterns of representability) constitute models for constructing a narrative structure of any kind. If they are compared to type sentences, along the lines of what we have been saying, then the narrative structure will be the discourse which these sentences form. And such a discourse will have to be coherent, like any discourse.[25]

3.6. Plot and Fabula

The Russian formalists, when they employed the concept of motif for the breaking down of narrative texts, provided a workable method for individuating content and for segmentation of the text. Tomashevsky writes: "After reducing a work to its thematic elements, we come to parts that are *irreducible*, the smallest particles of thematic material: 'evening comes,' 'Raskolnikov kills the old woman,' 'the hero dies,' 'the letter is received,' and so on. The theme of an irreducible part of the work is called the *motif*."[26] For such segmentation not to remain inert, deprived of speech, attention must be paid to the way the units individuated are linked together. The links will come to the surface when *plot* and *fabula*, two other structures revealed by the formalists, are compared. Here is Tomashevsky once again: "Mutually related motifs form the thematic bonds of the work. From this point of view, the story /*fabula*/ is the aggregate of motifs in their logical, causal-chronological order; the plot is the aggregate of those same motifs but having the relevance and the order which they had in the original work."[27] In the fabula, therefore, narrative content will be paraphrased, while the causal-temporal order, often violated in the text, will be respected; the plot, on the contrary, will paraphrase content and keep to the order in which the units are given in the text.

It is well known that the formalists made particularly able use of the plot/fabula pair. This applies to Shklovsky, who was especially sensitive to problems of montage. (These were the best years of Eisenstein, and the formalists were much involved in film making.) It applies no less to Tomashevsky, who was fascinated by the typology of plot and fabula. Shklovsky, with a great deal of visual imagination, has described "stair," "ring," and "brochette" constructions and pointed to constantly used devices like "retarding." He also illustrated different ways in which separate tales can be linked and made to form coherent collections of tales. He commented, too, on overall construction procedures of the kind employed in works like *Don Quixote* and *Tristram Shandy*.

Narrative has always made use of analectic retrievals[28] (for temporal sections anterior to the basic narrative), of inserted narratives (the *Orlando Furioso* here again is a forerunner of *Don Quixote*), of multiple, interlacing plots (the *Orlando Furioso* itself is a prime example, but so is Boiardo's *Innamorato* and chivalric poems in general),[29] of the displacements of the fabula. The formalists have taught us to motivate infractions against the "natural" order, to study the means for activating passage between narrative units belonging to different periods of time, to explain the function of combinations and alternations.

Useful integrations derive from research into time. There is, first and foremost, the relation between *erzählte Zeit* and *Erzählzeit*, between the time of the tale told and the time of its telling.[30] In dealing with content, we meet with retarding devices, ellipses, and shifts of perspective, and these must be related to the weight events will have with respect to the plot. All of this is only possible on the basis of a segmentation of content units, one which will correspond to individuation of the motifs.

3.7. Narrative Functions

3.7.1. Simply saying that motifs are the actions which constitute the plot does not explain very much. In any narration at all, actions and events will be innumerable, and their importance for the determination of the plot will vary, for it will depend upon how broadly the plot is being considered.[31] The first chapter of *The Strange Case of Dr. Jekyll and Mr. Hyde* contains this action: "Enfield sees a man run into and trample a little girl." But the analysis might be more detailed: "A Mr. Enfield tells his friend Utterson, a lawyer, that one black winter morning, as he was going home, he saw a man and a little girl running rapidly along two streets which met at a corner. The inevitable collision ended with the man trampling over the child's body." Or again: "During one of their Sunday walks, Mr. Enfield and his friend, the lawyer Utterson, found themselves in a bystreet. They stopped in front of a building two stories high which showed no window and whose door was equipped with neither bell nor knocker. Mr. Enfield lifted up his cane and, pointing to the door, began an extraordinary tale. Once, about three o'clock of a black winter morning, as he had been returning home, he had seen a 'little' man and a girl of maybe eight or ten, each hurrying down two streets which met at a corner. Inevitably, they had run into each other. And the horrible thing had been that the man had trampled over the body of the child."

It will be noted that in the first paraphrase Enfield appears as a mere eyewitness to a violent and disgusting action. In the second paraphrase, he has become an heterodiegetic, extradiegetic narrator as well. In the third analysis, Mr. Enfield at first assumes the role of an intradiegetic character, like Utterson who will then become the tale's extradiegetic addressee. Enfield will then become the heterodiegetic, extradiegetic narrator.

In the first analysis, action is reduced to the essentials: to the two actors (the man and the girl) and to the predicates arranged in a logical and chronological sequence (collision and trampling), as well as the predicate (saw) which qualifies the "eyewitness" as such and which projects the action into the past. In the second paraphrase, the memorable action is broken down into an occasional component (the inevitable collision) and an intentional one (the trampling). Besides the two anthroponyms required for the utterance act of the tale (Mr. Enfield and the lawyer Utterson), the second of them qualified professionally, we find chrononyms (a winter morning), toponyms (a street), temporal qualifications (while), qualifications of spatial perception (at a corner), and kinetic qualifications (haste), and all of these make possible the definition of a chronotopos.

In the third paraphrase, over and above the elements just mentioned and susceptible of integration in a chronotopos, we find a differentiation or articulation of habitual actions (one of their usual walks) with respect to an accidental event (the collision) and to a horrible and unusual one (he trampled over her). The sequence of the actions is contextualized metalinguistically (Mr. Enfield points to the door with his cane) and qualified still further in the time of the narration (three o'clock of a black winter morning), in its characters (a "little" man, a girl of eight or ten), and in the inanimate elements of the scene (a door with neither bell nor knocker). The more the paraphrase is expanded, the more it specifies the structure of the intradiegetic narration, the situation of the utterance act, as well as the modalities of what is narrated, the contradictory indications of horror and of the extraordinary memorability of the impression made upon the mind of the narrator.

3.7.2. Tomashevsky was aware of this problem and sketched a solution for it:

> Usually there are different kinds of motifs within a work. By simply retelling a story /fabula/ we immediately discover what may be omitted without destroying the coherence of the narrative and what may not be omitted without disturbing the connections among events. The motifs which cannot be omitted are **bound motifs**; those which may be omitted without disturbing the whole causal-chronological course of events are **free motifs**.[32]

Tomashevsky then goes on to distinguish *dynamic motifs* (those which modify the situation) from *static motifs* (those which do not) and warns us of the existence of motifs which are static but tied, given that their introduction into the story may be without consequences in the immediate circumstances, though they may become determinant at another point.[33]

In the wake of Tomashevsky, Barthes distinguishes between function and *clues* (which do not refer to "a complementary and successive act, but to a concept more or less diffused though essential to the sense of the story; character clues /*indices caractériels*/, which concern the persons in the tale, items of information relative to their identity, notes for 'atmosphere'", etc.); he also sets up a hierarchy of importance for functions: whereas *cardinal* functions (or *nuclei*) constitute the real hinges upon which the tale turns, *catalisis* functions "do no more than 'fill up' the narrative space which separates hinge-functions."[34]

The drawback in the analyses of both Tomashevsky and Barthes is that they are two-dimensional; it is almost as if it were merely a matter of bringing to the fore, in the text, parts solidly causal and of variously toning down the others.[35] In reality, the text as discourse is entirely a matter of circumstantial evidence: its principal actions are often the outcome of a complex of secondary actions, and they may be implied without being named. Cause and effect can be enucleated only through paraphrases, while paraphrases synthesize contents to a greater or lesser degree, depending upon whether what we wish to grasp is subtlety of texture or the bold lines of the text. At the level of fine texture, we have, in Stevenson's tale, a consequentiality in the extraordinary and horrible impression produced upon Enfield by the event narrated. The horrible and the extraordinary are unfolded gradually, and they intertwine at the end of the first chapter of a tale which belongs to the genre of fantasy. But, even in the most synthetic paraphrase, the synthesis of the extraordinary and the horrible is already made manifest in such a way that it is readily comprehensible. The action paraphrased allows no ambiguity and leaves no lacunae unsaturated.

3.7.3. It was Propp, a scholar closely connected with the formalists, who put investigation of motifs on a solid basis (although his aim was not literary but ethnographical; he was looking for reliable criteria for the classification of folk tales). The term he introduced was *function*, and he defined it as follows: "Function is understood as an act of a character, defined from the point of view of its significance for the course of the action."[36] Functions are motifs seen in their relation to the unfolding of the action. Propp's aim was to individuate the invariants behind the variables, to group together actions which, though they are different in different folk tales, nonetheless all have the same function. Hence, Propp's idea of function is not limited to single texts, but, in general, is one which holds good for groups of texts whose structure is analogous. In an impressive attempt at unification, Propp drew up a list of a very small number of functions (31), valid for the classification of all of the actions present in his corpus of one hundred magic folk tales; in correspondence, and as a consequence, he discovered a constant structure in all the folk tales he examined. The tales differ from one another primarily because of the kinds of action each function is used to represent, by the elimination of some functions, or by the insertion of groups of differently realized functions (which constitute extra *movements*).

It should also be noted that Propp was well aware both of the problem of relations between motifs and plot and of the possibility of arriving at a higher degree of abstraction than that of the functions. Concerning plot, he wrote: "All *predicates* give the composition of tales; all *subjects, objects,* and other parts of the sentence define the theme."37 With recourse to the syntactic nucleus of the motifs (illustrated above), what is being said is that the predicates (i.e., the actions) provide the composition for a tale, in short its structure, whereas subjects and complements concern its plot. This is not a very precise formula, because subjects do not change (e.g., the villain in place of the hero), but their features and names do (the villain may be the devil, or a dragon, or an ogre, or an enemy). But, in any event, it should be noted that Propp, unlike the literary formalists of his time, makes no distinction between fabula and plot. The reason for this becomes quite clear when we recall that shifts in chronology, and other kinds of montage, are not found in folk tales.

It was perfectly clear to Propp that his sequence of functions did not represent the simplest type of composition, one not susceptible of further breaking down:

> Morphologically, a tale *(skazka)* may be termed any development proceeding from villainy (A) or a lack (a), through intermediary functions to marriage (W*), or to other functions employed as a dénouement. Terminal functions are at times a reward (F), a gain or in general the liquidation of misfortune (K), an escape from pursuit (Rs), etc. This type of development is termed by us a *move (xod)*.38

This outline serves to show (1) that Propp had no intention of furnishing tools for literary analysis, which he states explicitly (typical is his elimination of the plot/fabula pair which critics find so useful); (2) that his list of functions holds good, and will only hold good, for the hundred folk tales of his investigation (the complementary character of the operations effected in order to unify the motifs as functions, and the segmentation of all the folk tales in the corpus, authorizes the inference that a different corpus would have led to classifications somewhat, perhaps greatly, different); (3) that the "significance for the course of action" posed no problems for Propp, on the basis of what we have affirmed under (2); Propp himself recognized the existence of other levels of abstraction.

Ideally, investigations of plot and fabula will move along superimposed levels (the plot will be above, given its greater articulation and specification, and the fabula below, because it is more concise and simplified); they are levels which occupy an intermediate area between the surface level, that of language (or discourse), and a deeper level, that of the narrative model made up of functions. Thus, if we take the findings of Shklovsky, of Tomashevsky, and of Propp and bring them together as a reasoned whole, we can formulate39 a four-stage model capable of embracing the whole:

    I. Discourse;
   II. Plot;
  III. *Fabula;*
  IV. Narrative Model.

This model has been applied and tested, and its practical advantage is that it gives a visual representation of the scale of generalization (cf. §3.4) against which analytical data can be measured. Thus, it is possible, from the outset, to assess any research project whose approach is "narratological." When historiographical applications are called for, see below (§4.4).

3.8. Narratology[40]

3.8.1. The method applied by Propp is valid within a specific data system and when a well-defined program of analysis has been formulated. A strong temptation existed, naturally enough, to apply it to other texts and to other types of narrative texts, to upgrade it and make it a general schema for narration. Such a temptation should have been resisted. Not only is Propp's corpus an extremely limited one, it is also made up of tales which are objectively alike; thus, the ease with which they can be reduced to a unified schema should not illude us into imagining that any real possibility exists of arriving at a general model for all types of narration. The speculative energy expended in such attempts to render Propp's method generally applicable has nonetheless served to bring to light exigencies which must in some manner be satisfied.[41]

We might, for example, point to the logical requirements expressed by Lévi-Strauss.[42] Among functions there will exist transformation relations (*prohibition* is the negative transformation of *order*), possibilities of unification (*departure* and *return* are the two extremes of one single function, *separation*), and so forth. On this basis, Greimas has reduced Propp's list of thirty-one functions to twenty.[43] It was again Lévi-Strauss who pointed out the possibility of breaking down the terms which designate functions into even simpler semic elements. This should make it possible to link together functions which contain semic elements in common and, thus, to arrange ideally the series of functions to be met with in a tale, not just horizontally within a paradigmatic network but also vertically (bringing into correspondence semically similar functions) within a syntagmatic framework.

In other words, we must realize that Propp did not solve the problem; he merely posed it, though he did so brilliantly. Attempts to apply Propp's analyses to other texts, particularly to literary texts, should be rejected because of an inadequacy which Propp himself was the first to point out. But there is an even more impelling motive for rejecting them. They take to themselves the terms which for Propp designated functions, and they take no account of the characters, whereas for Propp it was the characters alone who could act as subjects for the predicates these terms stand for. For example, *reconnaissance* for Propp means "the villain makes an attempt at reconnaissance"; *mediation* means that "misfortune or lack is made known; the hero is approached with a request or command; he is allowed to go or he is dispatched."[44] If, as Propp's improvident disciples do, we apply *reconnaissance* to acts carried out by persons other than the villain, or *mediation* to acts which do not concern the hero, then it is Propp's whole system which will fall apart. It is, in fact, a system where practically only one single subject exists, the hero, with an antisubject, the villain; it is they who have a monopoly of all possible actions. This is quite a different matter from what usually happens in literary narrative.

3.8.2. It thus seems obvious that any other closed list of functions can be delimited only in relation to a given corpus and only once a common plot (narrative model) has been individuated and found to be present in all the components of the corpus.[45] On the other hand, in terms of the aims of literary analysis, so radical a stripping down is less productive of results than an analysis which remains more faithful to the surface of the discourse, i.e., to plot and fabula. It is important to decide from the outset the level on which the analysis is to be conducted. This though is never done. There exists, as I have stressed (§3.3), a scale of generalization to which all research so far carried out, and all research to come, must be referred. The need to take this scale into account in any analysis "above" the plot is already clear from what has been observed concerning the first chapter of *The Strange Case of Dr Jekyll and Mr Hyde*; the possibility of applying it "below" the level of functions as well is, as we have seen, something of which Propp himself is well aware.

Among examples of maximum generalization, I might mention that of Labov and Waletzky, with its five points (orientation, complication, evaluation, resolution, coda).[46] This is purely formal, because it is open to absolutely any kind of semantic content. Or there is the example of Bremond[47] who applies Propp's phrase cited above and moves from improvement to be obtained to processes of improvement and so to improvement obtained or not obtained or, again, from deterioration foreseen to processes of deterioration and thus to deterioration effected or avoided. In this case, the semantic content is not named at all; a positive or negative sign is used to stand for the values in play. It still remains to be seen whether all three phases that Bremond discusses are really realized or whether some of them do not remain implicit.

The semantic element has considerable importance in any descriptive employment of the scale of generalization. When Propp brought together under one single term a number of different actions, he was guided not by considerations of semantics but by types of function. Actions very different in kind could be made to fall under the same label because of the identical function they achieved. It was the narrative paradigm which conditioned designation of the functions. But if one wishes to designate an action in general terms, without any reference to a corpus, the semantic problem, which is extensional in character, must be faced. It is a matter of finding a minimal lexicon of nouns to assume the largest possible number of those actions (one might hope, all actions) which lend themselves to being narrated. Such a lexicon would show them all at the same level of abstraction. This is rendered very problematical indeed by the diversified wealth of subdivisions to be met with in the lexical fields of any natural language and by the connotations which have accrued to each of its terms.

3.8.3. These problems, and those of plot analysis, can best be illustrated by comparing three different analyses of a tale from the *Decameron*, that of

Andreuccio (II, 5).[48] We should, though, bear in mind that almost all narratological analyses remain on the level of plot or fabula, even when they are modeled on Propp and even when it is Propp's terminology they use. The two conditions which would justify reference to a "narrative model" are, in fact, absent: a corpus and an archi-fabula.

When the tale is analyzed with Propp's method, it proves possible to obtain no more than the following schema:

> (initial situation: name and condition of the protagonist 3); *absentation:* Andreuccio sets out for Naples 3, *interdiction:* he is not to make display of his money 3; *violation:* Andreuccio makes display of his money 3; *reconnaisance:* Madonna Fiordaliso seeks information about Andreuccio 7; *delivery:* Madonna Fiordaliso gains possession of this information 8; *trickery:* Madonna Fiordaliso seeks to hoodwink Andreuccio 9; *complicity:* Andreuccio falls into the trap 14; *villainy:* Andreuccio is robbed by Madonna Fiordaliso 40; *branding or marking:* Andreuccio is covered with excrement 38; *return of the protagonist:* Andreuccio comes back to his lodging 55; *the first function of the donor:* the thieves suggest taking shares in the bishop's ring 63; *pursuit:* Andreuccio is left in the well 68; *rescue:* Andreuccio is transformed into a diabolical vision 69; *the first function of the donor:* as above 70; *the hero's reaction and provision or receipt of a magical agent:* Andreuccio takes possession of the ring and tricks the thieves 77; *pursuit:* Andreuccio is shut up in the tomb 78; *rescue:* Andreuccio emerges and seems 100,000 devils to the priest and his accomplices 83; *return:* Andreuccio comes back to Naples 85.

As for Propp's analysis, the names of his functions are all that, in reality, remain. The order in which they appear is violated (branding or marking cannot precede the donor function; pursuit must follow liquidation of the lack and the hero's return and precede the difficult task, and all these functions are absent here). And their designation is not particularly convincing. Flaunting one's money is imprudent; it is not the violation of an interdiction; the ring is not a magical agent; falling into a latrine must of necessity be described as branding or marking; an act of egoism and, later, a vendetta are both described as pursuit. Of Propp's archi-fabula there is no sign, and Boccaccio's tale, with its determining traits left out of account, has been seriously distorted.

3.8.4. If we follow Todorov we obtain something of this kind:

> $XA + Y - B \Rightarrow (X - A)$ opt. $Y \Rightarrow Ya \Rightarrow X$ $(YC) + Yb + Y - C \Rightarrow X - A + (XA)$opt. $X + (XA \Rightarrow Xb)$ cond. $Z + X - A' \Rightarrow Xa'' \Rightarrow XA' + (XcZ)$ opt. $X \Rightarrow ZcX \Rightarrow X - A' + X$ $A \Rightarrow Xa''' \Rightarrow XA' + Xa$.

The symbols employed are X = Andreuccio; Y = Fiordaliso; Z = the two thieves; A = rich; B = happy; C = sister; a = modify; b = steal; c = punish; opt. = optative; cond. = conditional; $X(...)$ = false vision for X; $+$ = succession; $\Rightarrow$ = implication; $-$ = negation. The result is a series of successions ($+$) and implications ($\Rightarrow$), which is almost undifferentiated given that the actions which are possible are a bare three (modify, steal, punish), while the results can be no more than the continuation or loss of four states (rich, safe, happy, endowed with a sister).

Overall, Todorov's schema is more malleable than any pseudo-Proppian approach. It has the further advantage of taking account of modalities (the optative, etc.); it is, finally, disposed to accept indication of attributes. On the other hand, it arbitrarily restricts the semantic possibilities of the verb, any value criterion being restricted to a positive-negative opposition that is all too vague. The result is that the story is reduced to a succession that is not very meaningful. *To steal*, whether it is followed by *to punish* or not, alternates with the wide class of change in situation. In short, what Todorov gains in the indication of values he loses in the description of actions.

3.8.5. Now we come to Bremond. He would, in all likelihood, find three phases in our tale: initial state, modified state, restoration of initial state. In substance, what we will have is a process of deterioration (loss of the five hundred florins) followed by a process of improvement (acquisition of a ring worth five hundred florins), which brings Andreuccio back to his original state. Two deterioration processes are inserted into the third phase (abandonment in the well, abandonment in the tomb), though they are not carried through. In his most recent model, Bremond also takes into account the active or passive position of characters.[49] This will then give us, in the first sequence, Madonna Fiordaliso regarded as an agent of improvement with respect to a passive Andreuccio; in the second, she appears as an agent of frustration and deterioration; in the third, the agent is Andreuccio, though he is egged on by his counselors (the two thieves) to initiate a process of improvement (gaining possession of the ring); the counselors, in their turn, are obstructors and deteriorators and twice abandon Andreuccio when he is in difficulty (i.e., in expectation of foreseeable deterioration).

Bremond's model is, from one point of view, a more malleable one (the analysis sketched here is reasonably faithful to Boccaccio's tale); it is also better orchestrated because the possibility exists of its reconciling analyses carried out on various levels (in our example, a three-phase analysis, followed by another which breaks down the final phase). No less noteworthy in Bremond is his final table. It determines for each phase of the story—not just the process, which would be the function in the strict sense—the agent and the patient of the process itself as well as the syntax of the processes (succession, simultaneity, causality, implication), their phases (eventuality, actualization, effective realization), and volition on the part of the agent.

To come back to our problem, which is the scale of generalization, what leaps to mind is the contradiction between the characters, named as they are named in the text in all their individuality, and the functions, which are always maintained at a high level of abstraction. We find ourselves inside a universe where the results of all actions fall into two broad categories—improvement and deterioration—and where characters cannot be other than agents and patients. In our tale, which hardly relies on an excess of subtlety, no way exists for distinguishing the different kinds of improvement desired by Andreuccio and

Fiordaliso (sexual satisfaction and the possession of money), nor can any weight be given to the fact that improvement to Andreuccio would have caused no harm to the woman, had she consented, whereas that of the woman involves dispossessing Andreuccio. It is difficult to record the concomitance of the two desires, and it is even worse when such concomitance is found inside a single character, as when the thieves, at first improvers, are turned into potential deteriorators, out of fear in the case of the well, out of revenge in that of the tomb. Bremond's tables may be able to record change, but only at the cost of breaking down action excessively and of rendering it incomprehensible.

3.8.6. The way opened up by Bremond is, nonetheless, the most accessible if further progress in formalization is to be made. It does not, though, seem to be practicable for the study of plot and fabula where the objects of desire (money, power, mating, etc.) and actions also have of necessity to be named. Even when the aim is maximum simplification of the plot (accepting with Propp and Bremond their indications as to the possibility of tracing more or less summary composite schemata), we must remind ourselves that it is literature we are dealing with and that it will always prove more advantageous to maintain the explicit character of objects and actions, however broad the terminological extension we employ. The basic schema for Alexandrian romance will be:

promise of marriage→retarding accidents (= obstacles to eliminate → elimination of obstacles → obstacles eliminated) → marriage.

It will not be:

improvement to be obtained → process of improvement (= obstacles to eliminate → elimination of obstacles → obstacles eliminated) → improvement obtained.

More than half of existing narration would fall under the second of these schemata, and there would be few cognitive advantages. The first formula refers us to a specific tradition, one which takes in, along with much else, the tale of Ruggiero and Bradamante in Ariosto's *Furioso*, as well as the events of Manzoni's *Promessi sposi*.

A great deal of research has shown how productive schemata of this kind can be, for they help individuate direct sources, grasp persistence of archetypal narrative structures, or illustrate the transformations a theme undergoes when it is used afresh. Examples might be Ruffinatto's study of the theatrical "sequence" which links Cervantes to Lope de Vega and the latter to the former and my own work on the similarities and differences of Marie de France's *Eliduc* and *Ille et Galeron* of Gautier d'Arras,[50] on Lope de Vega's borrowings from the *Novellino* and from Boccaccio, and the sources of Boccaccio's own tales.

Research into narrative archetypes is even more promising: the schema of Gautier de Chatillon's *Alexandreis* in the Ulysses episode of the *Divine Comedy*

(*Inferno*, XXVI), the theme of the Golden Age from Virgil and Ovid to Dante and beyond, the persistence of models for the lives and sufferings of women saints in Sade's *Justine*,[51] and so forth. No less attractive is the suggestion that the immersion of Andreuccio in the well should be seen as a symbol of purification, while everything that happens to him is the history of an initiation.[52]

What must always be kept in mind is that denomination of the elements to be considered and individuation of relations are essential moments in the critical act; as a result, it can, and should, be effected at such a level of generalization, and of adherence, as will appear most opportune for each and every case. (Choice of more than one level for different moments of an analysis is indeed most useful.) As Lotman so acutely observes:

> *An event in a text is the shifting of a persona across the borders of a semantic field.* It follows that the description of some fact or action in their relation to a real denotatum or to the semantic system of a natural language can neither be defined as an event or as a non-event until one has resolved the question of its place in the secondary structural semantic field as determined by the type of culture. But even this does not provide an ultimate resolution: within the same scheme of culture the same episode, when placed on various structural levels, may or may not become an event. But since the general semantic ordering of the text is supplemented in equal measure by local orderings, each with its own concept-border, an event may be realized as a hierarchy of events on more individual planes, as a chain of events, a plot. In this sense, that which on the level of the cultural text represents *one* event, may be transformed into a *plot* in some real text. One invariant construct of an event may be transformed into a series of plots on various levels. While constituting one plot link on the highest level, it may vary in the number of links, depending on the level of development of the text.[53]

This is a most important passage, above all because of the way it defines *event* (*action* in the terminology here adopted). By the reference he makes to the semantic field, Lotman underlines the fact that narrative actions are events only because they form part of a text which has semantic fields of its own. They are events only in relation to these semantic fields themselves. As a consequence, it is not the "real" importance of the action which counts when it comes to its being an event; it is its consequences for the movements of one, or more, character(s) from one semantic field to another. Naturally, Lotman believes that a work's semantic fields are a model of the world, a model which is immobile until plot intervenes. Plot is the "revolutionary element" with respect to a world picture. This is why "the movement of the plot, the *event*, is the crossing of that forbidden border which the plotless structure establishes. It is not an event when the hero moves *within* the space assigned to him."[54] Lotman thus abandons connections based on resemblances between the actions narrated and real actions which have connections of their own (cf. §3.10). What he stresses instead are connections based on semantic relations, such that they will either introduce an element of crisis into a model of the world or confirm it. On the other hand, since semantic fields are markedly stratified, one single episode may be seen as an event (action) in relation to one given semantic-structural level, while being considered a mere component of a broader event in relation to a higher level. Within a narrative text, it is possible to individuate a plot whose actions may, in their turn, be interpreted as forming a plot by themselves, and this may continue, with a progressive ramification of syntagmatic relations which will assume a downward-branching form.

It now becomes legitimate, indeed necessary, to formulate and put into effect a number of segmentation programs. They must be able to embrace cardinal points on a variety of levels, levels which are, as a rule, integrated. This does not involve the existence of different kinds of cause and effect. It means that the type of cause and effect which is operative in the literary text is different from that to be found in the natural sciences. It was Barthes who first observed that narrations generalize a kind of *post hoc ergo propter hoc*. On many occasions, a succession of events will be given an interpretation in causal terms by our instinct (this the writer will second and exploit); the aim will be to explain what would otherwise, strictly speaking, remain inexplicable. What is more, in the tides of men we often find (a) cause and effect whose nature is psychological, so that it moves not from event to event but from thought to event, and (b) a plurality of causes—and of this any good writer is well aware. Lastly, we should bear in mind that, in narratological analysis, motives either are not taken into account at all or are of necessity greatly simplified when they are taken into account. This is sufficient to explain why any number of chains of events can be individuated most plausibly for one single text.

3.8.7. Some thought might have been given to the different way in which events are combined in plot and in fabula. If certain facts are made known to the reader long after they have happened, this is often because, in the reality of the invention, they were unknown to the protagonists, their repercussions remaining submerged or taking effect only after a time. In short, an unknown *post hoc* impedes the action of a *propter hoc*. It is often the need to end the story in a certain way which accounts for a given line-up of events whose consequentiality will be anything but strict.

In general, it is worth meditating on Culler's observations concerning the priority of "the demands of signification" with respect to plot and of thematic structure with respect to content structure. The fabula should, as a result, be regarded "not as the reality referred by the discourse but as its product." According to Culler, "One could argue that every narrative operates according to this double logic, presenting its plot as a sequence of events which is prior to and independent of the given perspective on those events, and, at the same time, suggesting by its implicit claims to significance that these events are justified by their appropriateness to a thematic structure."[55] The conclusion will be that the fabula is to be read not merely in terms of its linearity (the movement from left to right as a diagram of its temporal succession) but backwards as well, given that, in the invention, causes and effects coexist. Not infrequently, indeed, it is the effect which determines the cause.

A narrative model is, then, an achronic model. It has been observed that any syntagmatic schema may be broken down and arranged in columns on the basis of semic affinities (cf. §3.8.1) and that in any element of a syntagm it is possible to see the compression on a smaller scale of an entire syntagm (cf. §3.7.2). And we now add to this that the syntagm should be read not just from left to right but from right to left as well. All this shows us the dialectic between a fictitious reality, to which the author gives form, and the techniques used in order to present that particular reality. A good way of perceiving this dialectic is to look at the events as if they really were subject to the laws of reality itself. Thus, fabula and plot will be the barest possible, the most obviously concise, way of representing events which the text in fact presents with great complexity, with nuances and calculated reticence. By so doing, it is imitating the never wholly transparent way in which events are in fact perceived in real life (cf. §3.13).

3.9. Narration, Description, Motivations

Narrative coherence is, to a considerable extent, entrusted to the concatenation of the actions. Quite another matter is the coherence of the different behavior of which the actions are part. What comes into play here will be possible psychological verisimilitude and, more importantly, the writer's commitment to motivating ways of behaving which will often be anomalous (though not, in themselves, unlikely). Narratives frequently take as their object the unusual, the astonishing, the unexpected.

For Propp, these problems are anything but pressing, given that, for the characters of folk tale, psychology is either absent or embryonic. They have been felt, though, and variously dealt with by those who have attempted to apply narratological analyses to literary texts. Todorov and Bremond, for instance, take into account the value systems which operate within the text and the kind of intentions characters have when undertaking actions (cf. §3.8.4–5). One does not, however, always find sufficient awareness of the fact that it is the very way in which the action itself is denominated at the moment of analysis which will connote it in the sense of values; this, on the whole, will correspond to that of the world which is realized in the text, though participation on the part of the analyst cannot be ruled out. (Actions like tricking, betraying, stealing, etc., are already marked to accord with a general morality, one which we share, but the consequences may make us uneasy when, in certain situations described or in certain types of text, such actions are, for whatever motive, justified, and even approved of.)

It is beyond question that motivations—whether general or particular, direct or indirect, causal or conditioning—will prove far more refractory to formalization than will actions. But the attempt can be made to arrive at formalizations not wholly oblivious to them. There have been moves in this direction. In practice, analyses like those described in section 3.1. should be made to converge with those described in sections 3.7–8.

Mention should at least be made of attempts along the lines of those of Greimas—attempts by Rastier, in particular. He uses a system of oppositions to analyze what he calls "invested contents," in other words, the set of social and individual values within whose framework the actions of the characters are inscribed. He further shows a correlation between recognized values and the attitudes by which it is attempted to realize or to oppose them.[56] For the field of the folk tale, we have Meletinsky's commitment to introducing into functional analysis oppositions relative to collective or individual conduct, to actions which are acceptable or unacceptable (in terms of a cultural assessment), together with other oppositions of a semantic, and indeed of a typological, character.[57]

Less fraught with consequences is the problem of description, for its responsibility in the organization of what is narrated is not crucial. It is no less difficult for all that—in part because of the lack of any pseudo-objective grid of the kind that links events and actions, in part because no behavioral grid exists of the kind that does service for motivations. Description, indeed, gives effect to an arbitrary temporalization, when elements which are copresent are passed in review in an order which is entirely dependent upon the choice of the writer. (Even if we admit that such choice will be in part conventional, progressions will be linear moving from high to low, from left to right, from near at hand to far away, etc., or vice versa; movement will be circular or elliptical, and so forth.) The few attempts that have been made are an earnest of things to come.[58]

3.10. Narratology and Reality

The attempt to individuate events and actions has followed the paths here touched upon in the search for a formal exactitude capable of revealing narrative structures without uncertainty. Since narration is predominantly narration of events, reality itself may also be used as a measure, or as confirmation, of contents narrated. To the chain of narrated events (which, whether real or imaginary, will always resemble real ones), the chain of narration will certainly be homologous (in ways that will need defining).

Only in appearance does such an undertaking constitute value assessment of the referent. (Linguistics tends to leave it out of account.) The term of comparison is not reality, whose status indeed is under discussion; it is our way of dissecting and naming reality. This in itself is already a linguistic and thematic operation (cf. §3.4). When we narrate, we necessarily have recourse to the same stereotypes which we employ when we perceive, interpret, and speak of day to day events.

"The theory of action," especially in the work of George Henrik von Wright,[59] sets out to define (with the aid of logical grids) possible types of events, human actions, and their connections, together with such aims and results as will lend themselves to definition. In short, his data are the same as those which narratologists have regarded as the load-bearing elements of narration, to be connected by means of the same temporal and causal links that man attributes to reality.

This theory, recently transferred to the narratological sphere,[60] links the concept of event to that of state (an event being a change at a given moment from one state to another) and distinguishes event-process from event-action (where the subject is human). In conjunction with various kinds of modal logic, the theory of action offers clear-cut classifications for the study of narrative functions. In an *alethic* system, we will encounter expressions of possibility, impossibility, and necessity; in a *deontic* system, of permission, prohibition, and obligation; in an *axiological* system, of goodness, wickedness, and indifference; in an *epistemic* system, of knowledge, ignorance, and belief, and so forth. Links between functions, already dealt with in the logical order by Lévi-Strauss and Greimas, can now in part be rearranged: "prohibition", "infraction," "punishment" are functions whose nature is deontic; "lack" and "elimination of a lack" are axiological functions; "recognition of the hero" is epistemic, and so on.

References to the real (to our descriptions of reality) have always proved to be absolutely essential for the understanding of any text of whatever kind. This is so whether reference is made to the "encyclopedia," i.e., to the sum of all the kinds of knowledge which make a text intelligible, or to the logical implications of any assertion. Our way of expressing ourselves is often elliptical, because we know that our utterances will be easily interpreted by our addressees through an immediate integration of all of their implications.

These implications are integrated with links that are a matter not merely of contiguity but of operative character as well. Utterances pertaining to any kind of action will immediately be referred, in their conciseness and ellipticalness, to the *action programs* in terms of which the corresponding action would be realized on the plane of reality.[61] I have visited someone in a distant city and have made mention of the fact; any reference I now make to a journey, to means of transport (trains, planes, and cars), and to preparations (booking, buying tickets, going to the station, etc.) will be related by their addressee to the *action program* and understood at once.[62]

Another profitable approach is the theory of "possible worlds."[63] Everyone knows the laws and properties which regulate the (empirically perceptible) course of the world and that of the objcts to be found in it. If the author of a text conforms to these laws and properties, and presents objects from its known repertoire, the possible world that he will bring to life will be entirely subject to the laws and properties in question. In other cases, a writer may bring into being a world wherein the objects that exist are different from real objects, a world inside which some of our laws and properties will not be valid, where different ones will obtain. Examples are the gothic novel, tales of phantasy, science fiction, etc. Definition of the rules in force inside a given (literary) world directly affects not only the sum of the addressee's "expectations" but also, and primarily, the causal connections of actions and, as a result, the structure of plot and fabula[64] and, together with them, of course, the whole system of implications and presuppositions. From the point of view of logic, it has for some time been debated whether one can speak of true and false with respect to literary characters, who have never existed, and with respect to their actions.

With the criterion of "possible worlds," a distinction can be made between inventions which maintain the same state of things to be met with in the real world and inventions which modify it. (With an approach of this kind, discussion of the concept of mimesis might be entirely transformed.) But literary truths also exist, and the true-false opposition can be applied to narratives as well. For example, a "pact" exists on the basis of which the reader accepts as true the statements of the narrator, while he feels free to exercise his own judgment with respect to those of the characters. In other words, the omniscient narrator is credited with "authentication authority."[65] This is diminished in the case of the narrator-character or the narrator-protagonist, and they will sometimes make the limitations on their possibilities of information explicit. It is in this sense that Doležel passes in review the typology of the addresser (§1.4–5) and illustrates the varying position of texts with respect to truth values, in particular, the twentieth-century vogue for texts deliberately deprived of "authentication authority" of any kind.[66]

3.11. Narratology and Point of View

The endeavors of critics to grasp the exactness of the connections between events have come up against the difficulties just spoken of; they can all be brought down to the fact that the writer cannot refer events which he has invented and which have involved his sensibility and his view of life to a merely anodyne world. The series of techniques grouped under the label "point of view" is dependent upon this (cf. §1.6). Point of view is concerned with the way facts are put forward, in short, with the angle from which each of the events which constitute the plot is revealed. The plot, therefore, links together vertically events which are presented at different distances and from within different perspectives. The composition of a narrative work depends on a variable equilibrium between the means of its presentation (points of view) and the things it presents (plot).

3.12. Multivoiced Discourse

The concept was introduced by Bachtin, who regarded it as only, or primarily, applicable to the novel. Bachtin also had in mind the internal stratification of the language into social dialects, professional and group jargons, literary currents and fashions, ideological and political dictates. He pointed out that many words and forms retain the contextual harmonics which link them to a specific sphere, a profession, a conception of the world. As a result, they function as *ideologems*. It is the copresence of expressions and words from various spheres which make it possible for the differences of opinion that we usually look for in authors to coexist from the outset in the language; they coexist in a kind of polyphony, or dialogue. Language is, for Bachtin, a "pluridiscoursive opinion about the world."[67]

Bachtin relates these observations to the field of stylistics, accusing the representatives of this discipline of having dealt with texts as though they were unitary wholes and of having, in consequence, attempted to define "the style of X" or, at least, "the style of writer X's work Y." On the contrary, in any (narrative) text a variety of stylistic-compositional units will exist: on the one hand, narration which the writer manages directly (and here we may speak of his style); on the other, the stylistically individualized discourses of the protagonists. In between lie the various stylizations of oral discourse (when a narrator-intermediary exists), semiliterary modes of narration (diaries, letters), and various forms of literary discourse (moral, philosophical, scientific arguments, etc.). Each of these units has its own style, or styles of its own, a subset with respect to global style. The style of the author, or at least that of the undisguised author, is simply one of these subsets.[68]

This might seem enough to make possible a quite new approach to stylistic research, which would devote its attention to the social registers and strata inside the text and see them as parts of its structural programming. But pluridiscoursiveness is a much more complex phenomenon, and it cannot be mastered merely by observing the way voices are distributed in the text:

> It is true that in the novel pluridiscoursiveness, is always personified, incarnated in the individual figures of persons with their disagreements and contradictions. But here these contradictions of individual wills and intelligences are embedded in social pluridiscoursiveness, and are thereby reinterpreted. The contradictions of individuals are here no more than the crest of the waves which rear themselves up from the ocean of social pluridiscoursiveness, an agitated ocean which impetuously renders them contradictory while saturating their words and consciousnesses with its own fundamental pluridiscoursiveness.[69]

The writer cannot, and must not, constrain the free flow of this multivoiced discourse; it is a constituent element of the language within which he and his characters have their being. Stylistic-compositive units effect a sifting process, a centrifugation, but they do not annul the pluridiscoursive forces which the language continues to emit.

It was by working on Dostoevesky that Bachtin was led to investigate this approach. There was a seeming contradiction between a polyphonic novelist like Dostoevesky, who makes very little use of language varieties, and monologue novelists like Tolstoy and Leskov, who nonetheless exhibit considerable linguistic variety. At this point, the concept of "dialogic angle" becomes fundamental; it is to be understood as an ideological-moral standpoint, one, though, which is not necessarily correlated to linguistic techniques. Fundamental, too, is the concept of "semantic position," under which language styles and sociolects are grouped together. Dialogic angle and semantic position make it possible to individuate stylistic varieties even when these are not realized through the mediation of the varieties which exist in the language.[70]

These concepts are part of a more far-ranging reflection. The writer certainly does not limit himself to regulating the various linguistic currents which flow together inside his text, and he does not adhere passively to the ideological positions he represents. His word is oriented directly toward objects when he expresses himself in the first person (it is, to use Bachtin's term, objectual), and it is not just toward objects that it is oriented; it is itself the object of the author's orientation when it is the characters who are speaking. Lastly, there exists a word within which two intentions coexist, that of the author and that of the character. They may coincide or divaricate, and an ideal phase difference will always persist. There is also the antagonist word, the only one expressed, although it implicitly refers to its opposite. With these clarifications, two of Bachtin's basic concepts—stylization and parody—come to the fore.

In stylization, the author's intention takes advantage of someone else's word to accord with his own personal intentions; in parody, someone else's word is pervaded with a diametrically opposed intention. In short, "the voices are not only isolated from one another, separated by a distance, . . . they are hostilely opposed."[71] Cases also exist in which someone else's discourse, while not quoted, indirectly transpires in that of the author: it is sized up and by implication rebutted.

The various types individuated by Bachtin are all involved with the subject-object relation, and this, depending on the case, may be found to be under the full control of the author. Again, it may be referred to fictitious mediators (narrators and characters) or signified by caricature, by antiphrasis, by hyper-characterization after the manner of parody, of unexpressed polemic, of stylization. Such a relation has more to do with the material that is being narrated than with the world being represented.

The sum of possible realizations of this interlacing of voices (those of author, narrators, characters) and of this overlapping or divarication of intentions (which gives material form to relations of doubling, of convergence or divergence between the author and the mediators he has conceived) is represented in concise form by the following table which represents discourse possibilities.[72]

3.13. Polyphony and Point of View

Bachtin's theory makes a positive contribution to studies of both stylistics and points of view. Point of view is an expression he himself uses in symptomatic sentences: "After all, what is important to the stylizer is the sum total of the devices associated with the other's speech precisely as an expression of a particular *point of view*. He works with someone else's *point of view*"; "someone else's verbal manner is utilized by the author as a *point of view*."[73] But we should not illude ourselves into thinking that the distribution of the different voices will coincide with the distribution of registers, of stylistic-linguistic varieties, of ideologems. We must not lose sight of the fact that pluridiscour-

I. Direct, unmediated discourse directed exclusively toward its referential object, as an expression of the speaker's ultimate semantic authority

II. Objectified discourse (discourse of a represented person)
   1. With a predominance of socio-typical determining factors
   2. With a predominance of individually characteristic determining factors

   } Various degrees of objectification

III. Discourse with an orientation toward someone else's discourse (double-voiced discourse)

   1. Unidirectional double-voiced discourse:
      a. Stylization;
      b. Narrator's narration;
      c. Unobjectified discourse of a character who carries out (in part) the author's intentions;
      d. *Ich Erzählung*

      } When objectification is reduced, these tend toward a fusion of voices, i.e., toward discourse of the first type

   2. Vari-directional double-voiced discourse
      a. Parody with all its nuances;
      b. Parodistic narration;
      c. Parodistic *Ich Erzählung*;
      d. Discourse of a character who is parodically represented;
      e. Any transmission of someone else's words with a shift in accent

      } When objectification is reduced and the other's idea activated, these become internally dialogized and tend to disintegrate into two discourses (two voices) of the first type

   3. The active type (reflected discourse of another)
      a. Hidden internal polemic;
      b. Polemically colored autobiography and confession;
      c. Any discourse with a sideward glance at someone else's word;
      d. A rejoinder of a dialogue;
      e. Hidden dialogue

      } The other discourse exerts influence from without; diverse forms of interrelationship with another's discourse are possible here, as well as various degrees of deforming influence exerted by one discourse on the other

Source: M. Bachtin, *Problems of Dostoevsky's Poetics*, Ann Arbor, The University of Michigan Press, 1973, p. 199.

siveness is a starting point; it is not a construction in the literary sphere. The writer himself, because he speaks the language, is a participant in its constitutional pluridiscoursiveness. What is more, point of view is not realized by the institution of persons and moods alone, for it is the outcome of continual shifts of focus which the author effects throughout the text for motives which can usually be defined but which cannot be provided for in advance.

Confirmation comes, unintentionally, from Uspensky's investigations of point of view, which broaden and render more explicit Bachtin's approach.[74] Uspensky passes in review and exemplifies all possible values for the concept— on an ideological, phraseological, spatiotemporal, psychological plane and concludes with remarks on the interrelation of points of view relative to the various levels of a work and to its constructive and pragmatic aspects. He attempts to determine, from within the author's discourse, various degrees of participation with respect to the facts narrated, as distinct from voice. This is a sense of *point of view* which might be defined as one of "conformity or unconformity" and which is not to be confused with any ideological acceptance. In fact, (narrative) conformity is possible without acceptance, while unconformity may coexist with acceptance. With Uspensky, in short, point of view is reduced to atoms. The various chapters of his book are typical ("The Nonconcurrence of the Ideological Point of View and Other Points of View"; "The Nonconcurrence of the Spatial and Temporal Points of View with Other Points of View"). And typical is his incontrovertible statement that "the whole narrative text can be sequentially divided into an aggregate of smaller and smaller microtexts, each framed by the alternation of the external and internal authorial positions."[75]

We must, it seems, resign ourselves to confusion. But it is with complication that we must end, a complication which is rationalizable on a theoretical level and which is, for this very reason, stimulating. At the origin of point of view and of many-voicedness lies the fact that it is impossible for a writer to put forward in disengaged fashion inventions which have involved his sensibility and his conception of life. The world of which he speaks, fantastic though it be, must always be presented as if it were real: the object of direct or indirect experience. For this reason he takes concrete shape as a narrator or else gives form to a narrator-character or to a narrator-protagonist, or he may have recourse to the expedient of a discovered manuscript (so that the experience is attributed to the author of the manuscript). Even when the author takes unto himself from the outset the attributes of omniscience and impartiality, he cannot avoid from time to time approaching his characters and, by so doing, limiting his own viewpoint to the horizon within which the characters move.

Hence arise two categories, person (or voice) and mood. There is a radical difference between them. Person, relative to the writer-narration relation, is disciplined grammatically (use of pronouns and deictics) and can, as a result, branch out in quite complex modes; for example, one character may tell of another character, who may then tell of a third, and so on to infinity. On the contrary, mood is relative to the writer-material narrated relation, and it may well happen that grammatical markings are not used to indicate it, for it is realized through movements which dislocate the limits of the horizon. Its individuation is a more delicate matter and is by no means beyond discussion.

Once this has been said about the direction of intersubjectivity, the opposite direction, subjectivism, needs to be taken into account. The imagined world is the work of a single subject who clearly enjoys measuring himself against his creation but who never forgets that he is himself the demiurge. A persistent dialectic of convergence and distancing with respect to the characters thus comes into play. The demiurge may be pleased to allow them to move and speak as if they were autonomous creatures, though more frequently he will wish to manifest his agreement or dissent. The polyphony that Bachtin individuates is a diagram of the confrontations and frictions between the author's conceptions, those attributed to the characters, and those of various cultural formations. In other words, what is at stake is the ideological position relative to the writer-sense relation.

3.14. The Tale Endowed with Form

Now that we have arrived at this conclusion, we may go back and complete our earlier observations concerning point of view and plot. The confusion which has reigned in work on point of view, though Genette has markedly circumscribed it, derives from the fact that a single term, all too pregnant, has been applied to phenomena of the most varied nature. Further clarification might come from awareness of the fact that person, mood, and ideological standpoint belong to three, ideally successive, stages of the process which endows the narrative text with form. In a very circumscribed model of text production, we will find ourselves in the space where plot and discourse combine. Plot is susceptible of mimetic, diegetic, or mixed realizations (in all their possible varieties); in discourse, on the contrary, everything is settled from the outset, definitively.

When plot is to be realized as discourse, the first thing to be organized is through which channels it is desired that the story be communicated to the reader (through which persons); subsequently, in a more detailed review of narrative contents, a choice is made, stage by stage (and outright to a greater or lesser degree) of the perception horizon within which these contents are to be situated (in which moods); lastly, and consubstantial with linguistic elaboration, is the variety of ideological standpoints assumed by the writer. Between persons and moods there exists not parallelism but combination (a narrator-character may, for example, assume perceptive horizons proper to the other characters of whom he speaks); in their turn, ideological positions are provided with a medium which will give them official status, i.e., persons (and we might recall the stylizations and parodies pointed out by Bachtin). They stand revealed, though, in the text's every part, thanks to phase-differences, slight though they may be, between the position of an I and that of the others whom the I in question has endowed with life; these are linguistic phase-differences which are to be glimpsed not only in referred discourse but also in the way in which the characters' horizons of perception are represented in narrative terms.

The successive stages of this endowing with form ideally succeed each other in the work of the writer; for the addressee, they provide a model for a real reading. By making use of this model, it is possible to work back from linguistic findings to organization of semiotic material in accord with the requirements of narration (persons) or in accord with the variety of observation points adopted (moods). Itineraries exist whose movement is vertical (from discourse to plot), others horizontal (and which move in the areas of plot extrinsecation). They explore correspondences between form and content (indeed, contents), between the linguistic and the semiotic, creating between the two pairs an imaginary interspace within which to see as a series of processes something which is really a definitive, indissoluble unity.

Notes

1. I call *dianoetic meaning* the discourse linking the ideas that inspire the work. The term is Aristolelian and has recently been relaunched by N. Frye.
2. An idiolect is a personal variety of a given language, the pattern imprinted on a language system by the use a single person makes of it (in our case by an author).
3. See D'A. S. Avalle, "Gli orecchini di Montale" (1965), in *Tre saggi su Montale* (Turin: Einaudi, 1970), pp. 11–90.
4. Stylistic vectors are those features of style (generally words and expressions) which most explicitly and directly evidence the text's dominant characters and ideas.
5. See Segre, *Le strutture e il tempo*, pp. 132–33 (English translation, p. 108).
6. See J. K. Ščeglov and A. K. Žolkovskij, *K ponjatii "tema" i "poetičeskij mir"* (1975). For the Italian translation, see "I concetti di 'tema' e di 'mondo poetico,'" in Prevignano, ed., *La semiotica nei paesi slavi*, pp. 392–425.
7. A. J. Greimas, *Du sens: Essais sémiotiques* (Paris: Seuil, 1970), p. 160. See also Greimas and Courtés, *Sémiotique*, pp. 29–33.
8. Greimas, *Du sens*, p. 160.
9. A. J. Greimas, *Maupassant: La sémiotique du texte; Exercices pratiques* (Paris: Seuil, 1976), p. 24.
10. Ibid., p. 61.
11. G. Sinicropi, "La diegesi e i suoi elementi," in *Strumenti critici*, 9 (1977): 34, pp. 491–922.
12. For this whole theme, much studied by contemporary linguistics, see, at least, O. Ducrot, "Dire et ne pas dire: Principes de sémantique linguistique" (Paris: Hermann, 1972), and "Presupposizione e allusione," in *Enciclopedia*, vol. 10 (Turin: Einaudi, 1980), pp. 1083–1107.
13. E. M. Forster, *Where Angels Fear to Tread* (London: Edward Arnold, 1959), p. 172.
14. Ibid., p. 173.
15. See M. L. Pratt, "Literary Cooperation and Implication," in *Essays in Modern Stylistics*, ed. Donald C. Freeman (New York: Methuen, 1981), pp. 388–89.
16. See Sklovskij, *O teorii prozy*.
17. T. A. van Dijk, in *Some Aspects of Text Grammars* (pt. 1, chap. 3) and *Text and Context* (chap. 5), uses macrostructure (as does M. Bierwisch) for the discourse, indeed metadiscourse, which synthesizes the content of a narrative text. Worth remarking is his observation (which can be verified experimentally) that such macrostructures should constitute the residue of information stored in memory: thus, they organize mnestic

information. In short, the macrostructures progressively individuated enable us to understand, and to arrange, any further information which is relevant to the argument. Compare van Dijk, *Macrostructures: An Interdisciplinary Study of Global Structures in Discourse, Interaction and Cognition* (Hillsdale, N.J.: Lawrence Erlbaum, 1980). The analyses of actions and functions here spoken of are thus an improvement on techniques which are proper to reading.

18. For example, J. Kristeva, in Σημειωτική speaks of *phenotex* and *genotext*, respectively, for the text in the proper sense (signifier surface), and for its deep, meaning structure; the former is, in Chomsky's sense of the word, "generated" by the latter. Both terms have been built upon the model of *phenotype* and *genotype*, derived from biology and introduced by Šaumjan into his generative linguistics.

19. See W. O. Hendricks, *Essays on Semiolinguistics and Verbal Art* (The Hague: Mouton, 1973); E. Agricola, "Text, Textaktanten, Informationskern," in F. Daneš and D. Viehweger, eds., *Probleme der Textgrammatik*, vol. 2 (Berlin: Akademie Verlag, 1977), pp. 11–32; D. Leeman, ed., *La paraphrase*, in *Langages*, 8 (1973): 29; and R. Martin, *Inférence, antonymie et paraphrase: Eléments pour une théorie sémantique* (Paris: Klincksieck, 1976).

20. For example, T. Todorov, *Grammaire du Décaméron* (The Hague: Mouton, 1969), uses capital letters for agents and attributes, lowercase italics for verbal actions, etc. But verbs and attributes are indicated with terms chosen by Todorov himself (there are, for example, three actions, and no more than three: *modifier, pécher, punir*. And it is the critic himself who so orders things that all the verbs used in the text will fall into the requisite categories). The formulae do no more than translate the critic's own paraphrase. What they ratify is really a highly personal classification.

21. The accent may be placed on events (happenings) or on actions, though there is a considerable difference between them. Actions are human and intentional; events may well be natural processes and as such unexpected. This difference is akin to that between a motivated sign and an arbitrary one.

22. A. N. Veselovskij, *Istoričeskaja poetika* (1940). Veselovskij's work was first published between 1897 and 1906. For a partial Italian translation, see *Poetica storica* (Rome: Edizioni e/o, 1981). See p. 290.

23. See K. Burke, *A Grammar of Motives* (Berkeley and Los Angeles: University of California Press, 1969), pp. XVff., 443–44; K. L. Pike, *Language in Relation to a Unified Theory of the Structure of Human Behavior*, 2d ed. (The Hague: Mouton, 1967), pp. 974–78; and E. M. Meletinski, *Principes sémantiques d'un nouvel Index des motifs et des sujets*, in *Cahiers de Littérature Orale*, 2 (1977): pp. 15–24.

24. I have dealt with this matter in *Semiotica, storia e cultura*, pp. 29-31. Compare what Veselovskij says of the motif: "By the term *motif* I mean a formula which, at the dawn of human society, answered questions which nature everywhere posed for man, or a formula which fixed those *especially lively impressions, derived from reality* which seemed important or which repeated themselves"; Veselovskij, *Istoričeskaja poetika* (Italian translation, 283; my italics).

25. The term *motif* is, unfortunately, a somewhat "overloaded" one. It may stand for (1) a pattern of representability, i.e., of action archetypes, quite close to (2) the minimal narrative elements which are recurrent in folk, or in literary, narration. But it may also stand for (3) a recurrent segment, at the level of signifier or signified, within a given text *(Leitmotiv)*. Another meaning is (4) an action which is determinant for the plot of a narration. This meaning was introduced by the formalists (and taken up, at times in the variant form *motifeme*, by Doležel, Dundes, etc.). The term dangerously multiplies an already considerable polysemia; it would seem preferable to use *action*, or *event* (cf. §3.8.6.) instead, or else *function* (cf. §3.7.3.) when it constitutes an invariant of the narrative model.

26. B. Tomashevskij, *Teorija literatury* (English translation, p. 67).

27. Ibid., p. 68.

28. *Analexis* is used by Genette, *Figures III*, pp. 77ff., to indicate postponement in the plot of an event in the fabula (or, to use his own terminology, of the *histoire* in the *récit); prolexis*, anticipation, is a symmetrical phenomenon.
29. The French in this respect speak of *entrelacement*.
30. See Genette, *Figures III*, pp. 228–31 (English translation, pp. 215–31); L. M. O'Toole, "Dimensions of Semiotic Space in Narration," in *Poetics Today*, 1 (1980): 4, pp. 135–49; and G. Zoran, "Towards a Theory of Space in Narrative," in *Poetics Today*, 5 (1984): 2, pp. 309–35.
31. See L. Doležel, "Towards a Structural Theory of Content in Prose Fiction," in S. Chatman, ed., *Literary Style: A Symposium* (New York: Oxford University Press, 1971), pp. 95–110.
32. B. V. Tomaševskij, *Teorija literatury* (English translation, p. 68).
33. Ibid.
34. R. Barthes, "Introduction à l'analyse des récits," in *Communications*, vol. 8, (Paris: Seuil, 1966), pp. 8–9. The different functional importance of a tale's various areas is also marked by its choice of tenses. For *close up* and *background* tenses, see H. Weinrich, *Tempus*.
35. On the other hand, it should be said that individuation of motifs is only one moment in Tomaševskij's overall strategy with regard to narration; he also takes into account characters and their relations, time, thematics, etc., in terms of a technique which proceeds from the empirical to its formalization as in the example of A. A. Reformatskij, *Opyt analiza novellističeskoj kompozicii* (1922). For the Italian translation, see *Saggio d'analisi della composizione novellistica*, in *Strumenti critici*, 7 (1973): 21–22, pp. 224–43.
36. V. Ja. Propp, *Morfologija skazki* (1928). For the English translation, see *Morphology of the Folktale* (Austin: University of Texas Press, 1968), p. 21.
37. Ibid., p. 113.
38. Ibid., p. 92.
39. Segre, *Le strutture e il tempo*, pp. 13ff. (English translation, pp. 9ff.). On page 246, n. 24, other proposals for the representation of narrative levels are listed.
40. The term was coined by Todorov to designate functional study of narrations.
41. There is a more detailed critical analysis in Segre, *Le strutture e il tempo* (English translation, *Structures and Time*), chap. 1. See also the exposition in van Dijk, *Some Aspects of Text Grammars*, chaps. 2, 8.
42. See C. Lévi-Strauss, "La structure et la forme: Réflections sur un ouvrage de Vladimir Propp," in *Cahiers de l'Institute de Science économique appliquée*, ser. M, 7, (1960): pp. 1–36.
43. See A. J. Greimas, *Sémantique structurale*.
44. V. Ja. Propp, *Morfologija* (English translation, pp. 28 and 36).
45. A specific corpus is the basis of E. Dorfman, *The Narreme in the Medieval Romance Epic: An Introduction to Narrative Structure* (Manchester: Manchester University Press, 1969), who uses *narremes* for the narrative units individuated. These, though, are complex episodes which are recurrent within the corpus (the insult, betrayal, the heroic act, etc.), and they are not individuated by means of functional criteria but merely as content segments. The same thing is true of M. Fantuzzi, *Meccanismi narrativi nel romanzo barocco* (Padua: Antenore, 1975). Thanks to its descriptive approach, this is a useful thematic repertoire for the baroque novel (in particular, for the novels of G. F. Biondi and G. Brusoni). Two spheres, love and a good-bad relation, embrace the whole variety of possible phases and types (for example, the repertoire of impediments to a successful outcome in love). Closer to Bremond's formulae is M. Romano, "La scacchiera e il labirinto. Struttura e sociologia del romanzo barocco," in *Sigma*, n.s., 10 (1977): 3, pp. 13–72. Of considerable interest is the attempt to individuate and arrange hierarchically the variants of a given poetical theme inside a corpus of

thematically related poems whose possible alternatives "ramify": A García Berrio, "Una tipologia testuale di sonetti amorosi nella tradizione classica spagnola," in *Lingua e stile*, 15 (1980): 3, pp. 451–78.

46. See W. Labov and J. Waletzky, "Narrative Analysis: Oral Versions of Personal Experience," in J. Helm, ed., *Essays on the Verbal and Visual Arts*, 2d ed. (Seattle, 1973), pp. 12–44. The relations involved can be represented by the following figure:

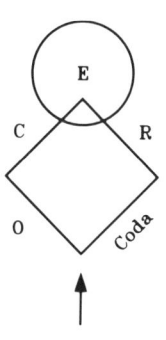

The starting point is the contemporaneous (= the arrow), and one is immediately faced with *orientation*, i.e., with the sum of all of the organizing notions (of place, time, situation, etc.). *Complication* follows, the sum of the events which transform the initial situation. *Evaluation* reveals, at the climax of the tale, the narrator's attitude toward his narration and brings to the fore determinant narrative units; this is generally followed by the *resolution*. The *coda* distances the facts narrated from the contemporaneous, which is why the figure returns to the arrow. The constituent element is, therefore, *complication* (which may well fuse with *orientation*) as a rule linked to *evaluation*; a tale gives a sense of completion when it also has a *resolution*. In other words, we are dealing with a construction which may prove complex to a greater or lesser degree.

47. C. Bremond, "La logique des possibles narratifs," in *Communications*, vol. 8 (1966), pp. 60–76. Completely asemantic is, on the contrary, the model put forward by G. Prince, *A Grammar of Stories: An Introduction* (The Hague: Mouton, 1973), which does make it possible to synthesize (with logical formulae, in terms of a generative model) any fabula or plot whatsoever, though without denominating actions and events. See also Prince, "Aspects of a Grammar of Narrative," in *Poetics Today*, 1 (1980): 3, pp. 49–63, and *Narratology: The Form and Functioning of Narrative* (Berlin: de Groyter, 1982). Another notable general arrangement is that put forward by G. Genot, *Grammaire et récit: Essai de linguistique textuelle* (Nanterre: Centre de Recherches de Langue et Littérature Italiennes, 1984).

48. For these analyses in the style of Propp and Todorov, I make slightly modified use of the elegant exercise of A. Rossi, "La combinatoria decameroniana: Andreuccio," in *Strumenti critici*, 7 (1973): 20, pp. 1–51.

49. See Bremond, *Logique du récit*.

50. See A. Ruffinatto, *Funzioni e variabili in una catena teatrale: Cervantes e Lope de Vega* (Turin: Giappichelli, 1971); Segre, *Le strutture e il tempo (Structures and Time)*, chaps. 2 and 4, and *Semiotica filologica*, chap. 8.

51. See D'A. S. Avalle, "L'ultimo viaggio di Ulisse," in *Studi danteschi*, 43 (1966): pp. 35–68, *Modelli semiologici nella Commedia di Dante* (Milan: Bompiani, 1975), and "Da Santa Uliva a Justine," in A. N. Veselovskij and D.A.F. de Sade *La fanciulla perseguitata*, ed. D'A. S. Avalle (Milan: Bompiani, 1977), pp. 7–33.

52. See Rossi, *La combinatoria*.

53. Lotman, *Struktura* (English translation, pp. 233–34).
54. Ibid., p. 238.
55. J. Culler, "Fabula and Sjuzhet in the Analysis of Narrative," in *Poetics Today*, 1 (1980): 3, p. 32. There are similar observations in M. Riffaterre, *La production du texte* (Paris: Seuil, 1979), pp. 153–62. Thematic structure may prevail over narrative structure, but any privilege accorded to action is logical in character rather than artistic (cf. §3.10).
56. See F. Rastier, "Les niveaux d'ambiguité des structures narratives," in *Semiotica*, 4 (1971): 4, pp. 289–342, and *Idéologie et théorie des signes* (The Hague: Mouton, 1972).
57. See E. M. Meletinskij, "L'étude structurale et typologique du conte," in appendix to Propp, *Morphologie du conte*, 2d ed. (Paris: Seuil, 1970), pp. 201–54; E. M. Meletinskij *et al.*, *Problemy strukturnogo opisanija volšebnoj skazki* (1969). (For the Italian translation, see "Problemi di descrizione strutturale della fiaba di magia," in *La struttura della fiaba* (Palermo: Sellerio, 1977), pp. 86–135.)
58. See, for example, Ph. Hamon, "Qu'est-ce qu'une description?" in *Poétique*, 12 (1972): pp. 465–85, and *Introduction à l'analyse du descriptif* (Paris: Seuil, 1981); M. Liborio, "Problèmes théoriques de la description," in *Annali dell'Istituto Universitario Orientale di Napoli: Studi nederlandesi, studi nordici*, 21 (1978): pp. 315–33; J. M. Blanchard, "The Eye of the Beholder: On the Semiotic Status of Paranarratives," in *Semiotica*, 22 (1978): 3–4, pp. 235–68; J. Garvey, "Characterisation in Narrative," in *Poetics*, 7 (1978): 1, pp. 68–78; "Il paradosso descrittivo: Atti del V Convegno italiano di studi scandinavi," in *Annali dell'Istituto Orientale di Napoli: Studi nederlandesi, studi nordici*, 23 (1980); J. Kittay, ed., "Towards a Theory of Description," in *Yale French Studies*, 61 (1981).
59. See G. H. von Wright, *Norm and Action* (London: Routledge and Kegan Paul, 1963), "The Logic of Action: A Sketch," in N. Rescher, ed., *The Logic of Decision and Action* (Pittsburgh: Pittsburgh University Press, 1967), pp. 121–36, and *An Essay in Deontic Logic and the General Theory of Action* (Amsterdam: North-Holland, 1968).
60. See T. A. van Dijk, "Philosophy of Action and Theory of Narrative," in *Poetics*, 5 (1976): 4, pp. 287–338, and *Text and Context*, chap. 6; L. Doležel, "Narrative Semantics," in *PTL: A Journal for Descriptive Poetics and Theory of Literature*, 1 (1976): 1, pp. 129–51.
61. See G. A. Miller, E. Galanter, and K. H. Pribram, *Plans and the Structure of Behavior* (New York: Holt, Rinehart, and Winston, 1960).
62. See T. A. van Dijk, *Text and Context*.
63. See J. K. Hintikka, "On the Logic of Perception," in *Models for Modalities* (Dordrecht: Reidel, 1969), pp. 151–83.
64. For applications of possible worlds to criticism, Th. G. Pavel, "'Possible Worlds' in Literary Semantics," in *Journal of Aesthetics and Art Criticism*, 34 (1975):2, pp. 165–76; D. Chateaux, "La sémantique du récit," in *Semiotica*, 18 (1976): 3, pp. 201–16; L. Doležel, "Narrative Worlds," in L. Matejka, ed., *Sound, Sign, and Meaning* (Ann Arbor: University of Michigan Press, 1976), pp. 542–53; L. Vaina, "La théorie des mondes possibles dans l'étude des textes: Baudelaire lecteur de Bruegel," in *Revue Roumaine de Linguistique*, 21 (1976): pp. 35–48, and "Les mondes possibles du texte," in *Vs*, 17 (1977): pp. 3–11; Eco, *Lector in fabula*, chap. 8; J. Heintz, "Reference and Inference in Fiction," in *Poetics*, 8 (1979): 1–2, pp. 85–99; L. Doležel, "Extensional and Intentional Narrative Worlds," in *Poetics*, 8 (1979): 1–2, pp. 193–211, *Truth and Authenticity in Narrative*, in *Poetics Today*, 1 (1980): 3, pp. 7–25; and Th. G. Pavel, "Narrative Domains," in *Poetics Today*, 1 (1980): 4, pp. 105–114. See also nos. 19–20 of *Vs*, devoted to *Semiotica testuale: Mondi possibili e narratività*.
65. Doležel, *Truth and Authenticity*, p. 11.
66. See L. Doležel, *Narrative Modes in Czech Literature* (Toronto: Toronto University Press, 1973), and *Truth and Authenticity*.
67. M. M. Bachtin, *Vosprosy literatury i estetiki* (Italian translation, p. 101).
68. Ibid., p. 70.

69. Ibid., p. 134.
70. See Bachtin, *Problemy poetiki Dostoevskogo* (1963). For the English translation, see *Problems of Dostoevsky's Poetics* (Ann Arbor: University of Michigan Press, 1973).
71. Ibid., p. 193.
72. Ibid., p. 199.
73. Ibid., pp. 189 and 190.
74. See B. A. Uspenskij, *Poetika kompozicii chudožestvennogo teksta i tipologija kompozicionnoj formy* (1970). For the English translation, see *A Poetics of Composition* (Berkeley and Los Angeles: University of California Press, 1973).
75. Ibid., pp. 153–54.

4.
The Text Historicized

4.1. Communication and History

The fact of regarding the text as part of a communication act automatically brings to the fore its links with the culture, and the perspective thereby established is a historical one. The codes employed by the addresser, and his motivations as well, derive from the cultural context within which he is inserted, while the addressee will have recourse to the codes at his disposition in order to interpret the text. Behind the problem of interpretation there lies, then, the serious problem of an encounter between two cultures, the possibility of one culture's understanding (and assimilating) an earlier one. Meaning systems are established inside a culture and constitute an integral part of it. Historical processes, as Uspensky observes, are communication processes; they coincide with the response of the social addressee to the new information the culture offers.[1] There is no need, therefore, for us to condemn a reading which confines itself solely to the text to the exclusion of its context; it is sufficient to realize that it is not possible.

The seemingly closed, autonomous nature of the text is immediately transcended in a reading, for reading is also interpretation. It is only a reading that can activate the communication circuit set up by the addresser, for the circuit will be complemented and so made capable of functioning only when the other pole of the communication, the addressee, has accepted the connection. The addresser-addressee line individuates the historical distance which the communicative capacity of the text transcends. The text in reality bridges much more, for it embraces all of the history which has converged on the text in the act of its composition.

The analysis-synthesis-analysis-synthesis cycle, though simple, represents the principal phases of the text's communicative life.[2] The addresser effects an analysis of the reality he has experienced (one which takes in all the elements of historical continuity). This analysis is synthesized in the text, with recourse to the codes the epoch offers. The addressee will analyse the text by having recourse to the codes of his own epoch and will then effect an interpretive synthesis of it.

It would seem, then, that history is revealed under two main aspects: the content is historical as is the character of the codes. On closer analysis, these two aspects will be found to be more homogeneous, because what is important in the text is not so much any datum or historical re-evocation as, to use an expression of Goldmann,[3] the "imaginary universe," i.e., history interiorized and structured as a system. This "imaginary universe" has the status of a model and constitutes a schema for the functioning of the codes.

This, in theoretical terms at least, is the most correct way of posing the problem of the historical aspect of texts. The many other ways possible (and frequently put into effect) usually dwell on historical content or the historical character of the addressers and addressees. This is all quite legitimate, but it must be made perfectly clear that, in such cases, the literary text is simply serving as a document for a reconstruction which will remain heterogeneous with respect to the text, because it is unrelated to its nature as a unified message.

4.2. Culture and History

Far more relevant are attempts to relate the text to its cultural context. The text belongs to the culture at the moment of its sending, and it will go on belonging to it during successive receptions. In its conformation, it is homogeneous with the other phenomena of the culture to which it belongs, and it is homologous with them. While relations of cause and effect, though they will not be immediate ones, may exist with respect to historical facts, with cultural facts there exists parallelism and concerted movement.

The influence, often indeed the impact, of historical forces (prevalently economic forces) is much more compellingly determinant for the cultural system as a whole than it is for single texts. Thus, analysis of culture is able to mediate between study of history and study of texts. Culture is, at one and the same time, a complex of human behavior modes (which means it belongs to the practical sphere) and an organized complex of expression systems (which means it belongs to the communication sphere).

4.3. Literary Historiography

It is not just possible but absolutely necessary to orient literary texts historically. The problem of a history of literature is quite another matter, and that it is constitutionally impossible has many times been asserted. While not wishing to return to the question, we will at least remind ourselves that the literary text is a semiotic structure and that its closely interwoven relations are connotative in type. As a result, if we follow the developments of any one element of the text, whether pertinent to expression or to content, this will, on an ideal level, involve disarranging its structure. The synchronic, here, is not just opposed to the diachronic as it is in the language; it also involves objects (such as signifying structures) which are heterogeneous with respect to the diachronic. Diachrony is concerned with codes and signs and their developments; it takes no account of the structures within which they have found employment and by whose means their potential for meaning has been multiplied.

To put the problem another way, the attempt has been made to distinguish the elements proper to textuality or, rather, to literariness[4] from others which are more steeped in direct experience and which are merely adopted by literature as its material. It was thought possible to grasp the historical development of what is peculiar to literature. Such a project involved setting aside the close-knit network which, at a variety of levels, links the development of society, that of literature as institution, and single literary works. Of this undertaking all that remains valid today is its requirement that any possible standpoint must be subordinated to the peculiar constitution of the literary text itself. The stress it laid upon historical conditioning (which it looked for in the biography of writers, in the situation of literary society, in the possibilities and modalities of distribution, in pragmatic efficacy) does undoubtedly pose problems of considerable importance; they are not, though, pertinent to literary criticism.

If the fact of seeing art as communication serves to underline how inevitable is historical consideration of it, it is a semiotic conception of culture which will allow us to avoid the pitfalls of simple-minded determinism and of primitive sociology. The definitions of culture offered by the Soviet semioticians, which we shall soon (§4.5) be looking at, can be related to those given by Western ethnologists and anthropologists, for example, by M. Mauss.[5] Whichever of these definitions we accept, certain axioms will hold good: culture is information (a nonhereditary storehouse of the information held in memory by a collectivity; a mechanism for producing new information); culture uses the language as its main tool; and language is not merely the most sophisticated means we have for communicating information but also constitutes a kind of filing system for safeguarding the massed information of the collectivity, its encyclopedia. As a consequence, reality is revealed to the collective consciousness only by means of signs, stereotypes, archetypes, i.e., by the language of knowledge, without which our perceptions would be no more than undifferentiated flux.

There is a further axiom: texts, and literary texts in particular, are among the principal purveyors of culture. This is why relations among the various tributaries of literature, those belonging to reality and more specific ones, will find themselves transferred through the stereotyping filter of a sign system which will render them homogeneous and susceptible of combination. In this way, the historical conditionings we have just eliminated are with us once more—in so far, at least, as the culture recognizes them and is disposed to express them. This way of looking at culture will also help us to avoid too violent a separation of the conditionings to which the addresser and his group are subject and the conditionings which are ratified by linguistic and literary institutions. In fact, it will be as well to distinguish conditionings of remote, or of more recent, date and thus different degrees of stereotyping. This, though, will leave unaltered the bi-unique, one-to-one nature of the writer-culture interaction. The writer will "recognize" his experience thanks to the means of which the culture disposes; the culture will assimilate the experience which the writer has realized.

4.4. Text Levels and Cultural Levels

4.4.1. Culture may be regarded as a complex of fields or spheres, each arranged as a system. Any synchronic conformation will reflect the state of the society which expresses it, and it will do so in two ways: first, hierarchization of the systems; second, the tendency of each of the component systems to adapt itself homologously to the kind of relations which characterize the corresponding society. It is to the former of these that Tynjanov[6] refers when he endeavors in outline to link the various fields or spheres (which he calls "series") and to individuate dominant "series" within a given society (Tynjanov explained transformation of literary genres in a similar fashion, on the assumption of a form of leadership on the part of one or another of them).[7] It is to the latter mode that Bachtin refers when (cf. §2.25) he conceives of the language as a monad within which are to be found—codified—both sociocultural levels and ideological variants ("ideologems" are words which convey ideological marks).

One way of inserting a text into its context might be to connect each of its levels with the corresponding level of the culture. What should be particularly remarked is the dialectic between innovative and conservative forces in both and their different degree and rapidity of development. If, for example, we take the four levels which it is possible to individuate in a narration (discourse, plot, fabula, and narrative model; cf. §3.7.3), it will be possible to relate them to the levels of the cultural context which correspond to them (the language, rhetoric, and metrics included; exposition techniques; anthropological materials; key concepts and logic of the action).[8]

The linking together of these four levels brings to light the mechanisms of the addresser-addressee relations as they move from the cultural context to the text and in the opposite direction. Here is a diagram:

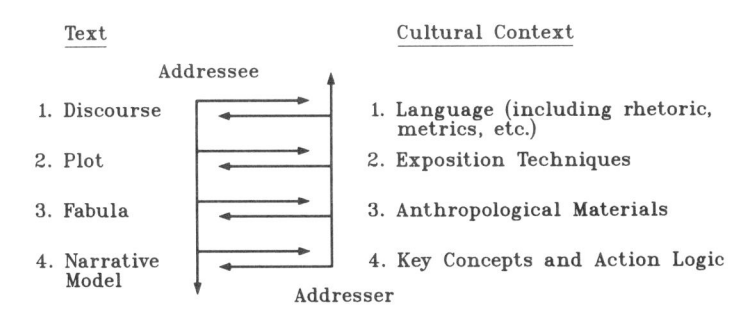

Text	Cultural Context
Addressee ↑	
1. Discourse	1. Language (including rhetoric, metrics, etc.)
2. Plot	2. Exposition Techniques
3. Fabula	3. Anthropological Materials
4. Narrative Model	4. Key Concepts and Action Logic
↓ Addresser	

The addresser, inasmuch as he is inserted into the context, will effect his inventive production while passing from zone 4 to zone 1 of the cultural context and will then find the literary signifiers and meanings which are to be introduced into the corresponding points of his text. In his turn, the addressee, the reader, will carry out his analysis by setting out from the text and working in the opposite direction (from 1 to 4); by so doing, he will come into contact with the corresponding points of the literary context.

Considerable historiographical implications are involved in the following statement: the four cross-sections which I have effected for the context demonstrate a degree of mobility and complexity which increases progressively. The same conceptual and logical system can be realized by means of a multiplicity of themes, myths, and stereotypes, and these, in their turn, may find expression in a wide variety of narrative modes. And thus we reach the point of the language itself, for the language is highly sensitive to shifts in culture and to passing fashion; so infinitely malleable is it that it can set up as many "idiolects" as it has speakers.

Under the heading *text* a considerable number of exemplars will be found to be reducible over time to the same narrative model, while the same fabulae, or ones composed of the same elements, will be realized, epoch by epoch, by means of different plots. The play of persistence and transformation is all the richer when functions and relations between characters are schematized—as I suggest they should be—as two distinct series. We will then discover that equal functions are produced by different character relations and different functions by equal relations.

A circumstantiated historical typology can be based on this. Narrative history will then consist of a history of the "types" which, as they move with constantly increasing velocity from section 1 to section 4, fall into disuse, or, in relation to the sum of the "types" extant in a given synchronic phase, and with fewer and fewer immediate repercussions, they will be transferred from sections 1 to 2, from 2 to 3, from 3 to 4. The sum of the "types" constitutes a system and its stratification, and it will be possible to describe and, perhaps, explain its transformations.

From a dynamic point of view, an explanation for the desuetude and birth of the various "types" might be looked for in the dialectic of codification and code innovation, but this should be related to the diversified vitality of cultural levels from epoch to epoch, because the writer, through his cultural context and by employing the semiotic materials it affords him, may reach the point not merely of innovating within a "type" but even of innovating the "type."

The above model is, naturally enough, a simplification, even when it is restricted to narrative. But the modes of literary explication are numerous, even were the list to include no more than the literary genres. Every genre can be sectioned according to different levels which will set up different relations with the same stratum or with other strata of the culture.[9] If we then take into consideration the copresence and concurrence of genres in any given literary period, it will become clear that the historicizing criteria we have sketched will serve to manifest the genres in all their manifold variety. Not only will relations exist between text levels and context levels, and inside a system of levels, we will find, too, that they exist from one genre to another as well, because each genre will have its own peculiar mode for establishing contact with the context. The model thus envisaged is a three-dimensional one, and its temporal axis should be capable of accommodating text-context relations and text-genre system relations as well.

4.4.2. Closing with a reference to genres a paragraph which began by breaking down into levels both text and culture serves inevitably to reaffirm the connection of all the content elements and the formal elements of the text, in accord with the production/fruition model which underlies the present pages. In rapidly reviewing its traits inside this new perspective, we might do well to start with the language. The language is made up of various subsystems which are the result both of a copresence of different diachronic phases and of its other differentiations: geographic (regional variants), social (varieties of level which depend on environment or on the superiority/inferiority relations of speakers), and functional (the different jargons of trades and research fields). In the drafting of any text a preliminary choice will inevitably be made among these aspects afforded by the language.

Choice of language is linked to an even more far-reaching choice, one which much more directly influences exposition modes and even their content. This choice, which concerns text types, is to a very large extent organized, in the literary sphere, by various poetics. These hold tacit sway even in periods seemingly not Aristotelian. A writer, once he has settled on his argument, is strongly conditioned to treat it in a given style, within a given literary genre, etc.

In this way a text realizes, within its complex organism, a solid interconnection of its major, minor, and minimal content elements and of its linguistic and stylistic expression forms, one which may perhaps involve narrative technique as well. Such "telescoping" is facilitated when a "program" exists, and this is the function of poetics. Poetics are techniques for the assembling of texts and, in general, of the typologies which are implicit in the texts.[10] But this connection between linguistic elements and content elements is homologous to that which exists in the cultural encyclopedia, where the primary modeling system, which is linguistic, serves to sustain secondary modeling systems (cf. §4.6.1–2). This makes it easier to perceive the links which tie a text to the culture whose expression it is.

Among the subsets of the language, *écritures* occupy a place of their own.[11] They conform not to content types but to ideological types, and as a result they are connected, if not directly to social formations, at least to explicit interpretations of the antagonism between such formations. This is an obvious case of the force of condensation to which, even inside the language itself, social tension and projects may give rise. The language, moreover, reflects the main lines of the sociosphere within which we move (cf. §4.5.1 and §4.6.5). Interactions between ideologies and poetics, between *écritures* and styles, are no less important; they are the most consistent and significant clues we have to the way culture and the socioeconomic spheres overlap or to the connective, mediating zone which is forged culturally as an image of the socioeconomic.

Considerations of this kind allow us to envisage an approach to literature which would move beyond unsubtle sociology and show itself capable of seizing upon the play, from model to model, of dialectic, the interaction of semiotic systems which will, to a greater or lesser degree, conform to the economic system. Such an approach will show how literature is engaged in putting forward new models (the reflection of shifts or crises in the social order), as a result of which it will also leave its mark on systems in force. Definition of models is not effected in the vast spaces of abstraction; it is a slow conquest of the territory of reality in movement; only in a sign-oriented perspective will such territory fall within the horizon of our understanding.

4.5. Culture and Models: The Self-Model

4.5.1. Over the last decade, thanks especially to the work of the Soviet semioticians, it has become possible to deal with the problem of how culture is to be defined in relation to communication and, in particular, to literary communication.[12] We may begin with this definition:

> From a semiotic point of view culture may be regarded as a hierarchy of particular semiotic systems, as the sum of the texts and the set of functions correlated with them, or as a certain mechanism which generates these texts. If we regard the collective as a more complexly organized individual, culture may be understood by analogy with the individual mechanism of memory as a certain collective mechanism for the storage and processing of information.[13]

It is even more evident that culture consists of a set of systems (such systems are anthropological, ethnic, political, philosophical, literary, etc.). We might adopt a formalist term and speak of a "system of systems." For the functioning of culture and for its interpretation as well, it is of prime importance that these systems, insofar as they are elements of social coexistence and thus of communication, are codes. "It is important to emphasize that the very relation of culture to the sign and to signification comprises one of its basic typological features."[14]

The system and its codes interact. One need only call to mind language, which is a code. Language is at one moment the vehicle, at another the principal interpreter, of all other codes. What we witness at work in culture is a permanent bilingualism, or plurilingualism. Indeed,

> For the functioning of culture, and accordingly for the substantiation of the necessity of employing comprehensive methods in studying it, this fact is of fundamental significance: that a single isolated semiotic system, however perfectly it may be organized, cannot constitute a culture—for this we need as a minimal mechanism a pair of correlated semiotic systems. A text in a natural language and a picture represent the most usual system of two languages constituting the mechanism of culture.[15]

Lotman and Uspensky go on to specify that these two "languages" must exist in a state of reciprocal untranslatability. This, as we shall soon see, explains why it is necessary to have a metacultural mechanism which will establish the relative equivalence of texts in the two languages.[16]

The priority of natural languages among cultural codices is evident. Of all the codes in play, it is the language which is the most "powerful" and the most malleable. The system of culture "is constructed as a concentric system in the center of which are located the most obvious and logical structures, that is, the most structural ones. Nearer to the periphery are found formations whose structuredness is not evident or has not been proved but which, being included in general sign-communicational situations, function as structures. Such quasi-structures /*kvazistruktury*/ occupy a large place in human culture."[17]

The semiotics of culture thus offers itself as a discipline capable of penetrating this concentric system and of seizing upon its correspondences and links. It is "the study of the functional correlation of different sign systems."[18] Other disciplines will, naturally enough, continue their autonomous examination of the peculiarities and functioning of each single system.

Culture, with respect to the social and communicative function of the various systems, is all-embracing. It is culture which makes sense of the world, because the world, before it is named, described, and interpreted, is nothing less than chaos. The sense of the world is our discourse about the world, and discourse about the world is only possible within a collectivity:

> The mechanism of culture is a system /*ustrojstov*, device/ which transforms the outer sphere into the inner one: disorganization into organization, ignoramuses into initiates, sinners into holy men, entropy into information. By virtue of the fact that culture lives not only by the opposition of the outer and the inner spheres but also by moving from one sphere to the other, it does not only struggle against the outer 'chaos' but has need of it as well; it does not only destroy it but continually creates it. One of the links between culture and civilization (and 'chaos') consists in the fact that culture continually estranges, in favor of its antipode, certain 'exhausted' elements /*otrabotannije*/, which become clichés and function in nonculture. Thus in culture itself entropy increases at the expense of maximum organization.[19]

It may therefore be stated that, in human society, culture is the sphere of organization (information), opposed to disorganization (entropy). We must go further though and add that this will hold good only "from within" the culture, because it is culture itself which decides what is to be considered as organized and what is not. As for the distinction between order and chaos, each society will adopt distinctive criteria of its own; it will make its own decisions. In any event, "culture is a generator of structuredness, and in this way it creates a social sphere around man which, like the biosphere, makes life possible; that is, not organic life, but social life."[20]

4.5.2. When it intervenes in chaos, culture has need of instructions. With no criterion not even culture could legitimately make pronouncements about the organization of the world. And it is here that the concept of self-model becomes operative. We might define it as the image of itself which is conceived and formulated by a culture:

> The essential mechanism which imparts unity to the various levels and subsystems of culture is its model of itself, the myth of the culture about itself which appears at a certain stage. It is expressed in the creation of autocharacteristics *avtocharakteristiki* (for example, metatexts of the type of Boileau's *L'art poétique*, which is especially typical of the age of Classicism; cf. the normative treatises of Russian Classicism), which actively regulate the construction of culture as a whole.[21]

The concept of self-model is essential to this conception. It emphasizes the intentions and initiatives without which the system of the culture would be, and would be seen to be, static, tautological, and sterile. The self-model (the concept is concomitant with that of text of the culture, of which more will be said later) operates, perhaps, as a polarization of the tendencies implicit in the system. It so orders things that these tendencies will be directed toward one single outcome or toward outcomes which will be related. In any case, the self-model authenticates awareness, autonomous programmatic engagement:

> The essential difference between cultural evolution and natural evolution lies in the active role of self-descriptions, in the influence exercised on the object by the representations of the object itself. This influence might be broadly defined as the subjective factor in the evolution of culture. Given that to the bearer of culture itself culture appears as a system of values, it is this subjective factor itself which determines the assiological aspect of a culture.[22]

We have seen how culture characterizes itself face to face with the world, i.e., with experience, and with its own representations of it. But a culture is characterized above all in relation to other cultures, since every culture is naturally antagonistic and potentially hegemonic (and it could not be otherwise; even when one culture casts itself in the role of mediator, with the aim of harmonizing other cultures, it will immediately see itself as superior to all the others).

The schemata for the contraposition of a given culture and other cultures are by now well known. They have been formulated (and designed, particularly by Lotman)[23] as oppositional pairs: *us-them* (the representatives of one culture and those of other cultures); *inside-outside* (what is external and what is internal with respect to the system of the culture); *this-that* (what is close and what is distant for the members of the culture). These schemata are malleable and will lend themselves to the most complex realizations. For example, *us-them* can be used to indicate, even graphically, the sense which the representatives of a culture have of being central or peripheral. With *inside-outside*, it is possible to represent, among other things, relations with the supernatural as superstitions, and religions cultivate them. Within the supernatural, enucleation of agents benign or malefic, or of agents who mediate between the terrestrial and the supernatural element, is also possible. Finally, *us-them* lends itself to manifold applications in all situations of dualism or of otherness.[24]

The nature of these schemata is topological because they represent mental situations in terms of space. They might revindicate their epistemological rights by invoking the Kantian categories of time and space, particularly the latter. It is with its aid that situations, already endowed in reality itself with spatial affinities, are formalized. What is even more interesting here is the fact that, in fixing these very general models, the metalanguage of the models has recourse to primitive, in a certain sense mythological, schemata. The architects of the models seem themselves to have sensed this, if statements of this kind are anything to go by:

> The choice of a discrete metalanguage of distinctive features of the types upper-lower, left-right, dark-light, black-white, to describe such continuous texts as those of painting or the cinema, may by itself be regarded as a manifestation of archaizing tendencies which impose on the continuous text of the object-language metalinguistic categories more characteristic of archaic systems of binary symbolic classification (of mythological and ritual types). But we must not rule out the fact that features of this kind remain as archetypal features even during the creation and perception of continuous texts.[25]

What is called for here is further discussion of the semiotic status of the models. Once it has been observed that their character is not linguistic, because they are visual or because their use of the linguistic element is prelinguistic and metaphorized, it is possible to go further and investigate the concept of metalanguage,[26] that of cultural metalanguage in particular. Stress should, for example, be laid on the fact that it is not possible to place oneself outside the perspective of a particular culture in order to deal with the problems of culture in general while at the same time retaining the language of the culture which served as one's starting point. A further problem needs to be debated. Can the semiotics either of the text or of the culture, as distinct from the language, postulate the existence of prelinguistic meanings, meanings of which different languages would be no more than the verbalization?[27] The Soviet semioticians provide an unintentional answer to this problem when they make appeal to the translatability of the languages within a culture: translatability from pictorial language to other languages cannot be effected by means of the language, even if it is true that the language may not unhelpfully collaborate.

4.6. Culture and Texts

4.6.1. These models may, in any case, represent primeval features of a culture, whether they are deduced from consideration of its totality or of single texts. What we must deal with here is the text-culture relation, for it is central to Soviet semiotics. The solutions outlined are two: the text may be symptomatic of a culture, at once its synthesis and a moment in its self-awareness; or the culture itself may be seen as a sum of texts, indeed as a single all-encompassing text. The concept of modeling system is the starting point for the first of these solutions: "By modeling system we mean the structured whole of elements and rules; such a system is found in relations of analogy with the complex of objects on the plane of consciousness, of awareness, and of normative activity. Hence, a modeling system may be considered as a language."[28]

Once we have been told that by model we are to understand "everything that reproduces the object in function of the cognitive process" and that the primary modeling system is the language, it is clear that the other modeling systems are the various cultural systems, art in particular, to be understood as reproduction of the world, as analogon of the world. Codification and decodification are the translations of reality into language or deductions from the language to the reality referred. The text, insofar as it reproduces reality, uses the language of culture; as a result, it is called a *culture text*:

> In defining culture as a certain secondary language, we introduce the concept of a 'culture text', a text in this secondary language. So long as some natural language is a part of the language of culture, there arises the question of the relationship between the text in the natural language and the verbal text of a culture. The following relationships are possible here:
> A) The text in the natural language is not a text of the given culture. Such, for example, for cultures oriented toward writing, are all texts whose social functioning implies the oral form. All utterances to which the given culture does not ascribe value and meaning (and does not preserve, for example), from its point of view, are not texts.
> B) The text in the given secondary language is simultaneously a text in the natural language. Thus a poem by Pushkin is at the same time a text in the Russian language.
> C) The verbal text of the culture is not a text in the given natural language. It may at the same time be a text in another natural language (a Latin prayer for a Slav), or else it may be formed by the irregular transformation of some level of a natural language (cf. the functioning of such texts in children's culture).[29]

B is the basic and most likely form. A refers to cultural self-censorship: from within the culture, expressions extraneous to its trends and preferential channels will be considered as nonexistent. C refers to the nonobligatory coincidence of natural language and secondary language: a culture may even consider texts in a different language as its own expression (the case of Latin holds, or used to hold, for all Catholic countries). Overall, it should be stressed that "culture texts" constitute no more than a subset of all texts which achieve their expression inside a culture. The following specification on Lotman's part is, I believe, of considerable importance. "A necessary property of a cultural text is its universality. A view of the world is related to the whole world and contains, in principle, everything. To pose the question of what is found beyond its boundaries is, from the point of view of a given culture, just as senseless as to pose it in relation to universum."[30] A view of the world cannot, in fact, be informative to a greater or lesser degree; it is a fact that the internal relations will remain the same even when variation exists in the elements employed for its description. Every culture text is, in this regard, a monad which reflects the model of the culture itself.

4.6.2. This connection between the culture, inasmuch as it is the matrix of a model of the world, and texts, inasmuch as they are potential suppliers of models of the world, constitutes an assertion which stands in need of the most detailed demonstration. The formulations of the Soviet semioticians are sufficiently pliable to admit (though no mention is made of the fact) that, over and above a functional hierarchy—in which the preeminent role is inescapably that of the language—and a prestige hierarchy—for which there exist epochs dominated by oral or written verbal codes (by a musical code, etc.)—there will also exist a pragmatic hierarchy of which account must be taken. It would describe, for example (cf. §4.4.2), the influence of poetics and *écritures* on the way models of the world are conceived and the influence of ideologies on their conception.[31] It is a field which is open to consideration of the pragmatics of culture: moving within it means avoiding undue emphasis on one aspect, "description of reality," at the expense of another, "intervention in respect to reality." All this does not take us beyond the limits of the theory of the models, for nothing is more familiar to an ideology than models (models may also take on the appearance of myths, and all ideologies are such).

It should further be pointed out—and the fact opens up new vistas for possible research—that "models of the world" and "theories of possible worlds" have a great many more things in common than the word *world* (cf. §3.10). The conditions to be met by any literary invention coincide with the parameters of the world as it is modelized in the corresponding culture. It becomes possible to consider any widening of scope, or any infraction with regard to the worlds that can be defined as "possible," as confirmations *ab absurdo* of such worlds or else as projects of, and aspirations toward, different worlds. Thus, logic may serve as a criterion for the measurement of innovative potentiality.

Relations between the modeling system of the culture and the single work of art seem to be fairly straightforward. If culture is susceptible to assimilation to a language, the work of art will be the equivalent of an act of *parole;* if the constitution of the cultural modeling system is semantic and paradigmatic in type, the constitution of the work of art will be primarily syntactic and syntagmatic. By analogy with the functioning of the *langue/parole* relation, we may believe that the models of the world put forward in a single text will be the realization (one of the many realizations possible) of a model of the world which is present in the culture as one of its potentialities and that every model of the world realized as a text will subsequently be assimilated into the culture, enriching or changing its model of the potentiality of the world.

4.6.3. In terms of the aims of literary criticism, it may well prove determinant and productive to verify the correspondence between the structure of the text and the model of the world it offers. If the conception of the model of the world immanent in a "culture text" is a valid one, the relations, close and regular as they clearly are, between the model and the forces which structure the text require investigation. Lotman himself has laid down useful guidelines, reformulating the problem of minimal narrative units while using as as yardstick the world framework into which such units are inserted.[32] The fact, for example, of defining actions (or events) as the shifting of a persona from one semantic field to another, or of qualifying as "revolutionary" a plot whose outcome is a modified vision of the framework of the world in contrast to other plots which leave it unaltered, is tantamount to marking out in the broadest terms the same interrelation among structures and the model of the world which is here postulated.

4.6.4. Culture can, in any event, be regarded as a "storehouse of information" for human collectivities. Day-to-day cultural activity consists in "translating a certain sector of reality into one of the languages of the culture, transforming it into a text, i.e., into information codified in a certain way, and introducing it into the collective memory."[33] But culture is not just an information bank; it is also a "mechanism creating an aggregate of texts,"[34] and, to my mind, it is with an approach of this kind, characterized by a potentiality-realization relation, that the theories of the Soviet semioticians will be made to yield their most positive results. The following is the clearest statement of the whole matter:

> From a semiotic point of view culture may be regarded as a hierarchy of particular semiotic systems, as the sum of the texts and the set of functions correlated with them, or as a certain mechanism which generates these texts. If we regard the collective as a more complexly organized individual, culture may be understood by analogy with the individual mechanism of memory as a certain collective mechanism for the storage and processing of information. The semiotic structure of culture and the semiotic structure of memory are functionally uniform phenomena situated on different levels. This proposition does not contradict the dynamism of culture: being in principle the fixation/*fiksacija*/ of past experience, it may also appear as a program and as instructions for the creation of new texts.[35]

Yet these very affirmations, when they speak of the "sum of the texts and the set of functions correlated with them," serve to suggest a different approach to the problem. That culture should be conceived as the sum of its texts is a proposal which has come from many quarters: at least Foucault must be mentioned. It is perhaps a direct outcome of the primary, indeed constituent, position attributed to texts that they should be seen as the connecting link between literary semiotics and the semiotics of culture. It is an invitation to broaden our concept of text, and we may be led in consequence to identify as a text "any vehicle of global ('textual') meaning—a ceremony, a work of the fine arts, or a piece of music."[36] But from such a standpoint the very nature of text would need to be considered differently from the way in which it is normally considered, and this would not exclude these pages.

4.6.5. The text, in as much as it is the prime element and the basic unit of culture, might be considered as a unanalyzable block in relation to culture. No longer a mere succession and combination of (linguistic) signs, and hence of discrete elements, the text for the culture would be a global sign, endowed with distinctive traits but not susceptible to segmentation into units of a lower rank. What is in play here is the distinction between discrete and continuous, and it will depend upon the point of view we adopt whether the text is to be seen as the sum of its discrete elements or as a continuous unity. And this is not all. It should also be possible to see as a text any set of texts which are homologous from some point of view. "The same message may appear as a text, part of a text, or an entire set of texts. Thus, Puškin's *Povesti Belkina* /Tales of Belkin/ may be regarded as an integral text, as an entire set of texts, or else as part of a single text—'the Russian short story of the 1830s.'"[37]

In this collective memory which is culture, input texts and output texts exist.[38] While it is easy to understand the concretization of texts as output, it is much less easy to imagine that text input may also be realized in the form of text stratification. The experience of the individual memory is a very different matter: except for the few cases of texts learned by heart, what memory conserves in rational order is content and formal elements, not whole texts. The collective memory is an abstraction, but it does not seem advisable to imagine it as different from individual memory other than in capacity. In all probability, in the term *collective memory* two images coexist: one concerns recognition and conservation to texts as the heritage of the community, the other their modelizing action in the single consciousness. Only for the first case is it possible to speak of integral text conservation. But what has already been pointed out must be borne in mind (cf. §4.1): texts are no more than a recording of graphic signs, until the moment at which they are subjected to a reading. If, on the contrary, we wish to allude to the active presence and the constant stimulus of texts, we must maintain that their presence in individual memories is of the selective and classificatory type here being discussed.

Much more valid and susceptible to development is the idea that, when compared to culture, texts do not present themselves as combinations of discrete signs but as continuous elements. Culture, in fact, assimilates not the explicitly syntagmatic character of signs (signifier and signified) in which the text as a product of language consists but rather a synthesis of its contents or, better, of such contents as culture has at a given moment recognized, or believes it has recognized. So true is this that the culture may contemporaneously assimilate different languages and codes, which, were there any question of their discrete elements, would be irreconcilable.

Here, too, comparison with the modes of individual assimilation will prove helpful. Whether the analysis is of a single text or whether it is the comparison of many texts (e.g., to take the case our semioticians give us, "the Russian short story of the 1830s"), the various breakdown techniques (individualization of motifs and themes, delineation of semantic fields, discovery of isotopies, etc.) will be brought into operation thanks to a metalanguage which will make it possible to overcome the heterogeneity and the incommunicability of the texts. In this operation, the sequence of discrete (linguistic) elements of the text is transcended, because one sets out from the results of comprehension, whose nature is continuous, and from distinctive traits. On the other hand, the elements arrived at, if they are to be pigeon-holed in memory, will have to be retranslated into language. This language, used with a metalinguistic function, is thus a language which is other, with respect to the natural language of the texts. It is after this conversion, from language to metalanguage, that a concentric system can be formed. At its center will lie the language (as system), and the other systems will surround it. The most highly structured (in Lotman and Uspensky's sense) will be closest to the center and the least highly structured farther out. This is why we have stated that culture is best seen as a synthesis of texts and as a producer of texts, rather than as a sum of texts.

Possibly the best definition of the way culture functions is the following offered by Lotman and Uspensky:

> The semiotic mechanism of culture created by mankind is constructed according to a different principle *[from that of non-semiotic systems]*: opposed and reciprocally alternating structural principles are essential. Their *relation to one another*, the disposition of particular elements in the structural field which emerges here, creates that structural regulatedness which allows the system to preserve information. It is crucial here, however, that it is not actually any specific alternatives whose number is finite and constant for the given system that are given, but the very *principle of alternation* itself, and that all the actual oppositions of the given structure are merely interpretations of this principle on a certain level. As a result, any pair of elements, of local regularities, of particular or general structures, or even of whole semiotic systems acquires the significance of being alternatives and forms a structural field which may be filled with information.[39]

This is a highly productive definition because it distinguishes elements, relations, and different kinds of information and allows for the possibility of linking the same elements together in different fashion, establishing thereby a variety of relations much more far-reaching than that of the elements in play. This makes it possible for us to describe the internal stratifications of culture (for culture is never, and never can be, uniform) on the basis of a shift in the relations of its elements or, obviously, of the participation of a greater or smaller number of elements within a structural frame. To complete our description, we should introduce ideologies here, for they set up polarizations among the elements of the system and, by so doing, orient or even dislocate its oppositions. Indeed, the heterogeneity of the conceptual system, whose nature is semantic, and the system of factual knowledge (historical, scientific, etc.) can be surmounted, once we are aware of the capacity of ideologies to classify knowledge or to break it down, in terms of the compartments of their dominant ideas.

4.7. History and Models

So far, we have been considering the malleability and the mobility of culture. It is because it is a synthesis of the experience of a collectivity that it will continually turn to its own advantage the results of any experience. This mutability can be observed inside an alternation of two counterpoised tendencies:

> In the union of different levels and subsystems into a single semiotic whole—"culture"—two mutually opposed mechanisms are at work:
> 1) The tendency toward diversity—toward an increase in differently organized semiotic languages, the 'polyglotism' of culture.
> 2) The tendency toward uniformity—the attempt to interpret itself or other cultures as uniform, rigidly organized languages.[40]

Apart from these antinomic tendencies, more specific antinomies are at work within culture, and they are no different from those met with in natural language. They belong principally to the spatial and temporal dimensions. Such are antinomies like native and foreign, modern and ancient. The second antinomy establishes a kind of diachrony inside synchrony. Any synchronic phase of the culture will contain elements of earlier phases, as well as anticipations of successive ones. This is exactly what happens in the language, where the young, adults, and the elderly coexist. This is why possible developments need never be abrupt. The first of our antinomies absorbs into the cultural sphere elements which derive from different, even distant, cultures. The polyculturality which results will multiply and enhance lifestyles and behavior; it will broaden the potential range of choice for programs of action and will encourage an experience of "something different" inside the community itself.

But the dynamism of a culture is first and foremost the product of its orientation, i.e., the dominant position it confers upon one specific semiotic system. This ensures that other semiotic systems which may be copresent will be pervaded and assimilated. Cultures exist which are oriented toward writing (text) or toward oral speech, toward the word and toward the picture.[41] The attribution of a dominant position to one semiotic system, determinant as it is for the establishment of any *unity of a culture,* is the most clear-cut consequence of the formulation of a self-model. It is thanks to the dominant system, or systems, that "the unified system is constructed which will serve as code for self-knowledge and for self-decipherment of the texts" of a given culture.[42]

A drive toward transformation is thus part and parcel of any cultural system. It makes it possible to carry out profitable investigation of the typologies of cultures and of their historical dimension. In general terms, the transformations of a culture may be regarded as the result of a confrontation between culture and chaos which, as we have already pointed out, is a constituent of any culture.

If, from the point of view of an inside observer, culture seen as organization and information stands opposed to chaos seen as entropy and inexpressibility, from the point of view of an outside observer,

> culture will represent not an immobile, synchronically balanced mechanism, but a dichotomous system, the 'work' of which will be realized as the aggression of

regularity against the sphere of the unregulated and, in the opposite direction, as the intrusion of the unregulated into the sphere of organization. At different moments of historical development either tendency may prevail. The incorporation into the cultural sphere of texts which have come from outside sometimes proves to be a powerful stimulating factor for cultural development.[43]

A history of civilizations might be outlined by following the different ways in which they have depicted order and chaos and the varied vicissitudes of a chaos which at one moment is expelled, at another is all-invasive, which is sometimes feared and at other times found attractive.

4.8. History and Typology

4.8.1. For a typology of culture, the semiotics of cultural models has also offered convincing suggestions. I am thinking, for example, of the differentiation of cultures oriented toward the "position of the speaker" from others oriented toward that of the listener (of addresser and addressee, we might say, of sender and receiver). In the second type of culture, the concepts of maximum clarity and of maximum validity coincide. Texts strive to be spontaneous rather than conventional, and favor is accorded to prose, to historical annals, to journalism. On the contrary, the tendencies of the first type of culture are esoteric; it prefers closed texts to which access is difficult and incomprehensible. It prizes poetry, prophecy, and perhaps secret languages. In a speaker-oriented culture, the audience for the text is modeled on the image of the addresser; in the other type, it is the addresser who conforms to the pattern of his audience.[44] Such oppositions as renaissance-baroque and classicism-romanticism are the most obvious historical actualizations of this polarity.

Another efficacious polarization is based on the distinction between cultures whose orientation is toward expression and others whose concern is content. The former see themselves as a system of texts, the latter as a system of rules; the former propagate themselves through manuals which take the form of generative mechanisms, the latter use catechisms and chrestomathies. Standard examples are European classicism and realism. In the case of classicism, theoretical models were regarded as eternal, as anterior to any effective creation. Judgment of texts and the degree to which they conformed to the rules were one and the same thing. In the case of realism, artistic texts functioned directly, without any need for the mediation of a theoretical metalanguage. A theoretician will elaborate his generalizations on the basis of the texts; he and the writer will often be one and the same.[45] Content-oriented cultures have a vocation for proselytism; the noncultural dimension is for them an open field. Expression-oriented cultures tend to keep themselves to themselves. They erect barriers against anything that is opposed to them; they identify nonculture and anticulture. Examples are medieval China and the Russia of Ivan the Terrible.[46]

Brilliant is the distinction made between cultures which realize an *I-him* type of communication and those whose type is *I-I*. The two communication types may be defined as follows:

In the one case we are dealing with information given in anticipation, which is transferred from one man to another, and with a code which remains constant within the field of the whole act of communication. In the other, instead, there is an increase of information, a transformation and re-formulation in terms of other categories; furthermore, it is not new messages which are introduced but new codes, while addresser and addressee coincide. In this process of self-communication what is effected is re-organisation of the personality, and this is linked to a very wide range of cultural functions, from a sense of one's own individuality, in certain types of culture essential to man, and self-identification and self-psychotherapy.[47]

Art, Lotman tells us, makes use of both systems of communication; indeed it oscillates within the field of their reciprocal structural tension. Aesthetic effects are produced the moment the code begins to be used as a message and the message as a code. This is because the text passes from one communication system to another, although it remains linked to both.[48] Now, it may happen that a culture will be oriented prevalently toward self-communication or else toward the kind of communication which is dominant in the system of natural languages. In the former case, we may well find intense spiritual activity, a tendency toward "the poetical" (when words are reduced to clues, when there is a tendency toward the cryptographic, while semantic connections are blurred and syntagmatic connections brought to the fore). A very self-contained dynamism will be the outcome. Message-oriented cultures, on the contrary, will tend to multiply immeasurably their tale of texts and make provision for a rapid increase of knowledge. Their character will be more mobile and dynamic. The culture of the European nineteenth century is a good example.[49]

4.8.2. Of those texts of Lotman available to us, one in particular represents the most ambitious attempt so far made to apply a typological interpretation to Russian culture (it is one which with few adjustments might apply equally well to the rest of Europe).[50]

Lotman's starting point is a matrix based respectively on the prevalence or on the limited importance of paradigmatic values, which Lotman calls semantic (sign-substitution relations), and of syntagmatic values (sign-combination relations). This is represented in the following figure:

II. (Syntagmatic meaning)

	1. I (+) II (−)	2. I (−) II (+)
	3. I (−) II (−)	4. I (+) II (+)

I. (Paradigmatic meaning)

These four possibilities are to be interpreted as follows:
(1) the cultural code constitutes the semantic organization only; (2) the cultural code constitutes the syntagmatic organization only; (3) the cultural code is oriented toward a rejection of both types of organization, i.e., toward rejection of the very nature of the sign; (4) the cultural code constitutes a synthesis of both types of organization.

The first type, defined as semiotic or symbolic, is that of the Middle Ages. The world was then imagined as word, and creation was the formation of the sign. All signs were to be referred in some way to one single meaning. What mattered was not their reciprocal relations so much as the way each sign gave rise to greater depths of meaning. The part, indeed, was homeomorphous to the whole, given that it could act as its symbol. A twofold division thus exists in the medieval model of the world: some phenomena are endowed with meaning; everyday phenomena are deprived of meaning. The result is a contradictory situation which excludes the biological and the day-to-day from its sphere of values and yet attributes value to facts which are impalpable but heavily symbolic. The everyday can be recovered only when it has been transformed into ritual. As such an individual enjoys no rights whatsoever; he must be a member of a group.

The semantic paradigm is built upon the basis of violent oppositions (heaven-earth, eternity-time, virtue-sin, etc.). The various semantic series which result from these can be deduced in such a way that nothing will be left over. Naturally enough, time is wiped out of this picture of the world. The beginning is not perfected in the end; it is a matter of eternity. Thus, whole families and peoples search for ancestors.

Defined as syntagmatic, the second type may be represented by the ecclesiastical-theocratic and absolutist conceptions of the sixteenth and seventeenth centuries and then by Peter the Great's "regulated state." What is now denied is any symbolic meaning of events and phenomena. Everything is projected onto the plane of church and state. Preference is accorded to practical knowledge, and common sense becomes the main criterion for reality. The parts (e.g., the individual) are no longer regarded as homologous to the whole; they are seen as fragments which are organized by the whole. It is within this framework that democratic ideals are developed.

In marked contrast to the semantic type, cultural objects are situated along a temporal axis, while movement, in general, is seen as improvement. The first term of the opposition old-new is seen as negative, while the second is positive. The concept of progress is born, but, since one takes for granted its subjugation to church and state, or that scientific knowledge will be broadened by it, what it leads to is a new semanticization, bureaucratic in character.

A culture like that of the Enlightenment may be defined as aparadigmatic and asyntagmatic: it laid claim to things as against signs, and as against words in particular and to biological and anthropological realities as against social organization. The antithesis natural-unnatural came to the fore, and the first element was the positive one. The arbitrary nature of the signifier/signified relation was discovered. Lastly, exclusive attention was devoted to the individual (as solitary, perhaps, as Robinson Crusoe); large-scale human groups were regarded as agglomerations.

With the affirmation of the bourgeoisie, the need was strongly felt to conceive a model of the world which would show it to be endowed with sense and unity. Historicism and dialectics developed, and it was with their help that "the idea of the world as a succession of real facts, which are the expression of a profound movement of the spirit, conferred on all events a dual sense: semantic, insofar as it was a relationship between the physical manifestations of life and their hidden sense, and syntagmatic, insofar as it was a relationship between these and the sum total of history."[51] The world, in short, seemed to be structured like a language, with a content plane and an expression plane. The attempt was also made, not always successfully, to insert into the system facts which were extraneous to it. This accounts for the attempts at evasion from this type of system, of which examples are still to be found.

4.8.3. At least in part, Lotman's models of cultural typology are applicable to our own culture as well; and engagement in such application would certainly lead to positive results. Descriptive and historiographical uses of Lotman's models for different historical spheres already exist.[52] Particular mention should be made of two contributions by Maria Corti.[53] They are devoted to medieval culture and deal with the triadic model of Indo-European origin, which preachers retained down to the twelfth century. It involved a conception of order as hierarchy, while hierarchy was the sanctification of the world. Its stereotype was the *Corpus Areopagiticum* of the Pseudo-Dionysius. Alan of Lille, for example, divided society into *orators*, *bellatores*, and *laboratores* and then went on to find this same pyramid structure in every social cell (in the parish, monastery, bishopric, etc.)[54] and obviously in the three virtues of the soul. From the point of view of the authority enjoyed by the models in certain periods, two orders of observation are important; one concerns the conflict between the model and thirteenth-century social reality; the other concerns the existence of an antimodel.

For the first point, Corti studies various ways in which the model was adapted to the emerging reality of a middle-class, mercantile civilization. Subclasses were multiplied to accommodate the *laboratores* (Honorius of Autun). The *ordines*, together with their hierarchical arrangement, were swallowed up in a sea of different statuses, primarily those of the professions (Jacques de Vitry). A new and more complex pyramid-shaped model was put forward with the aim of embracing all types of status (Humbert de Romans).

For the second point, Bachtin's theses concerning the comic and the carnivalesque are illustrated in the belief that popular culture, which the Middle Ages pushed to one side, created an antimodel.[55] This antimodel is a mirror image of the one accepted by the dominant culture, because it turns its topological ordering of oppositions upside down, exalting the humble and the meek against the mighty, pitting the body against the spirit, folly against wisdom. This is extremely clear in the *Dialogus Salomonis et Marcolphi*, and it is no accident that this text was imitated down the centuries, by the Bertoldo of G. C. Croce and also by Cervantes' Sancho.[56] The operation was, though, the work of a group of intellectuals whose aim was to break up "an ideal of perfect order, or, at the very least, <to> demystify it by presenting it to us upside down."[57] This is a formula which holds good for nearly all medieval attempts to put forward antimodels, given that it was impossible for those the Middle Ages discriminated against to elaborate a culture of their own. They could not even "take the floor."

Notes

1. See Uspenskij, *Historia sub specie semioticae* (1947). For the Italian translation, see Prevignano, ed., *La semiotica nei Paesi slavi*, pp. 463–71.
2. See Segre, *I segni e la critica* (English translation, *Semiotics and Literary Criticism*), pt. 1, chap. 2.
3. See L. Goldmann, *La création culturelle dans la société moderne* (Paris: Denoël-Gonthier, 1971).
4. For the Russian formalists' program for tracing a history of literariness *(literaturnost')*, see V. Erlich, *Russian Formalism*, 2d ed. (The Hague: Mouton, 1964), chap. 10. For the theory, see M. Marghescou, *Le concept de littérarité: Essai sur les possibilités théoriques d'une science de la littérature* (The Hague: Mouton, 1974).
5. An up-to-date bibliographical synthesis is I. Portis Winner and T. G. Winner, "The Semiotics of Cultural Texts," in *Semiotica*, 18 (1976): 2, pp. 101–56. A handy anthology is P. Rossi, ed., *Il concetto di cultura: I fondamenti teorici della scienza antropologica* (Turin: Einaudi, 1970).
6. See Ju. N. Tynjanovv, *Archaisty i novatory* (1929). For the Italian translation, see *Avanguardia e tradizione* (Bari: Dedalo, 1968), pp. 45–60.
7. Ibid., pp. 23–44.
8. See Segre, *Semiotica, storia e cultura*, chap. 2.
9. Useful suggestions for breaking down the poetic text have been given by G. Pozzi, "Codici, stereotipi, topoi e fonti letterarie," in *Intorno al "codice": Atti del III Convegno della Associazione Italiana di Studi Semiotici (Pavia 26–27 settembre 1975)* (Florence: La Nuova Italia, 1976), p. 41.
10. On genres and poetics as forms for a preliminary selection of materials, see Hempfer, *Gattungstheorie*, chap. 5; Corti, *Principi*, chap. 5; and Segre, "Genres" and "Poetics" in this book. See also M. Corti, "I generi letterari in prospettiva semiologica," in *Strumenti critici*, 6 (1972): 17, pp. 1–18.
11. See R. Barthes, *Le degré zéro de l'écriture*, chap. 2, p. 1.
12. There is a good synthesis in M. Pagnini, *Pragmatica*, pp. 34–46. The theses of the Soviet culturologists have been discussed by (among others) S. Zólkiewsky, "Quelques problèmes de sémiotique de la culture chez les auteurs est-européens," in the collective *A Semiotic Landscape*, pp. 204–20, and *Wiedza o kulturze literackiej: Głowne pojecia* (1980). For the Italian translation, see *La cultura letteraria: Semiotica e letteraturologia* (Bologna: Signum, 1982). See also Segre, *Semiotica, storia e cultura*, chap. 1, and "Culture et texte dans la pensée de Jurii Lotman," in M. Halle *et al.*, eds., *Semiosis: Semiotics and the History of Culture* (Ann Arbor: University of Michigan Press, 1984), pp. 3–15; and S. Miceli, *In nome del segno: Introduzione alla semiotica della cultura* (Palermo: Sellerio, 1982).
13. V. V. Ivanov *et al.*, *Tezisy k semiotičeskomu izučeniju kul'tur (v primenenii k slavjanskim tekstam)* (1973). For the English translation, see "Theses on the Semiotic Study of Cultures (as Applied to Slavic Texts)," in Thomas A. Sebeok, ed., *The Tell-Tale Sign: A Survey of Semiotics* (Lisse: Peter De Ridder, 1975), pp. 57–83.

14. Ju. M. Lotman and B. A. Uspenskij, *O semiotičeskom mechanizme kul'tury* (1971). For the English translation, see "On the Semiotic Mechanism of Culture," in *New Literary History*, 9 (1985): 2, pp. 217.
15. Ivanov et al., *Tezisy* (English translation, p. 75).
16. See Ju. M. Lotman and B. A. Uspenskij, "Postscriptum alle tesi collettive sulla semiotica della cultura," in Prevignano, ed., *La semiotica nei Paesi slavi*, p. 211. The most recent culturological work of Lotman translated into Italian is to be found in *Testo e contesto: Semiotica dell'arte e della cultura*, ed. S. Salvestroni (Bari: Laterza, 1980) and in *La semiosfera: L'asimmetria e il dialogo nelle strutture pensanti*, ed. S. Salvestroni (Venice: Marsilio, 1985).
17. Lotman and Uspenskij, *O semiotičeskom mechanizme* (English translation, p. 213).
18. Ivanov et al., *Tezisy* (English translation, p. 57).
19. Ibid., p. 58.
20. Lotman and Uspenskij, *O semiotičeskom mechanizme* (English translation, p. 213).
21. Ivanov et al., *Tezisy* (English translation, p. 83).
22. Lotman and Uspenskij, *Postscriptum*, p. 223.
23. See, for example, Ju. M. Lotman, *O metajazyke tipologičeskich opisanij kul'tury* (1969). For the English translation, see "On the Metalanguage of a Typological Description of Culture," in *Semiotica*, 14:2 (The Hague: Mouton, 1975), pp. 97–123.
24. In my chapter "Poetics," the opposition enables me to synthesize the progressive involvement in the literary sphere of what had earlier been looked upon as "otherness": "foreigners," "manual workers," the unconscious.
25. Ivanov et al., *Tezisy* (English translation, p. 64). See also E. M. Meletinskij et al., *Problemy*.
26. Metalanguage is, properly speaking, the use of language to speak about language itself (Jakobson identifies a metalinguistic function, cf. §2.5). See A. Giacalone Ramat and T. Kemeny, eds., *Linguaggi letterari e metalinguaggi critici* (Florence: La Nuova Italia, 1985).
27. See my "Linguistica e semiotica," in C. Segre, ed., *Intorno alla linguistica* (Milan: Feltrinelli, 1982), pp. 129–47.
28. Ju. M. Lotman, *Tezisy k probleme "Iskusstvo v rjadu modelirujuščich sistem"* (1967). For the Italian translation, see "Tesi sull'arte come sistema secondario di modellizzazione," in Ju. M. Lotman and B. A. Uspenskij, *Semiotica e cultura*, ed. D. Ferrari Bravo (Milan: Ricciardi, 1975), p. 4.
29. Ivanov et al., *Tezisy* (English translation, p. 67).
30. Lotman, *O metajazyke* (English translation, p. 101).
31. This proposal has been made in Segre, *Semiotica, storia e cultura*, pp. 7–24.
32. See Ju. M. Lotman, *Struktura chudožestvennogo teksta* (Moscow: Iskusstvo, 1970). For the English translation, see *The Structure of the Artistic Text* (Ann Arbor: University of Michigan Press, 1977), p. 328.
33. Lotman and Uspenskij, *O semiotičeskom mechanizme* (English translation, p. 50).
34. Ibid., p. 218.
35. Ivanov et al., *Tezisy* (English translation, p. 73).
36. Ibid., p. 62.
37. Ibid.
38. See Segre, *Semiotica, storia e cultura*, pp. 19–22.
39. Lotman and Uspenskij, *O semiotičeskom mechanizme* (English translation, p. 228).
40. Ivanov et al., *Tezisy* (English translation, p. 82).
41. Ibid., p. 83.
42. See Lotman and Uspenskij, *O semiotičeskom mechanizme* (English translation, pp. 66–67).

43. Ivanov *et al.*, *Tezisy* (English translation, p. 60).
44. Ibid., pp. 64–65.
45. See Lotman and Uspenskij, *O semiotičeskom mechanizme* (English translation, pp. 218–19).
46. Ibid., p. 221.
47. Ju. M. Lotman, *O dvuch modeljach*. For the Italian translation, see "I due modelli della comunicazione nel sistema della cultura," in Ju. M. Lotman and B. A. Uspenskij, *Tipologia della cultura* (Milan: Bompiani, 1975), p. 125.
48. Ibid., p. 129.
49. Ibid., p. 133.
50. See Ju. M. Lotman, "Il problema del segno e del sistema segnico nella tipologia della cultura russa prima del XX secolo," in Lotman and Uspenskij, *Ricerche semiotiche*, pp. 40–63.
51. Ibid., p. 59.
52. I quote, as an example, K. M. Boklund, "On the Spatial and Cultural Characteristics of Courtly Romance," in *Semiotica*, 20 (1977): 1–2, pp. 1–37, and "Sociosémiotique du roman courtois," ibid., 21 (1977): 3–4, pp. 227–56; C. Acutis, *La legenda degli infanti di Lara: Due forme epiche nel medioevo occidentale* (Turin: Einaudi, 1978); and A. Pioletti, "La condanna del lavoro: Gli 'ordines' nei romanzi di Chrétien de Troyes," in *Le forme e la storia*, 1 (1980): 1–2, pp. 71–109. These works should be compared with the study in Brasilian literature of the rhythm of oppositional pairs which are progressively dominant and interacting: L. Stegagno Picchio, "Opposizioni binarie in letteratura: Il caso della letteratura brasiliana," in the collection *Letteratura popolare brasiliana e tradizione europea*, ed. L. Stegagno Picchio (Rome: Bulzoni, 1978), pp. 15–35. For a study of literary systems in contact, see I Even-Zohar, *Papers in Historical Poetics* (Tel Aviv: Porter Institute for Poetics and Semiotics, 1978).
53. See M. Corti, "Modelli e antimodelli nella cultura medievale," in *Strumenti critici*, 12 (1978): 35, pp. 3–30. For the English translation, see "Models and Antimodels in Medieval Culture," in *New Literary History*, 10 (1978–79): pp. 339–66. See also Corti, "Ideologia e strutture semiotiche nei 'Sermones ad status' del secolo XII," in *Il viaggio testuale*, pp. 221–42.
54. The ternary model has been put forward continually down to our own day. See, for example, A. Jolles, *Einfache Formen: Legende, Sage, Mythe, Rätsel, Spruch, Kasus, Memorabile, Märchen, Witz* (1930). For the French translation, see *Formes simples* (Paris: Seuil, 1972), pp. 18–25. Jolles maintained that the main human activities are cultivating, fabricating, and interpreting to which the peasant, the artisan, and the priest correspond. For Duby's trifunctionalism (which in its turn derives from Dumézil) and for the ternary schemata, independent though akin, of Lotman, see M. L. Meneghetti, "Les modèles culturels: Ante rem, in re, post rem?" in Halle *et al.*, *Semiosis*, pp. 77–91.
55. See M. M. Bachtin, *Tvorčestvo Fransua Rable i narodnaja kul'tura srednevekov'ja i Renessansa* (1965). For the English translation, see *Rabelais and His World*, (Cambridge, Mass.: M.I.T. Press, 1968).
56. See P. Camporesi, *La maschera di Bertoldo: G. C. Croce e la letteratura carnevalesca* (Turin: Einaudi, 1976). See also the introduction to the volume edited by him in G. C. Croce, *Le sottilissime astuzie di Bertoldo: Le piacevoli e ridicolose simplicità di Bertoldino; Col "Dialogus Salomonis et Marcolphi" e il suo primo volgarizzamento a stampa* (Turin: Einaudi, 1978). See the corrections of F. Bruni, "Modelli in contrasto e modelli settoriali nella cultura medievale," in *Strumenti critici*, 14 (1980): 41, pp. 1–59.
57. M. Corti, *Modelli e antimodelli*, p. 28 (English translation, p. 364).

Part II
Themes of Literary Activity

Prologue:
Experience, Culture, and Text

1. From the World to the Text

There has been an extremely rapid extension in the uses made of a word like *text* (earlier an object of reflection only in the field of philology or in legal and religious codification), and the fact is typical of our epoch. Today *text* indicates not just a written text, a specifically literary one, but any coherent verbal utterance, even if it is oral. *Text* may even designate an articulated overall meaning carrier, such as a painting, a play, a dance, a rite. Finally, in the broadest extension, there is talk not just of textualized cultures but also of a whole culture looked at as a text.

Without going into the reasons for this terminological revolution, its most important implications and consequences can be pointed out here. In the attempt to revindicate an identity of origin for linguistic utterances of any kind, findings based on texts of a single type have been extended to the whole set. The totality of the utterances in a given language is our only source for practical (and theoretical) knowledge of that language and of its functions. When, for a general consideration at least, all the internal barriers are down, what lies before us is the whole field of the language in all its immensity: its contacts with the reality its names and catalogues, its institution of codes for representation, its conquest of an interpretative function (i.e., its acting as mediator for the various sign systems), its specialization for the production of informal and formal utterances, and, lastly, on another level, its renewed confrontation with reality, when this becomes the object of literary description.

This renewal of perspective (though not everyone is aware of the fact) is not unrelated to the affirmation of a semiotic mentality. It is thanks to this that the intelligibility of the world comes to be identified with an aptitude to employ signs to stand for things and their relations, with the need to communicate seen as a fundamental form of social cohesion, with the elaboration of metalanguages whose scope is to reconstruct the unity as communication of heterogeneous sign systems, and, finally, with the very conception of culture as a system of communication.

This multiplication of values has repercussions on the place occupied by the text in its original philological sphere. Text transmission is now seen as a striking example of communication over time (it is subject to inevitable interference) and of passage through different semiolinguistic systems. This leads us (and allows us) to reformulate our interpretations of the history of texts and our criteria for their reconstruction. We give weight now to the processes of tradition as against the mirage of restoration.

2. Language and Knowledge

The speaker does not stand disarmed in the face of his experience. The equipment he already possesses, the language, is of the highest precision. And this is not all. His experience, or an experience very similar to his, has already been that of millions of individuals, and they have contrived schemata, stereotypes, of the experience itself as well as syntactical formulae which, once they are codified, correspond to the stereotypes. Thus, the speaker is able at one and the same time (a) to analyze the basic elements of his experience into meaning units, (b) to interpret, in line with his sense of "cultural" causality, the mechanisms of the world he experiences, and (c) to denominate elements of experience and their relations by having recourse to a repertory of words, to their paradigms, and to the rules for their syntactical combination.

In short, operations that are linguistic in type are concomitant to, and in reality merge with, operations that are semiotic in type. It should also be added that, in practice, no "pure" experience is ever to be found. Any experience will form part of a well-defined finality, for it is inserted in the continual interactions which make up the life of individuals. This is the pragmatic aspect of the problem: confirmation of the textual unity of our acts, language acts included. These acts not only form part of an uninterrupted sequence of actions and reactions but are also, on every occasion, formulated in function of the replies foreseeable and take account of a given context.

3. The Discourses of Discourse

From a linguistic point of view, any text is a large, unified utterance, a *discourse*. Characteristic of discourse is its employment of an exclusively linguistic medium for the realization of a construction whose nature is semiotic. That this nature is semiotic can easily be demonstrated in the case of literary texts, given the inevitable presence in them of elements of connotation. Connotation brings to the fore a complex series of relations among the elements of a literary discourse which are not those regulated by grammar and syntax. Within the linearity of language discourse, connotation achieves a complex overlay of itineraries (real hypodiscourses), and these will involve a variety of fields, from the phonic to the semantic. It is this overlay which enlarges the communicative potentialities of discourse beyond the limits of mere information.

The semiotic nature of discourse can be verified without limiting ourselves to literature. A single observation may suffice. An infinite number of paraphrastic substitutions is possible: between a sentence and its various possible equivalents but also between two or more sentences which can be reduced to one in a summarizing paraphrase. As an extreme example, the contents of a whole book (however impoverished) can be synthesized in a few sentences. Chomsky's generative-transformational theory does not fully account for the operations under consideration, though it undoubtedly accounts for a part of them when it postulates the existence of deep syntactical structures which are variously articulated and ramified on the surface of the text and, even more so, when it postulates deep syntactical structures common to all languages. Between a text and its paraphrase, between one paraphrase and another, invariance is not linguistic in character but semiotic. (So true is this, that paraphrases can be made in any language at all or even by means of gesture, drawings, etc.)

Our minds are continually at work codifying and decodifying, from the linguistic to the semiotic and back again. This can be appreciated in the act of reading. It has been shown that we are not capable of taking in more than a single sentence at a time. And yet, as we move forward and read our text, we are linking up what we have already read with what we are engaged in reading, and all the time we go on reconstructing in memory all of the subject matter we have assimilated. This assimilated material is no longer organized linguistically. (At the outside, only fragments of our reading of the text are memorized.) It is arranged in quite other modes, which are determined by the conformation of our memory.

Analyses of the folk tale *(Narration/Narrative)* carried out by the formalists, apart from the critical and epistemological results obtained (establishment of narrative universals, of a "grammar" and a "logic" for functions), have subjected to strict verification the techniques of paraphrase. They have paid particular attention to the possibility of translating a discourse, itself the translation of other discourses, into an infinite number of further discourses. Between our perceptions and the text that utters them is located a series of processes analogous to that which links the thought which seeks expression to the discourse that expresses it. It is by moving through the dimensions of discourse that the activities of which the text is the conclusion and ratification can be verified.

4. What Communication Means

Communication has been the subject of much discussion, but because the most articulated communication of which man is capable is linguistic communication, it is easy to confuse communication with referentiality. Such an error can easily be confuted. One need only observe that language communication itself is often indirect; it coincides not with its referent but with elements implied by it and not named. Such oblique communication is no less frequent, and no less important, than direct communication.

This particularity is even more striking when utterances are examined as speech acts. It is well known that a command may be formulated as an observation, a question as a statement, and so forth. And this is not all. For a lengthy discourse which concerns topics that are, to all appearances, neutral, the immediate aim may well remain absolutely unexpressed on the referential plane.

In the case of artistic communication, the referent (apart from the fact that it is, in the main, fictitious) finds its range even more circumscribed. We need only call to mind the extreme example of music, which refers us to nothing but which, nonetheless, undoubtedly establishes communication between addresser and addressee. In literary communication, referentiality has confided to it the task of acting as vehicle for all values which are not referential in character. That a literary work does not confine itself to its literal meanings is known to everyone. What makes a semiotic structure of an artistic text is the capacity of its linguistic vehicle to communicate nonreferential meanings. This fact has been sensed by those literary critics who have spoken of some *je ne sais quoi, of aura*, etc.

Yet another fact needs to be recorded. Whereas the language text will generally lead beyond itself to what immediately preceded its utterance and to the context within which it was transmitted, an artistically elaborated text will multiply signification possibilities within itself, and it will involve the scholar in investigation of the techniques by which a succession of syntagms (all texts are such), when examined in terms of different reading programs, will prove susceptible to infinite mental reconstructions, each of which is productive of further sense.

Both these movements, the centrifugal toward reality and the centripetal within the sphere of the text, strive toward integration. The plurality of meanings unfolded by a text is one answer to our inability to say everything in explicit terms, to lay hold in words of every secret. Thus, the text will be all the richer in nonreferential communication, the more its sender is aware of the limits of understanding, of the obstacles to direct expression. The ineffable cannot be said. Its presence, though, can be communicated.

5. The Literary Difference

Differences between literary texts and other texts (which will be dealt with below) are not a matter of their nature but of their function and quality. So true is this that, between an ordinary text and a literary text, intermediate phases exist to which, as a rule, insufficient weight is accorded. Examples are oral narration of a happening when the scope is purely practical, institutionalized recitation of folk tales or myths, or singsong improvisation on basic vital rhythms. These are ordinary texts, and they prefigure or anticipate the literary text.

This fundamental unity is easily confirmed in the field of text materials—from symbols to metaphors, from motifs to themes. It is, in fact, a property of language, even of common language, to have recourse to techniques such as metaphor, metonymy, etc. (techniques which are thus not exclusively rhetorical). Literary language merely perfects the tendency. Even more interesting is the problem of theme and motif, because both must be united with all the stereotypes we employ to describe action and situations. In the wake of anthropology, folklore and literary analysis must work in common accord.

Among ways of illustrating the differences between the literary text and other texts, two are particularly efficacious. The first emphasizes the different character of the communication. Since literary communication is directed toward addressees who are quite unknown, and who stretch out into the future, it expects no reply, allows no feedback, introjects its own situation, and sets itself up as the code of itself. The second approach stresses a prevalence of the poetic function, i.e., the attention paid primarily to the form of the message rather than to any finality at the level of transmission or to any results to be obtained from the addressee.

I should like, though, to add a third mode, one less widely used as a formula for definition. Literature creates models of the world. This activity is an exact mirroring of the way we come to an awareness of the world by way of stereotypes in the cognitive order. Culture provides us with all the stereotypes we need to "express" reality, and they are arranged around the language. A writer, on the contrary, gives form to an internal reality, to a world, and he confers upon it a structure which is homologous to that of the world he has experienced. It is a model which is assimilated by the culture, and culture, when it does so, will render more effective, or will enrich, its heritage of stereotypes.

6. The Language System and the System of Languages

Linguistics and stylistics offer two seemingly contradictory images of the language. Linguistics, at least from the time of Saussure, has regarded the language as a rigid, functional system based on the concept of binary opposition (masculine and feminine, singular and plural, open and closed vowel, voiced and voiceless consonant, etc.) or, in the case of lexis, on the concept of semantic field. Words will unite to form sentences as rigid syntactic norms dictate. Despite a vastly different approach, generative linguistics has a not dissimilar image of the system.

Stylistics, on the contrary, stresses varieties within the system. It may present them as possible choices among words and forms which, while being semantically equivalent, are tonally different, or it may arrange into subsystems (registers, social varieties, trade jargon, etc.) the variants which the language offers, having them form strata of tonally connotated semantic equivalences. The language will then be seen as a set of subsystems.

The contrast is only apparent. Unity and rigidity do indeed apply to the system's phonetic and morphological elements. It is only with occasional variants that slight discrepancies or generational differences will exist, but they are never such as to compromise the whole. On the contrary, for lexis and sentence structure (for syntax to a lesser extent), the system breaks down into subsystems, though there will exist a substantial common, indeed predominant, connective of generally used elements. Difference in treatment is motivated by contents. Compactness will prevail for more abstract, formal elements; disintegration will prevail with material which is more sensitive to varieties in the sociocultural levels or in the occupational or ideological differences of the speakers and the variety of situations in which they may come to find themselves.

Thus, those scholars who have attempted to create a science of style have started out by correctly observing the fact that the language nearly always offers a plurality of choices with respect to referents whose denotation may be endowed with different tonal shadings. It is at this point, though, that the inadequacy of their techniques becomes apparent. In an overall study of the language, techniques have not been extended to embrace a description of the stratifications of the whole mass of speakers, while, in the study of literature, preference has been accorded to more explicitly intentional uses. It was not realized that in the literary text nothing escapes intention. What has no weight for one aspect (e.g., lexical choice) will have weight for another (e.g., for phonic values, for thematic cross-reference, etc.).

These considerations support the idea that study of the literary text should not be separated from study of other texts. On the contrary, what requires investigation is the special character of the use the literary text makes of what the language offers. Its main peculiarity is its commitment to the message as a semiotic whole. Each of its components will be linked in a close-meshed network of cross-references to all the others. This will be done in such a way that each element will reinforce the meaning potentials of the others.

One peculiarity to which adequate consideration is now accorded is the capacity of the literary text to reproduce in itself and to functionalize in terms of the addresser's intention, polarizations, and contrasts which, inside the language system, refer to stratifications and to antagonisms that are really present in the social structure. In this sense, the literary text, as well as being a model of the world, is a microcosm analogous to the macrocosm. The literary text, indeed, since it presents these polarizations dialectically, in a concise representation of the contexts within which they are realized (and which are evoked by art's capacity for illusion), in practice interprets them and moves beyond the static objectivity of a study whose character is descriptive.

7. Literary Production as Specialization

The so-called art of the word is of great complexity. Generation after generation of artists have striven to bring it to perfection and, in the form of the texts themselves, have handed down what they have discovered. The weight of literary influences is tangible evidence of this ideal continuity of endeavor. This is why, of all the subsystems of the language, literary language is one of the most tightly knit, one of the most resistant. Even in periods like our own, which attempt to break down the barriers of literary language, it still stands firm as a point of reference.

Literary language is sectioned in correspondence to the characteristics of genres. In any diachronic phase, genres will be clearly defined, though over time their characteristics and reciprocal relations will be mutable. While some scholars have attempted to stress the conventional nature of genres, and some have sought to seize upon evolutionary norms, others (first among them Goethe) have been prepared to believe that genres are, in some sense, categories. This is a conviction, not infrequently linked to an absolutization of Aristotle, which has proved too vital to be without foundation. The truth is that genres bring forth literary communication's different realizations.

Thus, we find an I-I communication in the lyric (where not only is an interlocutor unforeseen for the speaker but where the addressee is overshadowed or hidden by another, prior, intrasubjective addressee) and an I-YOU communication in theater, which simulates an everyday type of communication involving two or more speakers, each of whom in turn is addresser and addressee of the discourses. Epic and the novel make use of a narrative (diegetic) type of communication in which the addresser tells his addressee about third persons who are referred to as HE, SHE, and THEY, while their discourses are offered either directly (as in the theater) or indirectly, i.e., paraphrased, summarized by the narrator.

While these remain the three basic types of literary communication, the addresser-addressee relation has served as the starting point for other developments, in the sense that the "mediators" that a sender has decided to interpose between himself and his text's addressee are often complex and numerous. Thus, we find in the novel, alongside the narrator as protagonist or eyewitness, a plurality of points of view, a commutation series for participation or for ideal distancing. Theater, too, has admitted expedients which are diegetic in kind, and the "naturalness" of its dialogue is sometimes compromised, as is the I-YOU distinction of the actors and that of the spectators.

What remains fundamental, though, is recognition of genres as types of communication, and it is on this recognition that their distinctive function is based. Another analogous recognition is called for. Genres act as preselectors of communication. The fact that one is aware from the outset that a work belongs to a particular genre means that, to a considerable extent, information has already been given as to its type of subject matter, the mode of its treatment, its tone, etc. It is in terms of different forms (genres) that literary works introduce themselves.

Naturally enough, genres are not being put forward here as if they were primary forms of communication. They are historical individuals and can be classified most minutely into subspecies—various types of theatrical representation, various metrical forms (the sonnet, the *canzone,* the ode, etc.), various kinds of novels (sentimental, gothic, thriller, etc.). Genres and subgenres are, in such cases, rigidly codified—in the language used, in meter, in prose type, even in subject matter. The result is that the literary language, itself a subsystem of a given moment of the language, is further divided into subsets which correspond to the genres. This clear-cut apportioning of terrain ratifies a cataloguing of reality which has already been effected by the language.

8. Ideological Consequences

We have touched on the way in which language, even literary language, reflects differences, contrasts, and conflicts that are present in the body of society and are decisive for the way in which individuals come into contact with reality. This conflictual variety is in part determined, in part controlled, by ideologies, and no description of any state of the language can leave them out of account. In the field of literature, poetics constitutes a counterpart to ideologies. Every type of poetics is an ideology of literary production and obviously it is linked in some measure to socially current ideologies.

Whether we are faced with a poetics which is codified, and thus inevitably conservative, with a poetics which is a strongly motivated implied program, or, finally, with the kind of "shock-tactics" poetics to be met with in manifestos, we will always find ourselves dealing with a coherent series of literary programs, and of programs not merely literary, which the sender of a text will respect, though he may use his own personal tone of voice to do so.

Though it is linked to nonliterary ideology, poetics will not simply constitute its application to text practice. Since poetics is also a conception of the world and of life, what it does is to indicate points of reference for the modeling process which is the climax of a literary text's construction. For this reason, poetics, which in its construction aspects ensures the institution or application of genres, will also indicate the goals toward which they are (with all their formal specifications) to be directed. The history of poetics may be identified with the history of literature and of conceptions of the world, but due weight must be accorded to the dialectic between conservation and innovation, norm and transgression, tradition and invention. This is a dialectic which is brought into play by any activity but by artistic activity in particular.

9. Who Killed Invention?

What we have said so far has drawn attention to a marked degree of codification in verbal activity (and in many other activities not dealt with here). We have seen codification of our perceptions and representations, of the language with which we express them, of tonal varieties, of types of text, and of literary texts in particular, codification of content and of narrative causality, of symbols and of metaphors, and codification of conceptions of the world. The philosophers and literary critics who, especially in the wake of romanticism, celebrated the liberty of the creative act, might well have felt disconcerted.

Analogous considerations hold good for all the stereotypes whose existence has at one time or another been recognized: *topoi*, clichés, traditional metaphors, themes, and motifs. The very way in which we select reality in order to name it is, to a very large extent, preconstituted. But this stereotyping does not involve language and cultural products alone. There also exists a stereotyping which demonstrates the very conditions of our existence in the world and the categories of our perceiving, and the modes of our interpreting, reality. It is along this road that we must advance if we are to discover universals of narration (or, better, of discoursiveness).

We are far from celebrating any triumph of mechanicalness. It is merely a matter of transferring to other aspects of literary production what has long been known about language. With all its closed or at any rate stable repertoires, with all its rules and its norms, language does not exercise a repressive action on our need to express ourselves. Indeed, its very codification acts as the premiss for the freedom of our discourse. Given that language, first and foremost, must communicate so that it can be understood, it follows that its objective elements must be conveyed in such a way that they will conform to an institution whose validity is general.

On the model of the language, it is possible to describe the position of the addresser of any text, whether ordinary or artistic, and to see it as one moment in a semiotics of sign production in which all of us participate. As Peirce has shown, each of our representations is already a sign which, together with its explanation, constitutes another sign. It will require for its explication yet another explanation, and will thus institute yet another sign and so on to infinity (unlimited semiosis). In sign processes, in short, we seize upon the transition from the sphere of sense to that of thought, from configuration to construction, from imitation to transformation. In no sense is inventive (or creative) activity being denied: it is merely being pointed out that such activity will operate inside sign processes, transforming or variously combining signs rather than creating them. (The elaboration of systems of signs is a slow process, one which is collective and which is not conscious).

Considerations of much the same kind may be applied to the relation between invention and reality. Fiction would be insipid and unintelligible were there no references to the world of our experience. The worlds the writer forges are possible worlds, homologous in whole or in part to our own. They interest us precisely because of what they say about the world we know, about how it was, how it is, how it might be, how it should or should not be. Thus, the text, formulated in the first instance on the basis of reality, is in a position to break away from reality, but it does so in order to show it in another light. Our living and our imagining is a movement from one text to another.

References

Bachtin, M. M.
    1975. *Voprosy literatury i estetiki*. Moscow: Chudožestvennaja literatura. (English translation. Holquist, M. 1981. *The Dialogic Imagination: Four Essays by Mikhail Bakhtin*. Austin: University of Texas Press.)

Beaugrande, R.-A. de, and Dressler, W. U.
    1981. *Introduction to Text Linguistics*. London: Longmans.

Chomsky, N.
    1975. *Reflections on Language*. New York: Pantheon Books.

Hempfer, K. W.
    1973. *Gattungstheorie: Information und Synthese*. Munich: Fink.

Humboldt, W. von.
    1841. *Werke*, vol. 3, *Schriften zur Sprachphilosophie*. 3d ed. 1969. Darmstadt: Wissenschaftliche Buchgesellschaft.
Lotman, Ju. M.
    1970. *Struktura chudožestvennogo teksta*. Moscow: Iskusstvo. (English translation. 1977. *The Structure of the Artistic Text*. Ann Arbor: University of Michigan Press.)
Lotman, Ju. M., and Uspenskij, B. A.
    1975. *Tipologia della cultura*. Milan: Bompiani.
Peirce, Ch. S.
    1931–1958. *Collected Papers of Charles Sanders Peirce*. 8 vols. Cambridge, Mass.: Belknap Press of Harvard University Press.
Segre, C.
    1974. *Le strutture e il tempo*. Turin: Einaudi. (English translation. 1979. *Structures and Time*. Chicago: University of Chicago Press.
    1979. *Semiotica filologica: Testo e modelli culturali*. Turin: Einaudi.
    1984. *Teatro e romanzo*. Turin: Einaudi.
Terracini, B.
    1962. *Lingua libera e libertà linguistica: Introduzione alla linguistica storica*. 2d ed. 1970. Turin: Einaudi.

1.
Discourse

1. The dictionaries give two main meanings of the word *discourse:* in one sense, it is the exposition of a given argument whether written or delivered in public; in the other, it is "the act of discoursing," "the act of language communication." Certain expressions stress a sense of development: one may "break off" or "take up" a discourse. And accidents can happen: one may "lose the thread" of a discourse. It is to the second meaning that language analysis refers us when it talks of parts of speech (or discourse). The discourse of the first definition is a product of the second definition's discourse. Less solemn products are day-to-day conversations, and they, in their turn, may be described as "discourses." (It is to them that grammar alludes when it speaks of *oratio recta* or *oratio obliqua:* of discourse or speech which is direct or indirect according to whether it is given in its original form or is transposed into an account of it given by a narrator). It is the semantics of the Latin word *oratio* which underlies this basic distinction; *discourse* in the Romance languages inherits the senses of *oratio* (including its grammatical senses).

Narrative texts are a good example of the semantic polyvalence of the word *discourse*. In fact, they will generally include discourses imagined as really pronounced by the characters (oratorial discourses or, more frequently, ordinary discourses), but, when they are considered as a whole, they make up one single discourse (an act of language communication) which has been composed by an author and is directed to a reader. Thus, inside discourse as an act of communication, it might seem possible to contrast narration, on the one hand, and written and spoken discourses, on the other. This is exactly what is done by Benveniste (1959), who specifies that the aorist, the imperfect, and the pluperfect are peculiar to narration, where use of the third person goes almost unchallenged; on the contrary, the basic tenses of discourse (which excludes only the aorist) are the present, the future, and the perfect, while the persons used may be the *I* and *you* proper to dialogue alongside the third person itself.

But written or spoken discourses often invade the space of narration. The best-known example is indirect speech. Propositions dependent on *verba dicendi* state what the characters are supposed to have said, i.e., in effect, discourses are narrated in the same way as actions and situations are narrated. The most typical case of this ambivalence between narration and discourse is so-called free indirect discourse, identified by Bally (1912) and much used in modern narration. Free indirect discourse differs from indirect speech because there are no *verba dicendi;* it differs from direct speech because the author of the statements is not referred to by means of a first person pronoun but by a third person pronoun and because, for the most part, the verbs used are not in the present tense.

What needs to be stressed most strongly is that transition from direct speech to indirect, or to free indirect, speech is not brought about by any mechanical transposition of the syntactical framework. It is clear that choice of a given discourse or narrative type will imply from the outset the specific orientation of the means to be used for its linguistic expression. This is an initial indication of the existence of laws proper to discourse, laws which precede, and which underlie, its succession of sentences.

In recent decades, the second of our two meanings, "act of language communication," has enjoyed a diffusion as symptomatic as is the fact that so few attempts have been made to mark off and define whatever changes or involutions in values may be involved. Hardly any dictionaries of linguistics define the word *discourse* (there are exceptions: among them, Dubois, Giacomo, Greimas and Courtés, etc.). Of the many books which include our term in their titles, only a few offer a definition. The fact is that the attention devoted to discourse is the result of a wide variety of interests and interventions. Only in part do they converge, and the word is in consequence allowed to accumulate connotations unchecked.

2. For reliable points of references we may have recourse to Saussure and his followers. Saussure's antinomy *langue/parole* and his conception of syntagm will amply repay careful consideration. For Saussure (1906–11), the *langue* is a superpersonal reality which is counterposed to such use as, at specific moments, single individuals will make of it. The antinomy *langue/parole* thus serves to distinguish "1) what is social from what is individual; and 2) what is essential from what is ancillary and more or less accidental" (p. 30; English translation, pp. 13–14). Those who belong to a given language group have in their language a treasure in common. Each member will possess it to a greater or lesser degree, but it is its collective possession which constitutes the factor of the group's linguistic cohesion.

When the language, the *langue*, is used, it is made to pass from potency to act. All of the personal factors (whether of the articulatory or of the psychological order) which constitute *parole*, or speech, then come into play. In short, *parole* is "an individual act of the will and the intelligence, in which one must distinguish: 1) the combinations through which the speaker uses the code provided by the language in order to express his own thought, and 2) the psycho-physical mechanism which enables him to externalise these combinations" (Saussure 1906–11, pp. 30–31; Eng. trans., p. 14).

Saussure's definition owes its clarity to the antinomic nature of its expression. We also learn that "a language is necessary in order that speech should be intelligible and produce all its effects. But speech also is necessary in order that a language may be established. Historically speech always takes precedence"

(p. 37; Eng. trans., p. 19). And we are told elsewhere that "linguistic structure we take to be language minus speech. It is the whole set of linguistic habits which enables the speaker to understand and to make himself understood" (p. 112; Eng. trans., p. 77). In any event, for Saussure the existence of two kinds of linguistics is essential. One will be for the language, the *langue*, one will be for speech, *parole*. It is to the former that most weight is given, and it is accorded preeminence on the theoretical plane. References to the virtuality that is *langue* do not, however, lead to a satisfactory definition. Saussure tells us that the *langue* is a "system of signs" (p. 32; Eng. trans., p. 14), and this would seem to involve primarily lexis and morphology. But, since we have just been told that "it [is] possible for dictionaries and grammars to give us a faithful representation of language" (p. 32; Eng. trans., p. 15), we might well expect a more complete involvement of grammatical and syntactical norms.

The drawbacks of this general distinction become evident in the treatment of syntagmatic and associative relations. Here is what Saussure says of syntagms: "Words as used in discourse, strung together one after another, enter into relations based on the linear character of languages. Linearity precludes the possibility of uttering two words simultaneously. They must be arranged consecutively in spoken sequence. Combinations based on sequentiality may be called *syntagmas*" (p. 170; Eng. trans., p. 170). Associative relations are discussed immediately after this:

> Outside the context of discourse words having something in common are associated in the memory. In this way they form groups, the members of which may be related in various ways. For instance, the word *enseignement* ('teaching') will automatically evoke a host of other words: *enseigner* ('to teach'), *reseigner* ('to inform'), etc., or *armement* ('armament'), *changement* ('change'), etc., or *éducation*('education'), *apprentissage* ('apprenticeship'). All these words have something or other linking them. This kind of connection between words is of quite a different order. It is not based on linear sequence. It is a connection in the brain. Such connections are part of that accumulated store which is the form the language takes in an individual's brain. We shall call these *associative relations* (p. 170: Eng. trans., pp. 170–71).

Syntagmatic relations are conditioned by the linearity of language, which rules out the possibility of pronouncing two elements at one and the same time. Associative relations, on the contrary, have their seat in memory, and they are not subject to spatial limitations.

Here, too, at first sight, everything is perfectly straightforward. On the one hand, we have effective relations *in praesentia*, and they are conditioned by the linearity which is proper to facts of speech. On the other hand, we have virtual relations *in absentia* (coexisting in memory) and it is of these that the *langue* is constituted. It is at once obvious, however, that the model used for associative relations (today we would describe them as paradigmatic) is that of lexical structure, whereas that used for syntagmatic relations is the syntactic model. In other words, the elements involved in definition of these two types of relation are not quite the same.

The difficulties encountered become clear as progressive attempts are made to assimilate ever-broader syntactic elements to the *langue*. Saussure at first accepted as syntagmatic the union of two or more consecutive units, because they were codified or at least lexicalized. From the compound *re-lire*, he went on to include subject + verb groups *(nous sortirons)*, habitual attributes *(la vie humaine)*, and whole concise sentences *(Dieu est bon*, etc.) (p. 171). He then left the way open to locutions and expressions "whose usual character results from the peculiarities of their meaning or their syntax" (p. 172) and ended up attributing to the *langue* "all syntagma types built up on regular forms" (p. 173). This includes sentences as well, insofar as they realize combination rules proper to the language.

And yet, if our earlier definitions of *langue* and *parole* are to be maintained, any sentence, spoken or written, so long as it is not lexicalized like the first examples quoted, will be the product of an individual initiative. Furthermore, it will unfold in terms of a strict linearity, and, as a consequence, it will belong to *parole*. Saussure is aware of this possible objection, though he does not help matters by considering that "the characteristic of speech /*parole*/ is freedom of combination: so the first question is whether all syntagms are equally free" (p. 127; Eng. trans., p. 122).

Let us take any grammatically correct sentence. If we say that it was already virtually present in the *langue*, then it will no longer be clear which language facts we ought to define as *individual* rather than as *social*, nor, to go back to the quotation from Saussure (p. 30; Eng. trans., pp. 13–14), what should be regarded as accessory and more or less accidental, other than phonation elements of little weight or perhaps transgressions against ordinary usage. Saussure himself is not prepared to move too far in this direction. Indeed, his conclusion has a conciliatory tone unusual for him: "Where syntagmas are concerned, however, one must recognise the fact that there is no clear boundary separating the language, as confirmed by communal use, from speech, marked by freedom of the individual. In many cases it is difficult to assign a combination of units to one or the other. Many combinations are the product of both, in proportions which cannot be accurately measured" (p. 173; Eng. trans., p. 123). The fact that post-Saussurian linguists have adopted the term *discourse* is in line with their attempts either to resolve the *langue/parole* antinomy or to clarify the nature and function of syntagms. Buyssens (1967), for example, returns to the distinction, already quoted, between "1) the combinations through which the speaker uses the code provided by the language in order to express his own thought, and 2) the psycho-physical mechanism which enables him to externalise these combinations" (Saussure 1906–11, p. 31; Eng. trans., p. 14). He reserves the term *parole* for the second element, i.e., for the "the flow of sound which comes from the speaker's mouth," and calls the first element *discours*. The relation between *parole* and *discours* for Buyssens is identical to that which exists between sound and phoneme. On the one hand, we have a signification act, speech or *parole;* on the other, its functional part, discourse or *discours*. The concept of *discours* is intended to eliminate the *langue/parole* dichotomy. If it is true that *parole* is made up of phonic and acoustic phenomena which are in no sense linguistic, it is, on the other hand, impossible to study the sum of states of consciousness and potential relations which are present to the members of a community of speakers and which form its *langue*. Discourse alone, for Buyssens, will enable us to determine the linguistic system. "There is but one linguistics: all the rest is no more than psychology, physiology or acoustics" (1967, pp. 40–42).

An unpublished note of Saussure himself, now in Starobinski (1971, p. 14; Eng. trans., pp. 3–4), shows that Saussure took the same path:

> Language is only created with a view to discourse, but what separates discourse from language? What allows one to assert at a given moment that language has *become active as discourse?*
>
> Various concepts are present in language (that is, clothed in linguistic form), such as *beef, lake, sky, red, sad, five, to split, to see.* At what moment, and by virtue of what operation, what interplay between them, what conditions, do these concepts form *discourse?*
>
> The sequence of these words, however enriched it might be by the ideas it evokes, will never make any human being understand that another human being, by pronouncing it, wishes to convey something specific to him. What do we need to indicate that by using terms available to language we wish to signify a specific thing? This is the same question as that of knowing what *discourse* is, and at first sight the answer is simple. Discourse exists, in however rudimentary a fashion and in ways we do not understand, to assert a link between two concepts invested with linguistic form. Language, on the other hand, only makes preliminary recognition of isolated concepts which do not acquire the significance of thought until links have been established among them.

Here, *langue* is already being matched against *discours* rather than against *parole,* and it is being suggested that discourse is linking the words of the *langue* together with the aim of signification.

Let us return to Buyssens, for he initiates a series of reflections on discourse that is no less significant. A discourse is a complete communication act; it is, therefore, one which may contain a considerable number of sentences. Hence, we may well find that the values "language communication act" and "exposition of a given argument" are identical. (Work on discourse is, at the moment, moving along these lines). By starting out from discourse, i.e., from the major unit, in order to arrive, by way of successive segmentations, at discourse and sentence units and then at words, monemes, and phonemes, Buyssens eliminates at one blow Saussure's problem of the relation between syntagms and *langue* (or *parole*). His approach, though, poses two further problems, and in more recent decades it is these that linguistics has attempted to deal with. The first of them concerns the links between successive discourse units, which, since they belong to a single act of communication, can hardly avoid conforming to formal rules of connection. The second concerns the arbitrary nature of the segmentation effected by the individual speaker. It is a fact that one and the same meaning unit can be articulated in such a way as to form sentences different in type and of different length.

Benveniste, on the contrary, carries Saussure's distinction between associative relations and syntagmatic relations even further. He has no hesitation in placing the sentence and more all-embracing units in the second group. Saussure's dichotomy is thereby maintained, but recourse must be had to a different antinomy, to *langue/discours* rather than to *langue/parole*.

> The sentence is substantially marked off from other language entities in so far as it does not constitute a class of distinctive units which, like phonemes or morphemes, are virtual members of higher units. Underlying this difference is the fact that the sentence contains signs, but is not in itself a sign. Once this has been recognized, it becomes clear that there is an antithesis between sets of signs met with at lower levels and entities met with at this level.
>
> Phonemes, morphemes, words (lexemes) can be counted; they are finite in number. Sentences are not.
>
> Phonemes, morphemes, words (lexemes) have a distribution on their respective levels but have a use on higher levels. Sentences have neither distribution nor any similar kind of use.
>
> The inventory of the uses of a word might well know no end; an inventory of the uses of the sentence could not even be begun.
>
> The sentence, undefined creation, varies without limit; it is the highroad of language in action. What must be deduced is that with the sentence we leave behind the field of language as a system of signs in order to enter another universe, that of the language as an instrument of communication and whose expression is discourse.
>
> The two universes are then quite different despite the fact that they embrace the same reality, and they give rise to two different linguistics despite the fact that their paths cross in continuation. On the one hand, there is the *langue,* a set of formal signs which are brought to light thanks to well-defined techniques, arranged in classes on different planes, combined in structures and in systems; on the other hand, there is the manifestation of *langue* in live communication.
>
> The sentence is a unit in so far as it is a segment of discourse, not because it might be distinctive with respect to other units of the same level, something which, as we have seen, does not happen. Nonetheless, it is a complete unit endowed with sense and reference: sense, because it is invested with significance, and reference, because it refers to a given situation. Those who communicate have just this in common, a certain situational reference without which communication as such cannot be effected, since sense is intelligible though reference remains unknown (Benveniste 1962, p. 274).

These affirmations, if taken to extremes, might seem to imply the exclusion of syntax from the sphere of the *langue* (an unacceptable decision, especially in the light of recent developments in linguistics). They are, though, particularly felicitous when they speak of a necessary connection between sentence and situation and stress that the aim is communication. A great deal of research has subsequently been undertaken in this sense; and, also in this sense, it has proved possible to surmount the divarication (implicit in Benveniste's statements) between semantics of the word and semantics of the sentence (see, e.g., Benveniste's 1969 article *Sémiologie de la langue*, where he makes the questionable suggestion that we should speak of the semiotics of the word and of the semantics of discourse).

Denial of the sign value of the sentence, which in Benveniste's analysis is uncompromising, would require more detailed investigation. If we require that signs should have a codified utilization value and constitute closed repertoires, then there is no doubt that sentences are not signs but sign complexes. Evident, though, is the fact that sentences have a signifier (the sum of the words that constitute them) and a signified, which may be delimited by the use of paraphrases which will be the equivalent, at least in substance, to the given sentences. And this is not all. The words which compose a sentence will usually have many meanings; it is their combination into sentences which selects from these meanings the one which will effectively prove valid in the discourse.

Thus, words are signs only within the sentence. This means that, whatever solution we offer for the terminological problem, it will be difficult to make any clear-cut distinction between the (semiotic) sphere of words and the (communicative) sphere of sentences and of discourse.

3. It is impossible to classify various discourse types empirically. Of great interest, though, are the different attempts that have been made to specify linguistic functions (i.e., the purposes the locutor attributes to his utterances). They are fundamental for the establishment of discourse. The frame of reference employed in these attempts is the communication schema, and functions are related to the predominance of one or another of the elements in play. Bühler, for example, set out from a triangle which has at its apexes the addresser, the addressee, and the object of the discourse. He then made a distinction between an expressive function *(Ausdruckfunktion)*, which enables the speaker to characterize himself; a representative function *(Darstellungsfunktion)*, whose aim is to describe extralinguistic reality; and a conative function *(Appellfunktion)*, which attempts to act on the listener. While following Bühler, Jakobson gave a far more complex representation, in line with the more complex verbal communication schema that he adopted (where the message lies between addresser and addressee and where account is taken of the context within which the communication takes place, of the code on the basis of which the message is formulated, and the contact, i.e., the physical channel and the psychological connection which make it possible to communicate). In relation to this schema, we have a referential function, which is oriented toward the context; an expressive or emotive function, which concentrates on the addresser and expresses his attitude with respect to the content of the message; a conative function, oriented toward the addressee with the aim of influencing him; a metalinguistic function, which serves to verify common possession of the code on the part of the two interlocutors; a poetic function,

which concentrates on the message; a phatic function, which establishes, maintains, or interrupts contact.

These functions are copresent in discourses, and their characterization will depend merely on the predominance of one or the other of them. "Although we distinguish six basic aspects of language, we could, however, hardly find verbal messages that would fulfill only one function. The diversity lies not in a monopoly of some one of these several functions but in a different hierarchical order of functions." Even within literary genres, a whole play of functions will exist. "The peculiarities of diverse poetic genres imply a differently ranked participation of the other verbal functions along with the dominant poetic function. Epic poetry, focused on the third person, strongly involves the referential function of language; the lyric, oriented toward the first person, is intimately linked with the emotive function; poetry of the second person is imbued with the conative function and is either supplicatory or exhortative, depending on whether the first person is subordinated to the second one or the second to the first" (Jakobson 1958, pp. 353 and 357).

The function system recently put forward by Halliday (1970, pp. 140–65) is ternary like that of Bühler. The ideative function serves for the expression of content in relation to the speaker's experience of the real world. The interpersonal function places the speaker in a position to interact with others on the basis of a preliminary definition of his own position with respect to the existence of social groups. Lastly, the textual function is concerned with the way language is linked to itself and to the situation in which it is used, and it puts the speaker in a position to construct and understand discourses. These functions represent three successive phases of sentence formulation, so that they are of little use when our aim is characterization of discourse.

Where attempts at empirical realization are concerned, mention should be made of Kinneavy (1971). He lists various types of discourse with reference to a ternary schema of the Bühler type. It takes in expressive discourses oriented toward the speaker, persuasive discourses oriented toward the hearer, and discourses oriented toward the sign which are divided into referential discourses and literary discourses. Comparison with Jakobson's proposals is illuminating. Lyric poetry, where Jakobson saw poetic and emotive functions as predominating, for Kinneavy should fall under literary discourse with a function that is prevalently poetic. Kinneavy, in fact, is forced to abandon Jakobson's "dialectical" definitions. What is more, once he dedicates a specific section to literary discourse, he blocks any possibility of differentiating literary genres on the basis of the presence of various functions. So rigid a position does help us, though, to appreciate the double level on which linguistic functions act. There is a level of immediate manifestation (for which it may be said that interjections belong to the emotive function and imperatives to the conative function); there is an artificial and symbolic level (and it is only within this that one can legitimately speak of an emotive function for an act like poetic invention, so eminently a matter of reflection). The second level may be further characterized on the basis of a statistical consideration, which will allow a discourse to be defined as emotive (because emotive elements are prevalent), poetical (because poetical elements are prevalent), and so forth.

It seems clear to me that findings for functions are far more consistent on the first level than they are on the second level and that their statistical consideration is inevitably approximate. Recognizing, for example, the prevalence of the poetic function in a literary text comes close to being tautological. On the other hand, other functions (let us say emotive or conative functions) are either present in symbolic form (there is no emotion, only representation of an emotion; there is no attempt to influence the listener but a representation of such an attempt; a theatrical text will come to mind), or they act in a way which is different from that which communication theory envisages (a poetic text may act on a reader or listener's behavior as well, though it will do so through the emotive reactions which it produces in him with the elements of its message rather than through any conative function).

The sphere within which recourse to functions might prove convincing is more probably that of borderline discourses. I am thinking of oratory, where the conative element is seconded by the poetic function, or of travel books or journalistic accounts, in which the referential function may well depend heavily on the poetic. In general, I believe that the function which combines most readily with the others is the poetic function. This is natural enough, given that it would be very difficult to send a message without at least a minimal amount of concentration on it. And, vice versa, concentrating on the message is absolutely unable to cancel the message itself; once deprived of its communicative aim, any message would cease to be such. Awareness of this may assist us on the way to even more subtle analysis of literary communication and, at the same time, will limit any potential taxonomy of linguistic functions.

4. Discourse is the maximum language unit. Its sense is self-contained, and it corresponds to a fully realized communication situation—hence, the terms *situationeme* (Koch) and *behavioreme* (Pike), which are used to indicate a *situation unit* to which a *discourse unit* corresponds (in §7 we shall return to the importance of situation). Discourse is made up of *utterances*, (in French, *énonciation;* in German, *Äusserung*), groups of sentences pronounced by a single person and delimited by silences, by distinct pauses, or by the utterances of other persons; next come sentences, which are syntactically complete units. Lesser elements (words, phonemes, etc.) enjoy no autonomy in terms of discourse. Obviously, discourse may sometimes be made up of one single utterance; and the utterance, of one single sentence.

Traditional studies of syntax and linguistics have always focused attention on the sentence. The aim of linguistic study of discourse is to discover the laws and regularities which in any discourse govern the cohesion between sentences and utterances, for the discourse itself assumes a trans-sentential dimension. Classical rhetoric gives evidence of many observations which are trans-sentential in character. Rhetoricians devoted their attention to *dispositio*, i.e., to the way in which the demonstrative moments to a speech are linked together, and to *elocutio*, i.e., to the way its linguistic elements are connected. The writers of classical treatises include a great many rhetorical figures whose role is to group a certain number of sentences under a single head. Thus, we have anaphora, repetition of the same word or word group at the beginning of successive elements (verses or sentences); epiphora, repetition at the end rather than at the beginning; *complexio,* which unites the peculiarities of the two preceding figures; *polyptoton,* which gives us the same word in different clauses while changing its inflection; *reflexio,* or antanaclasis, which in dialogic exchange gives us the same word with different meanings. Various kinds of parallelism among sentences are also found; sometimes they are related semantically (*interpretatio*), sometimes completely or partially differentiated in meaning (*subiunctio* and *disiunctio*). We find, in addition, antitheses and comparisons.

In the field of modern linguistics, the "functional analyses" of the Czech Mathesius (1928) had already moved beyond study of those ties which are internal to the utterance. Every utterance will normally contain a *theme*, i.e., a part which refers to facts earlier expounded by the discourse and to facts otherwise known or which are to be taken as read, and a *rheme*, a part which contains such new information as the utterance is framed to furnish. (American critics have used *topic* and *comment* instead of *theme* and *rheme*.) The importance of this analysis lies in the fact that *theme*, at the same time that it refers us to earlier parts of the discourse, takes us beyond the limits of the sentence. What is more, Mathesius and more recent representatives of the Prague School have effectively emphasized that the unity of a discourse is guaranteed by the very fact that it is an act of communication. (They speak of "communication dynamics.")

Present-day exponents of the Prague School analyze long discourses on the basis of a variety of types of progression between theme and rheme. We find linear progression, when the rheme (topic) of one sentence becomes the theme (comment) of the following sentence (I met a colleague. He said hello.); maintenance of the topic (My colleague is called John. He is an excellent scholar. His works are well known.); block progression, when the rheme is split up into a number of themes (We met two soldiers. The first . . .; the second. . . .), etc. (Daneš 1970).

Related to, and parallel with, these investigations of the Prague School are such fairly recent undertakings as Pike's *tagmemics* and the *Textlinguistik* of the Germans and the Dutch. It should be remarked that, although the term *discourse* is still used in the United States, the Germans, like Hjelmslev before them, prefer the term *text* (not very happily); for them it embraces not only written texts but oral narration, dialogues, etc., as well.

We shall limit ourselves here to underlining some of the elements which *Textlinguistik* has brought to light in an attempt to determine the unity of discourse. We shall not, however, dwell on the discussions to which each element might lend itself. For the moment, our exposition will be merely descriptive:

Recurrence: for example, "*I saw a* car. *The* car was blue."

Paraphrase: "*He lives* with me, at home. *Under* my roof."

Co-reference, i.e., a referent common to one or more words. The most frequent cases, which are also grammaticized, are those of pronouns and verb substitution forms like *to do, to make*, etc. With an extension of the rhetorical term, the use of substitution forms after coreferential terms is called anaphoric and, when it precedes them, cataphoric. Coreference is often effected by means of words which include or imply conceptually the concept expressed by words used earlier: "*Peter saw a* motor-bike. *The* machine *shone in the sunshine*" (Dressler 1972).

The phenomenon of semantic contiguity is a much more extensive one (and one much less easy to classify). It is found when the terms employed by an utterance share common semantic features: "*I was* driving *down the* motorway *when quite suddenly the* engine *began to make a strange noise. I stopped the* car, *and when I opened the* bonnet *I saw that the* radiator *was boiling*." Even before a *car* is spoken of directly, the word *motorway* has introduced us to the semantic domain of the automobile.

If we go on and examine a discourse (or text) in its totality, we will take note of the marks which serve as an indication of its beginning and end, while the unfolding of the utterances can be considered within the framework of the listener's or reader's expectation horizon (for, against this, the adequacy and correctness of each single utterance will be measured). The unfolding of the utterance can be defined further in terms of its succession of verbal moods, tenses, and aspects. When a text is read aloud, intonation plays a fundamental role in its clarification.

Of no less importance for its implications is Harris's article "Discourse Analysis" (1952, p. 1). Two problems are expounded, and attempts are made to resolve them. "The first is the problem of continuing descriptive linguistics beyond the limits of a single sentence at a time. The other is the question of correlating 'culture' and language (i.e., non-linguistic and linguistic behavior)." These two problems are complementary: if the language never achieves realization in the form of isolated words or sentences but always in the form of discourses, spoken or written, the connection between the sentences of such discourses will be effected by the situation within which they are articulated. Thus, it is probable, even if not inevitable, that similar situations will call forth similar discourses, and we might then go on and envisage as legitimate the possibility of a typology.

Harris does not dwell on relations with the situation. He does, though, bring a wide range of analytical techniques into play. We might turn to his own description:

> Discourse analysis performs the following operations upon any single text. It collects those elements (or sequences of elements) which have identical or equivalent environments of other elements within a sentence, and considers them to be equivalent to each other (i.e., members of the same equivalence class). Material which does not belong to any equivalence class is associated with

the class member to which it is grammatically most closely tied. The sentences of the text are divided into intervals, each a succession of equivalence classes, in such a way that each resulting interval is maximally similar in its class composition to other intervals of the text. The succession of intervals is then investigated for the distribution of classes which it exhibits, in particular for the patterning of class occurrence (pp. 29–30).

These are the easily identifiable accents of a distributional approach proper to Harris and to part of the American School (Bloomfield, etc.). If nothing else, it might be thought to enjoy the advantage of a mechanization of the techniques it adopts, since it takes no account of the meanings of words or of any intention on the part of the author. Subsequent developments of the method (for example, those of Hiz), and attempts to put it into practice, have forced recognition of the necessity to give weight to the semantic aspects of discourse. Among the expedients adopted for an automatic analysis of discourse, it will suffice to mention recourse to the mediation of a metalanguage with the intention of avoiding the synonymic, polysemic, and homonymic aspects of natural language, to say nothing of the syntactical turns of speech which are equivalent in meaning though not in form (allotaxies) or equal in form but not in meaning (homotaxies). This involves, first and foremost, the constitution of conceptual lexicons relative to the scientific spheres to which the texts belong and, then, the formulation of principles for syntactic rewriting which will make it possible to establish analytical relations among the key concepts that have been brought to light (Gardin 1974). On other occasions, recourse to electronic elaboration makes it necessary to schematize, in terms of operations of the utmost simplicity, the semantic and syntactic transformation processes which are as a rule effected by the reader-interpreter.

5. In giving details of discourse analysis, we have observed the inseparability (similar to that which exists for words) between sentential and trans-sentential signifier and signified. Perception of what is signified is effected, for the addressee as for the linguist, by listening to, or by reading, the signifier. Modern and contemporary linguistics has elaborated the most sophisticated techniques in order to describe this perception insofar as it concerns the meaning of sentences. We shall attempt here to deal with modalities of perception when larger units, the utterances or the totality of a discourse, are involved.

First and foremost, we should call to mind linearity, a principle already formulated by Saussure. The constituent elements of discourse (phonemes, morphemes, words, sentences, utterances) follow one another; they are never pronounced together. It has been maintained that the principle of linearity is violated by unsystematized prosodic elements, by intonation in particular (hence, the adjective *suprasegmental*, used to designate these facts). In effect, intonation rests on certain syllables rather than on others, or it imposes a given rhythm on a succession of syllables. But no reading of a sentence is without intonation; a different intonation will confer a different meaning. A sentence will always be intoned in one way or another, and two (or more) possible intonations of one and the same sentence will, in reality, be two different sentences. A language act, therefore, cannot divorce itself from the temporal dimension.

The understanding of discourse units is, on the contrary, effected in distinct moments and with different temporality. Whether listening or reading is involved, every sentence is assimilated as its elements succeed each other (so that the receiver is made to conform to the linearity of the discourse); comprehension constitutes a second moment, when what is seized upon conceptually is the overall meaning of the sentence, now distinct from linearity (in fact, different languages use different word order to represent the same meaning). This process is repeated for the sentence that follows, except that, at its end, what is realized is not just the overall meaning of the second sentence but (in a third moment) the overall meaning of both first and second sentences, when they belong to the same utterance. The same procedure will apply to all of the successive sentences of an utterance.

From this elementary description, two consequences of considerable importance can be deduced. First, the division of discourse into sentences is arbitrary: almost always what has been said in one sentence might well have been said in two, and vice versa. Second, as reading (or listening) goes forward, the adding together of the meanings of the sentences will become more and more summary, given the limits of our memory.

In fact, the specific conditions of a text's reading reduce the succession of the sentences of its discourse to a "synthesis in memory," given that it is impossible to bear in mind simultaneously all of the constituent elements while mastering any extension greater than that of the sentence (Segre 1974, pp. 15–19; Eng. trans., pp. 10–13).

What is assimilated in reading, what is subsequently retained of the text, is a paraphrase in a progressively summary form. And, however disturbing the thought, it must be recognized that there is no way out of the dilemma between (1) lingering over single sentences of the discourse as they are perceived in their original linguistic formulation and (2) dominating the discourse as a whole in the aspect of its synthesis in memory.

It must not be deduced, from what has been said, that linguistic elements are important only at the moment in which a sentence is read. Both reader and critic (the difference is merely one of awareness) undoubtedly effect a synthesis in memory of the discourse's denotative content, one which is paraphrastic. At one and the same time, they make observations of a formal character which have trans-sentential meaning elements (connotative in nature) as their object. Reading thus enriches the synthesis in memory by comparing, as the reading moves forward, the formal elements that have already been recorded with those progressively encountered. This is a dynamic representation of discourse assimilation, given that we have already shown that it is impossible simply to add up the meanings of the single sentences.

In such a dynamic representation, it is easy to accommodate findings which concern trans-sentential signifier-signified relations. I shall merely touch upon key words and theme words, which make manifest on the verbal plane (and in a way which can be evidenced through mechanical means) the predominance in a given discourse of concepts or concept systems and stylistic vectors, which in the lexicon of the discourse reproduce parallelograms of forces involving the leading ideas of the message. In general, it can be stated that these two main lines of approach—one based on content, the other formal—need to be integrated in any exhaustive analysis in the same way in which they are integrated in reading.

But are they always integrated? In some cases the signifier of the discourse seems to enjoy an autonomy of its own. One need only mention the visual effects which in written texts are produced by the way words and sentences are arranged on the page. The most obvious example is that of poetry, at least in periods when it is the custom to begin anew at the end of each line. In modern poetry, one will call to mind the importance of the "blank space" which stands opposed to the printed part of a lyric. Alexandrian and medieval *carmina figurata* made even more play with the graphic layout of the page, and we have Apollinaire's *Calligrammes* and "concrete poetry," etc. In compositions of this kind, words are employed as elements in a design whose overall iconic significance corroborates and accentuates that of the text.

If we limit ourselves to language execution, the first examples of the autonomous activity of the signifier are provided by onomatopoeia, in so far as phenomena of this type are to be found beyond the bounds of already lexicalized formulae. It is well known that every language has different onomatopoeias for the same meanings (English *cock-a-doodle-doo* is *chic-chirichí* in Italian, *cocorico* in French, *kikeriki* in German, and *kukareku* in Russian). An Italian would not be able to interpret *cock-a-doodle-do* as "the crowing of the cock." Akin to onomatopoeias are such phonosymbolic forms as *zigzag*. It must, though, be stated that, even when they are created extempore, onomatopoeias will conform to the phonetic tendencies of the language. The onomatopoeias in American comic books, which Italian publishers as a rule retain unvaried, often sound most exotic to the ears of their new public.

Even single sounds have values attributed to them—weight, energy, and so on (*i* is supposed to suggest the idea of the small and the acute; *t* and *k* seem hard with respect to the softness of *l* and *m*, etc.). Such values are frequently expressed in synesthesic form, for example, by making the vowels correspond to colors. Here we are dealing with impressions which do not lend themselves to generalization even for the speakers of a given language. At best, phonic affinities can be found for certain series of consonants: fricatives might remind us of rustling sounds, *r* of vibrations, etc. In general, though, these effects take on a real consistency when they can be estimated in terms of their convergence with the meaning of words or sentences. It is then that they often make their appearance inside already codified "figures of the word," such as alliteration:

> graffia li spirti ed iscoia ed isquatra (Inferno, VI, 18);
>   he scratches the spirits and flays and rends them;

> e cigola per vento che va via (Inferno, XIII, 42);
> and hisses with the air as it escapes;
>
> fin che si sfoghi l'affollar del casso (Purgatorio, XXIV, 72);
> until the panting of his breast is eased.

In the first line, for example, the imitative effect derives from the wealth of *s* sounds (flanked by double *f*) and of *r* sounds and from the coincidence of the initial alliteration *(isc-, isq-)* with anticipation of *s* before a consonant in *sp-*. It derives, too, from the pair of verbs whose meaning is related; both of them are accented *(iscoia ed isquatra)*, both end in *-a*, and so on.

What merits special attention, though, is that it is possible to activate, and to semanticize by means of discourse, the phonic properties of a single word or disseminate the phonic elements of a word along the discourse, thereby multiplying anticipations and echoes. Here is an example from Pascoli:

> Da un immoto *fr*agor di carriaggi
> *fer*rei, moventi verso l'in*fi*nito
> *tr*a schiocchi acuti e *fr*emiti selvaggi . . .
>
> *(Myricae, Ultimo sogno,* vv. 1–3).

The musicality of these lines "does not arise out of any elements of 'musicality' which they possess in the system of natural language but from the connection which is established inside the text among its verbal structures. Their resonance is not physical or natural; it is relative, conventional, a literary artifice. Outside these verses, *fragore, carriaggi, fremito, ferreo* have no "musicality," and the feeling of musicality which Pascoli has sensed in them, and which he intended to produce, would be quite extraneous to them in an amorphous, 'noneuphonic' text" (Beccaria 1975, p. 203).

Cases exist for which it seems that phonematic or graphemic elements of a discourse interact inside the discourse itself and form a new discourse. Use of the acrostic was widespread in Greek and Latin and in Jewish and Christian literature as well. In an acrostic, the initial letters of lines of poetry, read vertically, form names or sometimes quite lengthy sentences. One of the most sustained examples is provided by Boccaccio's *Amorosa visione*, where the letters which open each *terzina* are made to form two sonnets and a dedicatory madrigal. Sometimes such words and sentences derive from letters in the middle of the lines *(mesostic)* or at the end *(telestic)*. So rigidly programmed a device imposes a further degree of constraint on creative liberty.

Among techniques of this type we might mention anagrams. But the word *anagram* has been used in recent times concurrently with *hypogram* and *paragram* to stand for another case of the convergence of two discourses in one. This is the existence, investigated by Saussure in notes which have recently been brought to light (Starobinski 1971), of verbal *themes*, embedded in the lines or prose passages of authors both classical and modern. Such themes are held to allude to the explicit or implicit subject of the narration, at times to its author. For example, we find the name Aphrodite emerging from the letters which make up each of the initial phrases of Lucretius's *De rerum natura* or the names Philippus, Leonora, and Politianus rising out of Politian's epitaph for Fra Filippo Lippi (whose lover was a certain Leonora Butti). And there is *hystérie*, present, though incognito, in Baudelaire's *Vieux saltimbanque*:

"Je sentIs ma gorge Serree par la main TERrIble de l'hystérie."

In speaking of *theme*, Saussure is giving us the interpretive approach he prefers. On each occasion the author will set out from a verbal theme and then go on to construct his verses (or prose passages) out of words which, once broken down in terms of recognizable norms, lend themselves to the theme's representation inside their sequences of letters (or sounds). Although the motivation is different, this is not unlike the cryptograms that authors used, particularly in the Middle Ages, to insert the disguised names and events of their personal histories into their works. Saussure's theoretical framework did not accommodate the idea that anagrams might be realization at the urging of an unconscious obsession, that they might derive from the dominance of the author by the language—being, in short, a linguistic activity which transcends the poet's intentional craftsmanship. Hypotheses of this kind are today accorded credit (thanks in part to the stimulus of psychoanalysis). This, for example, is the formula suggested by Fónagy (1965):

$$\frac{\text{Form}}{\text{Content}} : \frac{\text{Unconscious}}{\text{Conscious}}$$

Whatever the proportions between intentional craftsmanship and the intimations of the unconscious may be, and they are certainly variable, our ears have by now become receptive to such discourse within discourse.

Such discourse comes to constitute, "above or beneath the semantic plane, a sort of nonmeaningful text devoted to the realization, through sublinguistic signification modes, of the form or forms of a transcontextual communication" (Agosti 1972, p. 197). This new noncommunicative (or transcommunicative) discourse is sometimes articulated as a series of words, sometimes as groups of phonemes (or letters). In the former case, the words involved are homonyms or synonyms, i.e., they are similar in their phonic or in their semantic aspect. The text, over and above (or prior to) its syntactical-semantic texture, will unfold as a play of cross-reference and contrast, often subsequently resolved, involving words which in some sense stand out. In the latter case, letters and syllables have come to pronounce a primigenial discourse, a cry from the unconscious. Such are the lines in which Montale invokes an interlocutor who has died. What comes to the fore in the Italian is *tu, te = you* (Agosti, 1972, p. 207):

Mi abiTUero a senTIrTI o a decifrarTI
nel TIcchetTIo della TElescrivenTE.

In general terms, such an hypothesis is unassailable, although in concrete instances it can be proved and counterchecked only with difficulty.

6. When it is a question of discourse meaning, a significant contribution to our understanding has been made by narratological investigation, from the Russian formalists onward. It suffices to mention their (indirect) contribution to the problem of discourse segmentation. It should be borne in mind that literary texts narrative in content were the primary concern of the formalists. Construction techniques as they defined them—circular construction, frame construction, "spit" construction—and the broader range of application that they envisaged for traditional rhetorical figures, such as parallelism, oxymoron, etc., make it possible to grasp the reciprocal relations which exist among large blocks of narration.

Their most important insights are the outcome of a search for structures that underlie the level of discourse. A narration, Tomashevsky tells us (1923, Ital. trans., p. 311), constitutes "a more or less unified system of events, which are linked to each other. The sum of such events in their mutual internal relations is what we call *fabula*." As a rule writers expound these events in an order which does not correspond to their (supposed) succession but which aims for effects that are, in a broad sense, aesthetic. "Distribution to form an aesthetic construction of the events of a work is called its *plot* (p. 314).

A research framework of this kind highlights, first and foremost, intentional transgressions with respect to the chronology and logic of the events narrated (temporal displacement, interruptions and resumptions, interpolations, and the like)—what now would be called montage. This means that the time within which the linear discourse unfolds and the time of the facts narrated, be they true or false, are not coincidental. And we can go further. Montage of this kind will have direct repercussions on discourse. It will determine the perspective of the discourse's verbal tenses and give rise to linkage or deferment zones to the point that, although the temporal character of discourse will, on the whole, serve to dominate the temporal character of the facts, the disequilibrium such representation produces will call for corrective markers and devices on the discourse surface.

The most striking consequences of the formalist approach are found in the way they determined the minimal units of narrative discourse.

> As we go forward in this breaking down of the work into thematic fractions, we will, at last, arrive at sections which are *not further decomposable*. These will constitute minimal portions of thematic material: "Evening came"; "Raskolnikov killed the old woman"; "The hero died"; "He received a letter"; etc. The theme of an indivisible section is called a *motif,* and in practice each proposition will possess its own. . . . Motifs, as they combine together, form the work's thematic

structure. From this point of view, the *fabula* is the sum of the motifs in their causal-temporal logical relations, while the plot is the sum of these same motifs in their succession, and with the relations they acquire, as they are put forward in the work (Tomashevsky 1923, Ital. trans., p. 315).

Thus, fabula and plot are made up of minimal elements which cannot be subjected to any further breakdown in narrative terms. These Tomashevsky calls *motifs*, more or less appropriately. It is evident that neither "hero" by itself nor "he died" by itself have narrative value. The narrative element only appears with the sentence "The hero died." For a narrative nucleus, the least that is required is a subject with its predicate, though not all subject-predicate syntagms will constitute narrative nuclei. And so it is that we find ourselves faced once more with the sentence. An attempt is made by those who investigate discourse to integrate it into broader units, the difference being that sentences will no longer belong to the language of discourse; they will be metalinguistic and constitute paraphrases which summarize the text. Each motif-sentence synthesizes what may be quite a broad segment of the discourse, together with all the sentences it contains.

The same thing holds *a fortiori* for further progress in schematization of the tale, along the lines of Propp. We are alluding to his individuation of functions: "Function is understood as an act of a character, defined from the point of view of its significance for the course of the action" (Propp 1928, Eng. trans., p. 21). Any narration is thus the development of a model made up of a series of functions. With respect to the fabula, this model is more simple, because a great many actions present in the fabula will not be determinant for the unfolding of the action. Hence, they will not constitute functions. But it is the very nature of the model which is different. When the actions of the fabula have been determined, they will prove to be the same (schematized) actions narrated or described by the discourse. "Raskolnikov killed the old woman" is indeed the synthesis of what the novel narrates at a certain point. When, on the contrary, it is functions we are determining, what we will take into account, as we have seen, will be their "significance for the course of the action." "If the receiving of a magical agent follows the solution of the task, then it is a case of the donor testing the hero . . .; If the receipt of a bride and a marriage follow, then we have an example of the difficult task" (Propp 1928, Eng. trans., p. 67).

In other words, what is function with respect to the unfolding of the tale is, from a narrative point of view, classification of semantic categories. Naming functions means distributing among a limited number of categories an unlimited number of possible actions. In *The Morphology of the Folktale*, for example, the function *villainy* embraces seventeen kinds of action: kidnapping of a person, seizure of a magical agent or helper, the forcible seizure of a magical helper, the ruining of crops, theft of daylight, plundering in various forms, etc. Each of these actions can be described by using a variety of terms which constitute a group of semantic variants; on the contrary, groups of semantic variants are not reciprocally homogeneous in semantic terms (there is no affinity between ruining crops and stealing daylight). They are homogeneous in the sense that the actions listed have an analogous function within the particular corpus Propp chose, and always in the same position.

In more recent analyses of the tale, a variety of classifications have been adopted both for actions (or motifs) and for functions. The difference between the two operations to be effected still persists. It is not just a difference between a lesser or greater degree of generality; there is also a difference between exact, nonsystematic, definition relative to a single text and definition relative to the sum total of a corpus (i.e., to all of the texts under consideration) which is systematic. The categories which serve to denominate functions can be determined only on the basis of their overall potential in terms of succession and composition. This is done by considering texts as large syntagms of functions and by determining from within the corpus the rules of their syntagmatic composition. Thus, between plot and fabula, on the one hand, and narrative model, on the other, a fundamental difference exists. In plot and in fabula, actions are indicated metalinguistically in general terms, along the same semantic axis as those used in the discourse; in the narrative model, the categories directly involve various semantic fields and take in different actions which may represent the same function inside an already defined model of narration.

The Russian formalists, in investigating plot and fabula and in determining narrative models, led the way toward various possible metalinguistic transcriptions of narrative discourse. It is beside the point to dwell here on what is lost in such transcription: what Tomashevsky calls *free motifs* and *static motifs* (which are negligible because they do not contribute to the causal-temporal connection of events or because they bring about no change in the situation); or what Propp calls *motivations* and *attributes* (in his view the more unstable and inconstant elements of the tale). What is important is the fact that narrative content can be determined and formulated. Narrative content is semiotic in kind, because it is the meaning (indeed, one of the meanings, i.e., narrative meaning) of the tale which the discourse expounds. If it is uttered verbally, it will come to constitute a metanarration (thus, I might expound in English the content of a tale written in Italian or vice versa), but it can also be indicated with abbreviations (examples are those used by Propp for functions or by Todorov for actions).

This is why narratological investigations loom so large in the study of discourse. They follow the line of least resistance by insisting on determination of the overall meaning of a discourse. If, in this sphere, we wish to consider such analytical techniques as have been put into effect (Hendricks 1973), we shall find that two fundamental approaches to synthesis exist. A vertical approach, along a specific-generic scale, synthesizes in simplified (essential) terminology the lexical variety by which one can indicate a single action or a group of actions considered as a unity. A horizontal direction links the presence of characters to moments of their actions in successive phases of the discourse and reconstructs a metaphrase in which character and action, connected syntactically, realize in one single solution what is expressed in different moments and aspects of the discourse. To simplify, we might say that the subject is determined on the basis of anaphoric references to it in the discourse: noun repetition, pronouns, periphrastic indications, etc. Its action is what can be deduced: from direct indication by means of verbs; by use of synonymic verbs; by use of various constructions whose substance is verbal; by the distribution of allusions to single moments of verbal action or to moments which precede or follow the action. Individuation of the subject is prevalently grammatical in character; individuation of a character's action is prevalently semantic.

It is possible to move in either of these two directions to a greater or lesser degree in terms of the requirements of one's program of analysis. In a terminological synthesis, the limit chosen may be a given level of generalization. In the synthesis of narrative moments, actions whose weight at the level of events is small may be included; otherwise, they may be lumped together with actions of more moment with no need for separate enumeration. I have already suggested that a narrative model can be put forward only when it is based on a clearly defined corpus, for it is on this basis alone that actions otherwise semantically distant can be reduced to a single term, a term which will designate their function with respect to the tale seen as an integrated succession of other functions analogously named. This highlights the two different concatenations which involve moments of the fabula and those of the narrative model. In the concatenation of the fabula, what counts are traditional, logical connections; it is important that successive actions should bind the characters together with a certain degree of consequentiality, to be measured against behavior models contemporary with the text. In the concatenation of the narrative model, on the contrary, it is the logic of the system which prevails; the succession of the functions will, at one and the same time, be the realization of syntagmatic norms (linear matching of functions) and of paradigmatic norms (relations over distance, opposition, etc., among functions). The system implies a closed corpus, even though, with an unrealizable hypothesis, it might be suggested that the sum of all existing narrative forms a corpus. A census of functions, however, would lead us away from the relation between discourse and narrative content; in fact, such a census is activated by comparing the narrative content of various discourses. Here the levels to be observed are those of fabula and of plot.

But, if it is possible (at least in abstract) to envisage techniques for actions with some degree of certainty, with characters the matter is more difficult. To begin with, should they be taken into consideration at all? Propp seems to take hardly any account of them. He defines them by starting out from functions, not the other way around; he deprives them of any physiognomy or character which precedes the action and transforms them into roles inside the course of the action. We should not, though, allow ourselves to be misled by the terms which he uses to indicate functions (they are nearly always abstract nouns, sometimes followed by an attribute or by a specification). In fact, these abstract terms stand for complete sentences, which means that they have a subject: *interdiction* = "An interdiction is addressed to the hero"; *reconnaissance* = "The villain makes an attempt at reconnaissance"; *complicity* = "The victim submits to deception and thereby unwittingly helps his enemy." For Propp, then, a series of characters and a series of functions exist. A certain number of functions corresponds to each character; for each function, the most suitable character or characters are already foreseen. In other words, it is the substantial uniformity of the Russian magic folk tales which authorizes (partial) concealment of character: in reality, the functions of these folk tales follow each other in terms of a ritual that indicates the agent and the potential patient for each group of functions.

Nonetheless, we should bear in mind that Propp's analyses remain on the level of the narrative model, which is beyond the scope of our present exposition. This applies even more to Greimas. We need only mention the way he reduces characters (or actors) of all kinds to a mere six *actants* (sender, object, receiver, helper, subject, opponent), actants which can be linked to the meaning of the functions. For example, the *contract* would constitute a link between sender and receiver (communication); *struggle*, a link between helper and opponent, etc. If we consider the levels which underlie discourse, every character may be seen (a) as pseudo-referent, with a proper name and personal details invented by the writer; (b) as an actor with blood relations (a father, a mother, etc.) or situational relations with the other actors (as husband, as lover, as friend, as enemy, etc.), and these are the relations which may be modified in the course of the narration; (c) as a type (or mask), definable with a bundle of physical attributes or attributes of character. While *a* implies, but goes beyond, *b* and *c* in terms of a total, though fictitious, individualization, between *b* and *c* no hierarchy exists. Once *a* is attributed to the plot, the importance of *b* and *c* for the fabula will depend on the pertinence of their elements, for the type of narration will also determine their degree of importance. In general, though, the elements of *c* can be measured against motivations (with which they in part coincide), but they are undoubtedly less determinant than are those of *b*. It has already been affirmed that, at the level of fabula, characters—or rather their relations—are quite as important as are actions. One need only think of stories whose whole approach is dominated by the marriage which brings them to a close or, on the other hand, of stories of adultery—those involving the Oedipus complex—or problems of inheritance, etc. In cases like these, changes in the polygon of the characters are the hidden mainspring of the action.

The characters (subjects, objects, receivers, etc.) are now within our grasp, and so are the actions they perform. If the content of narrative discourse is its metalinguistic synthesis, this, too, must be articulated linguistically, as a discourse underlying discourse. Such discourse will have characteristics of its own. It is a virtual discourse, which becomes act only through attempts at interpretation; by definition it is a discourse which (errors of analysis and intentional obscurities apart) will resolve the ambiguities of the explicit discourse. Acceptability conditions for the paraphrases in which such discourse is realized can perhaps be defined at the convergence of an action theory and a discourse theory. In other words, it is necessary, on the one hand, that the paraphrase should present linguistic characteristics which will make it comprehensible and exhaustive and, on the other, that it should be possible to see it as realizing the conditions under which a series of actions can be regarded as interconnected and performed. Oddly enough, present-day analyses of the tale, while they stress (verbal or formalized) representation of the actions, have not investigated the problem of the alignment of the actions in metanarration.

I would use the term narrative nucleus for the paraphrastic cell which makes it possible to synthesize a narration or a nodal part of a complex narration whose conditions will be met only with the union of a number of narrative nuclei. Clearly, roles that are indispensable will occupy the places destined for the different cases in the structure of the sentence. Thus, when Burke (1945), in the narratological sphere, indicates key terms for action *(act, scene, agent* and possibly *coagent* and *counteragent, purpose, agency,* and perhaps *attitude)*, we might well be led to sketch a comparison with the "situation(al) roles" listed by Pike *(actor, goal, action, causer, place, instrument, enabler, time, beneficiary)* and with the eight cases of Fillmore's most recent sentence model (1971): *agent, object, place, time, instrument, source, goal, experiencer* (cf. Dressler 1972, pp. 66–67).

Once again, the attempt has not yet been made. Reference to generative-transformational theory is implicit and may serve to clarify some points and to avoid misunderstandings. If, with the contribution of the transformationalists, we arrive at primary and ineliminable structures for sentences, we will have grasped the primary and ineliminable structure of narrative nuclei as well. But comparison of the relation between narrative nuclei and narrative discourse, and of relations between nuclear sentences and surface structures, can be legitimately made only if we wish to highlight the differences. The nuclear sentences of the transformationalists are models which are immanent to the intricacy of surface structures. From an operational point of view, they are invariants to which we may refer the syntactic realizations of the discourse. They effect a breaking down of surface structures into (syntactically) simple elements, without repercussions on meaning. In narrative nuclei, on the contrary, the overall meaning of the discourse is reduced to the elements of its narrative substance, a reduction which, since it is effected exclusively on meaning (so much so that its foundation is in paraphrase), will move beyond the boundaries of language and become quintessentially semiotic. Narrative nuclei belong to semiotic metalanguage (which is naturally articulated as language but which might equally well make use of abbreviations and formulae or of any other formulation). And it is not true that a linguistic product like discourse can be seen as a "transformation" of metalinguistic elements.

We are now in a position to understand why it is that, though it is relatively easy to analyze the tale (where we are faced both with the signifier of the discourse and with what it signifies), no comparably straightforward approach exists for the analysis of nonnarrative discourses or of nonnarrative parts of discourses which are otherwise narrative. If the description of an action is susceptible to synthesis, this is so because its result polarizes the convergence of the particulars of the action in question. For the description of a landscape or a state of mind, it is as easy to find a more or less applicable label as it is difficult to seize upon points or axes of convergence. We might elaborate one of Lotman's observations and say that action is the passage of a character from one semantic field to another. A shift is much more easily sensed and defined than is stasis. At the present moment, expedients for the semiotic transcription of nonnarrative discourse can barely be glimpsed. They might take the form of a search for connotations, of a schematization of idea-forces (especially when they influence action), of anthropomorphization of nature to reduce it, too, to idea-forces. But there is little sign of the kind of discourse underlying discourse which can be formulated for narrative elements.

7. Though researchers have dealt with it in so many different ways, discourse remains tied indissolubly to the situation within which it is expressed. As Morris (1938) was well aware, it is the pragmatic aspect of communication that we are dealing with. "By 'pragmatics' is designated the science of the relation of signs to their interpreters"; it "deals with the biotic aspects of semiosis, that is, with all the psychological, biological, and sociological phenomena which occur in the functioning of signs" (p. 30). "Pragmatics itself would attempt to develop terms appropriate to the study of the relation of signs to their users and to order systematically the results which come from the study of this dimension of semiosis" (p. 33). Although for the biological and psychological aspects, autonomous branches of research have been developed, in the communications field stress has been laid primarily on the situation (which some have called *context*, though others have used the word to mean the sum of the words which make up a text).

The situation can be brought into focus in different depth. Close up, we are given an image of the precise conditions under which an act of communication is formulated. What stand revealed are the relations between the speakers, especially with regard to their prior knowledge of the argument of their exchange, of its premises, connections, and partial realizations. From a maximum distance, it is possible to embrace all of the sociocultural conditionings to which speakers are subject at a given place and time and their relations with the groups to which they belong as well. What we grasp close up are the modes of putting language acts into effect, i.e., of formulating discourses. What we perceive from a maximum distance are preliminary selections operated on the language of a given epoch, irrespective of how the discourse will subsequently be formulated. For the former, I would speak of the immediate communication situation; for the latter, of the sociocultural situation.

The different descriptions of the communication situation, for all their different accentuations, bring to light fairly clear-cut elements. Even from a distributionalist standpoint, we find a distinct revaluation of the pragmatic aspects of the language act in Pike's "tagmemics," which sets against an "etic" description of language, seen as an object, an "emic" description, in which its elements are assessed as functions with respect to the cultural world ("etic" :"emic" = "phonetic : phonemic"). The minimal identifiable discourse units are called, in virtue of the fact that they depend upon the behavior of two or more interlocutors, *behavioremes* (Pike 1967).

One of the most all-embracing censuses of the constituent elements of language communication is that put forward by Wunderlich (1971). He takes into account not just the addresser and addressee but the moment of transmission, the addresser's stance and range of perception, presuppositions concerning the addresser's knowledge and capacity, his opinion of the knowledge and capacity of his addressee, of his stance and range of perception, of the social relations between addressee and addresser, the addresser's intention, and the interrelation between addresser and addressee; lastly, he places within this pragmatic framework the utterance itself and its cognitive content.

There is clearly a danger involved here, and it increases as such distinctions multiply. It is easy to lose oneself in a series of findings which shift unceasingly, whereas the object of analysis ought to be the invariable, the rule. Most apposite at this point is the distinction made by Bally between *utterance (énoncé)* and *utterance act (énonciation)*. An utterance act is an act of language in its aspect of a *hic et nunc* event; utterance is the result of such an act. Linguistics is in general concerned with utterances; its interest in the utterance act is limited to such traces of it as can be discovered in utterances. It can be stated as a general norm that, if utterances are to be studied, knowledge of the principles of the utterance act is essential. The measure of relevance of the situation within which the utterance act has taken place is, however, still awaiting determination.

In a dialogue, for instance, alternation of *I* and *you* will correspond to the subject of the utterances and to his interlocutor: thus, *I* stands for two persons, and so does *you*. Of these two persons, however, *I* will always be the one who is actually speaking and *you* the one spoken to. Similarly, adverbs of place and time *(here, there, today, yesterday,* etc.) will have a referential meaning only in relation to the time and place in which the utterance act takes place. Yet, for the analysis of the utterance, it is sufficient that one should be aware of this relational perspective. For deictics *(this, that,* etc.), the same comprehensibility conditions obtain. Or, again, the name of a person *(Barbara, Charles,* etc.) may refer to various individuals, but, in a typical utterance act situation, its reference is, as a rule, quite unambiguous. Where analysis is concerned, we only need to know that between the name and the given person a definite relation exists. The problem is, thus, how one is to determine in the utterance act those traits which are pertinent to understanding of the utterance.

What is in any case clear is that no clear dividing line exists between the language act and its immediate communication situation. Speaking is very often a way of acting, just as acting can be a way of communicating. Only part of our utterances have the exclusive function of describing a state of fact. Often, in the act of describing a speaker's action, utterances will also perform the action itself. This happens, for example, with a promise, because to pronounce it is, at the same time, to make it. Austin (1962) calls utterances of the first type *constative*, those of the second type *performative*, and it is to him that we are indebted for the theory of *speech-acts*. This theory discovers performative elements even in utterances which are not obviously performative, and thus further widens the range of discourse repercussion within situation. Every utterance, for Austin, effects three contemporaneous acts: a *locutionary* act, which is a speech act in the strict sense, an elaboration of phonic, semantic, morphological, and syntactical elements to form completely meaningful sentences; an *illocutionary* act, which produces changes in the relations between the interlocutors (it involves questioning, commanding, etc.) and is an act which can be highlighted by transforming the question or order into such sentences as "I am asking you whether . . ." or "I order you to . . ."; a *perlocutionary* act, not explicitly such linguistically, which consists in influencing the interlocutor in such a way that he will, or will not, do or believe certain things. A typical example is the rhetorical question, which does not depend on the speaker's ignorance but rather upon his desire to obtain an already foreseen reaction.

There is no doubt about the importance of illocutionary acts; indeed, generative grammar (Ross, McCawley, Parisi, and Antinucci, etc.) would supply an underlying performative verb for every utterance, i.e., any utterance is regarded as if it were preceded by "I ask you whether . . .," I order you to . . ." Statements, too, would contain an implied, "I declare that . . . ." Searle (1969), though, defines illocutionary acts as acts whose status is dependent on constituent rules which, if not obeyed, exclude reciprocal comprehension, whereas perlocutionary acts are acts whose status is dependent upon normative rules, since a difference in the level of understanding of the interlocutors is accepted, indeed taken as given. This merely reaffirms, most illuminatingly, the different degrees of validity of the combination rules proper to the language and the way such rules as exist can be bent and made to accommodate aims which are in the broadest sense psychological. The distinction will be seen as most opportune when the perlocutionary aspects of any utterance are examined in relation to its immediate situation. "It's pouring down rain" in perlocutionary terms might mean "I advise you not to go out" in a situation in which (1) two persons are linked by friendship or affection; (2) they find themselves under shelter; (3) the person to whom the sentence is directed has expressed his intention of going out; (4) the weather really is bad, etc. These are type-situations which would at once disappear if, let us say, the person set on going out was strongly attracted by stormy weather or if his friend took pleasure in meteorological observations irrespective of their implications. Perlocutionary meaning is not so much to be derived from the rules of language as it is to be deduced from customary behavior, perhaps widely generalized, of the following kind: "It is inadvisable, not good for one's health, etc., to venture out when the weather is bad."

Such investigations, at present in their infancy, may well prove to be the natural outcome of a series of empirical observations. It often happens, for example, that a discourse contains pronouns or deictics which have no anaphoric reference or, perhaps, elliptical sentences whose value is a matter of opinion. In such cases, the speaker presupposes in the person he addresses an awareness of the elements of the situation which thus have no need of explication or which show clearly which possible values are applicable to the sentence as pronounced. This fact may have considerable repercussions, for we should recall that the meaning of many words changes in terms of content, type of discourse, etc. It would be hopelessly uneconomical, though, to attempt to formulate a general model for all possible situations. The exceptions are well-codified cases like etiquette-dictated exchanges, which are themselves governed by differences in age, sex, and social status. The starting point for an investigation so conceived must be recognition that pragmatics provides a framework within which discourse elements, which cannot be fully accounted for by a linguistic analysis, can be justified and explained. Such elements, which for any isolated sentence of a discourse would be all too numerous, shrink progressively as we turn our attention to the sum total of the context (of the discourse). Through the play of their cross-references, sentences put into effect a technique which eliminates those interpretations which are in conflict with the situation and which points the way toward the correct interpretation.

This does not lead us to conclude that we should leave to pragmatics such areas as remain inaccessible to an all-inclusive analysis of discourse. On the contrary, what must be looked for in the pragmatic situation are all of the possible conditions which make for the coherence of discourse. These conditions achieve explicit realization both in the formation of single sentences and, indeed even more so, in their concatenation (hence, the importance of opening sentences or, in written texts, of titles). It must be stated that syntax is very well able to introject, by grammaticizing, the greater part of pragmatics. It is true that an unexpressed, ungrammaticized residue will always remain ungrammaticized. In such cases, we ought not to regard pragmatics as a key, for it would be an unserviceable one. We need only remind ourselves that pragmatics, already partially absorbed into syntax, still contains ill-defined areas which will require more than just linguistic means for their probing.

The distinction between various types of discourse now becomes obvious. There exist two extremes, conversation and literary discourse. The former can be understood only in relation to its immediate situation, for it is integrated to such a point that it can leave unexpressed elements which may well be quite substantial. The latter is hardly tied to its immediate situation at all. Indeed, it is addressed to "potential" receivers whose overall coordinates are quite unknown. The former develops in the immediate present a perlocutionary capacity and exhausts itself thereby. The latter concentrates on locutionary aspects, while it shows a more subtle perlocutionary, practically unlimited, potential. These observations fit into the overall approach earlier outlined: the communication situation of a dialogue has a minimal extension, duration, and (as a rule) importance, whereas the situation within which a literary text is circulated involves a considerable measure of the culture, i.e., the sociocultural situation—the everyday as opposed to the general (and, as an extreme, the universal). It is a useful comparison, I maintain, because it serves to show that a study of pragmatics should not insist on a typology of situations; it should, rather, define the pertinence to the discourse of the situations themselves. To this end, analysis of the literary text readily offers itself.

In saying that pragmatics determines the coherence conditions for discourse, what we are attributing to it is a kind of supervision over the admissibility of utterances, whether taken singly or as a whole. In effect, it is on the basis of a given communication situation that certain utterances will be possible or impossible, comprehensible or incomprehensible. The implication is that utterances can be measured against two kinds of compatibility: linguistic and pragmatic. The signification potentials of words and sentences limit themselves—among various possible worlds, among various customary logics—to the actual world which is established by the immediate situation and which has a logic of behavior and communication of its own. It should be added that, inside the literary text, the logic of behavior and communication has already been sketched for us, however allusively.

These aspects of the matter should lead us to realize the need for research into direct communication situations, research which will go beyond the immediately anecdotal. Reference to the utterance–utterance act relation and to the pertinence of discourse situations might serve to highlight lines of resistance. On the contrary, sociocultural situations can be dealt with in the pragmatic sphere (and may perhaps be mechanized) by the employment of linguistic criteria. Language, in general, can be looked at as an invariant which renders possible discourse processes that fall into line with the specific conditions of their production. Such conditions will be determined historically by the ideological orientation of social groupings (Pêcheux 1975). In other words, when compared with the language seen as a system of possibilities, the utterance enjoys the status of a historical object. The semantic values of words would then be selected not just in light of their concatenation in the form of utterances but also because any utterance already belongs to a given discourse pattern (to a subspecies of ideological patterning). Hence, for example, a "religious ideological pattern" represents the dominant ideological form of the Middle Ages, and, to find related discourse patterns, we may turn to the sermon, in its rustic form or in the form it took when the clerical hierarchy addressed powerful nobles, and so on. This ideological pattern, with the various patterns of its discourse, determined particular choices and orientations within a basic conceptual system. An approach of this kind is clearly a historical one, for it stands in opposition both to any logical analysis of semantic relations and to any tendency to exaggerate the creative contribution of the individual. Ideological bases and sociocultural patterns are primarily responsible for choices in language. What we are dealing with, in Pêcheux's (1975) terminology, is discourse theory seen as the historical determination of semantic processes.

Discourse patterns (discourse types) thus constitute the subsystems of an ideological pattern. The sense of utterances must be determined by means of the series of paraphrases possible inside the discourse pattern itself. In short, it is, we realize, possible, inside the semantic fields of a given epoch and language, to seize upon other, more limited (though no less structured) groupings, which correspond to ideological patterns. A further delimitation of the field is effected by the various patterns of discourse. The image of a speaker to whom all the resources of the language are indiscriminately offered must be replaced by that of an individual historically predetermined in the choices he makes by his ideological formation and by the discourse pattern he adopts. It should (in my opinion) be stated, too, that discourse patterns exist whose degree of cogency may prove to be of greater or less urgency. The chances that exist of spreading certain messages abroad is determined by their own pluridiscoursive disposability, by their ability, partial though it may be, to cut across ideological boundaries.

8. What has been said up to this point falls within a conception of discourse as communication. Any discourse will be a message sent by an addresser to an addressee in accord with a common code. The context and the type of contact may change, but the individuality of the two principal subjects, addresser and addressee, will remain. Within this extremely general schema, discussion of the consistency, or free will, of the subjects might seem out of place, while absolutely evident are the cultural conditionings which can act on the breadth and quality of the language repertoire which, on every occasion, the addresser uses and which the addressee recognizes. The language, in short, is seen as a means (a code) employed—because, at least in part, mastered—for the formulation of a message.

Speculations concerning the consistency of the subject, from Nietzsche to Heidegger, might perhaps have left untouched the modest empiricism of communication, but it is reflections on language which have cast doubt upon the validity of the schema. Heidegger's idea that it is not man who thinks through language but language which thinks through man has found "scientific" support in Freud's discovery that only a part of our thought is conscious and autonomous. The consequent devaluation of the subject (and hence, in the literary field, of the author) and the enthronement of language in his place have been enthusiastically welcomed by Blanchot and by nearly the whole of the French *nouvelle critique*. This has led to a glottocentrism which enjoys at least two advantages: it has destroyed what was left of a positivistic, biographical approach, and it has brought to light the impressive weight of the language mechanisms by which the writer is effectively, and to a considerable degree, dominated. Otherwise, we can only regard as a brilliant *jeu d'esprit* any cancellation of the writer's responsibility for the production of the text, although we are free to impose as many limits as we wish on the fullness of his awareness and attribute all of the importance it deserves to the often-overwhelming action of linguistic and thematic structures.

It is Lacan who has most fascinatingly expressed this overturning of the subject-discourse relation. For him, the primary discourse is that of the unconscious. It is the discourse of the Other, eminently intersubjective. "The unconscious is that part of the concrete discourse, insofar as it is trans-individual, which falls short of the subject's disposition towards re-establishing the continuity of his conscious discourse" (1966, p. 252). This discourse of the Other has the nature of a chain of symbols—a chain which, for the Ego, is continually interrupted by the presence of synonyms (which correspond to the intervention of inhibitions and anxiety; in linguistic terms, they are metaphors) and by the appearance of substitution desires (by whose means the Ego attempts, metonymically, to unite itself with the Other). Lacan, in substance, is not rejecting the discourse of an Ego (without which the object of his analysis would disappear); he is seeing it as a pathological deformation, or a barely masked shadow, of a real and unique discourse, that of the Other.

This discourse of the Other is not a communicative discourse. Equally noncommunicative is the discourse spoken of by Foucault (1969), the primary object of his investigation. The epistemic structures which follow one another over time, by way of transformation rather than of development, should prove susceptible of analysis under the aspect of "discourse patterns." A civilization (or, within it, a scientific field) offers itself as a sum of discourse events among which relations, regularity, and correlations exist.

> In the case in which, among a certain number of utterances, it is possible to describe a similar system of dispersion and in the case in which among the objects, the types of utterance, the concepts, the thematic choices, it is possible to define a regularity (an order, correlations, positions and functionings, transformations), it can be said by convention that we are faced with a *discourse pattern,* thereby avoiding words too loaded with conditions and consequences and inadequate, what is more, for the designation of a dispersion of this kind, words like "science," or "ideology," or "theory," or "field of objectivity." We shall call *formation rules* the conditions which govern the elements of this repartition (objects, utterance modalities, concepts, thematic choices). Formation rules are conditions for existence (but also of coexistence, of maintenance, of modification, and of disappearance) in a given discourse sector" (1969, pp. 48–49)

Another term Foucault uses for these various systems of utterance is *archives,* and he stresses the fact that we are not dealing with the sum of the various things said, and even less with the content of utterances, but rather with the normativeness of the sayable within the system under consideration. The archive "is *the general system of the formation and transformation of utterances*" (p. 151).

For Foucault, too, the subject, individual or collective, is superfluous. There exists a discourse immanent to the infinity of the utterances proper to a given *episteme*—a discourse which does not link—as distinct from single utterances—an addresser and an addressee. Indeed, what advantage could there be for an addresser and addressee to share a message whose referent has been left out of account? Foucault says quite clearly that truth values and relations with reality are beyond the scope of formation rules whose formal character alone is important.

Foucault's discourse order is an extreme example of that reduction of reality to language which is characteristic of so many currents of contemporary thought. It is too easy to object that the discourse of which he speaks has nothing to do with that of the linguists; it is, indeed, an entity so abstract that it does not even take concrete form in the shape of words and utterances. As a result, Foucault's whole undertaking, instead of being a description of this discourse or of its laws, is a prophetic invocation of its existence. It is more profitable to return to the basic elements of communication (addresser, addressee, etc.), because they synthesize the function of language: to broaden and to strengthen contact with reality through the communication of will and knowledge. When we transform language or discourse into an hypostasis of Being, we are refusing to exist.

References

Agosti, S.
    1972. *Il testo poetico: Teoria e pratiche d'analisi*. Milan: Rizzoli.
Austin, J. L.
    1962. *How to Do Things with Words*. London: Oxford University Press.
Bally, Ch.
    1912. Le style indirect libre en français moderne. *Germanisch-Romanische Monatsschrift*, 4, no. 10, pp. 549–56, and no. 11, pp. 597–606.
Beccaria, G. L.
    1975. *L'autonomia del significante: Figure del ritmo e della sintassi; Dante, Pascoli, D'Annunzio*. Turin: Einaudi.
Benveniste, E.
    1959. Les relations de temps dans le verbe français. *Bulletin de la Société de Linguistique de Paris*, 54, fasc. 1. (Now in *Problèmes de linguistique générale*. 1966. Paris: Gallimard.)
    1962. Les niveaux de l'analyse linguistique. *Proceedings of the 9th International Congress of Linguists*. 1964. The Hague.
    1969. Sémiologie de la langue. *Semiotica*, 1, pp. 1–12 and 127–35. (Now in *Problèmes de linguistique générale*. 1974. Vol. 2, pp. 43–46. Paris: Gallimard.)
Bühler, K.
    1934. *Sprachtheorie: Die Darstellungsfunktion der Sprache*. Jena: Fischer. (Italian translation. 1983. Rome: Armando.)
Burke, K.
    1945. *A Grammar of Motives*. Englewood Cliffs: Prentice-Hall.
Buyssens, E.
    1967. *La communication et l'articulation linguistique*. 2d ed. Brussels: Presses Universitaires de Bruxelles.
Daneš, F.
    1970. Zur linguistischen Analyse der Textstruktur. *Folia Linguistica*, 4: 72–79.
Dressler, W.
    1972. *Einführung in die Textlinguistik*. 2d ed. Tubingen: Niemeyer. (Italian translation. 1974. Rome: Officina edizioni.)
Fónagy, I.
    1965. Le language poétique: Forme et fonction. E. Benveniste *et al*. *Problèmes du langage*. Paris: Gallimard.
Foucault, M.
    1969. *L'archéologie du savoir*. Paris: Gallimard.
Gardin, J.-C.
    1974. *Les analyses de discours*. Neuchâtel: Delachaux et Niestlé.
Greimas, A. J.
    1966. *Sémantique structurale: Recherche de méthode*. Paris: Larousse. (English translation. 1983. *Structural Semantics. An Attempt at a Method*. Lincoln: University of Nebraska Press.)

Halliday, M. A. K.
    1970. Language Structure and Language Function. J. Lyons, ed., *New Horizons in Linguistics*. Harmondsworth: Penguin. Pp. 140–65.
Harris, Z. S.
    1952. Discourse Analysis. *Language*, 28, pp. 1–30.
Hendricks, W. O.
    1973. *Essay on Semiolinguistics and Verbal Art*. The Hague-Paris: Mouton.
Jakobson, R.
    1958. Linguistics and Poetics. T. A. Sebeok, ed. 1960. *Style in Language*. Cambrige, Mass.: M.I.T. Press. Pp. 350–77.
Kinneavy, J. L.
    1971. *A Theory of Discourse; the Aims of Discourse*. Englewood Cliffs: Prentice-Hall.
Lacan, J.
    1966. *Écrits*. Paris: Seuil.
Mathesius, V.
    1928. On Linguistic Characterology with Illustrations from Modern English. *Actes du premier Congrès international des linguistes à La Haye*. Leiden. Pp. 53–63. (Now in J. Vachek, ed., *A Prague School Reader in Linguistics*. 1964. Bloomington: Indiana University Press. Pp. 59–67.)
Morris, Ch. W.
    1938. Foundations of the Theory of Signs. *International Encyclopedia of the Unified Science*. Vol. 1, p. 11. Chicago: University of Chicago Press.
Parret, H.
    1971. *Language and Discourse*. The Hague: Mouton.
Pêcheux, M.
    1975. Analyse du discours; langue et idéologies. *Langages*, 37.
Pike, K. L.
    1967. *Language in Relation to a Unified Theory of the Structure of Human Behavior*. 2d ed. The Hague: Mouton.
Propp, V. Ja.
    1928. *Morfologija skazki*. Leningrad: Academia. (English translation. *Morphology of the Folktale*. 1968. Austin: University of Texas Press.)
Saussure, F. de
    1906–11. *Cours de linguistique générale*. 1916. Lausanne: Payot. (English translation. 1983. London: Duckworth.)
Searle, J. R.
    1969. *Speech Acts: An Essay in the Philosophy of Language*. London: Cambridge University Press.
Segre, C.
    1974. *Le strutture e il tempo. Narrazione, poesia, modelli*. Turin: Einaudi. (English translation. *Structures and Time: Narration, Poetry, Models*. Chicago: The University of Chicago Press.)
Simonin-Grumbach, J.
    1975. Pour une typologie des discours. J. Kristeva, J.-C. Milner, and N. Ruwet, eds. *Langue, discours, société*. Paris: Seuil. Pp. 85–121.
Sinclair, J. Mc H., and Coulthard, R. M.
    1975. *Towards an Analysis of Discourse*. London: Oxford University Press.
Starobinski, J.
    1971. *Les mots sous les mots: Les anagrammes de Ferdinand de Saussure*. Paris: Gallimard. (English translation. 1979. *Words upon Words: The Anagrams of Ferdinand de Saussure*. New Haven: Yale University Press.)

Tomaševskij, B.
    1928. *Teorija literatury: Poetika*. Leningrad. (Italian translation. 1978. Milan: Feltrinelli.)

Wunderlich, D.
    1971. Pragmatik: Sprechsituation. *Zeitschrift für Literaturwissenschaft und Linguistik*, 1, pp. 153–90.

2.
Fiction

1. In Latin, *fingere*—the values of "shaping," "fashioning," and of "imagining, conceiving, and supposing" (i.e., of shaping with the imagination)—may shade off to become "feigning," "saying falsely." In other words, the concept is "lying." This concept is even clearer with the noun *fictus*, "hypocrite," and in the adjective *fictus*, which means not just "imaginary, or invented," but also "fictitious," "false." In *fictio* (from which the Italian *finzione* derives, though its n goes back to the verb *fingere*), we are dealing with a rhetorical term where the values that allude to linguistic and literary invention are the primary ones. Thus, *fictio nominis* is a calque (Quintilian, *Istitutio oratoria*, VIII, 6, 31) of the Greek *onomatopoiia*, and *fictio personae* is a calque of the Greek *prosopopoiia* (IX, 2, 29). In terms of the same schema, we may refer to a *fictio formarum*: "A common figure is the one which consists in giving form to unreal beings, as Virgil does with Rumour, Prodicus with Pleasure and Virtue—as Xenophon tells us—and Ennius with Death and Life when in one of his satires he has them debate" (36). The invention of an "exemplum," i.e., of a short narration used in illustration or for confirmation, is called, in the doctrine of the "loci," a *locus a fictione*.

The term *fictio* is thus very close semantically to *inventio*, except that the latter term is more concerned with the ideas to be dealt with in a work, and so with its rational content. These ideas are to be understood not as being created but as being rediscovered, in memory (this is why we say *heuresis, inventio*, "invention"). The definition of invention in the *Rhetorica ad Herennium* (I, 3) is "the capacity of finding arguments true or probable which will make a case convincing." And the creative act is reduced (as is the usual practice in Latin treatises) to an oratorical function. *Inventio*, nonetheless, enjoys pride of place in the treatises; it is, though, investigated in less depth than are *dispositio* and *elocutio*. As a rule, common-sense advice is given as to what is, or what is not, opportune. One need only recall Horace (*Ars poetica*, I): "Humano capiti cervicen pictor equinam /iungere si velit" ("If a painter has the idea of joining to a horse's neck a human head," and so on). It is clear that a conceptual framework for systematic consideration of *inventio* does not exist. More general implications were involved (philosophical rather than rhetorical) when the problem was the relation between literature and reality. It was a question which provoked controversy from the outset (and which is not yet settled). The word *fictio* itself is, though, a useful point of reference, because of the "valuational" connotations it is apt to assume, even though in classical rhetoric its sphere of application was limited, while its modern derivatives are fluid in meaning.

The terms of the debate were defined by Plato and Aristotle: art as lying (*fictio* in the worst sense) as against art as a depository of the truth; art as whore or art as instructor. The underlying belief is that literature imitates reality (mimesis); the difference is that, for Plato, this imitation is the reproduction of reproductions with respect to the ideas, which, in the world of sense, constitute true reality; Aristotle, for his part, can attribute to poetry an almost philosophical value. "Poetry is something more scientific and serious than history, because poetry tends to give general truths while history gives particular facts" (*Poetics*, 1451b, 5–6). Aristotle's pages have often been called a defense of poetry. But why should poetry need defending?

The fact is that literature, particularly narrative literature, sets up simulacra of reality. Even when the facts expounded in literature do not exist, they are isomorphic with facts which have taken place or which are possible. In the same fashion, literature evokes characters who, while they are not historical, yet resemble the people who move over the stage of the world. Where the characteristics and potentialities of characters are concerned, even though their actions may be different from the kind our experience meets with, the subsistence of a relation cannot be denied, and it only remains to examine, historically or in abstract, the potentialities for oscillation between real and imaginary. What interest impels us to accept and "enjoy" such verbal imitations of reality? In part, the problem is that of any kind of artistic activity at all, from the moment in which ritualistic and religious matrices were set aside. If debate on the autonomy or heteronomy of art has continued down to the present, it is because human beings find it difficult to conceive of an activity that is not finalized—in other words, an activity that has no subsequent repercussions on the reality which has served it as a model.

Whatever stand we take with respect to those philosophies which (though only in recent times) have managed to establish a zone of pertinence for artistic activities as against ethical, economic, and other such activities, what will remain symptomatic is the contrast between exaltations of freedom of invention as opposed to didascalic utility, of the sovereign imagination in place of the cognitive function, of abandonment against commitment. We shall see, as we move forward, that the contrast is inherent in the characteristics of the narrative work itself. Let us bear in mind, for the moment, that this contrast is the basis for any historical census of texts and of the ways in which they have been received. We might further remark that the orientation of single works of art is not always constant. What we are dealing with are polarities, which may prove to be stronger or weaker in terms of different epochs and of the different recipients of a work. It should be noted that the work of art, once it has been launched into a specific cultural context, will go on transmitting its message even when the contexts are totally different and will continue to do so practically to infinity.

Any unified solution would then be mistaken, necessarily so. When speaking in general terms, it may prove helpful to investigate the plurality of the utilizations to which works and types of work may prove susceptible, as well as the modalities employed by different readers and different environments which have given rise, or which give rise, to such utilizations. In this sense, it is possible to discuss the concept of literary "fiction"; it is in the context of this dialectic that the inventive aspects proper to narrative texts (and which include the fantastic or the absurd) come to the fore. Without jumping to conclusions, consideration of the concept will at least bring to light some of the mechanisms of the transmission and reception of narrative.

2. It is worth noting that in English the Latin word *fictio* has become an outright designation of the narrative text. The *Oxford English Dictionary* defines this sense of *fiction* as follows: "The species of literature which is concerned with the narration of imaginary events and the portraiture of imaginary characters; fictitious composition. Now usually, prose novels and stories collectively; the composition of works of this class." In the Romance languages, on the contrary, the sense oscillates (as does that of the verb *fingere*) between "simulation" and "literary invention," and it is not a technical term. The same thing is true of the German *Fiktion* (itself from the Latin).

Classical rhetoric measured fiction against imitation (mimesis), its opposite, and all discussion of the licenses narrators might be allowed fall under the heading of verisimilitude. Indeed, deviations from verisimilitude can serve for the classification of literary types. Thus, among the possible subject matter for poetry, the post-Aristotelians list what is probable, verisimilitude *(plasma)*, what is improbable *(mythos)*, and what is true *(historia)*, i.e., to use the terminology of the Latin treatises, *res ficta* or *argumentum, fabula*, and *fama*. In this case, the *res ficta* is, of course, invented, though it will remain within the limits of verisimilitude. "Invention is when a fact that is invented might nonetheless have occurred, the subjects of comedies, for example" (*Rhetorica ad Herenniuum*, I, 13). These are limits which the fabula goes beyond. It is in this light that Priscian's *species narrationum* (*Praeexercitamina rethorica*, 2,5) must be understood: "fabulous, pertaining to fables; imaginative, in the form of tragedies or comedies; historical, for the narration of real facts; civil, used by orators engaged in lawsuits." These are distinctions which, by way of a complex tradition, come down as far as Dante, who tells us that "la forma o il modo del trattare è poetico, immaginativo, descrittivo, digressivo, translativo, etc." (*Epistole*, XIII, 9).

What most interests us here are the free flights of fancy of writers. For writers (and poets) are accorded much greater license than, say, orators, given that "poetry aims to impress with the splendour of its form and . . . its aim is simply to please; it attempts to do this not only by imagining things fantastic but even things quite incredible" (Quintiliano, *Istitutio oratoria*, X, 1, 28), a passage which is perhaps not unmindful of Horace (*Ars poetica*, 338): "ficta voluptatis causa sint proxima veris" ("what is imagined so as to give delight should be close to the truth"). Such license is difficult but not impossible to justify on the basis of a criterion of verisimilitude. Once again, any discussion must begin with Aristotle. "If an impossibility has been portrayed, an error has been made. But it is justifiable if the poet thus achieves the object of poetry—what that is has been already stated—and makes that part or some other part of the poem more striking" (*Poetics*, 1460b, 24–26).

This is a passage which should be read alongside an earlier one which attributed to tragedy the description of "incidents which cause fear and pity," and Aristotle adds that such facts are all the more effective "when the incidents are unexpected and yet one is a consequence of the other. For in that way the incidents will cause more amazement than if they happened mechanically and accidentally, since the most amazing accidental occurrences are those which seem to have been providential" (*Poetics*, 1425a, 4–7). It should not be forgotten that Homer is praised because he was able "to dissimulate and make pleasant even the absurd" and because he "taught the others the proper way of telling lies." According to Aristotle, this is the use of the paralogism. "When B is true if A is true, or B happens if A happens, people think that if B is true A must be true or happen. But that is (in logical terms) false. Consequently if A be untrue but there be something else, B, which is necessarily true or happens if A is true, the proper thing to do is to posit B, for, knowing B to be true, our mind falsely infers that A is true also" (*Poetics*, 1460a, 18–25). His conclusion is that "what is convincing though impossible should always be preferred to what is possible and unconvincing" (2460a, 18–25), given that "for poetic effect a convincing impossibility is preferable to that which is unconvincing though possible" (1461b, 11–12).

3. Infringements of truth—in short, lies—find their justification in what is, after all, the poet's primary objective: to have himself heard or read. They fall within a set of artistic techniques by whose means the public's attention is attracted and held. But the admissibility of such lies, says Aristotle, should be measured not against their distance from reality but in terms of the connection with moments of the narration which their placing will establish (the comparison with paralogism is symptomatic). Indeed, any judgment of admissibility is superseded by a judgment of validity, and this will be related to the overall links of fabulation, inside which the elements that tell lies play a role that has been assigned to them. Aristotle's functional analysis underlines the fact that the component parts of a tale "must be so arranged that if one of them be transposed or removed, the unity of the whole is dislocated and destroyed" (*Poetics*, 1451a, 34).

The expectations of the public, which the sixteenth-century commentaries still stress, is seen as being "surprised" by the poet, because he puts forward events which are, as Vettori says, *praeter expectationem*. Nonetheless, it rarely happens that the addressee of a literary work really is surprised when impossible happenings are presented to him. The normative nature of literary genres determines in advanced the limits, and the type, of admissible infringements against the possible. Anyone who listens to a fairy tale regards it as obvious that fairies, ogres, and gnomes with their supernatural power should be found in it;

anyone who reads an epic poem regards it as normal when he meets with personifications, divine interventions, etc. If what we are dealing with is a Gothic novel, it would be strange indeed if there were no ghosts, animated skeletons, messages from the tomb, etc. The task would be unnecessarily arduous were our search for amazement to be pushed back to the inaugural moments of each literary genre (whose proliferation would then be pointless).

The first observation to be made might be this: the addressee is struck by impossible or marvelous events themselves, not by their mere presence. He is prepared to assist at something out of the ordinary but does not know from the outset exactly what he will be dealing with in any specific case. In fact, we would not be far wrong to think of a kind of competition among writers (particularly those of them who are most generous with their surprises) to see who can best contrive ever new incentives to astonishment. Apart from the fact that this primarily concerns literature as production, it can easily be observed that the repertoire of "tricks of the trade" and of "coups de théatre" is a somewhat limited one. Novelties in the field are more a matter of combination than of creation.

It is far more likely that the surprise element needs to be kept quite separate from enjoyment of the lie. Not only does the reader already know that a particular text will provide him with a certain dose of fiction, but it is precisely because he is aware of the fact that he will be all the more able to enjoy it when it appears. Astonishment at the unreal, the impossible, the absurd is only one among many of our exigencies, and the texts which provide it in good measure are fulfilling a specific task. Having recourse to fiction (inventing it or making use of the invention of others) means widening for a moment the confines of reality, and we thread our way through zones normally forbidden.

This is a movement of a kind well known to psychoanalysis, which draws a dividing line between the conscious and the unconscious and shows when the frontiers are crossed. It recognizes the means by which unconscious drives, when censured, find conscious legitimation in sublimation. Resemblances between oneiric processes and the processes of phantasy have always been recognized. Schleiermacher, in an age not as yet Freudian, accorded them due weight. This functional parallelism, however, does not imply, except to a limited extent, material in common. Literary fiction is tied, for the most part, to traditional repertoires, akin to those of symbols and metaphors.

For an understanding of the preconditions for telling lies, what Aristotle says, in the passages cited, about the way in which the elements are connected in a text is fundamental. Distance from possibility is unimportant; what is important is that such distance should be authenticated inside narrative logic. This is the rationality sought after by sixteenth-century Aristotelians like Castelvetro: "Impossibilità si può fingere per lo poeta, qualunque volta sia congiunta con la credibilità, cioè sia informata di ragione, percioché la impossibilità così fatta, d'impossibilità, per la ragione accompagnantela, diviene possibilità (1576, p. 610): "Impossibility may be feigned by a poet on such occasions as it is linked to plausibility, i.e., when it is endowed with reason, because impossibility so contrived is, because reason accompanies it, transformed from impossibility to possibility." On closer examination, the following exigencies must, it would seem, be met: (1) the work must remain within a coherent system of possible/impossible relations; (2) the presence of impossible elements must conform to a narrative logic which can be assumed to obtain within the given system. Any literary work (and when its character is fantastic this will be all the more true) in effect sets up a possible world which is different from the world of experience. It is necessary, and indeed sufficient, that it should be subject to the rules of its own cohesion.

The concept of "model" is at this point illuminating. Narrative literature, in effect, does no more than elaborate models of human life. It cannot provide a "quidsimile," nor does it wish to. It does more. It brings to the fore (or suggests) lines of force. The model thereby assumes a cognitive function. If it presents elements which are in disaccord with reality (or rather, with our experience of the real), it will do so in order to delineate more clearly, and to render more evident, the lines of force themselves. And this is not all. The various types of fiction can be classified on the basis of the kinds of roles that can be assumed by a model. It is a model which can describe human life, which can interpret it with deliberate deformations and exaggerations, which can provide a fantastic alternative to life or propose the replacement of its reorganization (utopia). It is a model which may lead us back to life or furnish us with the means of criticizing it; it may second evasion or illuminate aspiration. Thus, the ambivalence between the freedom of fancy and the abandonment of invention on the one hand, and cognitive and didascalic commitment on the other, corresponds to the different uses that can be made of the model. One may contemplate it and feast on it to the full or else relate it (by comparison) to the reality it reproduces fictitiously or anticipates by exemplification or both.

4. Mimesis and falsehood are two points of reference, and it is around them that literary conceptions and ideals are alternatively arranged. It is beyond question that, in terms of empirical assessment, texts are to a greater or lesser degree subservient to the possibilities (though not to the actuations) of the real, but, from the point of view of the constitution of a work, fiction as falsehood is a starting point that cannot be eliminated.

Only by a tacitly accepted convention can we admit, for example, that the writer (1) furnishes us with the verbal equivalents of events and persons for the most part nonexistent; (2) appears to be informed not only of the actions of the characters, real and fictitious, but also, in general, of what they think as well; (3) culls, from within the reality he imagines, only events adapted to the shape of his narration, attributing to them autonomy and coherence, exactly as if the causal order operated in a closed circle, in accord with his decisions. A writer takes unto himself the right of establishing possible worlds; he arrogates to himself omniscience with respect to these worlds and exercises (less so over recent decades) a selection which is functional in character.

The narrator is, in short, a licensed liar in terms of any true or false opposition. Even with a possible or impossible opposition, falsehood prevails if we regard as possible such things as may be met with in everyday experience and which, in terms of this experience, can count on a fair degree of statistical probability. With criteria of this kind we would have to regard as impossible not only any intervention of the supernatural, any hyperbolic *amplificatio*, but all expedients and plots.

Nearly all narration has worked with relatively limited repertoires of actions and with limited overall schemata for events (at least within single artistic movements and periods). All the time, there has been a tacit agreement with the addressees as to the acceptability (to take the example of classical and Renaissance comedy) of identical twins to be distinguished or not as the plot required, of disguises often transsexual, of agnitions which resolve and pacify, of the convenient device of the *deus ex machina*, and so forth. The fact is that, once narrative stereotypes have been established (and all literature works with stereotypes), the reader will no longer measure the statistical probability of an event in relation to the real world; he will do so in relation to the conventions to which the story makes reference.

Thus it is that literary conventions do not merely effect a functional legitimation of the impossible. They legitimate it even further on the basis of its repetition and utilization over a long succession of similar texts. The exceptional takes on a syntax and a paradigm; it enters into the structures of a grammar. Hence, what taken in itself would constitute an absurdity, and would have no validity as communication, enters into a system of values. The conventions of literature are the grammar of the impossible. One understands why literary theorists have spoken not of the possible and the impossible but of verisimilitude or the lack of it. It is the latter distinction which alludes more to a syntactic coherence and a paradigmatic recognition than to confrontation with the real (and we might recall Aristotle's "likely impossibility" and "unbelievable possibility"). On the other hand, mimesis really is, as Plato said, the replacement of reality as it is lived by its shadow or reflection. It is, though, a shadow which acquires (for there is no mystery about the process which produces it) a reality of its own, and it is left to the writer's discretion whether to accentuate or to underplay the isomorphisms.

Mimesis and fiction establish a dialectic: concrete relations with reality are relatively important (they are dealt with directly by literary conventions and mediated by underlying conceptions of the world). Vastly more important is the writer's intention to communicate, the scope he attributes to the formalization of models.

But relations with the real take on a different kind of importance in terms of the instinct of fabulation. The reader's propensity toward acceptance (in accord with civilizations and fashions) of narrations—possible, plausible, or at any rate coherent—must come to terms with a natural need to surrender to fabulation in order to move beyond one's own mundane experience toward the lives of others or toward another possible life. In this way, the "fallacy" of mimesis and the truth of falsehood become correlative elements.

Narrators are well aware of this. It is a fact that they multiply historical points of reference, that they often base themselves on authorities which do not exist, that their authoritative sources are often made up, that they introduce into their texts the (false) traces of a history of previous editions; it is a fact, too, that such efforts are multiplied when the subject matter breaks free of the real and the possible. We should also note that these authentications are often brought forward in undisguised bad faith where playfulness invites amiable complicity. Reflections of unreality are made to play upon simulations of the real.

Goethe's *Lust zu fabulieren* and Bergson's *fonction fabulatrice* (which seems to lie at the origin of myth and religion) have been discussed in various cultures and in various epochs. It can hardly be said, though, that their psychological bases have been adequately investigated either as they concern the addresser, the teller of tales, or the addressee, who profits from the fabulation. The field of child psychology is an exception. Two discourses need to be made. The first is a broad approach to the writer's capacity to give life to a possible world and to the reader's (or listener's) readiness to allow himself to be conducted by means of words into this world (the word is a guide to the programmed elaboration of the world which has been distilled in the word). A second, more specific, approach is to the existence of a need to invent stories or to have them told to one. This need might be regarded as universal if we call to mind, to cite only extreme cases, the importance in primitive cultures of the teller of tales and the diffusion of narrative in mass culture—the films, comics, and soap operas of today.

There has, on the contrary, been much discussion in abstract terms of the importance of fantasy among human activities. Whether or not it is distinguished from the imagination (and Albert the Great was the first to do so), fantasy has always been recognized as a creative faculty (the term Goethe uses is *Schöpfertum*). If the artist brings into being a new reality, it is equally true that creation itself (whomever it should be attributed to) is an act of fantasy which assimilates the creator to the artist. Thus, Fichte's theoretical spirit operates like an "I" that represents, and representation is "the marvellous faculty of the productive imagination." All of the activities of consciousness come under its head. In a totally different philosophical framework, the faculty of thought for Vaihinger achieves realization in a series of fictions, and it is thanks to them that we find our way in the fog of our senses and achieve an, at least temporary, dominion over reality. The study of consciousness is thus a study of fictions. Overestimation of the individual "I" and overestimation of empirical perceptions both lead, strangely enough, to very similar conclusions.

For the philosophers, fantasy acts on reality; according to some it constitutes it. In works of literature, it dances around reality, it keeps an eye on it as it draws away from it, or it rushes headlong toward it. Literary fiction considers reality a datum. The bolder the fiction (the more prone to the unlikely and the absurd), the more its user is compelled to verify the effective validity of the real, within, or it may be beyond, the limits of his conceptions. Flight from the real and return to the real are the two alternative directions of the activity of the *fonction fabulatrice*.

Let it be clear: reality and unreality, possibility and impossibility are to be defined in relation to the beliefs to which the text refers. It is difficult to speak of unreality or of impossibility with regard to a mythological text; and a hagiographic text by definition will admit, while considering them exceptional, divine interventions, ubiquity, thaumaturgic actions, communication with the dead, the whole range of miracles. As it projects itself toward the future, science fiction rationalizes, with (pseudo-) scientific explanations, extensions, at times astounding, of our capacities.

Even the horror tale, a genre where interchange between reality and unreality may be at a maximum, lies inside fairly well-defined cultural coordinates (belief in ghosts and in vampirism, parapsychology, and various types of occult phenomena); they are taken up in calculated stylization by the writers of a positivistic age, whose tastes are postromantic. For the authors of horror stories, the dialectic between mimesis and falsehood has been introjected—albeit, though not exclusively, in a poetic.

5. Down to the twentieth century, we may say that writers started out from empirical, but fairly stable, concepts of reality and had recourse, in their search for elements antinomic to it, to the sphere of the religious, the mythical, the magical, the legendary. The twentieth century turned this upside down. The certainty of reality is in crisis, while the sources of an "institutional" absurd (religion, myth, etc.) run dry. The dialectic between reality and unreality is mounted ex novo, but only on the terrain of a reality that is flawed and elusive.

This is why in contemporary narrative no well-defined zone of pertinence is established for the unreal or the marvelous. Once the properties of the real become elusive, identification of its opposite is compromised as well. The marvelous (always in a negative sense: the absurd, the nightmare) lies embedded in a day-to-day which it renders even more inaccessible, alien, incomprehensible. If the marvelous of tradition casts doubt on the physical laws of our world, the marvelous in its modern form refutes the interpretation schemata which man, in the course of a long parabola, has contrived in order to account for his existence. The new marvelous is a mimesis distraught with the horror of discovery.

For example, the concepts of law and guilt are those Kafka places for us in a perspective both unsettling and distressing. It is a law that is not expressed, that is enforced by a power which is capricious, omnipresent, and elusive and by a guilt not brought about by specific acts, by the violation of norms (which in fact do not exist), but which is nonetheless accepted even by the victims of the law. And guilt is accepted as being beyond expiation; the more so, the more the victims are, in the moral sense of the word, innocent. And Kafka does not merely question ordinary notions of crime and punishment, the idea that law is explicitly defined and transgressions punishable; since the laws of which he speaks are the principles of existence and even of essence, what he in effect dramatically overturns are accepted conceptions of the relation between man and the world.

Kafka's absurd enfolds man, it holds him in its power. It is an escatalogical solution, delineated but elusive, which rejects reason and the word. Man moves within the absurd, whereas his habits, feelings, projects are adapted to a reality as yet unexploded, waveringly shared. Beckett's absurd is, on the contrary, introjected by man; it guides the moves he makes toward an inevitable fall, if not annihilation. Man experiments in himself, in his tortured carnality and in the frustration of his every exertion, the suffocating embrace of a hostile and silent will. Kafka's laws are inexpressible and their validity is collective, even though they are verified through the experience of a single character. In Beckett, the two antagonists—the hidden, perhaps sadistic, legislator and his subject—are personalized; they face up to each other from a distance, though the outcome is never in doubt.

In Kafka and Beckett, the theater of the absurd is everyday life. Characters do not bedeck themselves as is usual; they remain ideally naked; their naturalness is without defense in the face of an external will and its rigors. Habits, fine feelings, tics are fragments of a harmony between man and the world which a negative revelation has fractured; the absurd floods in through the breaches of the disaster. The illogical, the nightmare are the signs of reality unmasked.

Face to face with this horrifying mimesis, with this realism of the absurd, fiction stands revealed as purely cerebral in its operations. Fiction is oriented toward the mind of its creator rather than toward the simulacra it produces; fiction turns upside down the relation of model to life, of book to reality. Hence, the tendency to have recourse to an alternative logic, to sophism, and paradox. Sophisms oppose the principles of identity and of contradiction. The best-known pre-Socratic paradoxes (Achilles and the tortoise, for example) are used by Borges (one of whose works is symptomatically entitled *Ficciones*) to effect a thoroughgoing subversion of the categories of space and time, in an extremistic authentication of absolutist idealism.

With instruments such as these, Borges ensures for himself the possibility of moving inside an absurd both regulated and structured. Hence, for example, the cyclical nature of events, the reversibility of time, the reciprocal exchanges between imagination and life, the mirror-image relation of the thinker and his thought are nests of boxes which multiply to infinity the relations of subject to object, of container to content. To this must be added skillful use of the law of probability and of large numbers, in virtue of which coincidences and repetitions are held to be possible, even though they are based on an incommensurable extension of chance.

Such "logical" instruments are always discovered or rediscovered. The techniques of the riddle and of the investigation intervene (one thinks of titles like *Inquisiciones* and *Otras inquisiciones*) and are used by the writer in his detective stories. Hence, each story is a passage from an initial disorder or anomaly, in terms of which the facts present themselves to the perception and common sense of characters and reader, to an order based on the norms of Borges's own "logic." At one and the same time, the need to interpret finds satisfaction (a riddle solved gives a sense of freedom) as does a desire for rationality, a rationality whose perfection lies in the fact that it is not entangled in the threadbare nets of the real.

These exercises, which might all too easily end up as sophisticated *jonglerie*, a mystification declared and accepted, always achieve their realization in a link between life and book which is the basic element of Borges's invention. It is an element shot through and through with vaunted erudition and mystification: nonexistent works and authors vie with choice polyglot quotation; authors who do exist are enriched with works not their own or with others never written; well-known titles migrate from one author to another; the same book can be composed twice and remain identical over a distance of centuries.

Such cultural sophistication becomes a conception of the world. The library of Babel collects all of the works that have been written or that ever will be written, and each work contains not only the meanings placed there by its author in relation to his epoch but also the meanings it would have had if it had been written by another, by others, or by mankind as a whole. It is through books that a nonhistorical past can be produced (that of Tlon), a past which can influence our present no less than real history. This approach might be regarded as an out-and-out exaggeration of the polarities of life and literature, reality and fiction. Borges takes a stand which is so absolutely on the side of literature and of fiction that life is seen as an epiphenomenon of literature, reality as a shadow of fiction. We are at the antipodes with respect to any disquisition on mimesis and verisimilitude. It is the omnipotence of literature that is being proclaimed, though only in the realms of fantasy can it ever find realization.

Such a discourse can become even more subtle. What counts for Borges is not primarily books as words (or letters). Words and letters (cabalistically) contain the world, and its shape is progressively the outcome of the activity by which we name and denominate. Words and letters in the infinity of their possible combinations contain not only all that has been, or that ever will be, said and done, but also everything which has never been and which will never be. In them alone, therefore, will lie any equivalence among possible worlds—one, and only one of which, is our own.

Exemplary result of a renunciation, the fiction of Borges compels us to rethink the logical and existential terms of our relations with the real; and to do so from the rarefied and purely mental distance of the word, of the literary.

This fiction, which is the antithesis of realism, serves to show up the weakness of a poetics too enamored of immediacy of representation, of inevitability of moral reactions or celebrations. Narration cannot confine itself to describing any more than painting can limit itself to photographing. By leaving reality behind, fiction renders our perception of reality more refined and more subtle; it strengthens our critical faculties; it uses paradox to reveal forces and motivations. This is all the more true if the reality one abandons really can be interpreted by the unreality into which one enters, if this unreality shadows forth a nonempirical logical system that, in certain of its aspects, is akin to that inside which reality is inscribed, or could be inscribed.

This is like stretching to the utmost the thread which ties us to the real. It is a thread that can be stretched not just beyond the limits of the real but within its limits as well. Hyperbole, *amplificatio*, sarcastic distortion—all of the techniques of an exasperated realism (which tend toward expressionism) are simply ways of transforming reality itself into fiction, ways of re-presenting experience to accord with points of view that are fabulous, unreal, and absurd. Fiction therefore does not so much set its sights on fantastic worlds as deform this world of ours, and it does so in such a way that its interconnections and its evaluations, extrapolated from their deceptive equilibriums, stand revealed to us in all their brutality. Alternative possible worlds are not what is being proposed. It is our own world which is put forward as impossible.

Whether it invents or deforms, fiction always measures the real by the fact of stepping back from it; it defines it from a distance which sets up new and unusual perspectives; it solicits it to the point of turning it upside down. Opposed attitudes toward the use of literature (evasion and involvement, detachment and commitment, hedonism and criticism) reveal themselves as two phases of something which, embarked upon as adventure, may well turn out to have been a cognitive undertaking, an initiation to praxis.

6. Fiction may be the invention of facts or of sequences of vicissitudes. It is this second aspect which has been most stressed here (and which is, in the usual meaning of *fiction,* preeminent). These vicissitudes are narrated through a discourse, and it is through the events of the discourse that the reader (or listener) comes into contact with those of the fabula. Content vicissitudes are the summing up of only one of an infinite number of itineraries realizable within the text. Each itinerary, in reality, is a vicissitude. Thus, the text as a whole (and each narrative text) may be regarded as a fiction—a polyvalent and polysemic fiction. Indeed, from the point of view of formal itineraries, no text exists which does not constitute a fiction, because the author "invents" the way he connects the words and arguments he wishes to communicate, often indeed seeking for effects of surprise or for the final catharsis of an intellective solution.

In this sense, the border between the work of fiction and other literary works becomes elusive. The same is true if we rely on the concept of mimesis, given that mimesis is often mimesis of an earlier work, of an earlier mimesis, rather than being directly related to reality. In such a case, the work imitated becomes the model for another model (accepting both meanings of the word), i.e., it offers, as reworked material, a part of its schematizations. In addition, any work of literature at all, when it has recourse to themes, stereotypes, and so on, will as a rule be far more indebted to literature and to culture than to reality. In the midst of conventions, reality must gain what space it can.

Such reflections are not meant to cast doubt on the individuality of the narrative text, for this is solidly based on the *fonction fabulatrice* and on clearcut formal rules. They do help, though, to explain why (in concomitance with the presumed present weakness of narrative fiction) literary criticism now seems prepared to put itself forward as a rival to creative literature.

As interpreter and illustrator of the work's semiological structures (and of their potentialities), literary criticism has the task of determining, achronically, the functional, conceptual, and symbolic systems temporalized in literary discourse, while bringing to light their initial, as well as their possible, implications. Criticism takes as its base the semiotic complex of the work, and no light contribution is made by the inventiveness to which it has recourse with the aim of isolating, correlating, arranging, and interpreting the elements of this complex structure and creating a new (critical) construction. This construction is undoubtedly a fiction. It does, though endeavor to re-present, in the most satisfactory manner, the materials of the literary construction. The guarantee is a philological attitude which consists in carefully checking basic semantic values both in the text and in its cultural context and which strives to recover the overall meaning of the structure. In short, it sets up a *Zirkel im Verstehen*, a back-and-forth movement among the parts and the whole, one which must involve not merely the work in its elements and as a whole but also the work as itself one element of a larger whole.

This does not mean restricting research to the author's desire for signification, in the belief that this can be disengaged with certainty, with nothing left over. Indeed, time confers on the structures of the message an increase in meaning; one of the properties of art is its capacity to speak from one generation to another, to unfold with the help of time. The semiotic structures of the work are not what is transformed; it is the observer who comes to perceive new relations, new vistas, within a series of points of view which can be regarded as inexhaustible. The constructions of literary criticism never are, and never can be, definitive. They cannot even be finite. We should say no more than that the critic applies himself totally to disengaging the semiotic structures of the work, which will also involve deriving from it such meanings as his epoch, culture, and personal insights will be able to reveal. He will know (or he should know) that truth will not be quite at one with the results of his analysis and that it will go on forever welling forth from the multiplicity of our analytical operations.

A creative tension exists between, on the one hand, a commitment to clarification of communicative contents and contexts and, on the other, the contribution of a combinative, associative, and prospective fantasy. Too strong an inclination toward the first pole will lead us to reduce literary criticism to narrow-minded and self-assured philology; allowing oneself to be attracted toward the second pole will easily induce us to accord too much weight to isolated elements of the text's semiotic structures and to arrange them so that they will form new structures—structures which, irrespective of their fascination, will usurp in fruition those of the work when they ought rather to give reasons for them and interpret them. Creative criticism, in other words, runs the risk of producing restructurings that will not lend themselves to verification in terms of the totality of a text, which will then become mere pretext, and of unleashing a purely literary imagination, one not called upon to measure itself against the real (nor even against that part of the real which is the text). This is spellbound contemplation of our own daydreaming, while the world escapes us. Literature withdraws into itself.

It would be anachronistic to defend the cognitive function of literature by distinguishing the sphere of criticism from that of fiction, just as one cannot now take refuge in the thoroughly discredited principles of literary genres. Moreover, the first to prevaricate were inventive writers themselves, especially with the essay-novel whose most illustrious example is still *Don Quixote*. And it should not be forgotten that, in the allied field of criticism of the visual arts, the critic often takes upon himself full responsibility for the communicative capacity of an (otherwise indecipherable) work and goes far beyond any defensible correspondence.

On the other hand, no one has the right to restrain the fiction of criticism, for it is a creative activity, (nobly) parasitic though it be. It is an activity which renews the message of the text, which, though it may change the tone, causes its voice to resound, and which multiplies its potential for evocation and perpetuation. It is an activity which out of one text can create as many others as there are interpretations to offer and which then entrusts to us this polyphony, these echoes, for further inexhaustible transmutations. Only in abstract is it easy to distinguish between a commitment to the text and a commitment which starts from the text: between hermeneutics and invention.

It is two different activities that we are speaking of (the one is applied to the real, the other to a text. They intersect and overlap in such a way that a text may well be its own criticism (or a criticism of other texts), while critical activity, though it sets its sights on the reality of the text, may do so in an attempt to discover, beyond the realities revealed and foreshadowed by the text, yet other fragments of reality. Between literature and criticism collaboration exists, but competition is not absent, even on the plane of inventive capacities. Both set their sights on the same target, and that target is knowledge.

What we have been saying so far has little relevance to the most recent positions of the *nouvelle critique* or to its theoretical bases. For the proponents of the *nouvelle critique* (and here their most lucid interpreter may well act as their ambassador), speakers or addressers are to be put firmly in brackets, as is the content of the message itself. The discourse of the text and critical discourse are to be considered as one and the same thing, because they take place inside a "discourse of the language" which pays no attention to the coordinates of communication. Such an undertaking is daring indeed, and it involves putting language in the place of the subject, be he author or critic. "The subject is not an individual fullness, which one has or has not the right to empty in language (according to the "genre" of literature one chooses), but it is, on the contrary, a void around which the writer weaves an infinitely transformed word (inserted in a chain of transformations). Hence, every writing *that does not lie* designates the absence of the subject instead of its interior attributes. Language is not a predicate of an inexpressible subject, or of one which language itself might serve to express, but it is the subject" (Barthes 1966, pp. 57–58).

The logical outcome is the impossibility of distinguishing between the work and its criticism. "Criticism and the work keep saying 'I am literature,' and, while they join voices, literature never utters anything other than the absence of the subject" (Barthes 1966, p. 58). "The work (even if it is classical) is not an external, closed object which may later be mastered by a 'different' language (that of the critic); it is not the support for a commentary (an accessory word, surrounding a solid, full center). Deprived of origin, wherever it is sited institutionally, it knows only one mode of existing: an infinite passage through other writings. What still appears to us as 'criticism' is only a manner of 'quoting' an ancient text, which, inside its own perspective, is itself shot through with quotations; the codes counteract ad infinitum. Thus, it is correct to affirm that, from the moment in which a science of writing, writing itself, is born, any literature, any literary criticism, will die." (p. 9) What does language communicate then? And what, since it is still feasible, does literary criticism reveal? "What it reveals cannot be a meaning (since this meaning backs away ceaselessly toward the emptiness of the subject) but only chains of symbols, homologies of relations" (p. 58).

Curious is the fact that, while Barthes recognizes the motivations of literary criticism in the usual sense of the term, he calls it *reading* and reserves the word *criticism* for the activity just defined. "Only a reading is enamored of the work and establishes with it a relation of desire. To read is to desire the work, to want to be the work, to refuse to submit it to any word extraneous to it. . . . To move from reading to criticism means changing desire, desiring no longer the work but a language of one's own. For this very reason, however, this is tantamount to taking the work back to the desire to write from which it arose" (p. 63).

The glad tidings of this central role of language and of writing (whose guarantors, it is clear, are Blanchot and Lacan) can be proclaimed; they cannot, though, be subjected to proof because any demonstration would require two subjects at least, an addresser and an addressee, not to mention the subject matter of the demonstration itself. And all of this would run counter to the theory. We will content ourselves merely by pointing to Barthes's contraposition of a criticism of contents (one which is, then, based on communication) and a criticism of language (which is understood as a suprapersonal production and epiphany of symbols). Despite his frequent contact with semiology, the most recent conception of critical activity put forward by Barthes is therefore a distinctly antisemiotic one (given that signs are instruments of communication and given that the language and the symbols of which he speaks have no communicative scope).

Thus, the creativity of literary criticism reaches the point of obliterating any distinction between literature and criticism. The critic misunderstands the communicative nature of the text (isolating it from its addresser-addressee circuit); he turns the code-message relation upside down (utilizing, in an inventive effort, elements of the code but isolating them from the message as a whole); he reinforces the hegemony of the language at the expense of those who use it. A semiotically oriented critic, on the contrary, will set out from the communicative function of the text and see it as a message however polysemic it may be, however ambiguous and rich in unconscious elements; he will attempt to seize upon the widest possible range of content and will defend the instrumental function of the language. The two conceptions which here stand in opposition are thus not a matter merely of literature; they involve the world.

The fascination of an invention (a fiction) which arises out of the fictions of other people is undeniable, as if we were to raise to the nth power imagination in its most unbridled aspects and enjoy to the full the infinite possibilities of the play of language. But such a choice is an ideological one as well. If it is true, as we have argued here, that flights of literary fancy take as their point of reference a vision and an interpretation of reality, and if it is true that alternative models, itineraries through possible worlds, really serve for a more satisfactory delineation of "one" model of our world and that escape is such only in relation to the place from which one is moving away, it is equally clear that this kind of dialectic will no longer function when literary criticism propagates one imagination inside another imagination, one linguistic activity inside another, and when, in the place of reality, one puts a book and, in place of praxis, a proliferation of symbols.

In the last resort, narrative fiction is no longer being reinforced; it is being taken beyond the point of no return, toward spaces where language rotates about its own axis, in an autotelic phantasmagoria. It falls to the task of semiotic literary criticism (all the better if its bases are solidly philological) to illuminate the fictions of writers, to attempt to interpret what they reveal—the condemnations, the hopes, the expectations which they continue, thanks to our insistence, to bring to light.

References

Barthes, R.
    1966. *Critique et verité*. Paris: Seuil.
Castelvetro, L.
    1576. *Poetica d'Aristotele vulgarizzata, et sposta per Lodovico Castelvetro*. Basel: Pietro De Sedabonis.
Quintilian
    1921. *Istitutiones oratoriae*, trans. H. E. Butler. Loeb Classical Library. Cambridge, Mass.: Harvard University Press.

3.
Genres

1. The root *gen*, whence *gigno*, links the Latin *genus* both to the idea of sex (hence, grammatical gender) and to that of race or lineage, as a principle of classification. Among literary uses of the word, we find *genus scribendi*, i.e., *style*, and literary *genera*, groupings comparable to those of the sciences. Here, too, there also exists a difference of generalization (*genus* against *species*), which, as we shall see, will find its correspondence in our argument. The vicissitudes of the Latin word closely follow those of Greek *genos;* but, in Greek, *eidos* was more commonly used for "literary genre" and stood specifically for "aspect," "form." The grouping of literary works into a limited number of genres was suggested and widely put into effect *a posteriori;* the doctrine of genres is, as a rule, cultivated in a period which follows that of their development (this holds good for Aristotle, as well as for the sixteenth-century theorists and for Boileau). In periods of strict literary codification, however, it may well assume a normative finality, and so look to the future. Genre, therefore, will sometimes have a nomenclative function, sometimes a projectual, or even normative, function. If we turn to periods unaffected by such classifications or extraneous to them, the development of genres can be looked at as a maturing of traditions, the establishment (through the imitation of prestigious models) of connections between certain contents and certain forms of exposition. Definition of genres will then be a way of verifying, in critical terms, the changing history of these connections, for they constitute the framework within which literary activity develops.

2. We may observe that Plato proposed a grouping which was binary and based exclusively on content: serious genre (epic and tragedy) and comic genre (comedy and iambics). A more subtle threefold division is also due to Plato (*Republic*, 392e–394b). It distinguishes *mimetic* or *dramatic* genre (tragedy and comedy), *expositive* or *narrative* genre (dithyramb, nòmos, lyric poetry), and a *mixed* genre (epic). This is based not on intrinsic characteristics but on variation in the relation between literature and reality, measured against the basic concept of *mimesis*, i.e., *imitation*.

This criterion is maintained, in its substance, by Aristotle, even though he is mainly concerned with tragedy and only secondarily with epic poetry (the unfinished *Poetics* has deprived us of his pages on comedy). But Aristotle, while he devotes his attention to tragedy (and often uses it as a paradigm for poetry, to the point of including epic in his observations), also adopts other techniques for distinction. These I give here schematically, extrapolating them from Aristotle's discourse, despite the fact that a classification of genres is not what he was aiming for:

(1) metrical form: tragedy uses iambic trimeters; epic uses hexameters.

(2) the quality of the characters: noble or better than we are in the case of tragedy and epic; humble or worse or, even more, ridiculous for comedy. This second criterion may be combined, when the scope is descriptive, with a relation to imitation. Sophocles comes close to Homer in the nobility of his characters, but, in terms of mimesis, he is closer to Aristophanes (*Poetics*, 1448a, 20–1448b, 1).

(3) duration of events: "Tragedy tends to fall within a single revolution of the sun or slightly to exceed that, whereas epic is unlimited in point of time" (1449b, 12).

(4) unity or plurality of action: "In tragedy it is not possible to represent several parts of the story as going on simultaneously, but only to show what is on the stage, that part of the story which the actors are performing, whereas, in the epic, because it is narrative, several parts can be portrayed as being enacted at the same time" (1459b, 24–26).

And this is not all. Immediately before his classification on the basis of mimesis, Aristotle had advanced, and then abandoned, another exclusively formal criterion as follows: art made up of harmony and rhythm (auletic or citharistic) or of rhythm alone (dance); art made up of language alone, in prose (mime and socratic dialogues) or in verse (elegy, epic, etc.), and, if in verse, unity or variety of meter; and lastly, art made up of harmony and rhythm and language (dithyrambs, nòmoi, tragedy, comedy) (1447a, 1–1447b, 27).

Artistotle's standpoint is that of the historian and critic who, at the same time, seeks as philosopher to arrive at general principles with which to justify his assertions. It was the authority of the philosopher which would later make it possible to read the *Poetics* as a book of literary rules, and it should be added that the history of the genres of ancient Greece, outlined by Aristotle at the beginning of his text (1448b, 4–1449a, 30), could hardly have appeared to him in any other light than as a process of perfection which had achieved, in the splendid literature of the Attic period, an organization which, in its magnificence, appeared to be definitive. Nonetheless, the *Poetics* makes no claim to be normative, let alone to define literary genres. Aristotle expresses opinions, puts forward suggestions, and is more concerned with the theoretical premises than with their effective realization. This is why even today the *Poetics* is a valuable work. It was rather in the field of rhetoric that Aristotle emphasized the didactic aspects of those classifications which relate to speech making, that vital activity of his time, and his *Rhetoric* will be imitated or "completed" many times.

Only in the Alexandrian period does a definite doctrine of genres mature. It is a kind of catalogue of a great literature which has been exhausted, or a repertory of choices for epigoni. Genres are placed in direct relation to styles and they are minutely classified. For example, for theater the triad tragedy-comedy-satyr play is established, corresponding to the high, low, and middle styles. Detailed observations concern the language of single genres (comedy for example), for it is understood that codification will involve the discourse plane itself. Furthermore, it is intended that the list be all inclusive, and an attempt is made to distinguish sub-genres *(polumerestate)*. Thus, for example, melic poetry, depending on whether it is devoted to the gods or to men, takes in hymn, prosodion, paean, dithyramb, nòmoi, adonic, "io bacchus," hyporkhema, and, respectively, encomium, epinikios, skolion, love song, epithalamium, hymenaeum, "syllos," threnos, epicedium. It is to the Alexandrians, and specifically to Dionysius of Thrace (170–190 B.C.), that we owe recognition of the lyric (or melic) genre. Aristotle had neglected it, perhaps because he found a poet like Pindar too distant and without following. The late recognition accorded to the lyric can be explained terminologically (lyric poetry is, strictly speaking, sung to the accompaniment of the lyre; therefore, it did not include everything that would now be understood as lyric poetry, while it did embrace the monodic sections of tragedy). And there are nomenclative considerations as well (the lyric in the Attic period was distinguished not merely from the melic and from choral poetry to the sound of the flute but also from iambic poetry, from satire, elegy, epitaph, epigram, threnody, hymn, etc.). These difficulties will persist in modern treatises because many short poetical compositions cannot be regarded as lyrics. Indeed, the canon of Dionysius of Thrace is a relatively open one (it takes in tragedy, comedy, elegy, epic, lyric, and threnody); some wished to add the idyll and the pastoral. On the whole, though, the triad drama-epos-lyric met with some favor, and it will become central to the meditations of the Romantics. When Greece handed over to Rome, the main genres and their subspecies had already been listed and grouped, as a rule in relation to the Platonic or Aristotelian doctrine of mimesis.

For Alexandrian men of letters (they were often grammarians and scholars), the main preoccupation was classification, and this is most clearly evidenced in the "canons" and explanatory lists of authors which they drew up (for example, the *pinakes* of Callimachus). Their intentions were normative: the "canons" look back to the cultural past and rearrange it, while the norms face future problems. Thereafter, the whole successive history of the theory of genres (down to the moment when, with romanticism and its aftermath, the attempt will be made to revise the canon as a whole) will consist of the mutable relation between literary activity, courageously and consciously opposed to the definitive character of the canon, and invocation of principles on the part of theoreticians who were not always deaf to new requirements and who were engaged in reconciling them with the principles themselves.

It is within this framework that the Aristotelian approach will continue to survive down to the baroque period, despite lengthy periods of eclipse. On the whole, we might say that it was the normative element which became more accentuated and uncompromising, and it should be added that, read in this light, the *Poetics* was an authoritarian presence feared in every period in which classical taste was predominant. The case of Horace and the *Ars poetica* is typical. It defends the primacy of tragedy and the threefold Alexandrian division of theatrical genres, at a time when the theater hardly existed and when, in the lyric poetry Aristotle had left aside, there had been new developments (thanks in part to Horace himself, who, however, is silent on the subject), as there had been in satire, a typically Roman product. Thus, the *Ars poetica*, which owes such originality as it has to its clear-cut definitions of style and composition, ends up being astonishingly anachronistic even for its own time, unless we wish to regard it as the manifesto of a classical revival which never took effect.

Once again, it was in the sphere of a classicizing program, that of the Late Renaissance and the Counter Reformation, that Aristotle's *Poetics* was energetically revived. In the Middle Ages, the classical genres had been completely overwhelmed, just as, with the passage from Latin to the vernacular, a new metrics had developed based on accent and quite different from Greek and Latin metrics. It was the very basis of Plato's threefold division which was incomprehensible, in an age which ignored the possibility of actually staging Latin plays and which consequently could not understand the meaning of mimesis. The words *comedy* and *tragedy* were understood in an exclusively stylistic sense and on the basis of the happy or unhappy ending. Thus, Dante saw the *Aeneid* as a tragedy (*Inferno*, XX, 113) and called his own poem a *Commedia* (Letter to Cangrande, 10).

Many literary genres were created *ex novo* in the Middle Ages. We might call to mind, of those destined to a long life, the romance (novel) and the *novella* (short story); drama, sacred at first and then profane, was established and was quite independent of any influence from Latin theater; a type of epic was developed, the *chanson de geste*, whose far-off echoes of Virgil merely served to underline how totally extraneous it was from any antique models. Such inexhaustible creativity gave rise in Italy to the psychological novel *(Fiammetta)*, to the *cantare in ottava rima*, and finally to romances of chivalry, these too in ottava rima.

This proliferation of forms and themes was not subjected to constraint at the level of theory. Different poetics collected the Late Latin rhetorical tradition and presented it anew, while the *artes dictandi* were concerned with epistolography and the harangues of the Communes. The development of single genres and of their system was governed exclusively by the rapid consolidation of traditions and by public demand. This situation persisted virtually down to the Late Renaissance, by which time knightly romance, pastoral, comedy, etc., had already given of their best.

Renewed discussion of poetics (which soon comes to center upon the *Poetics* of Aristotle) coincides with an attempt to consolidate and provide rules for Renaissance taste. Where genres are concerned, we might remark two salient points: the debate in defense of the romance, which enhanced, but also disturbed, the sector of *mixed* literature (at once diegetic and mimetic); and the question of tragedy, of the unities of time, place, and action in particular, and of catharsis (Guarini's later defense of the *pastoral* and the *tragicomedy* should be added). We should recall that Aristotle's failure to mention lyric poetry was remarked and replaced with forthright revindication (Daniello, Tasso, Guarini, etc.); this, despite the fact that no solution was, or could be, found for the difficulties of its definition. For some, the lyric is mimesis, because a lyric poet "imitates" himself; for others (for example, Minturno), it is a mixed genre, because in part it imitates action and in part narrates it.

Overall, the problem of genres does not seem to have been particularly urgent, at least where classification was concerned. What was urgent was investigation of *imitatio* (also understood, in humanistic terms, as including imitation of the classics and not just mimesis of reality) and investigation, the outcome of philosophical and religious preoccupations, of the ultimate aims of art. There undoubtedly was discussion of genres, often quite animated, but it concerned single texts (Dante, Ariosto, Tasso above all). In these cases, discussion centered on the choice of subject matter, the limits of the fiction, the structure of the fabula. It was, in short, a critical discussion based on argumentation which was general and theoretical in character. In this sense, treatise writers and polemicists of the sixteenth century advanced some quite subtle arguments, which do not deserve neglect or, worse, derision.

We shall not deal here with more recent attempts to classify genres—first among them, for its historical importance and influence on European theorists (Luzan, Dryden, etc.), the *Art poétique* of Boileau (1674), which still belongs to the sphere of classical revival. Alongside the genres of the Aristotelian tradition—epic, tragedy, comedy—equal status was accorded to the various subgenres of contemporary poetry which Boileau lists (idyll, elegy, sonnet, ballad, rondeau, chanson, etc.), although there is no reference to any general principles of classification. From a naturalistic and rationalistic standpoint, genres are regarded as immutable over time (new genres, such as melodrama, are condemned, and Molière is dealt with belittlingly). The mythological element seems to be regarded as fundamental for the epic, but minor genres are defined with formal criteria.

3. The problem of the genres was posed anew when attempts were made to establish it on historical and philosophical bases. Vico (1744, ed. 1976, pp. 414–15), for example, while he retained the traditional subdivisions, saw in the development of genres and in their interrelations an *"istoria ragionata"* of humanity, an explanation of history. He distinguished between primitive epic, which documents a period when the only history was poetry, and reflected epic, populated by heroes who incarnate ethical and philosophical concepts, or between the ancient lyric poets, who raised their hymns to the gods, and those who later celebrated *"gli eroi trapassati,"* dead heroes; last came the melic poets *"de' quali è principe Pindaro,"* for Pindar leads them, and Horace the Romans. Vico sketched in historical terms the interlacing of tragedy, comedy, and satire, from their remote origins to the Latins, on the basis of their types of character (first came gods and heroes, then real public figures, then private,

invented figures). Vico's is an ideal history but, where the ancients are concerned, one which is based directly on the texts, however daring their interpretation. The model is a brilliant one.

Goethe *(Westöstlicher Divan)* represents an opposite, extratemporal view of things. With him genres are no longer principles of classification; they become poetical categories. Disdaining minor genres and subgenres, Goethe confines himself to Aristotle's two categories and to the lyric and sees them as the genuine, natural forms of poetry (as "echte Naturformen der Dichtung"). It is because they are categories rather than pigeonholes that the three forms (epic, lyric, and drama) can be found contemporaneously in a single text (in early Greek tragedy, the choruses are prevalently lyrical). Indeed, Goethe maintains that the three forms can be arranged to form a circular pattern, in such a way that the different genres that are realized can be defined on the basis of their respective distances from each of the three forms. This schema has a historical validity as well, when he remarks that "an epic poet narrates an event as if it was entirely in the past, while the dramatic poet describes it as entirely present" (Goethe and Schiller 1797, ed. 1960, p. 249). Goethe goes on to discover that genres in the literature of his own time tend to converge on the dramatic (one example is the epistolary novel), and, in general terms, he accepts that the separate character of genres is compromised.

Goethe's circular schema has recently been revived by Julius Petersen, who designs a tripartite wheel within which the genres, linking together the three spokes of drama, epic, and lyric, are arranged from the center to the circumference in the order of their progressive codification. It is a schema which aspires to be at once historical and universal, and, for this very reason, apart from the doubtful nature of specific labelings and reciprocal positions, it appears unacceptable.

The most advanced point in reflection on genres (though mention should also be made of August Wilhelm Schlegel and Schelling) is undoubtedly that reached by Hegel in his *Vorlesungen über die Ästhetik*, where one of his aims was to integrate a historical with an extratemporal standpoint. The triadic pattern typical of Hegel's thought (and on the basis of which art, too, is placed among the activities of the spirit, to be followed by religion and philosophy) was there, ready to hand in the case of genres. Once again they are epic, lyric, drama. The criterion for distinguishing these three genres was provided by the antithesis of objective and subjective. Epic, in fact, "presents what is itself *objective* in its objectivity" (1817–1829, Eng. trans., p. 1037), whereas the content of the lyric is "the subject, the inner world, the mind that considers and feels, that instead of proceeding to action, remains alone with itself as inwardness, and that therefore can take as its sole form and final aim the *self-expression* of the subjective life" (p. 1038). Drama is a synthesis of the two former attitudes, given that here "we see in front of us both an objective development and also its origin in the hearts of individuals. The result is that the *object* is displayed as belonging to the *subject,* while conversely the individual subject is brought before our eyes, now in his transition to an appearance in the real world, now in the fate which passion occasions as a necessary result of its own deed" (p. 1038).

This criterion of definition is, however, integrated with another, that is, relations with reality, basically that of Platonic and Aristotelian mimesis (though it is quite differently understood).

> Lyric poetry does envisage specific situations within which the lyric poet is permitted to draw a great variety of matters into his feeling and reflection; but in this kind of poetry it is always the form of the inner life which is the fundamental model and this at once excludes the detailed illustration of external reality. Conversely, the dramatic work of art presents characters to us, and the occurrence of the action itself, in actual life, so that in this case a description of the locality and the externals of the agents and the event as such is excluded from the start, and what has to come into the speeches is rather inner motives and aims than the broad connection between the agents and their world or their real situation in it. But in epic, over and above the encompassing national life on which the action is based, both inner life and outer reality have their place, and thus here there is spread out before us all the detail of what can be regarded as the poetry of human existence (p. 1078).

How happily these two criteria dovetail is made clear, for example, from Hegel's considerations on drama, which, like epic, has for its object "a happening, a deed, an action." But

> its first step must be, above all, to strip externals away and put in their place as the ground and cause of everything the self-conscious and active individual. For a drama does not fall apart into a lyrical inner life and an external sphere as its opposite, but displays an inner life and *its* external realization. It follows that in that case the happening does not proceed from external circumstances but out of an agent's inner will and character, and it acquires dramatic significance only by its relation to an individual's aims and passions. Nonetheless, it is equally true that the individual does not remain shut in to an independence of his own but finds himself brought into opposition and conflict with others owing to the nature of the circumstances (in which his character and his aim determine what he wills), as well as the nature of this individual aim itself. In this way, action is at the mercy of complications and collisions which, against the will and intentions of the agents, lead to an outcome in which the real inner essence of human aims, characters, and conflicts is revealed (p. 1160).

A further criterion, less developed though brilliantly alluded to, is that of time. "The outpouring of lyric stands to *time*, as an external element of communication, in a much closer relation than epic narrative does. The latter places real phenomena in the past and juxtaposes them or interweaves them in rather a spatial extension, whereas lyric portrays the momentary emergence of feelings and ideas in the temporal succession of their origin and development and therefore has to give proper artistic shape to the varied kinds of temporal movement" (p. 1136). This is projected onto the formal plane of its metrical realization: it "implies (i) a rather variegated ranging of longs and shorts in a broken inequality of rhythmical feet, (ii) the varied kinds of caesura, and (iii) the rounding off into strophes which in themselves and in their succession may have a wealth of variation both in the length and shortness of single lines and in their rhythmical figuration" (p. 1136).

The three genres defined thus by opposition and synthesis are subsequently represented in motion as metahistorical and historical developments (though there is no clear-cut taking of sides, one way or the other). Metahistorical, or at least pertaining to an ideal history, is the succession epic-lyric-drama. Epic, for example, must fall into "that middle period in which a people has awakened out of torpidity, and its spirit has been so far strengthened as to be able to produce its own world and to feel itself at home in it" (p. 1045), and in which, on the other hand, since religious norms and civil and moral law had not as yet been definitely fixed, they remained "a living attitude of mind from which no individual separated himself," since there was still "no separation between feeling and will" (p. 1045). Lyric poetry, on the contrary, and subsequently dramatic poetry, would properly belong to those epochs in which the confines between individual and collective, between feeling and will, are well defined.

Hegel's division of the texts of all three genres into three basic periods is, though, a historical one. Oriental is defined as *symbolic;* Greek (and Roman, by way of imitation), is defined as *classical;* and medieval and modern are defined as *romantic*. There is a rider: the "perfect figure" will always be met with in the classical period. Finally, two further modes for historicizing exist: the first, which may be quite detailed, consists in following up the developments of one single genre (and here Hegel turns literary critic, with observations subtle even when questionable and which include contemporary writers); the second groups the various subgenres under the three principle genres, almost as though they were unsuccessful attempts or belated echoes. To the epic are assimilated, on the one hand, the epigram, gnomic and didascalic poetry, theogonies, and cosmologies and, on the other, the idyll and descriptive poetry; to the lyric are assimilated hymns, dithyrambs, paeans, psalms, while drama is subdivided into tragedy, comedy, and drama (satyr plays, tragicomedy, etc.). Of interest, given its resemblance to Goethe's ideas, is the considerable space Hegel devotes to such transitional subgenres as romances and ballads, which lie halfway between epic and lyric. In general, the attempt to reconcile observation of the texts with the rigidity of the schema produces, time after time, fascinating pages: those on the *Divine Comedy*, classed under epic, those on the novel, defined as "the modern popular epic" (p. 1092), because it, too, reflects "the wealth and many-sidedness of interests, situations, characters, relations involved in life, the wide background of a whole world." The difference is that the novel "presupposes a world already prosaically ordered; then, on this ground and within its own sphere whether in connection with the liveliness of events or with individuals and their fate, it regains for poetry the right it had lost" and describes "the conflict between the poetry of the heart and the opposing prose of circumstances and the accidents of external situations" (p. 1092).

4. After this exposition of the impressive synthesis attempted by Hegel, a

moment of reflection is called for. It will be remarked that almost none of the theorists so far considered attempted any inductive technique of definition akin to the scientific passage from individual to genre to species. It is a procedure which, in fact, cannot be put into effect. The Aristotelian simplification was a choice effected within those genres which were historically documented for archaic and classical Greece; in no sense did it pretend to embrace the whole terrain of literature. The choice once made was progressively generalized (as if other genres could not possibly exist) and rendered ontological (almost as if genres were categories of the spirit). Thus it was that, with lyric added, the epic-lyric-drama triad imposed itself and enjoyed a prestige which survives even today. It was in relation to this triad that philosophers and treatise writers were to exercise their abilities, as (while mixing the real history of the genres with an ideal history of mankind) they engaged in an attempt to bring it into line with moments of human history or with phases of the life of the spirit. Other genres, when attention was paid to them, were arranged "around," or "fell under," the main genres or were regarded as mixed forms, midway between one genre and another.

At a certain point, it was realized that it was the nature of genres and of so-called subgenres to be different. Indeed, the "major" genres had been considered alternatively (and often contemporaneously) as leader genres, dominant genres (which surpassed subgenres in prestige and duration, while being substantially akin in their nature), or else they had been regarded as universal categories, which absorb the different subgenres in their historical development. On the other hand, the so-called subgenres (whose reality was further corroborated by specific formal features) were sometimes seen as part of a process of development, as affiliated to the "major" genres, and sometimes as part of a hierarchy of generalization, which implied a genre-species relation with respect to the "major" genres. Hence arose (for example, in Goethe and Viëtor) a distinction between *Naturformen* and genres: *Naturformen* are the "major" genres understood as universal literary categories, whereas genres (identified with what are usually called subgenres) are their partial and contingent realizations. And this is not all. The "major" genres, in their turn, have been also regarded as categories, or as historical genres, as *Grundbegriffe* or as *Sammelbegriffe* (Staiger). This is the source of the grammatical distinction between *das Epische* and *Epik*. In short, the relation between genres and subgenres is different from that which exists in science between species and genre; indeed, it is impossible, on the basis of shared constituent elements, to move back from subgenres, with all their historical discontinuity, variety, and malleability, to any such genres as may exist outside and beyond history, at least if their traditional pattern is to be maintained.

If we wish to be even more radical, the very components of the triad on investigation can be shown to be not really homogeneous. Even if, within the category of the drama, medieval and modern developments can be regarded as variants which are, in terms of overall definition, not really revolutionary, the difficulties to which the epic gives rise are far more serious. Germanic poetic compositions and the *chansons de geste* fit the category uncomfortably, while procrustean adaptation is needed for romances of chivalry (which explains the sixteenth-century polemics). Lyric poetry poses anew, and in a more exasperated form, all of the difficulties which hindered its initial recognition. There are too many short poetical genres which will not fall under the label, and yet distinctly "lyrical" quality may well be present in any literary form whatsoever. If it is possible to define and authenticate the lyric as category, the existence of a genre which will correspond to it is anything but obvious, and it is not difficult to understand why attempts have been made to see it not as a category but as the very essence of poetry.

As for the novel, which today is the most important genre, it floats free of the classical triad and constrains us to establish a class of "mixed genres," under which all literary production will in practice be grouped (though the proportions will vary). Again, it is interesting to observe that the novel is not a genre which embraces minor genres like the detective story, the horror story, science fiction, etc. Such "qualified" novels are developments, specializations, of the novel, to be arranged in terms of historical progression, not as part of any hierarchical classification.

Debate on classification of genres can be renewed with profit only when we have resolved the ambivalence between history and categorization—in other words, only when we have made a choice between an empirical description of genres in terms of their development over time (in which case, clearly, any distinction between genre and subgenre will disappear) or when an attempt has been made to define *ex novo*, in terms of coherent criteria, such categories as will furnish a full account of total literary production.

It will surprise no one to learn that the first of these solutions was put forward in the positivist period. Indeed, it has been all too easy, in more recent times, to note the more mechanistic aspects of Brunetière's evolutionism. Nonetheless, his rapid panoramas of the development of different genres (e.g., the sequence *chanson de geste*, courtly romance, epic novel à la Scudéry, *roman de cape et d'épée*) acted as excellent antidotes against forced attempts at categorization. When the problem was posed in a diachronic dimension, what came to light was a series of continuities which did not necessarily involve substantial nuclei or immutable formal structures. The task of maintaining coherence was entrusted to history. No less important is the conception of a competitive relation among genres (on the pattern of Darwin's struggle for survival). Literary history then appears as a competition among different genres, as a network of differentiations and convergences, of hierarchies which constantly change as first one genre and then another comes to the fore. Thus, one of the most striking phenomena of modern literature would be the assimilation by the novel of techniques which were proper to tragedy, of themes which once were the preserve of essayists, etc.

Although so closely tied to the positivism of his day, Brunetière gives expression to exigencies which totally different approaches would find no less relevant. He sought an "histoire littéraire" which would, from the outset, contain within itself a principle sufficient for its own development, and he sought to define, beyond and above external influences, the way work acts upon work, "la grande action . . . des oeuvres sur les oeuvres" (1890, ed. 1898, p. 262). These same exigencies were championed by the formalists. One of them indeed, Tynjanov, put forward the conception of a competition between genres in terms of the new structural concepts. In Tynjanov's writings, we find an employment, at once well-defined and wide-ranging, of the concept of system. "The study of isolated genres outside the features characteristic of the genre system within which they are related is impossible" (1929, Ital. trans., pp. 70–71). We also find an employment of the concept of function. "The variability of the functions of a given formal element, the rise of some new function of a formal element, and the attaching of a formal element to a function are all important problems of literary evolution" (p. 72). The persistence of an evolutionistic approach should also be noted: *evolution, dynamism,* and, especially, "for phenomena of literary evolution . . . the principle is *struggle and mutation*" (p. 28).

On the other hand, Tynjanov is opposed to any conception of literature as progressive evolution because, for him, it moves forward by leaps and bounds, and its development is not uniform. Every genre, observed at a given moment, will allow one to distinguish fundamental traits and secondary traits. It is the secondary traits—"casual" results and deviations, errors even—which in the history of genres bring about mutations so marked that they, to some extent, annul continuity. Continuity can be spoken of for the notion of "extension," which opposes "main" forms (the novel, the long poem) to minor forms (the short story, the short poem), and for "constructional elements" (rhythm in poetry for example, and semantic coherence—the plot—in prose) or for materials. For the individual character of the genre, what changes is far more important: it is the constructive principle which will lead to constantly renewed ways of utilizing constituent factors and materials.

Shifts within the genre system, and within the genres as systems, can be reduced to attempts on the part of writers to break free of an automatization to which any constructive principle is, by its vary nature, prone. It will become rigidly normative, extend its range, assume hegemony, and beget heirs—hence, the reaction: renewal, or a different functionalizing of the secondary traits of a form, the reappraisal of less canonical forms, and recourse to cultural spheres still regarded as extraliterary. "The genre as system may in such cases oscillate. It arises (from deviations and from the elements of other systems) and declines, transforming itself into the elements of other systems" (p. 26). Thus, we assist at a "breaking up" of traditional genres and at the affirmation of new genres which arise out of what remains of preceding genres or "from the trifles of literary production, from the hidden corners, the innermost folds /of culture/" (p. 27).

This dynamic vision has as its aim explanation of transformations rather than comprehension of entities, by virtue of the fact that it excludes a priori any existence of such entities other than a relational one. Entities such as extension, construction elements, and materials are solid enough, but the way they combine to form works and genres can only be defined in relation to other works and to other genres within an omnicomprehensive conception of a literary system, which is, contemporaneously, defined and explained by comparing it with earlier and successive diachronic sections.

Almost without exception Tynjanov's examples come from Russian literature of the eighteenth and nineteenth centuries, but his "model" is certainly applicable to other literatures and periods as well (one need but mention Even-Zohar's recent use of them). Naturally we still need to define the meaning within culture of genres, these wavering simulacra. Of this we shall speak in section 7.

5. As for attempts to re-establish the canon of the genres, mention must be made of the success enjoyed by a casual remark of Jean Paul (Richter). According to him, "Epic presents an event which develops out of the past, drama an action which reaches towards the future and beyond, lyric an emotion which is contained in the present" (1804, ed. 1963, p. 272). A definition similarly based on time is that of Dallas, a Victorian critic, who was heavily indebted to the German Romantics; for him, too, (1852), epic deals with the past, drama with the present, lyric with the future. In other words, drama and lyric change places with respect to Jean Paul, and the ease with which they do so might arouse suspicions as to the coherence of the principle itself.

But Dallas adds criteria no less general; drama represents plurality, epic totality, lyric unity. Or else, the three genres should be distinguished by the use they make of the persons of the verb; while epic is characterized by the third person singular and lyric by the first, the second person plural is proper to drama (on the basis of a psychological differentiation of "you" and "thee" which is not relevant here). Another of his attempts (1866) characterizes drama, lyric, and epic on the basis of the kind of relations (sympathy, fantasy, etc.) which exist between the poet and the objects of his poetry. This gives, respectively, the following three fundamental types: (1) I am that thing or like that thing; (2) that thing is me or like me; (3) that thing is that or like that.

The observations of Jean Paul and those of Dallas are given a strictly grammatical formulation in Jakobson (1935, French trans. p. 130):

> Reducing the problem to a simple grammatical formulation, we might say that the first person of the present is, at one and the same time, the starting point and the leading theme of lyric poetry, while this role is taken in epic by the third person of a past tense. Whatever the specific object of a lyric tale, it is no more than appendix, accessory, backdrop for the first person of the present; the lyric past itself presupposes a subject in the act of remembering. Vice versa, the present in the epic is distinctly referred to the past, and, when the "I" of the narrator begins to express himself as one character among others, this objectivated "I" is no more than a variety of the third person, as if the author was looking at himself out of the corner of his eye.

And we should note here the absence, perhaps with the aim of accentuating the oppositive formulation, of drama and its relative "you."

The clarity of these latter proposals would seem to invite systematic organization. One is attracted by the possibility of sketching a diagram—its abscissas, pronouns, and its coordinates' tenses—to see if such a closed series of combinations can be made to correspond to different genres and subgenres. It becomes clear at once, though, that this will not take us much beyond the limits of a clever game. The prevalence of pronoun over pronoun or tense over tense is in its nature not statistical; it is the outcome of a synthetic perception which does not admit of demonstration on the part of the critic. Nor, on the other hand, can it be maintained that our hypothetical table would constitute a universal matrix, given the inexhaustible potential for variation which the writer is allowed. The continual shifts in choice of a basic tense on the part of novelists may serve as a sufficient demonstration. The whole discourse could be turned upside down; we might observe, genre by genre, passages from one square to another in accord with times and places.

Frye, too, believed he had found an objective criterion for the distinction of traditional genres, plus narration; it should be looked for in "the radical of presentation" (1957, p. 247), i.e., in the fact that the word in literature may be recited (drama), said (epic), sung or declaimed (lyric), written to be read (fiction). Frye immediately warns us that these modes of presentation are "among the ways in which literary works are ideally presented, whatever the actualities are" (p. 247), and, then, with historical annotations, he proceeds to correct the clear-cut character of a distinction which, in any event, hardly seems very solid, even when it is taken in a genetic sense.

In this same volume, Frye outlined other criteria for definition and applied them to various "canons" of literary genres. He was not worried in the least, despite his seemingly systematic approach, by the fact that he contradicts himself. Here, for example, is his theory of *mythoi*, which is based on two contrasting pairs: tragedy and comedy, romance and irony. The latter falls inside "a cyclical movement within the order of nature" (p. 161), between innocence and experience; the former is realized by movements downward or upward, from innocence toward the catastrophe of a collision with reality or from threatening complications toward innocence rediscovered. Or, again, there is his theory of the "modes of invention," founded, thanks to a hint from Aristotle (cf. §1), on differences of degree between the hero and the reader or environment. We have *myth*, in which the hero is "superior in kind both to other men and to the environment"; *romance*, with a hero "superior in degree to other men and to his environment" (p. 33); the *high mimetic* mode (taking in epic and tragedy), in which the hero is a leader "superior in degree to other men but not to his natural environment"; the *low mimetic* mode (comedies, realistic novels, and short stories), in which the hero is "superior neither to other men nor to his environment," where "the hero is one of us"; lastly we have the *ironic* mode, when the hero is "inferior in power or intelligence to ourselves, so that we have the sense of looking down on a scene of bondage, frustration, or absurdity" (pp. 33–34). It is a list which excludes many possible combinations, while it is extremely difficult to bring into line with it (as Frye would wish) the principal stages of literature over the last fifteen hundred years.

More than for its results (further compromised by the impossibility already referred to of arriving at any extrahistorical canon on the basis of a list of historical genres ancient and modern), Frye's attempt is notable in that it seeks to arrive at classification criteria which are not formal in type and which will allow, in reciprocal combination, a characterization of genres (Frye includes, among these criteria, the oppositions verisimilitude and inverisimilitude, comic and tragic). If the outcome is failure, this is due to the heterogeneity of the theoretical techniques adopted, to the inconsistently absolutist character attributed to hints drawn from classical culture, and to the uncertainty of the overall approach.

Among the attempts that have been made to arrive at the matrices of literary genres, that of Jolles is currently gaining ground after years of neglect. His investigation, in reality, converges only in part on the traditional problem area of the genres. Of the nine "simple forms" studied by Jolles (*Legende, Sage, Mythe, Rätsel, Spruch, Kasus, Memorabile, Märchen, Witz*), not one fully coincides with the genres of the Aristotelian or post-Aristotelian list. For this very reason, Jolles's considerations might well offer insights toward a reformulation of our problems or show the auroral moments of what would later be transformed into genres in the strict sense.

The forms he analyzes are those "which are produced in language and which grow out of the working of language itself, without the intervention, so to speak, of a poet" (1930, French trans., p. 81). So far, such studies have been the preserve of ethnography rather than of literary criticism, though the literary critic frequently catches sight of them as the original nucleus of his text. The working of language reproduces the principal phases of human work, that of peasants, of artisans, of priests, that of cultivation, manufacture, interpretation. It reproduces them by intervening in the confusion of the universe, by organizing it in words and so giving it form. The simple forms are remodelings of the world effected by language.

"Every time that an activity of the spirit leads the multiplicity or diversity of being and events to crystalize and to assume a certain figure, every time that this diversity—perceived by the language in its prime and indivisible elements and having become a product of language—is able contemporaneously to *wish to say* and *mean* a being or an event, we shall say that a simple form has been born" (Jolles 1930, French trans. p. 42). For such *event units*, which tradition, down to the formalists and beyond, called *motifs*, Jolles prefers the term *verbal gestures* (cf. Mukarovsky's *semantic gesture*). They are "the place in which certain experienced facts have become crystalized in a certain way under the action of a certain mentality and, at the same time, the place in which this mentality produces, creates, and signifies experienced facts" (p. 43). The simple form becomes a form which is actualized in terms of a particular orientation and in terms of the importance attributed to verbal gestures.

Despite the stress he lays on language, despite a repeated distinction between simple forms and actualized forms, one notes that Jolles aims not so much to isolate verbal gestures and define them morphologically as to grasp the *mental dispositions* which should effect their orientation. It is a mental disposition which in *saga* constructs the universe as a family and interprets it in terms of clan, of genealogy, of blood ties; it is a mental disposition which in *Kasus* represents the universe as an object that can be assessed and judged to accord with norms; it is mental dispositions which make it possible to differentiate *Mythe* from *Rätsel*. "If myth is the form which 'provides' the *answer*, riddle is the form which exhibits the *question*. Myth is a reply which contains a preliminary question; riddle is a question that seeks for an answer" (p. 105).

It is improbable (and Jolles does not try to make us believe otherwise) that the simple forms constitute a complete catalogue of basic mental dispositions. Therefore, it is not possible to undertake any interpretation of literary texts which would see them as a combination, however mutable, of simple forms. What Jolles does is, at best, to follow the progressive articulation of simple forms in the shape of actualized complex forms, their reappearance in different guise over time, and the development of possible anti-forms (such as, in the case of legend, the anti-saint and the anti-legend). Hence, we are invited to verify the affinities between legend, Pindar's triumphal odes, and the sporting pages, which in the newspapers are devoted to football players and cyclists; and to observe in the Greek epic the original traits of saga (which will come to the surface once again in great narrative cycles like Zola's *Rougon-Macquart* or the *Forsythe Saga*) and the transformation of the folk tale, the *Märchen*, into the short story (and here we are on more familiar ground; indeed, it is Jacob Grimm who is quoted).

The framework used by Jolles brings together an inspiration which is still romantic (the search for roots, the concept of popular as against sophisticated poetry) and formalistic insights which, even though not investigated in full, are quite remarkable. "As well as a comparison of all simple forms as such, a task still awaits us. We must study the activity, the function, and the structure of verbal gestures in each simple form and, respectively, compare the verbal gestures of different simple forms" (pp. 211–12). Particularly worthy of note—although unfortunately the only information available comes from a letter written by Becker and quoted by Schossig in his preface to the 1956 reprint—is an attempt to organize the simple forms (now increased to ten, with the addition of the fable) in terms of two axes of orientation, made up of modes of uttering (*Aussageweise*) and of an opposition between real form and ideal forms. This takes the following form:

	Interrogative	Indicative	Silence	Imperative	Optative
Realist	*Kasus*	*Saga*	*Rätsel*	*Spruch*	*Fabel*
Idealist	*Mythe*	*Memorabile*	*Witz*	*Legende*	*Märchen*

Overall, Jolles's work is more brilliant than solid, more attractive than useful.

The arguments of Stender-Petersen (1949) also do not quite escape subjective impressionism, despite the fact they start out from the still-stimulating schemata of glossematics. They are based upon the concepts of *instrumentalization* and *emotionalization*, to be referred respectively to the expression plane and to the content plane. Genres, which for Stender-Petersen have become four (lyric, epic, drama, and narrative), are to be defined with a bidimensional schema, on the basis of their reproduction of reality (direct—subjective—in the lyric and in drama and indirect—objective—in the epic and in narrative) and of their measure of instrumentalization and emotionalization—and thus of "fiction" (which is at a maximum in lyric and epic, at a minimum in drama and narrative). Thus we have:

	Maximum Instrumentalization and Emotionalization	Minimum Instrumentalization and Emotionalization
Direct Reproduction	Lyric Genre	Dramatic Genre
Indirect Reproduction	Epic Genre	Narrative Genre

Stender-Petersen then makes provision, though on the basis of an abstract combinative schema, for a series of mixed genres, whose number—twelve—is predetermined by that of the four underlying genres: lyrical-dramatic, lyrical-narrative, lyrical-epic, dramatic-epic, dramatic-narrative, dramatic-lyrical, narrative-epic, narrative-lyrical, narrative-dramatic, epic-lyrical, epic-narrative, epic-dramatic. As a contribution to the theory of genres, it is none too solid.

More elastic, though it also starts out with the four-genre canon, is the representation offered by Hernadi (1972). Its inclusiveness is not due primarily to its fourfold internal division of every genre (which embraces varieties and modes within genres rather than subgenres in the strict sense); it results from its twofold polarity: *authorial* and *interpersonal* (corresponding approximately to diegetic and mimetic), *private* and *dual*. The authorial pole constitutes the "thematic *presentation*" of a vision; the interpersonal pole, the dramatic *representation* of an action. Perpendicular to this axis is a second one with, at one pole, the *dual* pole, *envisioned* action, a combination of authorial perspective of vision and fictive interpersonal perspective of action: at the other pole, the *private*, the time and perspective of the *enacted vision*. In this the extratemporal qualities of thematic vision and the temporal subjective development of dramatic action are combined. The four genres are arranged along these two axes, as are also, in their respective areas, the varieties connected with them. The following figure is Hernadi's representation:

GENRES 215

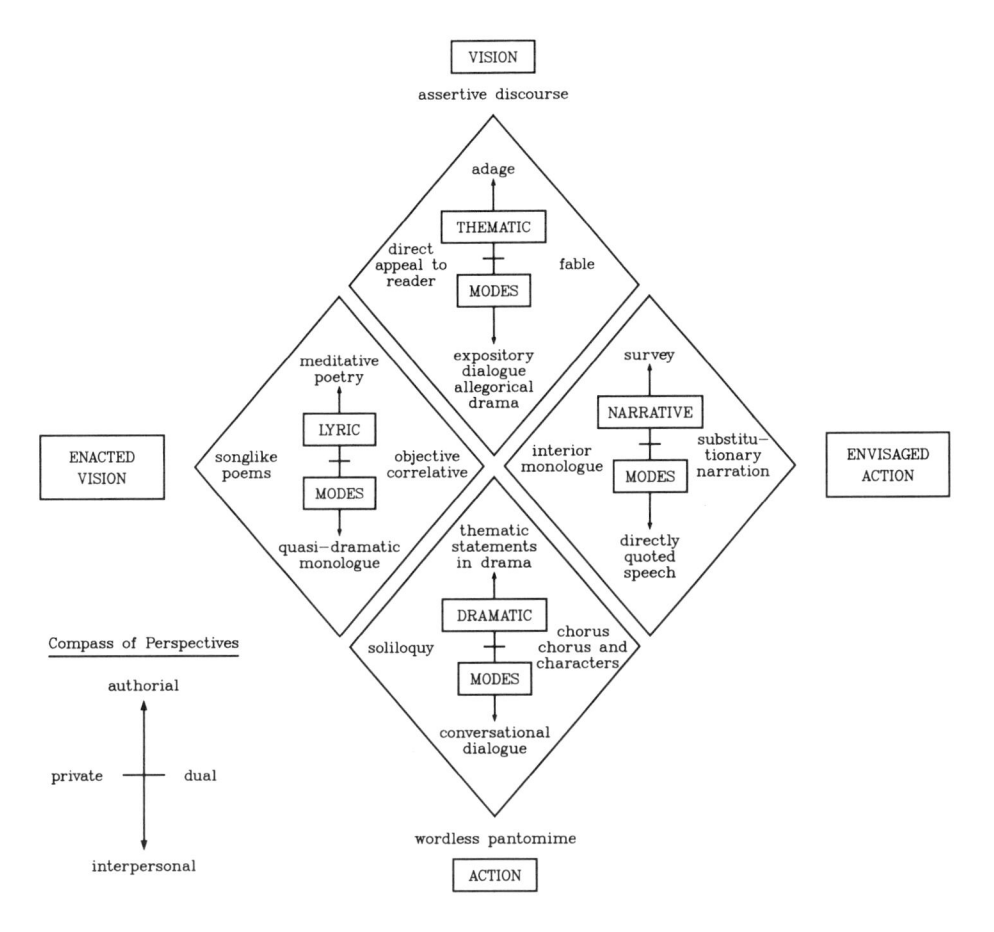

```
                           VISION
                      assertive discourse
                            adage
                              ↑
                         ┌─────────┐
                         │THEMATIC │
              direct     └─────────┘      fable
              appeal     ┌─────────┐
              to reader  │  MODES  │
                         └─────────┘
                              ↓
                         expository      survey
           meditative    dialogue       ┌──────────┐
           poetry        allegorical    │ NARRATIVE│
                ↑        drama          └──────────┘  substitu-
           ┌───────┐                    interior  ┌───────┐ tionary
ENACTED    │ LYRIC │     objective      monologue │ MODES │ narration    ENVISAGED
VISION     └───────┘     correlative              └───────┘              ACTION
           songlike      ↓                            ↓
           poems     ┌───────┐                    directly
                    │ MODES │                     quoted
                    └───────┘                     speech
                         ↓
           quasi-dramatic   thematic
           monologue        statements
                            in drama
                         ┌──────────┐
                         │ DRAMATIC │     chorus
                         └──────────┘     chorus and
                         soliloquy        characters
                         ┌─────────┐
                         │  MODES  │
                         └─────────┘
                              ↓
                         conversational
                         dialogue
                      wordless pantomime
                         ┌────────┐
                         │ ACTION │
                         └────────┘

Compass of Perspectives
         authorial
             ↑
   private ──┼── dual
             ↓
        interpersonal
```

The interest of Hernadi's systematic arrangement lies above all in the mobility it accords to exemplars of each genre inside this kind of quadrant—to the point of admitting shifts whose character is historical and even varieties of polarization within a single text. Hernadi has come back to his double polarity (1976) and has defined both its axes in different fashion. He now calls the horizontal axis which links writer and reader the "rhetorical axis of communication," while the vertical axis which links language and information is the "mimetic axis of representation." Hernadi's goal is a general description of critical operations, and he fills his schema with details derived from the theory of speech acts and from the concept of implied author—all this, within a distinctly semiotic framework. It is possible though to discern in this arrangement a contribution to the theory of genres, for genres might, I believe, be defined on the basis of coordinates corresponding to their relative positions on the two axes.

6. The most radical reactions to the theory of genres are those which defend

the creative liberty of writers; genres are regarded as sets of rules which literary critics artfully impose on them. Giordano Bruno (*Degli eroici furori*, 1585) had already declared that "there are as many genres and species of true rules as there are genres and species of true poets" (I,1); and Gravina is no less forthright in his *Discorso sopra l' "Endimione"* (1692). Perhaps Victor Hugo, in the 1826 preface to his *Odes*, took the most uncompromising stand against the validity of genres and their differentiated prestige. The only valid distinction should be that between good and bad, true and false. His opposition is, however, more energetic than coherent. In his *Préface du "Cromwell"* (1827), we are faced once again, though in a somewhat free and antitraditional form, with a whole history of humanity in terms of genres: from the hymn of primitive peoples to classical epic to Christian and modern drama.

Secondary, though substantial, contributions toward the breakdown of genre theory were made by those poets and critics who, while not rejecting the idea, laid stress on a preeminence of the genre which least readily lends itself to definition—the lyric. They considered it not in terms of its possible formal aspects but as itself the quintessence of an aptitude for poetry. The lyrical can spread the wings of its own inspiration inside other genres, when these are at their most inspired. Schelling places the lyric at the head of the other genres because, as in music, it is the finite (the subject) which there holds sway, ready and able to express the infinite. Leopardi calls the lyric "a genre which, just as it is first in time, is also eternal and universal, i.e., proper to man perpetually in every age and in every place, as poetry. And at the beginning poetry consists of this genre alone, and its essence always lies principally in this particular genre to the point almost of being confused with it. And it is the most truly poetic of all kinds of poems, for they are not poems except insofar as they are lyrics" (*Zibaldone*, 4475).

Implicit in an approach of this kind, although not always conscious, is an abandonment of the concept of genre as a principle of classification and a shift toward a new tonal meaning: no longer *the lyric* but *the lyrical*. It then becomes possible to encounter the lyrical in poetry of all kinds, and this legitimates its (not always uncontrasted) celebration as the purest moment of aesthetic synthesis. Indeed, Croce, who saw art as one moment, the aesthetic moment, of the Spirit, postulated lyrical intuition as the whole basis of artistic expression and saw the lyrical and the poetical as very nearly one and the same thing. It was he who gave formal expression to the most thoroughgoing criticisms of the whole concept of the literary genre. One need only turn to his *Estetica* (1902, pp. 40–44), where he states that genres have nothing to do with lyrical intuition; they belong to a second stage in reflection when intuition has been split into form and content: it is only for cataloguing purposes that works can be grouped together on the basis of their formal affinities. These criticisms are given systematic expression in the *Logica* (1909), which opposed concepts to pseudoconcepts. Genres should fall under the class of pseudoconcepts, whose value is practical and empirical rather than theoretical and which, while they serve for classification, exercise a negative influence on judgment.

What lies behind these pages of Croce is, one senses, the age-old, recurrent objection to any idea of using the concept of genre as a criterion for judgment. The objection is so well founded that one can hardly avoid accepting it. And yet what becomes more and more clear in Croce is the recognition he accords to the utility of genres, not merely for naming purposes but in historiography as well (cf., for example, 1933). Such acknowledgment is extended and taken even further by Fubini (1956), when he studies genres in the light of stylistic traditions and shows how important is "a history of those elements or modes which artists assume from tradition into their works and which they regard as lying beyond the artistic synthesis that will make them the integrating part of an organism; they thus precede the work of art and are the heritage not of any single artist but of many others whose tastes and culture are akin" (p. 168).

What, though, remains exclusively a part of Croce's own theory, one which is no longer acceptable today, is the clear-cut distinction he made between a moment of intuition, absolutely independent of any action on the part of the institutions of language or of institutions yet more formal, and a successive, intellectualistic moment, which is proper to the literary critic but not to the writer. If it does pertain to the writer, this will only be when he is acting as a critic. Today, we are more inclined to see the writer within a dialectic between intuitions and expressive institutions, between his personal freedom and customs or norms. Linguistic and formal orchestration exists prior to the production of a text, even though the text tends to licenses, infractions, or lacerations. The genres themselves are part of this orchestration.

7. Once we have reduced genres to their real nature as historical products, and have placed in their right perspective attempts to ontologize what may be useful for the identification of poetic tonalities or approaches but which will only partially coincide with real genres, what remains to be dealt with is the specific nature of genres within the total overall discourse of which they form part. In short, what distinguishes the various types of literary discourse, the genres, from other language discourses?

To begin with, it is evident that literary discourse is a very special kind of speech act, for it is without any immediate communicative aim (in fact, it will still be found valid by readers who are distant in space and time). If practical aims do exist (flattery of those in power, the creation of political propaganda, successful courtship), they are sought after by presentation of the product itself or by means of oratorical devices which, as a rule, will only marginally involve the nature of the text. Even success in utilitarian terms, when it is achieved (immediate payment, royalties, etc.), is not solicited directly by means of the message (which otherwise would consist, at its deepest level, of a petition, "pay me my fee"); it is the result of pleasure found in its form and themes.

And yet a literary message does communicate. In certain cases, it may prove capable of changing the way we look at the world. Its seeming lack of aim, in contrast to the importance of its effects, depends on the quite special mode of its communication. The addresser (the writer) carries his work forward to the point at which the message is complete, no further; the addressee (the reader) sets out from the message in order to interpret it, without interrogating his addresser. It is a two-stage communication with no feedback. This situation remains unvaried even in those few cases for which an addresser-message-addressee contact does exist, because, in general, the literary message (apart from extempore poetry) has been formulated in advance and the addresser's function, during contact, is merely to act as a channel.

This breaking down of the literary message into two phases (addresser-message, message-addressee) is an institutionalized fact and, as such, is far more symptomatic than any peculiarity in the text's actual transmission: the fact that it is sung, read aloud or silently, acted, etc. On the whole, and with the obvious exclusion of theater, the silent reading of texts is by now almost unopposed (unless, with the extinction of the Gutenberg Galaxy, vocal and mimetic performance of it will reappear). The literary message is entirely entrusted to such readers as it will happen to encounter: it is a message for the future.

It is these properties of the literary text which make necessary a strictly codified structure which will take the place of all the acts of syntonization, of amplification, of correction to which recourse may be had in ordinary discourse. The literary text must not only communicate a message but communicate what kind of message it is that the addresser has adopted, and, at every point, it must refer to its peculiarities. Knowledge of the types of literary message that are possible constitutes for those who use it what Jauss calls their "horizon of expectation."

The same motives that govern the addressee in his perception of discourse type were earlier at work when the addresser determined his choice of type. There exists a competence common to addresser and addressee, and formulation of a message in terms of one of the possibilities contained within such competence constitutes a performance. These terms taken from linguistics will assist us toward further clarification.

The language constitutes a code which an entire community possesses. Limits to the extension, or to change, of this code are determined by the requirements of communication. Rules exist for the construction of any discourse of whatever kind, and they are sufficiently elastic to offer a wide range of possibilities from which an addresser may choose. Lexical, morphological, and stylistic choices are to hand when a sentence is to be constructed, and to this must be added the different ways of connecting sentences: formal choices, discourse choices (trans-sentential links).

The nature of the literary text, as discourse not directly communicated to the unknown addressee and which admits of no reply, confers on it a particular sign density. It is frozen into definitiveness. Literary discourse is an autotelic structuring of signs. The intelligibility of this discourse does not depend exclusively on knowledge of its linguistic elements; it depends, too, on knowledge of the norms of its cohesion. This is why any analysis restricted to the linguistic, stylistic, or metrical characteristics of a literary text is so often disappointing. What actually characterizes it is the way it connects these peculiarities in relation to the means it adopts for the presentation of contents. This comes down to saying that literary genre is really this particular type of relation between a variety of formal peculiarities and their content elements.

Just as the value of the words can be understood only by starting with sentences, so the function of the formal elements of a text can only be seized upon if one starts from the totality they form. Specialization in literary language is directly dependent on the institution of registers for the exposition of the materials which pertain to various types of text. The variety of metrical forms, the repertoire of *topoi*, the grouping of themes, different exposition techniques have all been elaborated in relation to specific types of text. Thus, Hjelmslev's well-known fourfold division—content form and content substance, expression form and expression substance—should be borne in mind in its totality and in all its eventual subdivisions whenever we speak of literary genre or of a text as belonging to a genre.

The author, in short, has at his disposal a series of possible contents on the one hand and a series of discourse techniques on the other. While each of these techniques will, taken in itself, constitute no more than a convention, the convergence of stylistic, discoursive, expositive techniques (within a given culture) will form a code. In other words, the literary culture to which the writer belongs has already established for its techniques a canon of preferential relations. It thus provides him with a set of "programs" for his performance (cf. Corti 1976, chap. 5).

With genres, then, Saussure's concept of synchrony is rendered even more specific. Within the semiotic synchrony of a given time and place, a subsystem will exist relative to literary expression. Within it, other subsystems will be found. Far less extensive, they relate to genres and provide rules for the selection of material and for its combination as content and form. While language or single thematic elements may belong to various subsystems, they will, each time they appear, be harmonized with, and arranged within, each subsystem and conform to its links between content and expression.

It will at once be clear that genres are even further disontologized on the basis of these observations. If the contribution of formal aspects is so determinant, it will be no easy matter to bring together texts in different languages under any single label, except in cases where some genetic descent or affinity can be vouched for. If, with respect to two parallel or successive literatures, we are led to speak of the same genre, this merely means that we are underlining the common presence (or persistence) of techniques which are assessed as significant by the literary historian on the basis of a choice that is arbitrary— because it breaks down the convergence of factors in a sign unit—although in many cases justifiable.

And how, other than arbitrarily, is one to establish a limit beyond which elements in common will be less decisive than contrasting elements (pronouncing judgment, for example, as to the continuity, or lack of continuity, in the case of Greek epic, Latin epic, *chanson de geste,* or in the case of medieval romance and the modern novel)?

At the same time, if genre is defined on the basis of norms of cohesion, it becomes possible to define the technique of literary production. These norms constitute a well-tried set of instructions which save the writer from the need to excogitate on each occasion the way his inventions are to be expressed in words. What is thus regulated is the use of an equally predetermined series of expositive and descriptive stereotypes, of themes and commonplaces, techniques, lexemes, rhythmical patterns, and so forth. Literary expression is a highly conventional activity; it makes use of experience accumulated over centuries, experiences which cannot possibly be neglected. Our very perception of reality is effected through stereotypes, and, finally, norms of cohesion have reached the point of being introjected, not just as a technical fact but as reflection of the surrounding culture.

Precisely because they regulate, however approximately, materials whose nature is varied, these norms are not rigid, and this is the case even for epochs when they are given a, very limited, codification. And moments exist which are, in literary terms, revolutionary—when writers overthrow the norms, renew or establish genres, or change the relations among genres. Much more frequently, the writer's personality comes to the fore because of the way he makes use of some of the materials—expanding, circumscribing, transposing. Every performance will, to a greater or lesser degree, leave its mark on overall competence, and in the course of time a change will be effected in the relations between formal peculiarities and the content elements which the norms formalize. Thus, the norms themselves will change. This accounts for the unbridled dynamism, described by Tynjanov, inside single genres or between one genre and another.

It should be remarked, though, that unless we deal with epistemic discontinuity (the case of the Middle Ages) the existence of genres will not be interrupted by their negations. The anti-novel is not something completely different from the novel; it is simply a novel in which certain constituent elements have been turned upside down. Abandonment of metrical regularity for poetry can be correlated to recovery of prosodic structures and phonic cross-reference inside what seemed license. Again, negation of genres in itself will, as a rule, merely establish new genres: the anti-novel is again a good example. Norms for sign cohesion are, therefore, indispensable. This is only natural, for any communication requires codes in common for addresser and addressee, because it is impossible to proffer signs that are so totally different from those in current use that they would prove unintelligible.

The semiotic nature of these cohesion norms implies that they form part of the cultural-semiotic system itself. This approach to the problem brings to the fore the correspondence (though it is not coincidence) between changes in the cultural-semiotic system and changes in genres and their norms. It is along such lines as these that a sociological interpretation of literary production can be undertaken, one that is based not merely on the ideology of writers, on "relevance" of subject matter, on market factors, etc. Individual works do not, or do not always, afford a direct reflection of society but rather an analogy between the norms of sign cohesion for the whole of the literary texts of an epoch, seen as malleable and sociologically representative components of the cultural-semiotic system with their own dynamics.

References

Behrens, I.
   1940. *Die Lehre von der Einteilung der Dichtkunst, vornehmlich vom 16. bis 19. Jh.: Studien zur Geschichte der poetischen Gattungen*. Beihefte zur Zeitschrift für romanische Philologie, 92. Halle: Niemeyer.

Brunetière, F.
   1890. *L'évolution des genres dans l'histoire de la littérature: Leçons professées à l'Ecole normale supérieure*, vol. 1, Introduction: L'évolution de la critique depuis la Renaissance jusqu'à nos jours. 3d ed. 1898. Paris: Hachette.

Corti, M.
   1972. I generi letterari in prospettiva semiologica. *Strumenti critici*, 4, 1, pp. 1–18.
   1976. *Principi della comunicazione letteraria*. Milan: Bompiani. (English translation. *An Introduction to Literary Semiotics*. 1978. Bloomington: Indiana University Press.)

Croce, B.
   1902. *Estetica come scienza dell'espressione e linguistica generale. Teoria e storia*. Milan: Sandron.
   1909. *Logica come scienza del concetto puro*. Bari: Laterza.
   1933. *Poesia popolare e poesia d'arte. Studi sulla poesia italiana dal Tre al Cinquecento*. Bari: Laterza.

Dallas, E. S.
   1852. *Poetics: An Essay on Poetry*. London: Smith, Elder.
   1866. *The Gay Science*. London: Chapman and Hall.

Even-Zohar, I.
   1978. *Papers in Historical Poetics*. Tel Aviv: Porter Institute.

Frye, N.
   1957. *Anatomy of Criticism: Four Essays*. Princeton: Princeton University Press.

Fubini, M.
   1956. *Critica e poesia*. Bari: Laterza.

Goethe, J. W. von, and Schiller, F.
   1797. Über epische und dramatische Dichtung. *Über Kunst und Altertum*, 6 (1827): 1, pp. 1–7. (Now in *Goethes Werke*. 1960. Hamburg: Wegner. Vol. 12, pp. 249–51.)

Gülich, E., and Raible, W., eds.
   1972. *Textsorten: Differenzierungskriterien aus linguistischer Sicht*. Frankfurt am Main: Athenäum.

Hegel, G. W. F.
   1817–29. *Ästhetik*. 1955. Berlin: Aufbau-Verlag. (English translation. 1975. *Aesthetics: Lectures on Fine Art*. 2 vols. Oxford: Clarendon Press.)

Hempfer, K. W.
   1973. *Gattungstheorie: Information und Synthese*. Munich: Fink.

Hernadi, P.
   1972. *Beyond Genre: New Directions in Literary Classification*. Ithaca: Cornell University Press.
   1976. Literary Theory: A Compass for Critics. *Critical Inquiry*, 3, pp. 369–86.

Jakobson, R.
   1935. Randbemerkungen zur Prosa des Dichters Pasternak. *Slavische Rundschau*,

7, pp. 347–74. (French translation. *Questions de poétique*. 1973. Paris: Seuil. Pp. 127–44).

Jauss, H. R.
- 1970. Littérature médiévale et théorie des genres. *Poétique*, 1, pp. 79–101. (The French translation of the following item.)
- 1972. Theorie der Gattungen und Literatur des Mittelalters. H. R. Jauss and E. Köhler, eds. *Grundriss der romanischen Literaturen des Mittelalters*. Heidelberg: Winter. Vol. 1, pp. 107–38.

Jean Paul (J. P. F. Richter)
- 1804. *Vorschule der Ästhetik nebst einigen Vorlesungen in Leipzig, über die Parteien der Zeit*. Hamburg: Perthes. (Now in *Werke*. 1963. Munich: Hansen. Vol. 5, pp. 7–456.)

Jolles, A.
- 1930. *Einfache Formen: Legende, Sage, Mythe, Rätsel, Spruch, Kasus, Memorabile, Märchen, Witz*. Halle: Niemeyer. (French translation. *Formes simples*. 1972. Paris: Seuil.)

Petersen, J.
- 1939. *Die Wissenschaft von der Dichtung: System und Methodenlehre der Literaturwissenschaft*. Berlin: Junker und Dünnhaupt.

Rossi, L. E.
- 1971. I generi letterari e le loro leggi scritte e non scritte nelle letterature classiche. University of London, *Institute of Classical Studies Bulletin*, 18, pp. 69–94.

Rüdiger, H.
- 1973. *Gattungen in der vergleichenden Literaturwissenschaft*. Berlin: de Gruyter.

Ruttkowski, W. V.
- 1968. *Die literarischen Gattungen: Reflexion über eine modifizierte Fundamentalpoetik*. Bern-Munich: Francke
- 1973. *Bibliographie der Gattungspoetik*. Munich: Hueber.

Stender-Petersen, A.
- 1949. Esquisse d'une théorie structurale de la littérature. *Travaux du Cercle linguistique de Copenhague*, 5, pp. 277–87.

Tynjanov, Ju. N.
- 1929. *Archaisty i novatory*. Leningrad: Priboy. (Italian translation. 1968. Bari: Dedalo.)

Vico, G.
- 1744. *La Scienza nuova giusta l'edizione del 1744*. 5th ed. 1967. Bari: Laterza.

Wellek, R., and Warren, A.
- 1942. *Theory of Literature*. New York: Harcourt, Brace.

4.
Narration/Narrativity

1. The bases for a definition of narration are laid down, very well indeed, in Aristotle's *Poetics*. His starting point was the theory of imitation already elaborated by Plato, and he wrote:

(1) "it is possible [as a poet] to proceed either partly by narration [or] partly by assuming a character other than your own—this is Homer's method—or by remaining yourself without any change, or else [you may] represent the characters as carrying out the whole action themselves" (1448a, 21–24). Thus, as distinct from dramatic form, in which actors imitate the gestures and pronounce the discourses attributed to the characters (mimesis), in narrative form it is the poet's discourse which effects a verbal equivalent of the action (diegesis) and which may then perhaps go on and give us, in direct or indirect form, the discourses of the characters.

Aristotle was thinking of the epic poem as the main form of narration. And it was with reference to epic that he determined the fundamental qualities of narrated action (or fable):

(2) "Clearly the story must be constructed as in tragedy, dramatically, round a single piece of action, whole and complete in itself, with a beginning, middle, and end, so that, like a single living organism, it may produce its own peculiar form of pleasure. It must not be such as we normally find in history, where what is required is an exposition not of a single piece of action but of a single period of time, showing all that within the period befell one or more persons, events that have a merely casual relation to each other" (1459a, 18–25). He insisted on the coherence (indeed, on the organic nature) of the facts and on the self-contained character of the narration, which was to be autonomous in the sense that it had to have a beginning and an end sufficiently defined to justify its extrapolation from the flux of events (cf. 1450b, 22–1451a, 15).

Lastly, he laid stress on a relation of reciprocal necessity which was to subsist among the parts of the action:

(3) "As then in the other arts of representation, a single representation means a representation of a single object, so, too, the plot being a representation of a piece of action must represent a single piece of action and the whole of it, and the component incidents must be so arranged that if one of them be transposed or removed, the unity of the whole is dislocated and destroyed" (1451a, 30–33). Clearly, Aristotle is speaking of literary narration and of that alone. But, on the

basis of his affirmations, we may go back, by affinity or contrast, to the characteristics of narrating as one of the activities of man as a speaking animal. Narrating is a mediated linguistic realization, whose scope it is to communicate a series of events to one or more interlocutors and to do so in such a way that the interlocutors will participate in this knowledge, and so widen their own pragmatic context. Narration is oriented toward artificiality and, in the last resort, toward art, when the communication will concern facts that are invented (as deliberate falsehood or for mere pleasure) or, even better, when no immediate finality is involved, and when the narration (true, held to be true, or invented) is cut off from its pragmatic context and structured in an autonomous form.

Folk tales and myth are the most obvious examples of the intermediate stage of narration—half-way between practical communication and art. They are transmitted orally, and on each single occasion they are reformulated. They are, however, predetermined in their structure, and they are autonomous with respect to their vital context. Their position is intermediate from a genetic point of view as well, if it is true that the short story arises out of myth and, even more, out of the folk tale (including intermediate forms of which the *exemplum* is primary in the West). It is thus altogether natural that studies of narration should have been undertaken in the first instance by ethnographers engaged in determining invariables and laws of composition in the sphere of myth and folk tale. But, although literary diegesis constitutes a subclass of all possible discoursive narrations, it should nonetheless be pointed out that diegetic narration is not the only kind that exists. If we refer once more to the second passage quoted from Aristotle, we shall realize readily enough that the properties of action are not proper to diegesis alone; they form part of a much wider sphere. The tale is not a prerogative of diegetic realizations; it is to be found in mimetic realizations as well. So true is this that Aristotle's statements do no more than re-echo for epic what he had said of the theater (cf. 1450b, 22–1451a, 15). What exists then is a narrative content (to use Aristotle's term, a fable) and its realization, which may or may not be diegetic, which may be verbal but also nonverbal, or not merely verbal. A fable may be narrated or it may be represented; it may be narrated with words or with gestures (mime) or through an orchestration of words, gestures, sound, etc. (films).

It is the first passage from Aristotle which best illustrates the dichotomy between action and realization. A number of realizations of one and the same fable are possible because a fable constitutes a well-articulated and autonomous referent. It is an invariant which can be represented by many variables (hence, possible transpositions from one type of realization to another). It is an autonomous referent, because, however it is uttered, an action will have an unequivocal nature of its own; it is an articulated referent because, among the different actions of the fable, there exist logical or at least chronological relations and these can be enucleated without taking into account the mode of utterance. The concrete character of the referent (or pseudoreferent, if the narration is fictitious) is much more fluid, or it no longer exists when we deal with lyrical, psychological, reflective, and other such contents.

Of our three passages from Aristotle, the first may be considered valid in general for any kind of narration. In the second, the comparison with historical narration is no longer valid for everyday narrations, which may well have an historical structure, i.e., a coherence not identifiable with the continuity of action of the characters. This applies equally to the exigencies formulated in the third passage. As for the opening of the second passage—unity of action—it should be noted that in everyday narration there exists a possibility of integration from the pragmatic context of data known to the interlocutor. In consequence, the action may also be narrated in an incomplete or disjointed form. It is less important to stress the well-known linguistic notion that everyday narration, as distinct from literary narration, may also have recourse to nonverbal means (gestures, etc.).

2. Systematic analysis of narration was initiated by the Russian formalists in the years 1915–30. They followed up the proposals that had been made by Veselovsky, the great folklore investigator, and it was Propp, another expert on folklore, who in the same period did most to develop a method of analysis. This research has been taken up again since the 1950s, and there has been a convergent contribution on the part of ethnologists (from Lévi-Strauss to Dundes, from Maranda to Meletinsky) and of literary theorists (Todorov, Bremond, etc.).

Apart from the interest of such research for the description and classification of the texts of myth, folklore, and literature, it should be added that analysis of narration immediately showed itself to be a particularly efficient instrument for the study of discourse (and this is an aspect of the matter we have already discussed in the relevant chapter). In fact, the signal success in the investigation of discourse meanings is obtained when, as is the case with narration, these meanings (or signifiers) correspond to actions easily isolated, which are joined together by links of succession or, even better, of causality.

Without going into problems dealt with in the first chapter of this section or entering into the history of the research itself, we intend to deal here with certain aspects of descriptive interest: (a) minimal units of narration; (b) the concepts of action and function; (c) the syntagmatic and paradigmatic links between the actions and between the functions; and (d) the overall construction of narration. We shall subsequently move on to the modalities of narrative performance.

3. When faced with an action narrated in verbal form or in another mode, both the critic and the linguist cannot avoid repeating the operation which any ordinary listener or reader will carry out. They will mentally reformulate and "summarize" the content of the narrative discourse. Metanarrative reformulations are the result, in substance paraphrases. Even in the case of nonverbal narrations, our reformulations will reduce them to discourse. An attempt may be made to limit to the utmost the arbitrary nature of such paraphrases, but it is impossible to find any more objective way of determining actions (Hendricks 1973). The inevitability of the paraphrase depends on an objective fact: an action cannot be formulated conceptually otherwise than with sentences. It

ought to be pointed out that, between the nuclear-sentence and the corresponding section of the discourse, no equivalence exists: the nuclear sentence is the content of the discourse section reduced exclusively to what may be considered action.

Paraphrases are therefore short sentences, with a subject and a predicate, plus any objects and complements there may be. But not all predicates utter actions. Predicates of action or process (in the latter, the agent is not a person) are opposed to predicates of state, and these do not concern the narration (Doležel 1976). Furthermore, every action may be defined in terms of greater or lesser generality. The action "Hitler seized power" may also be uttered as a series of sentences which will correspond to the single political actions in which this seizing of power was articulated, and each of these actions might be broken down still further into the various acts and crimes which constitute it.

From the grammatical point of view, the series of minimal elements of a paraphrase will be found to coincide with the general sentence schema which post-Chomsky linguists seek to identify. Further restrictions are to be applied, however, where action is concerned, on the basis of its semantic value. One of Lotman's statements seems to apply here: "An event in a text is the shifting of a persona across the borders of a semantic field," given that "it is not an event when the hero moves 'within' the space assigned to him" (1970, Eng. trans., p. 233 and p. 238).

To the opposition between act, or process, and state, between act with or without semantic transfer, another fundamental opposition must be added: action against function. The formalists, and Tomashevsky in particular, had already marked off within narrative actions (called *motifs*) those which were determinant for the integrity of the causal-temporal connection of events *(tied motifs)*. It was, however, Propp who, as well as being the first to employ the term *function*, best clarified its constructive value: "Function is understood as the act of a character, defined from the point of view of its significance for the course of the action" (1928, Eng. trans., p. 21). The difference between action and function does not lie, or does not just lie, as might at first appear, in its importance (in the sense that many actions are not determinant for the unfolding of events) or in its generality (in the sense that the weight of an action with respect to an event may be indicated by a nonspecific, but broader, definition of its content). It lies in the fact that the function, as distinct from the action, calls for a general semantic framework.

It is this framework which makes it feasible to undertake narratological analysis, i.e., to determine, from among all the actions narrated, those which constitute the narrative structure. Any narration, in fact, will be made up of quite a long succession of actions: from the lighting of a cigarette to the provoking of a catastrophe. The measure of their importance is something that can be assessed not on its own terms but in relation to other actions; lighting a cigarette (in Svevo's *La coscienza di Zeno*) or eating a *madeleine* (in Proust) may, from a narrative point of view, prove much more decisive than provoking a catastrophe in a place far removed from the story and without repercussions upon it.

Fundamental here are the concepts of syntagm—the connections between actions along the discoursive (temporal) chain—and of paradigm—the semantic correspondence of actions located at different points along the same chain. For the syntagm, the most elaborated model is that of Propp who, from a corpus of one hundred magic folk tales in Afanasief's collection, isolated thirty-one moments which, in whole or in part but always in the same order, were to be met with in the totality of the tales. Verbal definition of these moments, which are identical with narrative functions, makes it possible to relate to their corresponding categories a whole variety of actions carried out by the characters in the tales.

As for the paradigm, Lévi-Strauss has put it to good use, as have the Russian folklore investigators (e.g., Segal). It is a matter of defining actions not only as they relate to contiguous actions but also in terms of the way in which they recall each other, even at a distance, by the fact of belonging to one or another semantic field. The various semantic fields, which as a whole make up the overall sense of the tale, can be represented as lines which vertically connect the horizontal lines of the temporality narrated.

The set of Propp's thirty-one functions constitutes a model for all the folk tales of his corpus (though, most unhappily, it has been used by more recent authors to cover tales extraneous to that corpus). On the contrary, the "score," in terms of which Lévi-Strauss sets out actions like music, is deduced from the interpretation of a single text (in his case, a myth). We are faced with the distinction, in studies of narratology not always a clear one, between narrative model and fabula. Fabula is a term already adopted by the formalists to indicate the succession of the actions which are determinant for the narrative and which can be deduced from a text once its nondeterminant actions have been eliminated. These actions are then rearranged to accord with the succession of events, a succession which writers in their art rearrange. The model, though, enjoys a general validity with respect to a corpus; its actions are defined as functions, i.e., in terms of the relation they establish with other functions in a syntagmatic dimension which is valid for the whole set of the texts of the corpus (Segre 1974, chap. 1).

In a closed model like that of Propp, one can already observe the presence of *post hoc* and *propter hoc* sequences. In fact, the coherence of a narration is based not only on the continuity of its character or characters but also on the consequentiality of its actions (though due weight may be attributed to casual undertakings or events, which will thus occur *post hoc* but not *propter hoc*). Hence, Propp notes the dual presence of each of the following pairs: "interdiction and its violation; the attempt to find out something and the transmission of information; deception (fraud) by the villain and the hero's reaction to it; fight and victory; marking and recognition" (1928, Eng. trans., p. 109). Here the second term of each pair implies the first.

But a closed model takes no account of eventualities which are not realized in the corpus. It was in the act of proposing an open model that Bremond stressed the existence of alternatives, of dichotomies. Any action may succeed or fail. Characters move inside a garden of forking paths; they take now one direction now another in accord with the outcome of their actions. Bremond's model is derived not so much from the texts as from reality itself: "This engendering of narrative types is, at the same time, a structuring of human conduct whether imposed or suffered. They provide the narrator with a model and material for an organized unfolding which is indispensable to him and which he would be incapable of finding elsewhere" (1966, p. 76).

On the one hand, there exists a predetermined sequence of functions; on the other, a sequence of alternatives. The problem of logically constraining relations among functions remains, however, an open one. Only recently has any attempt been made to apply the techniques of logic to the different kinds of "human conduct whether imposed or undergone" to which Bremond's model refers us. I am thinking of George R. von Wright's action theory. In the first attempts made (Teun van Dijk, Doležel), the aim was to fit narrative nuclei, on each occasion, into various kinds of logic: alethic (possible, impossible, necessary, etc.), deontic (permitted, prohibited, obligatory, etc.), axiological (good, bad, indifferent), epistemic (involving knowledge, ignorance, belief). For example, the logic of the functions interdiction-violation-punishment would fall under deontic logic.

Such studies will perhaps make it possible to arrange, other than empirically, the series of the functions to be found in a text. They should further make it possible to effect a more rigorous grouping of functions into large units segmenting the text. For the moment, we attempt, while drawing attention to sequences, to establish, on the basis of content, text divisions which are made up of a number of functions or actions and which constitute unified blocks. Otherwise, what we determine are the basic moments of any kind of narration. We set out from Aristotle with his abstract observation that a tale must have a beginning, a middle, and an end, and arrive at Propp, for whom a tale is "any development proceeding from villainy or a lack, through intermediary functions to marriage, or to other functions employed as a dénouement. . . . Terminal functions are at times a reward, a gain or in general the liquidation of misfortune, an escape from pursuit, etc." (1928, Eng. trans., p. 92). We set out from Labov and Waletzky (1967) with their fivefold schema—*orientation, complication, evaluation, resolution, coda*—and arrive at Greimas who, between the extremes of breakdown of order and alienation and reintegration and restoration of order, locates the intervention of a hero who is to prove himself and carry out a mission (1966, pp. 199–202). For the cohesion of the whole, there is a forceful expression of Horace, who warns us "primo ne medium, medio ne discrepet imum" (*Ars poetica*, v. 152).

Many of these schemata, though, show signs of their folk tale origins; it is easy to express doubts as to the possibility of generalizing them. It would be much better to have schemata even more abstract, like that of Bremond which gives concrete form to Aristotle's triad in the sequence virtuality–actualization (or its absence)–scope attained (or not obtained) and that of Teun van Dijk which singles out (1) a state and actors, (2) causes of a change in state, (3) impact of the actors on this state, (4) action of the actors when confronted with a state, and (5) state and actors in the situation which results (1972, p. 294).

4. The nucleus-sentences of which we have spoken in the preceding paragraph act as a nucleus in two senses. In one sense, the nucleus-sentence may be regarded as the most synthetic paraphrase of content; the events and characters of more detailed paraphrases can be inscribed as developments or diversions or as insertions with respect to the content of the nucleus-sentence. In the other sense, the nucleus-sentences are the equivalent of actions and functions, so that the complex of what is narrated consists in the interconnection of nuclear-sentences.

It might seem possible to state that the nuclear-sentence in the first sense is the synthesis of the nuclear-sentences of a narration in the second sense: the sum of the actions or functions realizes an all-embracing action or function. But this does not hold for all narrations. While, for some, the predominance of a general schema is evident, others exist where the separate moments narrated achieve greater autonomy (and where the general schema becomes not so much that of an action as that of an experience or an epoch). It may also happen that different plots intertwine reciprocally (so that the general scheme will be made up of the contrasts or parallelisms of the plots). From the different patterns of relations between actions and functions and general schema, a typology of narrative texts might easily enough be undertaken. The successive stages of the picaresque novel or of the *Erziehungsroman* might be compared with the unified parabola of Arthurian romance, with that of the sentimental novel, or with the tight-woven web of Ariosto's epic.

This phenomenology is determined by the type of action and by the strength of the bonds which link them. But a thoroughgoing illustration could only be provided by having recourse to other elements which of necessity are eliminated from such an X-ray perception of narration. These are elements of character and motivation, conflicts of feelings, etc., what critics in the English-speaking world, when they speak of an overall narrative pattern, describe as *action*. Clearly we must add the mainsprings, for the most part psychological, which provoke the actions themselves to the objective, often logical, consequentiality which ties one action to another. If work on this aspect is not particularly forthcoming, it is because mainsprings of this kind are less easy to enucleate, and can be described with far less accuracy, than can actions themselves.

Here we need do no more than mention the status of the characters. In folk tale texts, characters are virtually identified with the actions or the series of actions they perform, whereas in literary works they take on a psychology of their own, complete with contradictions, and, as a result, the way they operate through actions is not so clear-cut and direct. Certainly, if they are reduced to the role they play in the action—if, in short, they are considered as *actants* (so that several characters may function as a single actant, and a single character may take on a number of actantial roles)—it will then be possible to achieve a radical reduction in the number and attribution of functions. This has been done, with use of convergent arguments, by Propp, Souriau (1950), and Greimas (1966, pp. 172–82). Let us consider the most highly elaborated model, that of Greimas.

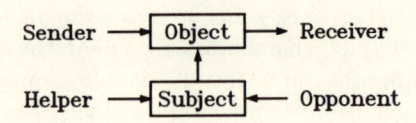

```
Sender  ⟶  Object  ⟶  Receiver
                ↑
Helper  ⟶  Subject  ⟵  Opponent
```

It is at once clear that this is too general to adapt itself to the varied way in which characters intervene in narrative reality. It would perhaps be more satisfactory to determine, insofar as this is possible, the idea-forces which drive the characters and the way they evolve in the course of events. It is more simple to determine relation changes in the characters which are the consequences of actions. A tale might be seen as a succession of functions which bring the characters together or which separate them (in relations of love or friendship, as fellow workers, etc.) and which will at each stage constitute different polygons of conjunctive or separative relations.

When we speak of relations between nuclear-sentences of different degrees of generality, and of the variety of connections between actions and functions, we are already faced with one of the main themes of narratology: the biplanar plot/fabula relation. The technique of not recounting the facts in chronological order has been widespread from classical times, when it was customary to begin *in medias res*, initial events being communicated subsequently in retrospective narration usually by one of the characters. A plurality of plots will of itself involve a breaking up of any strictly chronological order, and artistically motivated intervention on the part of narrators will add to this. It is a question of art. Indeed, techniques of this kind are typical of more complex forms of narration, whether epic poems, novels, or films. In oral tales (e.g., in the folk tale), deviations from the natural order of events are rarely to be found.

The difference between plot (in Russian *sjužet*) and fabula was underlined by the Russian formalists, though literary criticism in English had long since made a distinction between plot and story. Plot is the exposition of the events of a narrative in the order in which they appear in the text; fabula is the exposition of the same events in their chronological and logical order. Such exposition, precisely because it brings together and reconstitutes connections dislocated by the narration, is much more than a simple rearrangement. It is also an act which determines the functional value of the actions and, hence, a decisive stage on the way toward our elimination of nonfunctional actions and toward construction of a narrative model. Determining the fabula is thus the equivalent of beginning discovery of the logical-temporal relations among actions. Once the fabula has been defined, it will constitute a term of comparison for the techniques realized in a text and, when the field of research is widened, for classification of techniques as they relate to historical periods, literary genres, etc.

The order of events in the fabula is, therefore, chronological. But the time factor, as well as being deeply involved in dislocations typical of the plot, is still further compromised because there exists no synchronic equivalence between the events related and the space accorded them (the lines, or pages, or minutes in which they are represented). A narration may dispose of many years in a single sentence (or it may leave them out) and then go on for page after page to dwell on a few minutes. Furthermore, and this brings us closer to the sequence of the actions, it may attribute to one action a singulative aspect, to others a durative or iterative aspect (Genette 1972, pp. 122–82).

Order, duration, and frequency are thus the three principal manifestations of temporality. They should not be considered exclusively in the material evidence of their transgression of the synchrony with respect to the temporality of narrative realization. They also involve the nature of this realization: breaks in order are modulated by back reference and by connectives (in the film we regularly find fade in or fade out); differences in duration correspond, for the most part, to oppositions like summary and description, utterance and dialogue, or reflection, etc.; and the aspect (frequency) of the action calls for a particular use of tenses, conjunctions, adverbs. These manifestations are part of the powers which the narrator arrogates to himself with respect to his material.

5. But, if we go back to the origins of the narrative manifestation, we will realize that the range of choices a narrator can make is an extremely wide one. Once he has a subject, a narrator has first and foremost to decide what means he will use to communicate it: an oral tale, a film, a television play, a stage play, a novel, a comic, etc. Even if the choice for any given narrator is not really an open one, in abstract these and other possibilities do exist, and it is possible to "decant" from one medium to another, even after the communication has been effected (a film, a television play, a stage play, etc., can be narrated orally; from a novel a film can be made, or from a film a novel, and so forth). There is no need to insist on the fact that such "decanting" will bring to light, when competences are well matched, the peculiar character of the different media.

An initial choice already in part determines the type of utterance. One has only to think of the sharp distinction between mimesis and diegesis, between what is called in English *showing* and *telling*. In the former, the author is eclipsed behind his characters; he speaks to us with a tone and in words which he puts into their mouths. In the latter, he directs the narration himself. But since diegesis is hardly ever to be found in unadulterated form, what we usually find is an alternation of narrative and of discourses (more diegetic when indirect, more mimetic when direct), and this involves a definite standpoint with respect to the material. In other cases, use is made of letters (the epistolary novel), of fictitious memoirs, etc.

An observation must now be made. In artificial (literary) narration, more than in mimesis or in lyric poetry, the author seeks to keep the communication circuit alive by creating a mediator between himself and the narratee (the addressee of the narration). The communication circuit will then have the following appearance: addresser→ (narrator)→ narration→ addressee narratee. If no difference exists between the addressee and the narratee (who is not to be identified with the reader), the addresser (author) and the narrator are indeed distinct. It is the narrator who will often converse with the reader and who will have recourse to metanarratives and render explicit the organization of the material; it is the narrator who will make observations concerning the material and at times suggest connections and anticipate events or even how things will end. In short, it is the narrator who says *I*, even when he is not identifying himself with a character.

The addressee seeks to move behind the narration to the narrator and perhaps to the author, but, hoodwinked by a double fiction—the narrator and the narrated content—he is likely to confuse author and narrator or even author and narration when (as in first person accounts) the narrator is also protagonist or a character. Such ambiguities keep the contact between narrator and narratee alive, and they should not be eliminated by any codification of possible combinations. The interlacing of codifications is active and ever variable.

On the other hand, the narrator is also a mediator between addresser and narration. It may be taken for granted that the addresser knows everything that he wishes to know concerning the narration, since he has invented it himself. It must then be added that the narrator constitutes a regularizing exigency for this omniscience, one able to limit it or to mete it out as the story moves forward. And since overall knowledge of the story itself is shared between narrator and characters, a basic threefold division applies: narrator > character: the narrator knows more than the character(s); narrator = character; the narrator knows, or comes to know, as much as the character whose point of view he assumes; narrator < character: the narrator knows less than the characters, whose behavior and discourses he describes without claiming to understand them (Pouillon 1946; Todorov 1966).

The position of the author with respect to his material—the distance from which he describes the facts—can therefore be situated along the axis which links narrator and character(s). The whole problem has been repeatedly dealt with under the label "point of view." The narrator may identify himself with the protagonist of the story and present it to us as an autobiography; he may appear in the guise of a secondary character, an eyewitness of events he has been involved in; he may, while remaining outside the story, still adhere to the point of view of the protagonist or else, turn and turn about, act as the interpreter of the thoughts and feelings of all the characters, and so on.

Without going into all possible cases (the possibilities are numerous indeed), we may content ourselves here with the groupings which arise out of Genette's proposed fourfold division (1972, pp. 275–79 and 291–300). He describes as *heterodiegetic* the case of a narrator absent from the story narrated and as *homodiegetic* one in which the narrator is presented as a character (hence, a tale in which the narrator is the protagonist, and not just any character, will be *autodiegetic*). Furthermore, with reference to narrative levels, he calls *intradiegetic* a tale unfolded by a narrator once removed who belongs to the level of the action (Ulysses who tells his own story in books IX-XII of the *Odyssey*) and *extradiegetic* a tale unfolded by a narrator once removed who belongs to a narrative level different from that of the principal action (the characters of the frame, often itself narrative in form, who in many classical collections tell the tales themselves). Thus, we have four types of narration, and they depend on the position of the narrator:(1) *extradiegetic-heterodiegetic* (the narrator is absent from the tale he narrates); (2) *extradiegetic-homodiegetic* (a narrator directly recounts his own tale); (3) *intradiegetic-heterodiegetic* (a narrator once removed, thus already a character of a tale, tells stories from which he is absent); and (4) *intradiegetic-homodiegetic* (a narrator once removed tells his own story).

6. We have been moving upward from the fundamental structures of narration toward the modes of its manifestation. Our observations have brought to light, first, structures common to any kind of narration and, then, techniques which are primarily literary. When, for example, we take the film, which seems to have at its disposal so complex a narrative orchestration, we find many equivalents to the techniques here under discussion, but the inevitable distance between camera and actors severely limits potential points of view. They will be fundamentally heterodiegetic, even when disembodied voices, titles, or such (instruments literary in kind) lend the film a homodiegetic or autodiegetic appearance.

In cinema, then, any personalization of the narrator as distinct from the author (except when use is made of the expedients mentioned above) is extremely awkward. It is not possible to develop that dialogue with the narratee which has, beside phatic or perhaps distensive functions, the dialectical potentialities of a comment as well, being sometimes in agreement, sometimes at odds, with the narration. We have earlier stated that the narrator enlivens the communication circuit. We will find this confirmed when we consider the inevitably authoritarian form of cinematic narration, for the only alternative it offers is refusal to receive it. In cinema, the possibility of our assuming the point of view of a character, in however deformed a guise, is a severely limited one, given the seeming objectivity of images fixed on film and the presence of the actors in the sights of the lens.

Even where point of view is concerned, what should be noted as peculiar to literary narration is the fact that it makes it possible for us to get inside characters, inside their very thoughts. This is done not merely by utterances in assertive form (indirect speech) and in mimetic form (direct speech whose modes may well be close to the irrational and the random, i.e., free association and stream of consciousness) but also by the use of syntactic forms to signify reception of thoughts on the part of the narrator (free indirect speech). Once again, only in literary narration is it possible to distinguish differences of duration—the singulative and the frequentative from the durative. And varieties of style and register should not be neglected, for they go far beyond a choice between a mimetic dialogue (where, from one character to another, account is taken of all the peculiarities—of psychology, sociology, character, language, etc.) and any dialogue translated into standard language. Expressive potentials can be broadened to cover diegesis as well, and variety will then be practically infinite.

If these indications are followed up, we shall discover that what we are discussing is the novel rather than narration in general. A distinction between the one and the other might have helped clarify discussion of the crisis and death of the novel. Narration is, in all likelihood, a substantial activity among all human activities (and it is no accident that, while the novel was allegedly in its death throes, narration was alive and well in the mass media and in other mass-produced forms). The crisis involves no more than the novel as genre, and what it challenges are specific conventions like the autonomy of the plot or the omniscience of the writer. Less frequently is doubt cast upon the totality of the orchestration which we have here, however rapidly, surveyed. (So true is this that many kinds of novels have been born or given a new lease on life: essay novels, "behaviorist" novels, *collage* novels, and the novels of the *école du regard*). I believe that it is misguided to stigmatize as arbitrary the right, perhaps the need, to propose, and to utilize, possible worlds and courses of events (and thus meditations and conversations). The real crisis is that of the individual "ego," of the world, and of relations between the one and the other. The novel should, if anything, follow up these developments, reflecting and, who knows, anticipating the solution (if a solution exists).

References

Booth, W. C.
  1961. *The Rhetoric of Fiction*. 2d rev. ed. 1983. Chicago: University of Chicago Press.
Bremond, C.
  1966. La logique des possibles narratifs. *Communications*, 8, pp. 60–76.
  1973. *Logique du récit*. Paris: Seuil.
Champigny, R.
  1972. *Ontology of the Narrative*. The Hague: Mouton.
Chatman, S.
  1978. *Story and Discourse: Narrative Structure in Fiction and Film*. Ithaca: Cornell University Press.
Dijk, T. A. van
  1972. *Some Aspects of Text Grammars: A Study in Theoretical Linguistics and Poetics*. The Hague: Mouton.
Doležel, L.
  1976. Narrative Semantics. *PTL: A Journal of Poetics and Theory of Literature*, 1, pp. 129–51.
Genette, G.
  1972. *Figures III*. Paris: Seuil (English translation. 1979. *Narrative Discourse*. Oxford: Blackwell.)
Greimas, A.-J.
  1966. *Sémantique structurale*. Paris: Larousse. (English translation. 1983. *Structural Semantics*. Lincoln: University of Nebraska Press.)

Hendricks, W. O.
  1973. *Essays on Semiolinguistics and Verbal Art*. The Hague: Mouton.
Koselleck, R., and Stempel, W.-D., eds.
  1973. *Geschichte-Ereignis und Erzählung*. Munich: Fink.
Labov, W., and Waletzky, J.
  1967. Narrative Analysis: Oral Versions of Personal Experience. J. Helm, ed. *Essays on the Verbal and Visual Arts*. Seattle: University of Washington Press. Pp. 12–44.
Lotman, Ju. M.
  1970. *Struktura chudožestvennogo teksta*. Moscow: Iskusstvo. (English translation. 1977. *The Structure of the Artistic Test*. Ann Arbor: University of Michigan Press.)
Meletinskij, E. M., et al.
  1969. Problemy strukturnogo opisanija volšebnoj skazki. Σημειωτική: *Trudy po znakovym sistemam*, 4, pp. 86–135. (Italian translation. 1977. *La struttura della fiaba*. Palermo: Sellerio.)
Pouillon, J.
  1946. *Temps et roman*. Paris: Gallimard.
Prince, G.
  1982. *Narratology: The Form and Functioning of Narrative*. Berlin: de Gruyter.
Propp, V. Ja.
  1928. *Morfologija skazki*. Leningrad: Academia. (English translation. 1968. *Morphology of the Folk Tale*. Austin: University of Texas Press.)
Scholes, R., and Kellogg, R.
  1966. *The Nature of Narrative*. New York: Oxford University Press.
Segre, C.
  1974. *Le strutture e il tempo: Narrazione, poesia, modelli*. Turin: Einaudi. (English translation. 1979. *Structures and Time: Narration, Poetry, Models*. Chicago: University of Chicago Press.)
Souriau, E.
  1950. *Les deux cent mille situations dramatiques*. Paris: Flammarion.
Todorov, T.
  1966. Les catégories du récit littéraire. *Communications*, no. 8, pp. 125–51.
Tomaševskij, B.
  1928. *Teorija literatury: Poetika*. Leningrad. (Italian translation. 1978. Milan: Feltrinelli.)

5.
Poetics

1. The various meanings which the word *poetics* has assumed over the course of time can be traced back to the program formulated and carried out by Aristotle in his *Poetics:* "Let us here deal with Poetry, its essence and its several species, with the characteristic function of each species and the way in which plots must be constructed if the poem is to be a success; and also with the number and character of the constituent parts of a poem, and similarly with all other matters proper to this same inquiry" (1447a, 1–13). We should remark that *eidos*, here "species," is used, for the most part, to signify "genre"—and this is the way some translators render it here—but it can, in a wider sense, mean "differential 'form,' and element of a whole," as Gallavotti tells us (1974, p. 263). The designation *poetics* was adopted both for treatises of this type and for their content, and it is from the second of these senses that all other meanings of the word derive.

Poetics stands for *poietike techne*, which is "the art of poetry," and its etymon (*poiein*) refers to literary production from the point of view of the craftmanship involved. This is a constituent element of Aristotle's exposition, although it is transcended in terms of a general theory of literature. Other authors have oscillated between discovery of techniques and theoretical generalization, either because they desired to furnish writers with practical advice or because they were attracted by problems of institutionalization. A similar dichotomy exists between a normative, prescriptive reading of the *Poetics* and one which is philosophical and, thus, necessarily historical.

Nonetheless, Aristotle's treatise is the paradigm. Almost all future poetics will be composed with reference to it, with the exception of a long interval during the medieval period, during which (since no one knew the original) a derivative, Horace's *Ars poetica*, was used. Horace's book is a lightweight work in theoretical terms but a lively one when it comes to advice on taste, and it is pleasingly polemical. It made its mark not only during the period when the *Poetics* was unknown, but even after its (sixteenth-century) rediscovery, and this was due in part to the idiosyncratic empiricism of the teaching it offered.

2. In Aristotle's conception, poetics and rhetoric are integrated. Aristotle himself wrote a work entitled *Rhetoric*, and he refers us to it in the *Poetics* when he is speaking of language and thought in the literary work. "All that concerns Thought [*peri . . . dianoias*] may be left to the treatise on Rhetoric; for the

subject is more proper to that inquiry" (1456a, 33–36). Thought *(dianoia)* includes the argumentative aspects of discourse: "proof and refutation, the arousing of feelings like pity, fear, anger, and so on, and then again exaggeration, and depreciation" (1456a, 38–1456b, 1; cf. 1450b, 5–12).

Re-elaborated by the Romans down to the *Rhetorica ad Herennium* and to Quintilian, the rhetoric which the *Poetics* takes as understood became, in the Middle Ages, the almost exclusive argument of those who wrote treatises on literature. The many works entitled *Poetria, Ars versificatoria,* and so on (Faral 1924), are in effect treatises on rhetoric (classifications and definitions of tropes, figures of words, and of thought). They may well be rounded out with references to Horace, whose own schema was rhetorical in type. His *Ars poetica* falls into three parts: *inventio, elocutio,* and *artifex* and is based on the Alexandrian triad *poiesis, poiema, poietes* (cf. Rostagni 1930, chap. 5). The doctrine of genres was expounded, always succinctly, in terms of a correspondence which the commentators found between the works of Virgil and the three styles as Cicero had defined them: *Aeneis* for the lofty style; *Georgica* for the middle style; *Bucolica* for the humble style. In this way, a canon was established. Its starting point was the three Alexandrian genres (tragedy, comedy, satyr drama), though the third of them was replaced by satire or, in some cases, elegy or else a fourfold division was created to accommodate them both (Mengaldo 1978, pp. 200–10).

These arts of poetry often defined possible defects of the three styles; usually a matter of mistakenly inserting words which should rightly pertain to different levels. This paved the way for the kind of investigation of relations between genres and registers which has been undertaken in more recent times. Aristotle had already referred to the matter: "Of the various kinds of words, the double forms are most suited for dithyrambs, rare words for heroic verse and metaphors for iambics," etc. (*Poetics,* 1459a, 9–11). And the Alexandrians gave the idea consistent application.

3. Aristotle's *Poetics* breaks off just as it is about to deal with iambics and with comedy; as a result, it ends up concentrating entirely on tragedy and epic. What is more, a preference for tragedy, which at the end is stated explicitly, meant a subordinate place for epic, though (thanks to Homer) it is a conspicuous one. The absence of certain genres, and the different degree of interest in those which are examined, serves to show that systematic classification of them was not the author's intention. Aristotle also bases his synchronic descriptions on a diachronic exposition (on those developments of tragedy and comedy which were known to him). Thus, while the criteria for his judgments are expressed forthrightly enough, an experience of some subtlety serves for their corroboration. Genres are presented within the dynamics of a double progression: that of historical development and that of comparative evaluation. The superiority of tragedy lies in the fact that it represents the fullest realization of Aristotle's idea of literature (and, indeed, it was the leading genre at the time of the *Poetics*). In short, genres are dealt with by Aristotle in function of his literary theory, and this theory is based on a comparison of literature and reality. It extends investigation of one of the fundamental themes of Greek philosophy,

one which had already been touched on by the Sophists and by Plato, although their assertions had sometimes been contradictory.

With his theory, Aristotle activates a defense of literature (against Plato's condemnation of it) which consists of demonstrating its cognitive value. The concept of mimesis, which formalizes a relation with reality, is complementary to a gnoseological conception of art, since art contrives to produce pleasure in virtue of our recognition and understanding of the reality it represents, while it celebrates, as its ultimate effect, catharsis, which means overcoming the passions through knowledge. Thus, Aristotle subordinates to his gnoseological theory potentially hedonistic or psychological orientations while not denying them and does so by identifying a cycle of mimesis-pleasure-knowledge.

Mimesis is imitation not of concrete facts but of the universals of human actions: hence, the importance of the concepts of possible, verisimilar, and necessary and a preference for the truth-like impossibility over the incredible though possible (1460a, 27–29) as well as the explicitly affirmed superiority of poetry as a "general view" with respect to history, for history will always be history of the particular (1451b, 6–12; cf. 1459a, 21–25).

It is from within a theory so conceived that the most striking anticipations of the formalists are to be found: interconnection of the parts of the action (1451a, 30–36), classification of types of connection (1452a, 12–22) and of change in the action (peripeteia, agnition, and disaster), and distinction between the plot and accessory motifs (1455b, 16–23). It might almost be said (though from a modern standpoint) that the *Poetics* is a large-scale theory of the fabula.

4. The fame enjoyed by the *Poetics* is also the history of its continual misrepresentation. Tragedy and epic had been distinguished by Aristotle by means of distributional criteria—their different combination of means, objects, and manner of imitating (1147a, 14–29)—and with taxonomic criteria: length, type of metre (1149b, 9–19). These hints at definition of genres were forthwith developed to form canons, and these included in their lists not just the main genres but the subgenres as well. Such canons were severely tested when faced with totally extraneous medieval and early Renaissance works—from Dante's *Divine Comedy* to romances of chivalry—or when new genres, created by the sixteenth and seventeenth centuries, needed to be justified (cf. §6).

The "degeneration" of the Aristotelian system is even more apparent in the way the concepts of mimesis and verisimilitude were manipulated (for Aristotle, they had been closely interconnected). Mimesis will often (from Dionysius of Halicarnassus to Scaliger) become imitation of classical masterpieces—an already sublimated mediation between nature and literary expression—or direct reproduction of facts and persons. To verisimilitude and inverisimilitude will be added, on the basis of distinctions which are often quite subtle, the absurd and the marvelous. The Alexandrians had already differentiated between *plasma (res ficta), mythos (fabula)* and *historia (fama)*, and the Latin rhetors were to follow them. Catharsis and pleasure would, in their turn, be reinterpreted in the light of new ideologies like Christianity, the Enlightenment, sensism.

One striking consequence of normative interpretation is the importance the treatise writers attributed to unity of action and unity of time. To these Castelvetro added a unity of place of which Aristotle had known nothing. He, indeed, having conferred a clear-cut preeminence on tragedy, had allowed it a great range of descriptive techniques. And it was the playwrights themselves, from Lope de Vega to Victor Hugo (in his preface to *Cromwell*, 1827), who challenged the validity of the rules.

But the misrepresentations referred to are the outcome of the vitality of Aristotle's model, for it was assimilated by different philosophies and by different currents of taste, all of whom found in it a wealth of techniques for description and classification which they could continually perfect. There is no basis, however, for the belief that sixteenth- and seventeenth-century poetics form a solid block or that they correspond to a conventional scholastic framework. Indeed, at times they contain extraordinarily penetrating insights into literary criticism and literary history.

A history of poetic treatises would not, in any case, coincide with a history of literary theories, for the following reasons: (a) the authors of poetics sometimes, though not always, represented the most advanced positions of reflection on literary activity, positions which often found expression in attitudes that were partial or temporary or polemical; (b) there exist periods when poetic treatises were rare or absent but when literary thought was actively elaborated; (c) the formulation of rules for poetic production has a tendency to develop autonomously (in consideration of changes in the literary system as a whole), whereas theorization of the artistic phenomenon will, from the eighteenth century onward, progressively neglect descriptive or institutionalizing moments.

5. Although it had been translated into Latin by William of Moerbeke, the *Poetics* was still unknown down to the end of the Middle Ages. Even the translation of Averroes' commentary, which had been made by Hermannus Alemannus (twelfth century), began to circulate only with its printed version, *Determinatio in poetria Aristotelis* (Venice, 1481). The text became fully known only when Valla translated it into Latin (1498), thanks to Aldo Manuzio's edition of the Greek text (1508). From 1541 onward, public lectures on it by Lombardi and Maggi were held in Padua, Ferrara, etc., and a considerable number of commentaries appeared: Francesco Robortello (1548), Bartolomeo Lombardi and Vincenzo Maggi (1550), Pietro Vettori (1560), Antonio Riccoboni (1599)—all in Latin; in Italian, Lionardo Salviati (1564), Ludovico Castelvetro (1570), Alessandro Piccolomini (1572), and yet others. No less than three translations into Italian exist. An exegetic undertaking of this kind is quite impressive, and it left its mark on those who composed poetics on their own account.

It should be noted that it was only in the second half of the sixteenth century, almost in parallel with the commentaries, that other poetics begin to model themselves unequivocally on the Aristotelian pattern. Earlier, the main source had been Horace: not only for Vida's *De arte poetica* (1527) but for the first four parts of Trissino's *Poetica* (published in 1529 and which also made use of the newly discovered *De vulgari eloquentia*), for the *Poetica* (1536) of Bernardino Daniello (who like Trissino was oriented entirely toward Italian texts), and for the schematic and rule-bound *Arte poetica* (1551) of Girolamo Muzio. Aristotle *(Poetics* and *Rhetoric)* came to the fore only in Books V-VI of Trissino's *Poetica* (1562, but written about 1549). Trissino quotes whole passages though he contaminates them with Plato, Dionysius of Halicarnassus, and Dante. Horace was still present in Capriano's *Della vera poetica* (1555), in Viperano's *De poetica* (1579), and in Minturno's eclectic dialogue *De poeta* (1559), and Plato, Cicero, Quintilian, etc., were not absent. But Aristotle was the most influential, and every treatise writer dwelt on his basic concepts: Capriano on the relation between imitation and invention and on the hierarchy of genres (divided into natural and moral poetry); Minturno made a threefold division for each of the three major genres and based it on the three levels of style and character. Even more original, in the last two decades of the century, were the writings of Patrizi *(La deca istoriale, La deca disputata* (1586); the other eight would follow), who grouped under the headings of divine, natural, and human the three main classes of literature and defined their products according to the mode of their communication and pragmatic functions. And Denores *(Poetica,* 1588) stressed that the ultimate aims were moral and civic and highlighted, with a sensibility that was already prebaroque, a sense of wonderment seen as a means for ensuring efficacy of imitation. The most complex theoretical level was probably, together with Castelvetro's commentary, that of the *Poetices libri VII* (1561, but written before 1558) by Giulio Cesare Scaliger. In this weighty work, Aristotle's thematic framework was rendered strictly systematic even at the risk of contradicting Aristotle himself. Scaliger's linguistic approach is of interest (words are regarded as mediators between men and things, the poetic discourse as a mediator between the moral and the natural sciences). Scaliger, too, set up a hierarchy for genres, with a scale which descends from God and embraces the most miserable of mankind.

The influence of the Italian treatise writers (Scaliger first among them) was immense. Pinciano's *Philosophía Antigua Poética* (1596) framed its descriptive sections to correspond to a philosophy of artistic creation. The attempt was made to arrange Spanish medieval and humanistic genres so that they would conform to a documentation which was essentially classical. The influence of Tasso can be felt in what is said about epic. Cascales, too, was linked to Tasso, while the normative framework of his *Tablas poéticas* (1617) was modeled on Horace and on Aristotle's *Rhetoric* rather than on his *Poetics*. Scaliger still dominated the Dutch writer Daniël Heinsius in his *De tragoediae constitutione* (1611) and also the work of the Dutch-German Vossius, whose *De artis poeticae natura ac constitutione, Poeticae institutiones, De imitatione* (1647) was an arrangement of preexisting arrangements. Philip Sidney's *Apologie for Poetrie* (1597), which dealt with the English poetry of its time, was fully influenced by the Italian writers as were the poetics of the French "Pléiade," which were Horatian as well. This applies to Ronsard (1565, and particularly to the posthumous preface to his *Franciade)* and to his successors down to Vauquelin de la Fresnaye (1605). Only in 1610 did there appear in France a poetics comparable to that of the Italians: the *Académie de l'Art poétique* of Pierre de Deimier.

6. In a history of poetics, it is important not to lose sight of works which are devoted to a single genre or to a single work. These are as a rule, polemical (they exalt, or belittle, contemporary or, at any rate, fashionable compositions), and for this reason they involve an often revealing clash between theoretical principles and an active or passive experience of art. Furthermore, precisely because single genres or single texts are their focus, they leave aside any concern with an overall framework and the obligatory symmetries it entails. Many such writings can be defined as pamphlets or manifestos, and they show the limited temporal orientation and the apologetic approach which is typical of texts of this kind (cf. §14).

When Aristotle's *Poetics* came to enjoy a new lease on life, the overall framework within which texts were inscribed was totally different from anything Aristotle himself had known. This explains why many treatise writers (among them Scaliger) preferred to confine their references to classical literature, to the Greeks and the Romans (whereas pre-Aristotelian poetics had been concerned almost exclusively with literature in the vernacular, e.g., Trissino and Daniello, or even with contemporary texts, e.g., Thomas Sibilet, 1549, Jacques Pelletier, 1555, etc.).

But any escape from literary reality was impossible. The problem did not arise in Spain, because the repercussions of poetics on artistic life remained limited. When Lope de Vega wished to prove that he was up to date theoretically, he wrote *El arte nuevo de hacer comedias* (1609), a not very convinced homage to the rules of tragedy, which stands in stark contrast to the tradition and to the popular taste to which real comedies, those of Lope himself first among them, in fact conformed. But, in Italy, the cult of Dante's *Comedy* went unchallenged, while the knightly romances of Boiardo and of Ariosto were extremely successful and highly esteemed; theoreticians authenticated this heritage in the light of the doctrine. For the *Comedy*, not easily assimilated to the epic poem and even less, despite the attempts made, to tragedy or comedy, the following should be mentioned: Castravilla (1572), Jacopo Mazzoni (1572 and 1587), Sassetti (1573), Borghini (1573), Bulgarini (1576, 1579, 1588), Capponi (1577). Its supporters pointed out its moral, allegorical, and sacred element and turned their attention to its perlocutionary potential. They preferred, as a rule, to defend the quality of the poem rather than its regularity, with an inductive rather than a deductive orientation.

Debate on the romance was divided into two phases which partially overlapped, because classification of this genre, after the appearance of Tasso's *Gerusalemme liberata*, took the form of a confrontation between the new text and Ariosto's *Orlando furioso;* each text had its ardent supporters. In the first phase, Fornari (1549), Pigna (1554), Giraldi Cintio (1554), Orazio Ariosto (1585), and others advanced, in the context of an opposition between "ancients" and "moderns," the historical and aesthetic reasons why the romance had developed in the neo-Latin world as a replacement for the moribund epic poem, and the difference of its norms (multiplication of plots) was remarked. Indeed, Patrizi (1585) turned the problem inside out and contested Aristotle outright. In a second phase, Tasso's poem held the center of the stage; it was measured against the theorizations and defended, by the author himself among others, with considerable intelligence. To the problems which had earlier come to light (e.g., unity of action, observed by Tasso but not by Ariosto), others were now added: the relations between truth and history and, since Tasso's inspiration was Christian, allegory and the use of religious themes. Among those who took part in this *querelle*, mention should be made not just of Tasso himself (1585, 1586, 1587, 1594) but of Salviati (1585, 1586, 1588), Pellegrino (1585), Lombardelli (1586), Guastavini (1590, 1592), Malatesta (1589, 1596), etc.

Elsewhere, it was the legitimacy of new genres which came under discussion—tragicomedy, for instance (Guarini, Denores, Alberti, Ingegneri, etc., were involved, and the argument centered on the *Pastor fido* of Guarini himself, 1586 and the years following). Those who wished to exclude the work remained blindly attached to the correspondence between genres and social levels which Aristotle had hinted at but which were emphasized in the sixteenth century: a literary system had to be the mirror of an unchanging model of the world. Furthermore, any mixing of levels was denounced as a threat to the pedagogic-moral function of art. In fact, the current which supported Guarini not only insisted on the continual mutability of the literary system but also pronounced itself strongly in favor of a hedonistic interpretation of literature. There were even discussions involving those genres which, in homage to Aristotle, had been artificially restored. This was the case for Speroni's tragedy *Canace e Macareo* (ca. 1541), and we may add Giraldi's *Orbecche* (1541) and *Didone* (1542) and others of an even more classical cast. Here—and the dates should be noted—Aristotle's arguments were rendered more trenchant and were more closely dissected, though no doctrinal novelties were forthcoming (for the whole question, see Weinberg).

Between general poetics and debates, a certain distance exists. A historical poetics matured in polemics, pamphlets, and manifestos, and an awareness of the autonomy of literary criticism was achieved. Certainly one already senses in these texts a productive convergence between theory and practice in art.

7. The suggestion that poetics has exercised a repressive influence on literary life finds little to support it. What may, rather, call for investigation is the degree to which, in the climate of the Counter Reformation, poetics themselves were instrumentalized. It is a fact, though, that the times and places in which Aristotelian legislation was most vigorous were the same ones which saw the affirmation of a classicizing and rationalistic taste which found its natural correspondence in the *Poetics* and its interpreters. The most positive example is that of the so-called Classical Age in France.

France had taken almost no part in the sixteenth century's elaboration of literary theory; it had neglected or rejected the Aristotelian unities; it had celebrated, during the Pléiade, a "modern" literature and been attracted, at the beginning of the seventeenth century, by mixed genres, especially in the theater (tragicomedy, pastoral drama, and mock heroic poems as well). Around 1630, though, France became the country of the Aristotelian unities and of tragedy. But though the rules were the same, the motivations were not: imitation (authorized by Scaliger) looked to the great models rather than to reality; verisimilitude was linked to credibility as a necessary vehicle for a moral function and to a *decorum (bienséance)* which was fundamental for an aristocratic and hierarchically minded culture. The very acceptance of Aristotle acquired a tone of its own, for it was based on the affirmation of a coincidence between his rules and the dictates of reason. What is more, the unities served to second the increasingly psychological approach of the tragedy: "Unity of action, unity of time, unity of place are three parallel, even though at times independent, forms of one single law which is essential to the Classical spirit, the law of concentration" (Bray 1957, p. 288).

This lively period of reflection on poetics has at its center a great debate on the unities (1632-39) which reached its climax with the battle over Corneille's *Cid* (1638)—and we might recall this author's discerning reference to "unity of plot or of obstacle to the protagonist's projects." The most numerous contributions to this debate were those of Jean Chapelain (who also defended Marino's *Adone*, presented by him as an example of modern epic); the most systematic conclusions were those of the *Poétique* of La Mesnardière (1639), which breaks off—and it is no accident—with dramatic poetry. Boileau's *Ars poétique* (1674) is no more than a rearguard action of consolidation, and that it is much closer to Horace than to Aristotle is significant. It was not so much a theory as a pamphlet, full of clever jibes at the expense of literary enemies, of practical advice and statements of taste.

The task that fell to Martin Opitz's *Book of German Poetry (Buch von der Deutschen Poeterey,* 1624) was the organization of a set of rules which would act as a guide for developments already under way in the German literature of the time. The book is no more than a scant summary of Heinsius and of Italian poetic principles, and many of its examples are drawn from French poetry. But it contains original observations on Germanic prosody and on rhyme. It is an example of a reduction on the synchronic plane of a diachronic experience (in which Germany had played no role). The problem of bringing a national literature, seen as standing in need of guarantee, into line with poetics can also be sensed in Dryden's *Essay on Dramatic Poesy* (1668), and it is found in a markedly xenophile form in the late *Poética* (1735) of Ignacio de Luzán, who upheld his neoclassical ideals by exalting Corneille and Rapin at the expense of Lope, Góngora, and Calderón. This standpoint was shared by Gottsched's essay on poetic criticism, *Versuch einer kritischen Dichtkunst* (1730), an attack on baroque "bad taste," which was to be replaced by clear rules in keeping with the ideals of the Enlightenment.

8. From the baroque period onward, the treatises became more free in form

and turned their attention to particularly problematical areas of literary production (e.g., the metaphor). They proclaim that they belong to specific cultural tendencies, favoring now the use of conceits or Arcadia, now the Enlightenment or neoclassicism. It is the eighteenth century especially which assisted at the birth of aesthetics as a philosophical rather than a literary tradition. There is no need to follow this intellectual adventure in all its phases. Leibniz and Kant shared a common view of art as knowledge; for the former, it lay midway between sense and intellect; for the latter, between theoretics and the moral will. It was a pupil of Leibniz, Baumgarten, who wrote the first *Aesthetica* (1750), "the science of sensory knowledge." The succession (an ideal one) from Vico to Schelling and Hegel saw art as a specific moment in development or in the cycle of knowledge. It was primeval for Vico and Hegel; for Schelling, the most sublime moment, that of the Absolute, an overcoming of the nature-spirit antithesis. It might be thought that an interest in art that was so all-embracing as to refuse to confine itself to literature alone, that had so dynamic a framework and a tendency so opposed to precept, could only have led to the elimination of any trace of poetics. But this was not the case.

Centuries of treatise writing had determined and formulated problems central to the ultimate aims of art or to the constitution of the literary text. On the other hand, the original catalogue of genres in all likelihood embraced, if not the main texts, at least texts which were clearly characterized and which could be traced back to the principles of general order. It is easy to understand why, in Vico and the chief representatives of idealism, quite consistent traces of Aristotle's schemata are found. Vico, for example, sketched an ideal history of genres and subgenres and related them to the three ages of the civic life of mankind. Friedrich Schlegel envisaged a historical poetics as the basis for a theory of poetry, on the grounds that a work cannot be assessed without taking its genus and species into account. Hegel followed the model of the treatise writers in his innovative analysis (and history) of genres.

The most extreme point reached by aesthetic reflection is that of Croce (1936), who makes a clear-cut distinction between aesthetic judgment and empirical judgment. It is as if the aim were to bring order into, and to clarify, the contaminations just outlined.

> The aesthetic judgment, which is formed thanks to mental categories or pure concepts, is substantially philosophical and not empirical; likewise philosophical and not empirical is aesthetics, the methodology of a judgment or science of the category of the beautiful. . . . All of this in no way alters the legitimacy either of an empirical judgment of the beautiful as an aesthetic or any empirical poetic made up of empirical concepts, whose special office is classificatory and not cognitive or discriminatory. . . . An empirical poetics would not exist and would consist merely in the series, continually increased by progressive specification, of these two orders of representational concepts: the first of which can be called evaluation, or rather reprobation, and the second, qualification, or rather characterization (Croce 1936, ed. 1963, pp. 160–61).

Such statements are questionable in terms of philosophical validity (the opposition of pure concepts and empirical concepts), and they exacerbate a demarcation between assessment of the "beautiful," which should leave out of account the forms in which historically art has found expression, and a definition of poetics seen in an exclusively normative and classificatory function. What is entirely neglected is the frequent convergence between poetics and the tendencies in taste or the expressive commitment of artists. Such statements might be turned inside out polemically in order to highlight the real continuity which exists when poetics are elaborated in relation to cultural situations, rather than the absolutism of an aesthetic judgment, valid only if one accepts and considers definitive (as under no circumstance it could ever be) the premises of a philosophical theory.

9. It is now apparent that poetic treatises are always the result of a compromise: between principles for the most part inherited and contemporary tendencies of the culture. The proportions will vary in terms of the polemical engagement of the treatise writer and his sensibility to his times. The poetics implicit in single works, in single authors, or in strongly characterized literary phases are quite another matter. Such poetics are the formal awareness of artists and epochs and can also be deduced from their practice as well as, obviously, from the explicit taking of sides. The succession of such poetics and the life of literature are one and the same thing. Research into this aspect was carried out especially in post-Croce Italy (Binni), particularly in the phenomenological sphere (Banfi, Anceschi), with the aim of vindicating the awareness of artistic production (Pajano 1970).

A program of this kind coincides in part with exigencies expressed by Schlegel (cf. §8) and put into effect, among the first, by Blankenburg, 1796–98, before the Russian formalists found a different expression for it. It was they who first envisaged the history of poetics in more concrete terms, as a way of arranging the study of forms and styles along historical coordinates and, as in Tynjanov, literary genres as well. While the Italians, conditioned by their dialogue with Croce, limited themselves to definitions whose nature was general and which fell within the terms of a debate where the tone was (not unprofitably) philosophical, the Russians brought together an extremely rich harvest of formal and thematic observations, which called for, and even predetermined, an overall arrangement. Perhaps the most synthetic definition of how much in the formalists' program can be transformed from descriptive poetics to historical poetics is to be found in these statements of Vinogradov: "Literary poetics contains in itself a study of historical development and of the transformation of styles, of aspects, and of literary genres in their typical or typological incarnations, and it is based, and this is one of its principal foundations, on the historical stylistics of artistic literature, not just from a purely linguistic point of view or aspect but also from a point of view relative to the science of literature. The specific quality of poetics as a historical, autonomous discipline lies in just this" (1963, Ital. trans., pp. 232–33; cf. pp. 192 and 208). In our conclusions (§18) we shall return to this, but first we must touch upon the more innovative aspects of the formalist revolution, those which led directly to structuralism and to semiotics.

10. The formalists initiated a new way of reading and underlined the difference between ordinary use of the language and its literary use and reached the point of seeing in literature an epiphenomenon of literariness; thus, they attempted to found a kind of general poetics. Todorov, in a recent analysis which is almost a synthesis and conclusion, works along these lines and alludes to an opposition between the referential and the poetical. Poetics, as study of the characteristics of the poetic function which literariness puts into effect, sets itself the goal of determining its elements; it sets out, in short, to formulate "a theory of the structure and of the functioning of literary discourse, one which will provide a framework of literary potentialities in such a way that existing literary works will be seen as particular cases which have been brought to realization" (Todorov 1968, p. 102). Poetics, then, ought not to concern itself with single literary works but with the possibilities offered by literary discourse, these being regarded as "abstract organizations, logically anterior to their manifestations" (p. 106). They are possibilities which can be grouped together on various levels: that of discourse (pairs such as utterance and utterance act; abstract discourse and figurative discourse; denotation and connotation; direct style and indirect style, etc.); that of narration in relation to its different points of view; and that of the organizing structure (the logical, temporal, spatial order). The concept of verisimilitude is once again taken up and transformed, subordinated from the outset to the concept of genre (verisimilar is what the rules of the genre hold to be such); in the second instance, it is subordinated to common belief which "acts . . . as a genre rule valid for all genres" (p. 149).

Todorov's hypothesis, too, ends up with an exigency historiographical in character: if evolution does not exist in literature, an evolution of the properties of literary discourse undoubtedly does; if genres do not exist in the abstract, they do exist in the history of their constituent traits. Thus, "it is necessary . . . to place oneself at the level of poetics in order to keep track, while following its subdivisions at the level of literary realizations, of the metamorphoses of one or another aspect of literary discourse. This type of study is new; it stands in opposition to description but, like description, it is tied to an elastic notion of literary history" (p. 153).

But the separation of ordinary discourse and literary discourse, although it was stimulating in the search for the constituent elements of literature, cannot be carried any further than this. This explains why the heir apparent of the formalists firmly ushered the poetic back into the fold of the language and regarded it as a function which, though in variable measure, will always be present, a function which, though, will be predominant in literary discourse, even if other functions will not be excluded. These functions are six in number, and they correspond to the six constituent elements of communication (addresser, context, message, contact, code, addressee). They are emotive, referential, poetic, phatic, metalinguistic, and conative). And it is Jakobson who attributes to poetics the study of "the poetic function in its relationship to the other functions of language"; thus, "poetics in the wider sense of the word deals with the poetic function not only in poetry, where this function is superimposed upon the other functions of language, but also outside of poetry, when some other function is superimposed upon the poetic function" (1958, p. 359).

If the study of ordinary language requires the contribution of the poetic in cases where the corresponding function is involved, the study of literary language will, in its turn, invade the terrain of ordinary language; this is because the poetic function will never be found in an adulterated state. Genres, as a result, can be defined anew: "The peculiarities of diverse poetic genres imply a differently ranked participation of the other verbal functions along with the dominant poetic function. Epic poetry, focused on the third person, strongly involves the referential function of language; the lyric, oriented toward the first person, is intimately linked with the emotive function; poetry of the second person is imbued with the conative function and is either supplicatory or exhortative, depending on whether the first person is subordinated to the second one or the second to the first" (p. 191).

Now that he has so staunchly vindicated the unity of language, Jakobson can move forward in his search for what is "specific" to poetic language. His references involve the omnipresence of rhythm, the integration of a metaphorical tendency (prevalent in romanticism) and of a metonymic tendency (prevalent in realism), ambiguity effected by superimposing the poetic function on the referential function, and the fact that, in general, the poetic message concentrates on itself. All of these aspects achieve coherence in one general principle: "the poetic function projects the principle of equivalence from the axis of selection into the axis of combination" (p. 358), i.e., the words a speaker selects from the vertical paradigm of synonymic possibilities (equivalences) are subjected by the writer to internal laws of cross-reference, harmony, repetition, alternation. This is done inside the syntagm (combination), which becomes a horizontal axis of equivalences. It is a vast canvas, and it establishes general and atemporal elements for poetic language, together with potentialities. For us, though, (at least within the limits we have set ourselves), it will prove more productive to retain the word *poetics* in its historical senses, variegated though they are.

11. We might think of treatises on poetics as maps of literary activity which are as complete as possible. They have been drawn either with an inductive method (data derived from existing literature) or with a deductive method (which sets out from general principles believed to be valid or, as is often the case, from a comparison between the frame provided by Aristotle and the Aristotelians and the literary situation being observed). Sometimes, induction and deduction will be mixed, and the fact may not be unrelated to different theorists' different degrees of philosophical coherence.

In these maps, literary genres play an important part, given that they constitute conformation types for texts to which, as a rule, other forms will be subordinated. Thus, literary genres and an Aristotelian approach to poetics are closely related. In fact, epochs which challenge the validity of genres, or in which genres undergo marked transformation, are also those in which poetical treatises are not written.

Styles are among the forms whose study is made possible only by a definition of genres. Here the word *style* is to be understood as a subsystem of literary language which is employed, or which lends itself to employment, in the field of certain specific genres in order to express certain specific contents (cf. §2).

We may well believe that the overall organization of literary activity effected by treatises of poetics constitutes not just a model of literature but a model of the world. Among the many proofs that might be adduced, the well-known "wheel of Virgil" will suffice: to the three styles *(humilis, mediocris, gravis)*, three classes correspond *(pastor, agricola, miles)* as do three types of character *(Tityrus* and *Meliboeus, Triptolemus* and *Coelius*, Hector and *Ajax)*, three animals *(ovis, bos, equus)*, three tools *(baculus, aratrum, gladius)*, three territorial sectors *(pascua, ager, urbs* and *castrum)* and, finally, three plants *(fagus, pomus, cedrus)*. The wheel of Virgil is thus a model of the world which is inscribed within (subordinated to) a literary model. This model is clearly a topological one; one need only observe the fact that its localization separates, on the one hand, the *pascua* and the *ager* and, on the other, in a position both central and dominating, the *Urbs* and the *castrum*.

Its very classification of styles is topological, because between *humilis* and *mediocris* there exists a difference of what would today be called level, while the *stylus gravis* is also called *high* or *sublime*, i.e., it is the maximum level. These levels of style are obvious metaphors for the corresponding social levels.

12. We have already seen (§5 and §6) how often poetics makes appeal to a model of the world. It is a tendency which persists in works which have long since abandoned any idea of a poetics-informed schema. Innovative, though today overrated, is the attempt made by Jolles to define *einfache Formen*, simple forms of expression corresponding to "event units." It makes reference to an explicit model of the world. Jolles reduced all human activities to three which are fundamental: cultivating, manufacturing, interpreting. These correspond to a primordial division of labor among peasants, artisans, and priests. Language itself, Jolles believes, cultivates, manufactures, interprets; its materials are elements of the universe which it determines and reorganizes. "Each time *language* takes part in setting up such a *form* ('a form that can be grasped as an object, and that possesses a validity and a cohesion of its own'), each time that it intervenes within this form to bring it to order, or to change its order, or to remodel it, we may speak of *literary forms*" (Jolles 1930, French trans., p. 26).

For his part, Frye appeals to another typology, one based on the opposition between high (noble) and low (popular or vulgar). I am alluding to his theory of "modes of invention," which is an elaboration of what is stated in *Poetics*

(1448a). According to Frye, we have *myth*, in which the hero is "superior in 'kind,' both to other men and to the environment"; *romance*, with a hero "superior in 'degree' to other men and to his environment"; the *high mimetic* mode (epic and tragedy), in which the hero is a leader, "superior in degree to other men but not to his natural environment"; the *low mimetic* mode (comedies and realistic fiction), in which the hero is "superior neither to other men nor to his environment," "where the hero is one of us"; lastly, the *ironic* mode, when the hero is "inferior in power or intelligence to ourselves, so that we have the sense of looking down on a scene of bondage, frustration, or absurdity" (1957, pp. 33–34).

We may legitimately speak of a model of the world in another sense. When the theorizers of poetics propose that their discipline ought to be inscribed in a rigid schema of human activities (as was commonly the case in the sixteenth century), they tend to confine it to a well-defined zone, with well-defined aims and "justifications." It is as if, once all possible activities have been listed, their ambition were to project onto their review of activities a map of the world which could be taken as immutable.

Those critics who, over the course of time, have dealt with one or another of these poetics have always attempted to measure its degree of normativeness. If matters are reduced to the terminology of linguistics, we would have the difference that exists between an utterance in imperative form ("You must act so," etc.) and one in assertive form ("Things are so"). It is a difference which is almost negligible.

Once it has been stated that the world is ordered in a certain manner, and that the literary system is, to a marked degree, homologous with it, no very wide-ranging initiative is left if one then turns to poetics for guidance. In general, this explains why the periods or environments in which poetics have flourished have been periods of establishment, conservation, or restoration. It is also the reason why, in such periods, polemics for and against poetics have always run riot.

Already more than once foreshadowed, and more evident, is the observation that every revival of Aristotle's poetics has further implied an anachronistic transposition of the world model of Aristotle's time to a reality many centuries distant. On the other hand, recent works on poetics have shown the limited validity of solutions of a romantic or idealistic type, which reject en masse the applicability of any concept of literary genre and look on rhetoric as a blunt, outworn instrument. They celebrate the poet's liberty of invention in the face of all of the schemata offered by the tradition and the culture of his time. Since the development of historical poetics, it has been ascertained that literary history is, in reality, made up of the history of forms, i.e., of their shifts, their resettlement in the form of new systems subject to the driving forces of successive cultural approaches (cf. §9).

13. The discourse on historical poetics must be taken up anew on the basis of the thesis of §12, which refers to modeling systems. The weakness of poetics is

the fact that the model of the world it refers to is implicitly regarded as immutable. But merely replacing immutability with a concept of mutability will hardly be enough.

The basic fact is that every model of the world implies an antimodel. I shall quote the way the Soviet semioticists approach this problem:

> To describe them from the outer point of view, culture and nonculture appear as spheres which are mutually conditioned and which need each other. The mechanism of culture is a system which transforms the outer sphere into the inner one: disorganization into organization, ignoramuses into initiates, sinners into holy men, entropy into information. By virtue of the fact that culture lives not only by the opposition of the outer and inner spheres but also by moving from one sphere to the other, it does not only struggle against the outer "chaos" but has need of it as well; it does not only destroy it but continually creates it. One of the links between culture and civilization (and "chaos") consists in the fact that culture continually estranges, in favor of its antipode, certain "exhausted" elements, which become clichés and function in nonculture. Thus, in culture itself entropy increases at the expense of maximum organization.
>
> In this connection it may be said that each type of culture has its corresponding type of "chaos," which is by no means primary, uniform, and always equal to itself, but which represents just as active a creation by man as does the sphere of cultural organization. Each historically given type of culture has its own type of nonculture peculiar to it alone. . . .
>
> Thus, from the position of the outside observer, culture will represent not an immobile, synchronically balanced mechanism, but a dichotomous system, the "work" of which will be realized as the aggression of regularity against the sphere of the unregulated and, in the opposite direction, as the intrusion of the unregulated into the sphere of organization (Ivanov *et al*. 1973, Eng. trans., p. 58 and p. 60).

This dialectical vision of culture, with only the slightest shift in terms, fits literary activity to perfection. No one better than the writer has an intuition, more or less conscious, of those shadowy zones which as yet have not been organized and which are not patent. His intuition is a form of fascination. It is writers who assay or unveil the antimodels and who, occasionally or definitively, move beyond the confines of the known, of the ordered. It is they who modify these limits, in exaltation or anguish, and they do so discretely or by main force.

If the model of the world implied by poetics does not subsist, this is because it aspires to be not just definitive but also exhaustive; it does not even hold good for its own epoch. Shifts in the literary system may be regarded, with Tynjanov, as the outcome of shifts which involve the interrelation and prestige of single forms (or literary genres)—in short, as the diachronic repercussions of synchronic restabilizing. It still needs to be added that such shifts reflect the different positions of a comparison between model and antimodel.

14. From the sixteenth century onward, a new kind of literary planning began to emerge, and in the modern period it became a dominant. It found its expression in the form of prefaces, literary pamphlets, and manifestos. Prefaces,

pamphlets, and manifestos (for brevity, we shall use only the latter term) are, in general, characterized by (1) a clear-cut diachronic point of view, in the sense that they contest the currently accepted literary system or at the very least propose, for the most part sectorially, changes in such systems; (2) reference to a model of the world, in the sense that they justify a necessity for renewal by reference to exigencies in contemporary culture which the system in force does not satisfy; and (3) substitution of an exhortatory, optative formula for the normative formulae typical of poetics.

These three characteristics are obviously well motivated. The first is a consequence of the fact that nonacceptance of the literary system cannot but lead to the planning of another system, which is abstract invention. An author or a critic can do no more than underline that particular point of the system which he regards as the most backward or most in need of change. Time alone will show what repercussions such change will have on the system as a whole. The second characteristic depends on how aware one is of a connection between the literary system and one's model of the world: realizing that changes have taken place in the model of the world means verifying the inadequacy of the literary system. The third characteristic is a verification of powers: anyone who speaks in the name of a model of the world which everyone recognizes as valid can be imperative; anyone who speaks in the name of his own vision of a connection between present and future must seek to convince and to overwhelm.

15. Between poetics and manifestos we find the same dialectical relation that exists, to govern the life of language, between the product and the act, *ergon* and *energeia*.

Poetics describe the whole of a literary system (mirroring a model of the world which the corresponding culture recognizes as valid). Manifestos express innovative intentions—not necessarily destined for success—which will inevitably dislocate the system by insisting on its single components or on sections of it and by including in the model areas which pertain to the antimodel.

The synchronic, and generally conservative, framework of poetics can consider as implicit its underlying model of the world: what is immutable can be taken for granted; what is definitive can be regarded as natural. Anyone who operates inside a poetics will make innovations, for the most part formal ones, while believing that they do not endanger his model of the world. Time alone will show whether innovations in the quantitative sphere will effect a qualitative change: i.e., whether they will express and confirm changes in the model of the world.

Prefaces and manifestos begin by perceiving that the model of the world which is in force is both obsolete and limiting; the new developments which they champion—in a tone now apologetic, now prophetic—often seem to center on technical matters, on language, etc. (though, in modern times, they progressively come to involve contents as well). But there is explicit reference to the macroscopic fact that the world faced by literature is no longer that implied by the poetics.

Just as in the language, the act cannot be realized other than by using, at least in the first instance, the product. A writer cannot invent a language which is totally unknown to his listeners and readers. In like fashion, he cannot avoid taking account of the genres and forms in force. He may modify them, turn them upside down, contaminate them, fuse them. This will not depend merely on the exigencies of communication. The author himself is part of a cultural society, and he reasons in terms of its codes.

Language can teach us even more. Innovations of whatever kind always involve isolated elements—however numerous, however striking such elements may be. No one even dreams of renewing the language system as a whole. Changes in the system are consequences, which cannot be planned and which are not easy to foresee, of a sum of innovations which concern isolated elements. This is why manifestos rarely plan for a new type of literary system; what they advocate are changes—often outright revolutions—whose character, however, is always sectorial. When the future is breached the breaches may then widen and prove uncontrollable.

16. The dialectic between poetics and manifestos has an exclusively theoretical value. In literary history we meet with only one central period (say, between the sixteenth and seventeenth centuries) during which poetics and manifestos (however they were called) coexisted. From then on, poetics, more or less deprived of authority, become more sporadic.

The progressive multiplication of manifestos is undoubtedly linked to the affirmation of literary conceptions which privilege the subject with respect to the tradition, deviation with respect to the norm, originality with respect to the conventions. These developments can be seized upon in more concrete terms once it has been observed that the history of literature is also the history of progressive disengagements of literary production from public functions, and even from the representative functions which it enjoyed in antiquity and which, only for brief periods, it has since regained. Such disengagement has accorded more and more freedom to individual initiative. It has, though, compelled writers to make explicit on each occasion, in what may at times turn into a kind of balancing act, a relation with the collectivity which, in earlier times, constituted the starting point. This relation with society (and often—and this is the negative aspect—with authority) justified from the communication point of view, and favored from the point of view of execution, the stability of the system. With a unified model of the world, those who commissioned a work, those who used it, and those who brought it to realization were all in a position to verify their ideological solidarity. In confirmation, it can be observed that even today genres which are destined for a mass market are extremely refractory to any innovation which is anything other than superficial.

17. The dialectic between product and act, between systems in force and proposed innovations, has given rise to widely differing patterns, on the basis of the development of different types of models and antimodels of the world. It may be said that, until the modern period, the model and the antimodel showed an unambiguous topological distribution. The well-known schema US/ THE OTHERS may have a number of possible realizations. I shall mention the

three which to me seem the most important. The first is transcendental in nature. Recognition and definition of the transcendental, whether divine or diabolical, lie at the heart of all religions, whether they are prehistoric or historic. The connection, originally a very close one, between literature and religion highlights an opposition between the everyday (US) and the transcendent (THE OTHERS). Such opposition, in its most elaborated Christian form, becomes threefold: heaven (THE OTHERS, positively), earth, and hell (THE OTHERS, negatively). More insubstantial is the collocation, and the very existence, of Purgatory (See, in this respect, Lotman 1969):

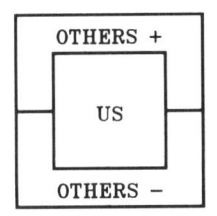

```
+-------------------+
|     OTHERS +      |
|   +-----------+   |
|   |           |   |
|   |    US     |   |
|   |           |   |
|   +-----------+   |
|     OTHERS -      |
+-------------------+
```

The same opposition between everyday and transcendent is to be found in folklore conceptions of a spirit world which is beneficent or malign. With the necessary modifications, this will be borrowed by the Gothic tale, the horror story, etc.

The second realization of the schema is ethnic and geographical in character. From the Greek *polis*, which saw all foreigners as barbarians, we move toward the gradual acquisition, within the model, of the original antimodel made up of "those who are different from us." Literature seconds the history of conquests and of geographical discoveries, progressively storing the mental structures of the "others," making them part of its own model of the world:

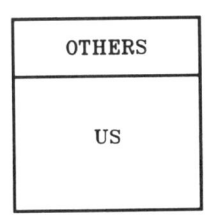

```
+-------------------+
|      OTHERS       |
|                   |
|                   |
|        US         |
|                   |
|                   |
+-------------------+
```

Along these lines we might annex such extraterrestrial civilizations as there may be, in accord with the anticipations of science fiction.

The third realization I wish to mention is based on class. Literature is nearly always the heritage of dominant classes, and it is biased toward regarding the world of workers, of the uneducated, of outcasts as an antimodel. But over the centuries it has come to devote closer and closer attention to the antimodel, to the point of assimilating it to its overall vision. This takes us from Christianity, a revolution both linguistic and rhetorical (Auerbach), down to naturalism, realism, and the many similar currents of today:

```
┌─────────────┐
│  (OTHERS)   │
│- - - - - - -│
│  US │OTHERS │
│     │       │
└─────────────┘
```

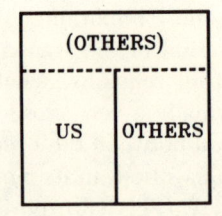

Scientific investigation of folk poetry and art and its imitation are a part of this phenomenon.

Effectively and potentially, these model and antimodel pairs have now resettled to form more open models which provide adequate space for their antimodels. These antimodels were such that, though important, they did not endanger the basic models or, as a consequence, literary institutions. Indeed, these were in a position to give expression to a recognition of their antimodels, even at the cost of drastic rearrangement.

The last hundred years have seen the dominant presence of a different antimodel, whose character is psychological. It is a centripetal antimodel, not a centrifugal one. The Other is no longer to be looked for outside the individual or outside the community; it is within the individual himself, in the most inaccessible and uncontrollable zones of consciousness:

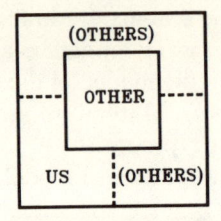

```
┌─────────────────┐
│    (OTHERS)     │
│   ┌───────┐     │
│---│ OTHER │---- │
│   └───────┘     │
│  US  │(OTHERS)  │
└─────────────────┘
```

Psychoanalytic terminology, rich as it is in hypostases, manages to name—certainly not to master—those spheres of consciousness which escape the rationality of logic and of communicative discourse.

This new antimodel renders problematic the compact character of "us," with whom the "others," while being topologically counterposed, still gave clear signs of homology: the excluded social classes and the barbarians themselves readily revealed to the impartial eye a structure which was substantially identical with that of "us"; in its turn, the transcendent, present only in its silence, was imagined by "us" as a copy of the world, governed by more inflexible rules, with legislators and inhabitants who were distinctly anthropomorphic.

The new otherness now discovered underlines the common resemblance of every "I," on the one hand, and thereby constitutes an authentically ecumenical "us," on the other, but it entails a fracture, indeed a feud, inside every single "I." When literature accepts this new perspective, the dialectic between the system and its innovations is biased in favor of the innovations, and irruption of the antimodel is openly proclaimed.

18. The attempt to link poetic treatises to a model of the world (cf. §12) is destined to failure for another reason which can now be explained: art in itself constitutes a model of the world. The world is a chaos, devoid of structure until such time as it is perceived and ordered by us. The models offered by art are among the most sophisticated and exhaustive of all models. The literary work, in particular, is the realization of a privileged structure inside the structures of a culture. We might remind ourselves that, according to the conceptions of Lotman and other Soviet semioticists, cultural elements are stratified in such a way as to form differently structured levels around language, while language is the culturally structured nucleus par excellence. The literary work is the realization of a maximum of modelizing with respect to the objects it wishes to describe, because it confers upon them all of the possibilities for structuring allowed by use of the language, which is an instrument not just of communication but for the establishment of worlds. At the same time, the literary work structures the language itself in function of the model to be realized and leads the potentialities of the language system toward purposeful actualization.

This twofold task of modeling both the world and the language is not plotted out *ex novo* by each new writer. It is established by comparing earlier models, which have been assimilated, accepted, or in part rejected, and by using the semiotic rules for setting up models. Culture is a text which unceasingly produces other texts. It is at this point that poetics comes into its own. This is not true of treatises on poetics, because in them the consideration of the past and programming at table have far too much weight; it is not true of implied poetics, those which can only be deduced a posteriori by analyzing the texts. It does hold good for whatever in the treatises, or in explicit or customary codifications, acts as a stimulus toward the practice of literature; whatever, expressed as intentionality in prefaces and manifestos, organizes or is capable of organizing the means of expression; whatever is present in the collective consciousness as a repertoire of stereotypes, as thematic and stylistic tradition. All of this can be verified by analysis, but only once its action has already been exercised.

Understood in this way, poetics are akin to (and within) ideologies, in the sense that they provoke a polarization of possible contents which, while it is efficient for the purposes of communication, already hints at an interpretation of the world. What we are dealing with are substructurings of the cultural system which, "if . . . they are partially differentiated in contents, are more frequently differentiated by the position accorded to the contents themselves in their model, by their varying oppositions among constant elements"; given that "the cultural system is traversed by movements and tensions, it is continually deconstructed and reconstituted, it presents alternatives and compromise solutions" (Segre 1977, p. 17). What is proper to poetics is preselection and functionalization of linguistic-stylistic techniques, which they distribute into preferential sets (which are not closed). These are useful to the producer, who adopts them as a *langue* on the point of becoming literary *parole*, and useful to the user of the work, who is the more ready to ascend from the *parole,* or speech, of the author to the literary language or *langue,* rather than to any generic and all-embracing *langue.* These preferential sets are endowed with a signification of their own when they are brought together in the service of an interpretation (modelization) of the world and concomitantly in the service of the structuring of possible contents. The use the writer makes of these linguistic-stylistic sets adds further significations, and these can be determined and interpreted in the light of the preselections made.

Poetics, therefore, embrace the sum total of the semiotic instrumentation to which the writer (the artist) has recourse in the act of giving form to his inventions. We are dealing with a complex of signification possibilities within which we find reflected—thanks, too, to combinations and commutations—all the elements of a culture (Segre 1977, p. 30). Just as the language has its universals, its long-term structures, and its more rapidly mutable traits, so do poetics embrace oppositions and "empty forms," whose validity is general, and codes of greater or lesser strength. But what characterizes poetics is an aptitude for connecting together the forms and stereotypes of reality, thereby effecting a continual osmosis between language and nonverbal cultural codes. It is thanks to this aptitude that the artistic text is able to convey its multiform communication.

References

Aristotle
- *Poetics.* W. Rhys Roberts, trans. 1927. Loeb Classical Library. Cambridge, Mass: Harvard University Press.

Bray, R.
- 1957. *La formation de la doctrine classique en France.* Paris: Nizet.

Croce, B.
- 1936. *La poesia: Introduzione alla critica e storia della poesia e della letteratura.*Bari: Laterza.

Faral, E.
- 1924. *Les arts poétiques du XIIe et du XIIIe siècle: Recherches et documents sur la technique littéraire du Moyen Age.* Paris: Champion.

Frye, N.
- 1957. *Anatomy of Criticism: Four Essays.* Princeton: Princeton University Press.

Gallavotti, C.
- 1974. Introduction, Comment, and Indexes to Aristotle. *Dell'arte poetica.* Milan: Mondadori.

Ivanov, V. V., *et al.*
- 1973. Tezisy k semiotičeskomu izučeniju kul'tur (v primenenii k slavjanskim tekstam). M. R. Mayenova, ed. *Semiotyka i struktura tekstu; studia poswięcone VII Międzynarodowemu Kongresowi Slawistów, Warszawa.* Wroclaw: Ossolineum. Pp. 9–32. (English Translation. "Theses on the Semiotic Study of Cultures (as Applied to Slavic Texts)." Thomas A. Sebeok, ed. *The Tell-Tale Sign: A Survey of Semiotics.* 1975. Lisse: Peter De Ridder.)

Jakobson, R.
- 1958. Linguistics and Poetics. Th. A. Sebeok, ed. *Style in Language.* 1960. Cambridge, Mass.: M.I.T. Press. Pp. 350–77.

Jolles, A.
    1930. *Einfache Formen: Legende, Sage, Mythe, Rätsel, Spruch, Kasus, Memorabile, Märchen, Witz*. Halle: Niemeyer.
Lotman, Ju. M.
    1969. O metajazyke tipologičeskich opisanij kul'tury. *Trudy po znakovym sistemam*, 4, pp. 460–77.
Mengaldo, P. V.
    1978. *Linguistica e retorica di Dante*. Pisa: Nistri-Lischi.
Pajano, R.
    1970. *La nozione di poetica*. Bologna: Patron.
Rostagni, A., ed.
    1930. *Arte poetica di Orazio*. Turin: Chiantore.
Segre, C.
    1977. *Semiotica, storia e cultura*. Padua: Liviana.
Staiger, E.
    1946. *Grundbegriffe der Poetik*. 1971. Munich: Deutscher Taschenbuch Verlag.
Todorov, T.
    1968. Poétique. O. Ducrot et al. *Qu'est que le structuralisme?* Paris: Seuil. Pp. 97–166.
Vinogradov, V. V.
    1963. *Stilistika: Teorija poetičeskoj reči; Poetika*. Moscow: Akademija Nauk. (Italian translation. *Stilistica e poetica*. 1972. Milan: Mursia.)
Weinberg, B.
    1961. *A History of Literary Criticism in the Italian Renaissance*. Chicago: University of Chicago Press.
Weigmann, H.
    1977. *Geschichte der Poetik*. Stuttgart: Metzler.

6.
Style

1. The small pointed stick *(stylus)* used for writing on wax tablets, and whose other, flattened end served for erasing, became, in Latin, the metaphorical equivalent of "way of writing, way of composing." For the present exposition we may start with these two fundamental values of the word *style*. (1) the set of formal traits which characterize (as a whole or at a particular moment) a person's mode of expressing himself or an author's way of writing; (2) the set of formal traits which characterize a group of works constituted on typological or historical bases.

In both cases, the formal traits may be linguistic (and thus peculiar to the sphere of discourse), but they may equally well belong to other modes of expression (figurative, musical, etc.). It was in the visual arts that the notions of Romanesque, Gothic, Renaissance, and Baroque styles (made canonical in the last century) found their most solid foundation.

With a further extension, *style* may be used to describe a way of behaving or, in general, of operating. The conductor of an orchestra has his style, and so has an athlete, and we speak of a person's style when his actions conform to certain stereotypes of behavior.

In the classical world, attention to the second definition of style (which embraced such denominations as *stilus atticus* and *stilus asianus*) was markedly predominant with respect to the first. The first meaning was present for the most part in a normative sense (the clarity Aristotle recommends to the orator; the purity, concision, and persuasiveness added to this by Theophrastus). As a result, it was turned upside down and became, in the sense of the second meaning, a unified ideal or a bundle of technical instructions which the work to be undertaken was to implement. In this lies the main difference between classical rhetoric and modern stylistics.

It is beyond question that classical rhetoric (whose most systematic organization is to be found in the *Rhetorica ad Herennium*) had already laid down guidelines along which formal analysis of texts could develop. *Inventio* and *dispositio* dealt, respectively, with choice of the arguments and with the order in which they were to be expounded, while *elocutio* was concerned with discoursive and stylistic techniques, and *actio* with intonation and gesture. But this set of instruments was not assembled for the purpose of characterizing or criticizing texts; its intention was the production of other texts. What is more, classical rhetoric was primarily concerned with oratory, and the operations it describes are related to different types of legal process and to the effects to be achieved when arguing cases before the courts. As a result, though we will find interesting digressions into the question of emotions, they, all of them, have to do with the making of successful speechs. Once this has been made clear, it can be added that Greek and Latin treatise writers did in part apply rhetorical categories to nonoratorical texts and that the armory of rhetoric, however changed or differently understood, has down to our own day continued to give proof of its descriptive utility. The classification of techniques was carried out so efficiently that it still holds good even when the scope of the analysis has changed.

Apart from *actio*, which concerns oratorical discourse in performance, *inventio* and *dispositio* stand in opposition to *elocutio* in the same way as a formalist analysis of the tale (work on plot and fabula, narrative functions, etc.) stands in opposition to study of stylistic techniques. Style in the strict sense, however, corresponds to *elocutio* (Greek *lexis*), and, from the time of Macrobius, it has been regarded as a variant of *elocutio* on the level of person or group or epoch. But, among *inventio, dispositio*, and *elocutio*, exchanges exist, so that, for example, "figures of thought," such as antithesis and the simile, realize content structures of *inventio* on the level of *elocutio*.

The fact remains that it was to the doctrine of *elocutio* that the most detailed attention was devoted by classical and medieval writers on rhetoric, and they have bequeathed to us a wealth of concepts and terms to which we still have recourse (however much we may reorganize and reformulate them). In general, everything can be brought down to the concept of *ornatus* on the basis of a distinction between an originally unadorned content and the addition of ornaments or colorings (the word used is indeed *colores*). These are capable of rendering content more agreeable, more efficient, etc. Such a conception is a necessary consequence of the standpoint chosen: the fact of offering a repertoire of stylistic techniques implies the chronological posteriority and the additive nature of such techniques, as opposed to the normativeness of a grammar which admits no exceptions.

It is this supposedly additive nature which makes possible a classification whose validity is general (and, therefore, disregards contexts). It depends on whether ornamentation involves single concepts—and thus takes in tropes—or sections of the discourse—and thereby involves figures, while these latter may be figures of the word, if they involve phonetic and syntactic material, or figures of thought, if they penetrate to the sphere of invention. The terms we are dealing with here are highly significant ones. *Tropos* in Greek is a "turning point," a semantic "deviation": a word is turned aside toward a meaning different from its ordinary one, so that the same signifier takes on a new meaning. *Figura*, on the contrary, seems to intuit the iconic value of the *dispositio* of the words in discourse. It is almost as if, by way of the patterning of their members and phrases, they were drawing attention to relations of parallelism, of repetition, or of contraposition at the level of thought.

Certainly, such definition of the tropes has proved precious for modern researchers in semantics (from Darmesteter onward), while the definition of figures has been taken over and improved by stylistics. The tropes are ten or so (metalepsis, periphrasis, synecdoche, antinomasia, emphasis, litotes, hyperbole, metonymy, metaphor, irony), and they have the most profound influence on language, although it remains true that they do enter into ordinary usage quite rapidly. When they do so, they assume a recognized semantic value and so lose any rhetorical value. Between figures of words (inversion, repetition, pleonasm, enallage, ellipse, zeugma, etc.) and figures of thought (allegory, prosopopeia, irony, apostrophe, etc.), an intermediate zone exists, and rhetoricians have attributed it to the second of the two groups. For these (antithesis, chiasmus, brachylogy, preterition, etc.), it is easier to see how thought and expression interlock. It is a good starting point to see rhetoric (or stylistics) as a study of discourse articulations, given that the more traditional figures are apt to characterize literary currents and epochs.

This observation will suffice to show that the conception of *ornatus* had already been superseded in fact by theorists of rhetoric, however unconsciously. In much the same way, the idea of the rhetorical figure as a deviation with respect to a hypothetical neutral form was abandoned (for example, by Fontanier). The real problem (as Genette notes) is how to identify a discourse unit by comparing it with, and implicitly opposing it to, what might take its place, a different, "equivalent" unit.

2. Tropes and figures are undoubtedly elements which pertain to style. It might be possible to base a characterization of texts on their use or varied presence (though only in recent times has the attempt been made). It would be possible, in this way, to arrive at bundles of distinctive traits proper to a work or to a group of works. Classical rhetoric, and medieval rhetoric even more, had already attempted an all-embracing definition of style, typological and normative in form though it was. I refer to the doctrine of styles seen as peculiar to literary genres and to the doctrine that style adjusted itself in relation to character types.

The latter forms part of the theory of mimesis. It should be noted that it was used as a critical tool by the Alexandrians, when they wished to demonstrate the superiority of Menander to Aristophanes, and by Horace (*Ars poetica*, vv. 114–18) as an argument against Plautus. Priscian (*Praeexercitamina rethorica*, 9), when he speaks of *ethopoiia*, writes, "The propriety of persons and occasions must everywhere be observed; there are words which are right for a young man, and others which are right for an old man: words for a man who is enjoying himself, and others for someone who is suffering . . .; the style that should be adopted is, then, that which fits the characters one introduces."

Far more important is the doctrine which links style to literary genre. Although from Didymus the Alexandrian to Cicero (*De optimo genere oratorum*, 1) and Horace (*Ars poetica*, v. 89) one speaks of tragic style, comic style, etc., a distinction soon comes to the fore which will last for the whole of the Middle Ages and beyond: that between low, middle, and high style. It is a distinction which originally involved only relations between *elocutio* and genres—this is the case for the *Rhetorica and Herennium* (IV, 8). But, on the basis of affirmations which go back to Aristotle, it was subsequently made to correspond to the social level of the characters. This is the distinction that Geoffroi de Vinsauf makes in his *Documentum de modo et arte dictandi et versificandi:* "Sunt igitur tres styli, humilis, mediocris, grandiloquus. Et tales recipiunt appellationes styli ratione personarum vel rerum de quibus fit tractatus. Quando enim de generalibus personis vel rebus tractatur, tunc est stylus grandiloquus; quando de humilibus, humilis; quando de mediocribus, mediocris" (II, 145).

That things did not end here is clear from the famous *rota Virgilii*, the exemplification of a correspondence, codified as such, between the three styles and the kinds of characters, proper names, animals, tools, residence, and plants which could most opportunely be attributed to them. The *Rota* uses Virgil as its touchstone—the *Bucolica*, the *Georgica*, and the *Aeneis*. For, to Virgil's works, the commentator Donatus had already attributed the status of model for the three genres within which the three styles were to be realized.

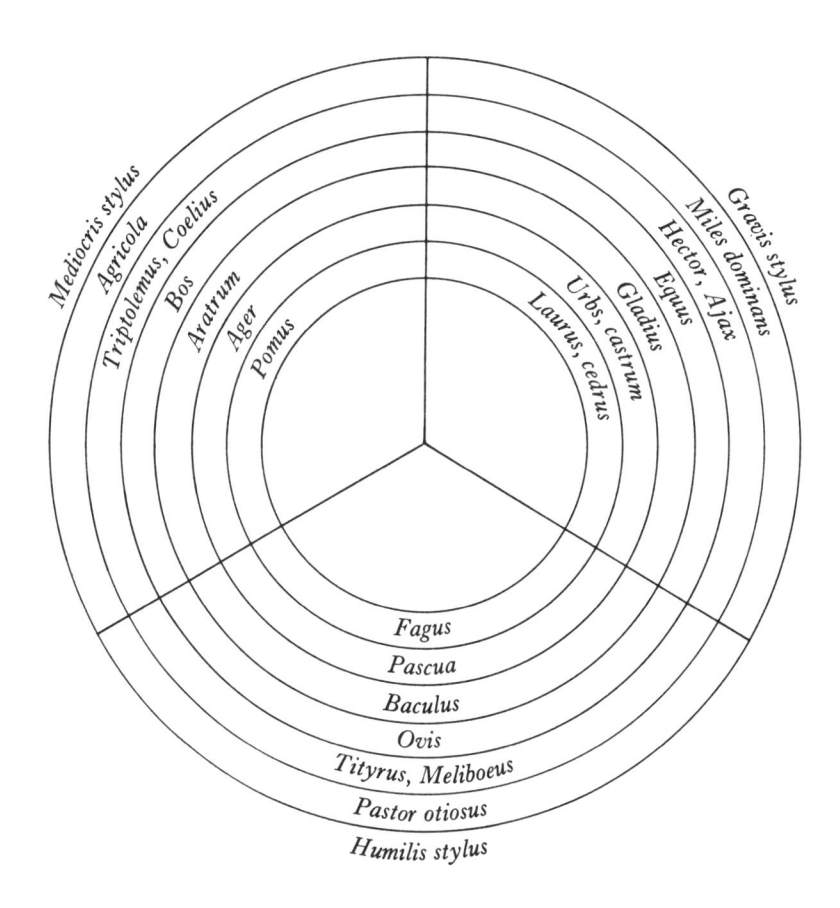

Such a schema, in a summary and almost symbolic form, stresses a connection between genres, human types, onomastics, environment, and style. In other words, it shows the indissoluble connection between *elocutio* and thematics seen as a whole, vertical links between form and substance. It evidences the existence of a genre polycode (a system of various codes).

Limiting ourselves for the moment to the field of linguistic expression, we are led to remark how frequently treatise writers insist on a necessary correspondence between lexical choice and style. For each style they often provide examples to be commended and others to be condemned—from Geoffroi de Vinsauf (*Documentum de modo et arte dictandi et versificandi*, II, 146–52) to Dante (*De vulgari eloquentia*, II, 6, 2–6). There is a growing conviction that choice of language is related to choice of genre—in other words, that what is implemented in every genre is a subset of an epoch's language system. This is a concept which was repeated down to the Enlightenment, by La Harpe, for example, and by Mauvillon, who, in his *Traité général de style* (1751), lists *face* and *demeure* as words belonging to lofty style, *visage* and *habitation* as middle style, *garbe*, *frime*, *frimousse*, and *manoir* as comic.

Ancient theories, in short, kept on surfacing, but they only did so in periods of classicizing taste. In reality, Christianity and the Middle Ages had thrown into disarray any style-content relation and had done so to such a degree that the history of literary culture can be read as an outcome of this revolution. It was Erich Auerbach who best clarified the "scandal" of the humble language of Holy Scripture with its "scripturarum mirabili altitudine et mirabili humilitate" alluded to by St. Augustine. This antithesis between the humble and the sublime was incarnated in Christ himself, in his life and passion.

The centuries from St. Augustine to Dante reveal a contrast between writers who were tied to the stylistic hierarchy of an involuted Latin which few understood and other writers (mostly preachers) who had grasped the fact that the *sermo humilis* was potentially capable of going deeper and of spreading much more widely. There exists a dialectic between a succession of "renaissances" and the driving force of popular expressivity, down to the moment at which the *rustica romana lingua* of the vernacular took on a role of its own. What was being effected was the total replacement of one language institution by another, not simply an interplay of the Latin registers of the lowly (realistic) and the sublime (abstract). From that moment on and for a long time thereafter, choice of style went hand in hand with a far more radical choice: that of the language to be used, Latin or the vernacular.

When the vernacular took on the dignity of literature, a different history of style was revealed. The new literature was first made to absorb the techniques of the classical *ornatus*, and, subsequently, between the *stilnovo* (a designation which says *style*) and Dante, it was led to elaborate a new range of possibilities which included the sublime. This history began with Christianity (Auerbach 1958), and it is still in progress today. This is has been made clear, once again by Auerbach (1946), in a vast canvas where the touchstone is realism, i.e., the *humilis stylus*. His text is, at the same time, a demonstration of the historical and sociological significance of styles, seen as codes for literary expression.

3. Both the concept of ornament and that of linguistic choice were formulated with reference to literary production. Only in the wake of Saussure, though, has there been any clear appreciation of the way every act of *parole* also constitutes a choice among the wide range of possibilities offered by the *langue*. Charles Bally (1905; 1909) took this as the theme of his stylistics. The word itself, though, is recorded for the first time in Novalis, who speaks of "stylistics or rhetoric" *(Stylistik oder Rhetorik)*.

Stylistics, Bally tells us, "studies the emotional value of the facts of organized language and the reciprocal action of the expression facts whose concurrence forms the means of expression at the disposal of the language" (1909, p. 1). "Stylistics thus studies the expression facts of language from the point of view of their emotive content—in other words, the expression of the facts of sensibility by means of language—and also the action of the facts of language on sensibility" (p. 16). Thus, a language expresses not just ideas but feelings as well, and it is impossible to grasp the way it functions if due weight is not given to thought and expression combined. When we express any thought we are always conditioned by the situation and by our emotional reactions to it. Hence, the language system is itself organized in terms of a series of options which are receptive to the ways we react. "Expression facts grouped around simple abstract notions coexist in latent form in the brain of speakers, and they are manifested thanks to reciprocal action—a kind of struggle—in the elaboration of thought and in its expression by means of language. . . . They attract and repel each other in an unceasing and complex interplay of *linguistic feelings;* relations of affinity or of contrast are thereby established by means of which they delimit each other reciprocally and are defined by being delimited" (pp. 15–16). In this manner, Saussure's schema of "associative relations" (1906–11, Eng. trans., pp. 173–75) receives substantial integration.

Bally measures the affective elements of the language with two yardsticks (which are totally ideal and determined by abstraction). The first is "the mode of intellectual expression," that of abstract language or of pure ideas—with which affective variants can be compared—and the second is the mode of ordinary language, by comparison with which it is possible to determine the sectorial varieties of a given language as it relates to the social environment and to practical use. It is by matching them against the "term of identification," representing the "mode of intellectual expression," that it is possible, in the case of synonyms, to determine affective characters, tied for the most part to notions of intensity (hyperbole, attenuation, etc.), of value (pleasurable, unpleasant, laudatory, contemptuous), and of beauty. On the other hand, it is with observations of a statistical nature that elements of ordinary language can be distinguished, as can those of various spheres and groups. These elements are proper to such varieties of ordinary language and produce "effects by evocation," which refer to the social position of the speaker and the collective evaluation which would normally be accorded it. The "synonyms" examined by Bally are not just words but complex expressions and whole sentences. In a certain sense, he reworks the terrain of the tropes and rhetorical figures, although his aim is descriptive. From a theoretical point of view, it can be remarked that, on the whole, he left very little for those who came after him to glean. Marouzeau does deserve a mention, however, since he developed and theorized the concept, which had been implicit in Bally, of stylistic choice. This involved having recourse to the activity of the speaker, and of the writer as well, and he thereby comes very close to stylistic criticism itself. If we refer back to the classic communication schema (addresser-message-addressee plus context and channel, though the latter may be neglected), we will have the impression that affective characters are primarily the concern of the addresser (and the considerable use Bally makes of psychologically oriented terminology would tend to confirm this), whereas his "effects by evocation" involve the addressee. But Bally is careful to point out that states of mind are being observed as a system of possibilities, one which coincides with the system of language possibilities, and that effects by evocation are valid first and foremost as clues to the sociocultural background of speakers. Thus, they themselves constitute a general system. This lays the foundations for a psychostylistics and a sociostylistics. Bally, however, pays little attention to the context within which these variants are uttered. To have done so would have led us from utterances to the utterance-act, from taxonomic neutrality to pragmatic implication.

4. From the eighteenth century onward, as the prestige of rhetoric declined, a new concept of style was developed; it was seen as an individual manner of expression considered in its totality and, indeed, identified with thought itself. Buffon's famous sentence "le style est l'homme même" is well illustrated by other affirmations of Buffon: "les idées seules forment le fond du style"; "le style n'est que l'ordre et le mouvement qu'on met dans ses pensées" (1753, ed. 1926, pp. 16, 15, 11). For the Romantics, style represented the highest point of artistic elaboration. According to Goethe, for example, it is based on "the deepest foundations of knowledge, on the very being of things, insofar as it is given to us to recognize them in visible and tangible forms" (1789, ed. 1954, p. 68). More and more frequently, one speaks of an author's style, though difficulty is experienced when it comes to describing it in technical terms. Here, for example, is Darmesteter, the father of semantics: "There is no need here to study the metaphor in style in order to perceive how in the writer, according to the way he feels and sees things, thought takes on different hues and clothes itself in material forms." And he adds in a note: "Such studies are the domain of literary criticism and of rhetoric; they have nothing to do with linguistics" (1887, pp. 65–66).

Linguistic study of individual style was first undertaken in the wake of historical-cultural formulations which go from Humboldt to Schuchardt. But it is to Vossler (who was also influenced by Croce) that we owe not just a series of separate analyses but the distinction between *Sprachstil* and *Stilsprache*, i.e., between the language data which make up the style of a work or of an author and those facts of style which become part of the development of the history of a language. Vossler, however, dealt primarily with all-embracing characterizations, or with period-by-period characterizations, of Romance languages and literatures. The study of literary style was really founded by Spitzer, whose links were not just with Vossler and idealism but with Freud as well.

Spitzer had an impressive background both in the philological and in the etymological field (and indeed he continued to work along these lines till the end, disengaging famous etymologies, like those of *trovare* and *race*, and philosophical and literary conceptions such as milieu, mother tongue, "tree of life," and "harmony of the world"). He himself rightly insisted on the links which exist between experiences of this kind and stylistic activity. Fundamental for Spitzer was the postulation (shared with Sperber) that "to each and every emotion—in other words, to any distancing from our normal psychic state—there will correspond in the expression field a distancing from ordinary language use, and vice versa a distancing from ordinary language is a clue to an unusual psychic state" (1928, p. 4). The first thing the critic must do, therefore, is to grasp these deviations from normal language use (in a different guise the "tropos," or "deviation," reappears) because they will serve him as clues to the writer's state of mind.

It then becomes a matter of confirmation and organization, i.e., of formulating general interpretive hypotheses. After that, one will return to the text, and, if the hypotheses are valid, it will furnish further linguistic evidence. This is a kind of abduction process, though Spitzer prefers to appeal to Dilthey and his *Zirkel im Verstehen*, or circle of understanding: details can be understood only in terms of the whole; and the whole, only when one starts out with the details. Spitzer uses an astronomical image and sees the mind of the author as "a kind of solar system into whose orbit all categories of things are attracted: language, motivation, plot are only satellites of this . . . entity" (1948, p. 14). At the center of this system lies "the common spiritual etymon, the psychological root, of several individual 'traits of style' in a writer" (p. 11).

The end result of this way of proceeding is dozens of fascinating essays like that on Charles-Louis Philippe, whose wealth of causal expressions and conjunctions *(à cause de, parce que, car)* and the (at times inappropriate) use of them leads us to recognize the presence of a "pseudo-objective motivation," a reflection of the ironical and fatalistic resignation which the author divines in his unfortunate characters and makes his own. Or there is the essay on Péguy, whose Bergsonian experience can be divined in the words he prefers (*mystique, politique*, compounds in *de-* and *in-*), in the parentheses which often open up perspectives to infinity, in the havoc wrought with commas, etc. Another essay shows an obsessive presence of blood images of a markedly sexual character in the writings of the pacifist Barbusse. Yet another brings to light in Racine a polarity between observation of the real and intellectualism, between emotive expression and a classical ideal.

Two progressively concomitant developments should be noted: stress is laid on the concept of text structure, and linguistic observations are no longer based on real "deviation" but on terms which may be neutral but which are rendered symptomatic by their grouping, by cross-referencing, and by contrast. I might mention the enthusiastic use Spitzer makes—right from the beginning of the final essay on Leopardi's *Aspasia*—of terms like structure, organization, and integrated perspective and the formula which he clearly derives from Saussure; "Poetry . . . may be rehabilitated if it is seen as a whole within which each part has its place and where subtle but clear correspondences connect the parts" (1963, ed. 1976, p. 252).

5. A convenient commonplace makes Bally the founder of a stylistics of the language and Spitzer the founder of a stylistics of the work of literature, of stylistic literary criticism. It should be added that Bally's stylistics describes possibilities, Spitzer's realizations; what Bally deals with are the premises of the utterance act, whereas Spitzer deals with utterances.

Before going on to discuss the two concepts—choice and deviation—which are basic for both Bally and Spitzer, there is a preliminary question which we ought to ask ourselves, one whose full implications became clear only after Bally. What is the system inside which the choice is made or with respect to which a deviation is effected? Where ordinary language is concerned, Bally was fully aware of the fact that alternatives will belong to specific language varieties as well, and for this very reason he set up the category of "effects by evocation." But "affective characters," which form the other large and complementary category, are in their turn conditioned by language varieties.

Modern linguistics has determined a series of language varieties (linguistic diatypes) relative to the social environments to which the speakers belong (sociolects, on the pattern of dialects) and to the conditions under which the utterances are realized (registers, which range from the courtly and learned to the popular and domestic). While it must be recognized that sociolects are not rigid because of circulation and contact among social strata, and that the classification of registers is fairly fluid, the fact remains that the system of language choices cannot be regarded as a unity. It must be broken down into partially overlapping subsets.

As Werner Winter writes, "A style may be said to be characterized by a pattern of recurrent selections from the inventory of optional features of a language. Various types of selection can be found: complete exclusion of an optional element, obligatory inclusion of a feature optional elsewhere, varying degrees of inclusion of a specific variant without complete elimination of competing features" (1962, p. 324). On these groupings of optional features, style markers impress their seal. These are words, expressions, etc., which are characteristic of one single language variety. So true is this that each variant might be defined on the basis of a list of its style markers. At the moment in which he expresses himself, the speaker does not have access to the totality of existing options but only to those that his sociolect offers him (the possibility of partial extensions exists) and, within these, to those which are authorized by the register he has adopted. One deduces that what is fundamental for choices is the social context, which is prerequisite, while the type of text within which the utterance is realized will serve as its conventional or ceremonial orientation. The individuality (the idiolect) of a speaker or group of speakers is manifested in the way in which different varieties of sociostylistics and of registers are brought into contact. Hence, in the same manner in which innovations impose themselves on language, the passage from one stylistic variant to other diatypes will become codified (as will any restriction). Thus, stylistic behavior is to a marked degree determined by pragmatics.

The problem of language varieties looms even larger in the case of literary stylistics. A writer does not measure himself against ordinary language (for, as we have seen, it is not homogeneous) but against one particular variety, literary language, whose subspecies are peculiar to genres and to their minor forms. At least, this is the case for eras when literary codification is strong. Today's state of affairs is even more complex because the writer takes account not just of literary language, whose weight is still considerable, but of different varieties of ordinary language as well, and he may at times seek, in outright contamination of literary language and language varieties, an originality which will be proper to the text he himself dictates.

Italian stylistics was the first to stress the relation between the writer and the language. The cultural polycentrism of the Italian peninsula, the vitality of its dialects, and the phase difference between literary language and "regional Italian" presented an unsettled situation which stimulated the interest of historians of the language. Of those who investigated style, Devoto, from the beginning, put forward a perspective all his own. The texts of writers were to be analyzed, but this was to be done in order to characterize them as they related to the language (unpremeditated, at least in terms of his programs, were the critical results of the operation). "Stylistics," he wrote, "begins to establish its sovereignty only once the notion of sociality appears with its consequentially dual relation between the author and the community to which he belongs" (1961, p. 30). "Style offers us a relation. It is the result of a dialogue between us and the linguistic institutions of which we make use, and on which the writer leaves his mark but by which he, too, is conditioned in his work" (ibid., p. 185). Devoto arrived at stylistic planes (which correspond to the three persons of the verb) and stylistic traditions (which correspond to genres, registers, sectorial languages). The writer's relation to these is a dialectical one, or he may find himself in conflict, and in moments of transgression he will appeal to his addressee to ensure that the innovations he puts into effect will be understood. Devoto, in short, saw the writer as a participant in a history (that of the language), with respect to which (through a mechanism of readjustments and infractions) he reacts with his style.

The writer, however, possesses a repertoire of expressive techniques within which there exist groupings that correspond to the varieties of spoken and of literary use. This repertoire is brought into operation through the production of discourses. We may well believe that, in such production on the writer's part, involuntary (or unconscious) moments and moments of awareness and of intention coexist, and it will not always be easy to distinguish their respective contributions or possible convergence. I shall mention, as a proposal which has found some following, Barthes's proposed distinction (intelligent but terminologically misleading) between style, seen as belonging to the germinative, biological, hypophysical order, as the product of a drive, and *écriture*, as an act of historical solidarity. "Language and style are objects; writing is a function: it is the relation between poetic creation and society, it is the literary language transformed by its social destination, it is form seized on in its human intention and thereby linked to the great crises of history" (1953, p. 14). These *écritures*—political, literary (genres), etc.—are the most highly institutionalized of language varieties. It is among them that the writer will make his choices, only to find himself fighting against them in order to affirm his freedom. It is a fight which Barthes does not then go on to describe in general terms (a definition of creativity would have been the result); he contents himself with it as it relates to a polemical *hic et nunc* situation.

6. The problem of language varieties does not, as might seem, merely involve definition of the sphere within which stylistic choices and deviations make their appearance and to which they refer. It should be added that language varieties constitute systems; they correspond to a structuring principle which governs from within, for each element of the whole, the range of its possible oscillations. Attention should no longer be devoted to the alternatives implicit in each choice but rather to the formal premises of the set of alternatives offered by a given language variety. Hence, definition of language variants constitutes an unavoidable premise for the structural study of the text.

On the other hand, it is clear that these structuring principles are susceptible of formulation only as general tendencies (they can, however, be documented, for the elements involved, with statistical approximation). The best vantage point for their individuation is the productive activity of the writer himself, for he situates himself, by means of a series of successive specifications, along a line that leads from the language to the language variety chosen and to the type of text realized. The impossibility of any taxonomic description is a consequence of extralinguistic motivations (ideological, poetical, etc.)—all of which can be referred to pragmatics.

It is clear, in the light of these considerations, how close twentieth century stylistics remained (until several decades ago) to classical conceptions of ornament. The presumption, in fact, was that, once choices or deviations had been left aside, content could be regarded as being substantially constant, unmarked; on the other hand, stylistic markings were made to depend directly on the animus of the writer, which, thanks to them, shone clearly forth. On a closer view, the distinction between stylistically valid elements and other invalid elements is too clear cut, and the space between artistic activity and its product is too narrow and altogether too barren. A discussion of the concepts of choice and of deviation will lead us to the same conclusions.

Let it be repeated, at this point of our discussion, that the two terms, though at times used without distinction, refer to two successive and different aspects of drafting: the former to the utterance act, and the latter to the utterance. Choice refers us to the moment of the utterance act, despite the fact that it starts out with the utterance. It is the critic who, faced with a form or an expression, imagines that it must, in the writer's mind, have had competing forms with respect to which is was preferred. He hypothesizes a choice to be made and sees it as lying behind a result which is unique. Deviation, which belongs unequivocally to the utterance, is instead the result of one of the possible choices on those occasions when it diverges to a greater or lesser degree from ordinary use. A difference of measure must then be added to this phase difference, given that a choice is effected among elements which are proper to the language or to its subspecies, whereas deviations constitute innovative elements which, in a certain sense, go beyond current usage.

For choices as a series of possibilities, as choices to be made, what has been said so far may suffice. But for choices made, the problems involved are more complex. Stylistic criticism enjoys greater liberty with respect to classical rhetoric when it comes to determining characterizing traits, which do not always belong to a codified repertoire. Nonetheless, discourse elements pertinent to language analysis will always exist, while others will be neutral. In like manner, classical rhetoric regarded discourse as a corpus to which ornaments and embellishments could be added or as an uninterrupted straight line, broken into by the presence of tropes and figures.

We might be led to think that Spitzer was influenced by his experimental research on a linguistically abnormal author like Rabelais (and, in fact, he later acknowledged that "deviation from usage will not always be outright unusual; often we have to do with no more than slight variations, like use of the pedal in music" (1928, p. 5); it should be kept in mind, though, that the concept of deviation survives in the formalists' assumption that an artist's individuality achieves realization by means of infractions against the linguistic standard and, in the axiom typical of information theory, that a word, a sentence, a discourse are all the more informative the less they are predictable inside a given norm. It is an axiom which statistical analysis of lexis easily documents.

Nonetheless, the concept of linguistic standard is a difficult one to pin down. Two extreme positions exist: the standard may be identified with the *langue* (regarded as use or as "average use") or else with the idiolect of the author. Midway between lie attempts to define the standards of various sublanguages which are specific to a greater or lesser degree. An attempt has already been made to use computers to compile lexicons of current average usage (though the results are always questionable)—and, in any case, this is something which we will never be able to do for the average usage of past decades or centuries). It is also possible to propose lexicons for the sublanguages of a given epoch.

Giraud's stylometrics comes under this heading. It estimates the *écart*, word for word, between the frequency proper to the language itself and that of a work or author. It determines key words and, on their basis, effects a thematic characterization. (Giraud's "richness index" is, however, autonomous (1945, pp. 52–55); the formula it puts forward is $R + V / \sqrt{N}$, where "V" stands for the number of words used by the author and "N" for the number of words the text contains). Of primary importance for its theoretical implications is the change thereby effected in the concept of deviation; instead of seizing on single deviations from the norm, what must now be measured, especially in the totality of an author's lexicon, are shifts in "rank," which involve every word. Within the totality of the lexicon, one will thereby arrive at a general deviation, systematic and symptomatic in character, which will affect even words not in themselves significant. In practice though, the difficulty still remains of defining the characteristics of one's touchstone: linguistic use or variety. Recent attempts at a transformational definition of style are comparative in character. It should be possible, it is held, to define models of competence and of performance proper to a text, on the basis of a comparison with the models of the language, because they will represent one possible application of such models. But the same insurmountable obstacle forever presents itself: the choices offered by the language or sublanguage do not necessarily coincide with those the author had before him at the moment of his utterance act. His choices were those proper to his own idiolect at the precise moment in which he was composing (or correcting). It is possible to know, in part, what they were, but only when the author's variants have been preserved.

Such considerations, in my view, force us to an extreme conclusion. If we study a text as a document of the history of the language, or of the history of stylistic institutions, it can, indeed it must, be compared with what is known of uses contemporary to it. What we arrive at, however, will in reality be not choices but differences (or else coincidences), symptomatic for the characterization of the text and for assessment of its possible influence. The concept of difference is objective and does not imply, nor should it imply, options really open to the writer within a range unknown to us. By analyzing differences, we will be in a position (a) to draw up a complete table of a text's innovative and conservative aspects; and (b) to determine its stylistic tone, which will be highlighted by a differential comparison with the characteristics of the language variety or varieties to which the text belongs. If what we aim for is an interpretation of the text as artistic product, its language will need to be looked at as an autonomous and autotelic system. What the 1929 Prague *Thèses* declare is no more than the simple truth: "The poetic work is a functional structure, and its various elements cannot be understood outside their *connection with the whole*" (*Thèses* 1929, 3, c). This, in the last analysis, is the same conclusion to which, by quite different routes, Spitzer himself came.

7. It is not enough, however, to adopt the methods of stylistics in analyses which have as their object the language of a writer. Once the safeguard of external comparison is removed, findings will be entirely dependent on the critic's intuition. This is true for Terracini who, within an idealistic framework which was already tendentially semiotic in some of its aspects, spoke not of deviations but of *punti distinti*. These were explicit and direct traces of symbolic value of which the whole textual complex was the carrier. Thus, *punti distinti* would be privileged points "of the process by which the symbol is articulated in the word" (1966, ed. 1975, p. 37). Despite all his efforts, it applies equally well

to Riffaterre, who describes a context (in the sense of text) as an alternation of microcontexts, some of which are marked (stylistic expedients) and others not. An effect would be obtained not by stylistic expedients but by their opposition to unmarked microcontexts. Nonetheless, it will always be the critic—or, rather, in the case of Riffaterre's preferred practice, the consensus of critics—who decides which microcontexts are marked.

Far more productive are various positions of Jakobson, such as his statement that "the poetic function projects the principle of equivalence from the axis of selection into the axis of combination" (1958, p. 358). By virtue of this, interest, withdrawn from the paradigm or axis of selection (i.e., in practice, from the stylistic choices offered by the language), is transferred to the syntagm or axis of combination, i.e., to the text considered in its overall self-sufficiency. This proposal (which should be related to formalist investigations of parallelism) has been followed up by Levin, among others. He lays stress on "couplings," i.e., on a succession of two segments of an utterance which are syntactically akin but semantically different, or vice versa. It is a technique which places us at the point of intersection of the syntagmatic axis (the linearity of the discourse) and of the paradigmatic axis (with its combinatorial series of possible substitutions). Against Levin's approach (not, though, against Jakobson who inspired it), a further objection might be made: the narrowness of the sphere to which it is applicable and the difficulty of generalizing its conclusions.

If subjectivity is the danger, then we might look with favor on the attempts that have been made to achieve an all-embracing characterization of style based on the presence or absence of distinctive features. One example among many is the table proposed by Doležel (1964, p. 262), which takes in direct speech, free direct speech, free indirect speech, speech proper to the narrator, and mixed forms of speech, and gives general indications as to their functions. Doležel, however, goes beyond the sphere of lexical, syntactic, and rhetorical phenomena (to which, in general, stylistics has limited itself) and opens the way to *en bloc* acceptance within the province of style of all of the phenomena of discourse.

An analogous, though independent, result is that of Bachtin (1963; 1975), and it is based on observations of a different order. It is the novel itself, and to a lesser degree other genres, which most dramatically calls into question any possibility of a unified definition of style. The author of a novel does not merely communicate his own reflections and feelings; he invents a world with situations and characters of its own, while its discourses are referred, whether directly or indirectly. He will practice a continuous mimesis with respect to the manner in which he imagines that his different actors (which the English language symptomatically calls characters) ought to express themselves. It is through his lips that they speak, while maintaining, as their author expressly intends they should, their own stylistic independence. The contamination is different (but it is contamination nonetheless) when what we are dealing with is "free indirect speech," which the narrator controls syntactically. Bachtin speaks of a plurality of voices and finds that it is present even where there is no direct dialogue, because, for the most part, the narrator will assume the point of view of one or another of his characters and, as a result, some measure of their linguistic peculiarities, of their idiosyncrasies, as well.

A text, especially a narrative or theatrical text, is thus seen by Bachtin as a stylistic patchwork where different people speak and where events and places are looked at through the eyes of different characters. The range becomes all the greater when we take into account, first, the fact that the author at times may confer a kind of power of attorney on a narrator or narrator-character and bestow on him a stylized language which diverges from his own personal style and, second, that, even when the author speaks in the first person, he is measuring himself against preexisting opinions, conceptions, and interpretations and that his expression can only be in implicit disagreement or agreement with such propositions, for these, too, will involve recourse to expressions and words, in short to stylistic markings. It is in this way that we discover intertextuality. Every text will be written in such a fashion that other pronouncements, other earlier texts, will show through. In other words, whether the author enters into dialogue with his characters and assumes their way of looking at things and their tone of voice, or whether he speaks in his own proper person and inevitably bears in mind the opinions of others, the result will be a series of stylistic divergences and convergences, such as to impede any overall, unified definition of style.

It is, in short, indispensable (1) to broaden the concept of style so that it will take in all discoursive phenomena and (2) to aim for a description, not so much of a work's *style* as of the *styles* which coexist in it, of how and why they harmonize. In the figurative arts, deprived as they are of a verbal element, the extension of stylistics to cover their every aspect, as well as the totality of their realization, is accepted without demur. A very clear distinction needs to be made, however, between the stylistics of the language and the stylistics of the literary work. This serves to implement the observations we have already made on the difference between study of a text as document or as organism. The stylistics of the language will furnish materials that will act as indicators and that can then be employed for a stylistics of the work of art.

8. Vicissitudes and aporias in the case of stylistics derive from the fact that the work of literature seems to be the product of language. It is only natural to hope that its interpretation might be derived from its linguistic aspects. In reality, the literary work is a semiotic product which is realized through the code-language. Few writers have attempted to give, and none of them will ever give exhaustively, a history of the cognitive and literary experiences which come together in a work. It is possible to glimpse, but only in the broadest terms, the linguistic experience which allows the writer, as he moves through the spheres of the language, of sectorial languages, and of literary codes, to express in words an invention inside which all his experiences will coalesce. What we do know, though, is already sufficient to reveal the stratification of meanings which underlies the linguistic surface of the message.

The history of this stratification may or may not allow of reconstruction. Being aware of its existence does mean, however, that due weight will be given to the complexity of the semiotic construction which is the work. The very concept of system, which brings to the fore the multiple relations that link one element to all the others, is not enough to measure the complexity of the literary message if it is considered only in terms of the linguistic system. What needs to be assessed is a semiotic system with all its variety (and its hierarchy) of meanings and of senses.

As I have suggested elsewhere (Segre 1969, pp. 29–35), the practice of the writer and that of the critic can be aligned in terms of a series: analysis 1–synthesis 1–analysis 2–synthesis 2. The expressive synthesis operated by the artist on the basis of the analytical elements of his experience (linguistic experience included) is subjected by the critic to a new analysis which has as its objective an interpretive synthesis. Analysis 2 no longer has in front of it the elements of analysis 1, given that synthesis 1 has already been effected and has set up a network of connections among the elements which enrich and orient them. Hence, stylistic data arrived at thanks to analysis 2, while they conserve their nature as style markers or as components of a linguistic-stylistic variant, are overdetermined by their functionalization within a new, self-sufficient system (which is semiotic).

The stylistics of a work of art cannot, then, be identified with the stylistics of the language, given that the latter has as its object the elements of analysis 1 while the former involves elements of analysis 2. But it cannot be identified with literary criticism either, because stylistics has as its object, by definition, elements or systems of elements of discourse, whereas literary criticism sets out to seize the network of the connections which link these elements—hence, the impossibility of attributing a precise status to the stylistics of a work of art. It lies midway between linguistics and literary criticism, between a history of forms and an assessment of functions. The best solution is to emphasize its linguistic aspects, while leaving to literary criticism functional interpretation of the aspects themselves.

The variety of meanings and of senses peculiar to the literary text authorizes, indeed encourages, delineation of an infinity of interpretive models. So true is this that the general models so far put forward have no more than approximative value. This applies to Ingarden's model with its levels and strata (i.e., in its most recent form, phonetics, morphology, lexis, syntax, meter, etc.) and to Hjelmslev's model as well, with its four fundamental sections (content substance, content form, expression substance, expression form).

However much our descriptive capacities may be refined, we may, I believe, take it as proven that the literary work is a connotative system, i.e., a system in which, as Hjelmslev tells us, the expression plane is constituted jointly by the expression plane and the content plane of a denotative system. The promotion of each verbal element from a denotative to a connotative function will involve multiplication of the meaning potentials of elements of the language, once they have been inserted into the semiotic construction which is the literary work.

Any idea that census or illustration of a stylistic feature will serve to define a "spiritual etymon" of whatever kind is one which may safely be abandoned. On the one hand, we run up against the meaningful pluridimensionality brought into being by the seeming linearity of the discourse; on the other, we come to realize that this pluridimensionality is so totally overwhelming, when compared with any conceivable definition of a "spiritual etymon," that it will replace it outright. The transcendent concept of "spiritual etymon" must be replaced by an immanent concept, by rules for structuring.

The aporias of stylistics throw a good deal of light on the particularities of critical practice. A text is an interweaving of signals which are primarily denotative, while connotative functions are activated by means of different, though contemporary, syntagmatic groupings (of sounds, of words, of sentences). The critic, once he has come to understand denotative content, must then go further and use the same signals as evidence of connotative values (and these he will be able to confirm through systematic exposition of analytical links). Furthermore, he may also find in the signals evidence to be referred, not so much to the text's connotative construction, as to the conditions which preceded its structuring. Every discourse element thus offers the critic circumstantial aspects rather than mere "signals." It is only when an interpretation is complete that part of the evidence will achieve the status of signals. The history of stylistics is the history of a never-ending hunt after evidence on the part of literary critics.

References

Auerbach, E.
    1946. *Mimesis: Dargestellte Wirklichkeit in der abendländischen Literatur.* Bern: Francke. (English translation. 1953. *Mimesis: The Representation of Reality in Western Literature.* Princeton: Princeton University Press.)
    1958. *Literatursprache und Publikum in der lateinischen Spätantike und im Mittelalter.* Bern: Francke.

Bachtin, M. M.
    1963. *Problemy poetiki Dostoevskogo.* Moscow: Sovetskij Pisatel'. (English translation. 1973. *Problems of Dostoevsky's Poetics.* Ann Arbor: University of Michigan Press.)
    1975. *Voprosy literatury i estetiki.* Moscow: Chudožestvennaja literatura. (English translation. 1981. In Holquist, M. *The Dialogic Imagination: Four Essays by Mikhail Bakhtin.* Austin: University of Texas Press.)

Bally, Ch.
    1905. *Précis de stylistique.* Geneva: Eggiman.
    1909. *Traité de stylistique francaise.* Heidelberg: Winter.

Barthes, R.
    1953. *Le degré zéro de l'écriture.* Paris: Seuil. (English translation. 1967. *Writing Degree Zero.* New York: Hill and Wang.)

Buffon, G.-L.
    1753. *Discours sur le style prononcé à l'Académie française (25 août 1753).* 1926. Paris: Les Belles Lettres.

Chatman, S., ed.
> 1971. *Literary Style: A Symposium*. New York: Oxford University Press.

Darmesteter, A.
> 1887. *La vie des mots étudiée dans leur significations*. Paris: Delagrave.

Devoto, G.
> 1950. *Studi di stilistica*. Florence: Le Monnier.
> 1961. *Nuovi studi di stilistica*. Florence: Le Monnier.
> 1975. *Itinerario stilistico*. Florence: Le Monnier.

Doležel, L.
> 1964. Vers la stylistique structurale. *Travaux linguistiques de Prague*, 1, pp. 257–66.

Enkvist, N. E.
> 1973. *Linguistic Stylistics*. The Hague: Mouton.

Enkvist, N. E., Spencer, J., and Gregory, M. J.
> 1964. *Linguistics and Style*. 3d ed. 1967. London: Oxford University Press.

Goethe, G. W. von
> 1789. Einfache Nachahmung der Natur, Manier, Stil. *Weimarer Ausgabe*, vol. 47. 1896. Weimar: Weimarer Goethe Gesellschaft. Pp. 77–83. (Now in *Gedenkausgabe der Werke*. Vol. 13. 1954. Zurich: Artemis-Verlag. Pp. 66–71.)

Granger, G.-G.
> 1968. *Essai d'une philosophie du style*. Paris: Colin.

Guiraud, P.
> 1954. *Les caractères statistiques du vocabulaire*. Paris: PUF.
> 1954. *La stylistique*. Paris: PUF.

Guiraud, P., and Kuentz, P.
> 1970. *La Stylistique: Lectures*. Paris: Klincksieck.

Hatzfeld, H.
> 1953. *A Critical Bibliography of the New Stylistics Applied to the Romance Literatures (1900–1952)*. Chapel Hill: University of North Carolina Press.
> 1955. *Bibliografía crítica de la nueva estilística aplicada a las literaturas románicas*. Madrid: Gredos.
> 1966. *A Critical Bibliography of the New Stylistics Applied to the Romance Literatures (1953–1965)*. Chapel Hill: University of North Carolina Press.

Hatzfeld, H., ed.
> 1975. *Romanistische Stilforschung*. Darmstadt: Wissenschaftliche Buchgesellschaft.

Hatzfeld. H., and Le Hir, Y.
> 1961. *Essai de bibliographie critique de stylistique française et romane (1955–1960)*. Paris: PUF.

Jakobson, R.
> 1958. Linguistics and Poetics. In Th. A. Sebeok, ed. *Style in Language*. 1960. Cambridge, Mass.: M.I.T. Press. Pp. 350–77.

Levin, S. R.
> 1962. *Linguistic Structures in Poetry*. The Hague: Mouton.

Mauvillon, E. de
> 1751. *Traité général de stile: Avec un traité particulier du stile épistolaire*. Amsterdam: Mortier.

Milic, L. T.
> 1967. *Style and Stylistics: An Analytical Bibliography*. New York: Scribner.

Riffaterre, M.
> 1971. *Essais de stylistique structurale*. Paris: Flammarion.

Saussure, F. de
- 1906–11. *Cours de linguistique générale*. Lausanne: Payot. (English translation. 1983. London: Duckworth.)

Sebeok, T. A., ed.
- 1960. *Style in Language*. 2d ed. 1968. New York: Mitchell.

Segre, C.
- 1969. *I segni e la critica: Fra strutturalismo e semiologia*. Turin: Einaudi. (English translation. 1973. *Semiotics and Literary Criticism*. The Hague: Mouton.)
- 1981. *Stilistica*, in *Enciclopedia italiana di scienze, lettere ed arti*, Quarta Appendice (1961–1978). Rome: Istituto della Enciclopedia Italiana. Pp. 490–91.

Spitzer, L.
- 1910. *Die Wortbildung als stilistisches Mittel exemplifiziert an Rabelais*. Halle: Niemeyer. Beihefte zur *Zeitschrift für romanische Philologie*, 29.
- 1928. Zur sprachlichen Interpretation von Wortkunstwerken. *Neue Jahrbücher für Wissenschaft und Jugenbildung*, 6 (1930): pp. 632–51. (Now in *Romanische Stil-und Literaturstudien*. Vol. 1. 1931. Marburg an der Lahn: Elwert. Pp. 4–31.)
- 1928. *Stilstudien*. Vol. 1. *Sprachstile*. Munich: Hueber. Vol. 2, *Stilsprachen*. Munich: Hueber.
- 1948. Linguistics and Literary History. In *Linguistics and Literary History: Essays in Stylistics*. Princeton: Princeton University Press. Pp. 1–39.
- 1959. *Marcel Proust e altri saggi di letteratura francese moderna*. Turin: Einaudi.
- 1963. *L'Aspasia di Leopardi*. *Cultura neolatina*, 23, no. 2–3, pp. 113–45. (Now in *Studi italiani*. 1976. Milan: Vita e Pensiero. Pp. 251–92.)

Style and Text: Studies Presented to N. E. Enkvist. Stockholm: Språkförlaget Skriptor AB. 1975.

Terracini, B.
- 1966. *Analisi stilistica: Teoria, storia, problemi*. 2d ed. 1975. Milano: Feltrinelli.

Thèses
- 1929. *Thèses presentées au Premier Congrès des Philologues Slaves*. In *Travaux du Cercle linguistique de Prague*, 1.

Ullmann, St.
- 1964. *Language and Style*. Oxford: Blackwell and Mott.

Winter, W.
- 1962. Style as Dialects. In H. G. Lunt, ed. *Proceedings of the Ninth International Congress of Linguists, Cambridge, Mass., August 27–31, 1962*. 1964. The Hague: Mouton. Pp. 324–30.

7.
Theme/Motif

1. Theme, from the Greek *thema* (Latin *thema*), is the material which is to be elaborated (or which has been elaborated) in a discourse. According to classical rhetoric, the plan on the basis of which the material was arranged (the *consilium*) was to be distinguished from the material itself. Relations between *thema* and *consilium* were regulated by the phenomenology of the *ductus*. This provided for calculated concordances and discordances and for various kinds of dialectic between *thema* and *consilium*. In the Middle Ages, in addition to the meaning of "material," the word *theme* further acquired that of "subject treated, proposition which is proposed for development" (Wartburg 1966, p. 303), and it was applied in particular (in the fourteenth century) to a passage from the Bible which was quoted at the beginning, in order to be developed and commented upon during the remainder of a sermon.

Closely akin is the sense taken on by the word *theme* in musicology (from ca. 1835). It is "a characteristic melody which serves as subject for a musical composition and furnishes the material for its developments" (Wartburg 1966, p. 303); "a piece of musical material in a complete, self-contained form, but used in composition for the purpose of development, elaboration or variation" (Borrel 1954, p. 409). It is from this use that the literary use derives: "an element, a group of motifs characteristic of a work or of a tradition" (Wartburg 1966, p. 303).

According to these definitions, a theme is the material that is elaborated in a text (it is significant that in German the corresponding term *Stoff* actually means "material"), or it is the subject whose development constitutes the text or the idea which inspires it. These first approximations allow us to sense a fairly marked antinomy, one which is not reflected in any clear-cut terminological distinction: an antinomy between content and germinal idea, between *mythos* and *dianoia*, to use Aristotle's terminology (*Poetica*, 1449b, 35). Rhetoricians, in dealing, for example, with *obscuritas*, had already drawn attention to a difference between literal meaning and sense *(rheton kai dianoia, scriptum et sententia)*. Goethe was well aware of this antinomy when, in the notes to his *Westöstlicher Divan* of 1819, he distinguished *Stoff* from *Gehalt*, material, or theme, from content. The former is supplied in abundance by the world which surrounds the poet; the latter flows spontaneously from his innermost plenitude. There are further, though not definitive, clarifications in Frye. He draws

277

a distinction between "the verbal structures that describe or arrange actual events" and "those that describe or arrange actual ideas" (1957, p. 79) and contrasts *mythos* and *dianoia*. "The *mythos* is the *dianoia* in movement; the *dianoia* is the *mythos* in stasis. One reason why we tend to think of literary symbolism solely in terms of meaning is that we have ordinarily no word for the *moving* body of imagery in a work of literature. The word form has normally two complementary terms, matter and content, and it perhaps makes some difference whether we think of form as shaping principle or as a containing one. As shaping principle, it may be thought of as narrative, organizing temporally what Milton called, in an age of more exact terminology, the 'matter' of his song. As containing principle it may be thought of as meaning, holding the poem together in a simultaneous structure" (p. 83). Note, too, the specification that "a *dianoia* is a secondary imitation of thought, a *mimesis logou*, concerned with typical thought, with the images, metaphors, diagrams, and verbal ambiguities out of which specific ideas develop" (p. 83).

Thus, Frye arrives at two types of opposition: one between movement and stasis, the other between subject and content. The first he formulates more specifically elsewhere in terms of temporality and simultaneity. "We *listen to* the poem as it moves from beginning to end, but as soon as the whole of it is in our minds at once we "see" what it means. More exactly, this response is not simply to *the* whole of it, but to *a* whole *in* it: we have a vision of meaning or *dianoia* whenever any simultaneous apprehension is possible" (pp. 77–78). These are the same oppositions that have reappeared at the center of those narratological theories which have attempted to apprehend, behind the concatenation of the functions, a constitutional model—an "elementary structure of meaningfulness, used, insofar as it is a form, for the articulation of the semantic substance of a microuniverse" (Greimas 1970, p. 161). This constitutional model is to narration what semantics is to syntax. It is achronic (as opposed to the temporal nature of the narrative model) and conceptual, as against the factual nature of the functions.

The contraposition of temporality and atemporality calls for further investigation. It is perfectly true that narrative or poetic discourse unfolds in time, that, indeed, it possesses a time of its own. The content schematizations that we call plot and fabula are themselves temporal in character. No less clear is the fact that the inspiration idea, the *dianoia*, needs no temporal extension other than that required for it to be thought or pronounced; it can therefore be considered as atemporal. But this rigid opposition is of little use when what we want is to differentiate content from subject, argument, or theme. Weisstein defines argument as follows: "One is faced with an argument in the strict sense only by ignoring action as movement whose development is more or less regular and, with a further abstraction, by taking a bird's-eye view of it" (1975, p. 165). He goes on to add that the argument is a synopsis, an epitome, a digest.

This point, an important one, is not taken into account by narratologists. (And it will be as well, here, to base our investigation exclusively on diegetic and mimetic texts, since no proposals for formalized analysis of content as yet exist for lyric texts). Plot and fabula are summaries as well, and the narrative model which can be derived from the fabula is a translation into abstract terms of the actions individuated. The narrative model is the most economical schematization possible with respect to a given corpus. It is economical in the minimal number of the actions it gives as determinant for the development of events and in its degree of abstraction, which makes it possible to designate with a single term similar actions in the texts or in different parts of texts.

The subject, it might be said, is a summary of the fabula. Such summary leaves aside not only the logical and temporal dislocations which are typical of plot but also all of the other actions which might be regarded as instrumental with respect to the basic action. It is a summary, though, and not a schematization, because actions are not reduced to their functionality; indeed, they maintain their semantic content and remain closely linked to the characters who perform them. For the subject, therefore, what counts most is the semantic determination of actions rather than their syntagmatic consequentiality. The subject, or argument, might be defined in the following way: it is an utterance of the substantial terms of a story. Such utterance is realized linguistically, and so in temporal terms; but it is comprehended in atemporal terms, as is the assimilation of the content of a sentence or of a short utterance.

A typical example is that of headings (and they, too, may be termed arguments). We find them for tales—in the *Decameron*, for instance—for the chapters of a book, for the books of a long poem, and for a book as a whole. Individuation of "substantial terms" is in some measure subjective, even when the headings are the author's own. But a principle objectivization does exist here, just as it does for functions. The objectivization principle for arguments is diachronic and comparative. I may define the argument of *Medea* by comparing Euripides' tragedy with its sources and with its derivations; the argument is the totality, as defined by the cultural tradition, of the narrative invariants which are peculiar to these texts.

2. A fundamental contribution to the distinction between content, subject, and inspiration-idea is that of Panofsky, who makes use of arguments from the history of culture. He distinguishes in a figurative work between primary or natural subject matter, secondary or conventional subject matter, and intrinsic meaning or content. Primary subject matter is arrived at by identifying pure forms, inasmuch as these are representations of natural objects, with any expressive characteristics they may have. "The world of pure *forms* thus recognized as carriers of *primary* or of *natural* meanings may be called the world of artistic *motifs*" (1939, p. 5). Secondary, or conventional, subject matter (e.g., a male figure with a knife = St. Bartholomew; a group of figures seated at a dinner table in a certain arrangement and in certain poses = the Last Supper) is arrived at by linking together artistic motifs and combinations of artistic motifs with themes and concepts. Motifs thereby stand revealed as images; their combinations form histories and allegories. The intrinsic meaning, or content, corre-

sponds to the basic attitudes of historically determined groups (attitudes which the artist has made his own); they may be interpreted with Cassirer as "'symbolical' *values*" (pp. 6–8).

Thus, for Panofsky, motifs are distinctly more far-reaching in their range than are themes. Themes are those motifs upon which history has conferred a secondary meaning which accords with cultural conventions (cf., too, Christensen 1929). These secondary meanings, in their turn, are resemanticized each time they are reused, on the basis of conceptions of which the artist is carrier (or creator). This is why the primary subject, already predetermined culturally, can take on new value in the field of artistic production and in the specific context within which it is inserted.

Panofsky's statements can be taken as they stand and applied to literature. One need only be aware of the identity of secondary subject matter and argument, of intrinsic meaning and *dianoia*, or sense. What Panofsky highlights is the fact that individualization of a text's theme (or argument) is an act which is primarily historical, because it is conditioned both by the culture of the person who effects it and by such vicissitudes as are specific to the argument itself. Some arguments, for example, are closely tied to the names of characters (Oedipus, Tristan and Isolde, Don Quixote, Don Juan, etc.). This is so true that any other treatment of them under other names will at once lead to their identification. Others exist where the names are variable while the event remains unchanged. (The biblical tale of the chaste Joseph is a folklore theme which returns again and again in the most varied guises). It is only history which gives any kind of credence to the distinction—a weak one terminologically—between *thèmes héroiques* and *thèmes de situation;* the former is linked to the character of an actor, the latter to specific historical situations (Trousson 1965).

Entrusting to history responsibility for the individuation and itemizing of themes means that one is recognizing themes as a synthesis of possible events (so true is this that some themes, such as Oedipus, have become outright paradigms), the self-awareness of mankind, as it were. As Trousson writes (p. 7), "Our myths and the themes of our legends are our polyvalence. They are mankind's exponents, the ideal forms of tragic destiny, of the human condition." On the other hand, themes are apt, over time, to take on ever changing meanings, which means that the study of thematics has an important place in the history of ideas: "Themes, like symbols . . . are polysemous: that is, they can be endowed with different meanings in the face of differing situations. This is what makes an inquiry into their permutations an adventure in the history of ideas" (Levin 1968, p. 144).

Terminologically speaking, Panofsky's distinction between subject matter and intrinsic meaning, or content, might seem attractive (apart from the difficulty of identifying content with *dianoia*) because it would eliminate the bivalence of the word *theme* ("argument" but also "idea inspiration"). Unfortunately, earlier and later use has preferred to maintain such ambivalence—not without some justification. Hence, we shall continue here to speak of content themes and dianoetic themes.

3. Panofsky's distinction between primary and secondary subject matter will be found to be fundamental for any further investigation. If a theme is a culturally recognized motif, it will occupy a place of its own within the whole of the conventional figurative material which coalesces to form the work of art. Such material can be related to a type or a pattern, and may, in some measure, be defined as cliché. Zumthor (1971; 1972, p. 355) speaks of "formal signs within the texture of works" which make it possible to individuate "the existence of the tradition," and he suggests that they should be classified on the basis of their belonging to expression forms, to content forms, or to both. In "epic formulae," minimal figurative content is linked to lexical choices and to rhythmical-syntactical modules. We are on a level which is close to that of expression forms, and there is no doubt that lexical and syntactical clichés peculiar to literary currents should be arranged under this heading. On the other hand, *topoi* belong to content forms. They are "types whose dominant is figurative, weakly lexicalized, and they are not endowed with any specific syntactic *mark*" (1971, p. 359); whereas there do exist other techniques (like the song-love equation of courtly poetry) which involve both content forms (for figurative elements) and expression forms (for lexical choices, which are, for the most part, highly codified).

Zumthor's analysis, though it needs more documentation, is noteworthy, because it sees thematic elements in terms of a whole set of stereotyping assimilation processes. By so doing, it demonstrates the vitality, through texts, of such "reutilizable material [as has] emerged from some archaic *bricolage*" (p. 354). Repetition is something which it is right to stress; it concerns not so much single texts (e.g., "epic formulae") as the totality of the texts of a culture. As clichés recur from one text to another, it is tradition whose passage is revealed. Tradition, as always, reveals itself in a dialectic between passivity and reaction against passivity: the cliché may be put forward mechanically or it may be the means of stimulating conceptual developments. The cliché can be renewed. What is important is the whole body of the functional relations which involve the elements of a cliché, for they guarantee its cohesion as it passes from one text to another. "A *type* will be any element of *écriture* at once structured and polyvalent, involving, that is, functional relations between its parts, and re-utilizable indefinitely within different contexts" (p. 354).

Since study of the theme will involve content forms almost exclusively, formal clichés may be left out of account here, and what Zumthor says of their affinities with figurative clichés is perfectly acceptable. On the other hand, we might well wish to be more fully informed as to such differences as exist between *topos* and theme. It is true that Zumthor, after proposing his fourfold division, does touch upon the existence of "types having no existence other than a figurative one. Thus, the death by betrayal of the hero probably perpetuates in epic an extremely ancient schema from folklore: love which implies an obstacle to love. . . ; [or there also exists] the 'constraining gift' recently studied by Frappier" (p. 360). Such types as these are, in fact, classed by literary criticism under the headings of themes and motifs. Zumthor does not take comparative definition of these types any further; some of his observations, though, will prove useful as we proceed. They are, he tells us, *types-cadre*, frame-types, abstract forms at quite a high level of generalization; in single texts, they undergo an *amplificatio* which "consists less of a digressive expansion than of a specification" (p. 361). The examples he provides are, in fact, types like the quest, the pilgrimage, the dream. In condensed form, they may be found as more or less ornamental elements of a text. They may also act as the very framework of an entire text, and this they not infrequently do.

4. Among the most consistent results of cultural stereotyping, *topoi* must certainly be numbered. So much so, indeed, that it was upon them that Curtius based a whole survey of literary themes from classical antiquity to the modern period. In classical rhetoric, the *koinoi topoi (loci communes)* were arguments which lent themselves to development in the service of a thesis within various discourse genres. Quintilian tells us that, taken as a whole, they constituted the *argomentorum sedes*. Memory was, in fact, conceived of as a physical space which contained places *(topoi, loci)*, and it was in these places that ideas were located. An orator had recourse to them when he was in search of arguments which would suit the situations and the sections of his discourse, especially in the case of a *quaestio infinita*, a problem whose character was abstract. In the Middle Ages—when political and judicial discourses were no longer in vogue—rhetoric extended the use of *topoi* to take in all types of text: "they became clichés, which could be used in any form of literature; they spread to all spheres of life with which literature deals and to which it gives form" (1948, Eng. trans., p. 70). Thus, from the ancient edifices of rhetoric a stockroom for rhetoric was established: "There one found ideas of the most general sort—such as could be employed in every kind of oratory and writing" (p. 79).

Curtius's book, which is an impressive survey of stereotyped material of classical and medieval derivation, ranges from strictly allocutive formulae (assumed modesty, claims to originality, formulae for endings) to philosophical considerations (on, for example, the decadence of the world), from encomiastic overlappings and contrapositions *(puer/senex, fortitudo et sapientia)* to hypostases (the goddess Nature), from repertoires of metaphors (the composition of a text seen as navigation, its reading as nutrition, life as a theater, the world as a book) to traditional descriptions of the ideal landscape (the *locus amoenus*). Curtius has considerably modified the rhetorical concept of *topos*. A *topos*, in fact, was any kind of assertion of acceptable validity which would lend itself to act as the basis for a line of reasoning, if not for a syllogism or an enthymeme. Curtius, on the other hand, comes much closer to the connotations taken on by its modern derivatives: *commonplace, lieu commun, luogo comune* (where recursivity and banality are present as well). But it is precisely shifts such as these which form the interest of Curtius's investigation, while one need no more than mention recent reformulations of classical topics (Nelson), now understood as the study of "categorizing behavior" as applied to "the parts of the inventive process."

What does deserve to be pointed out, however, is the fact that the definition of *topos* given by Curtius is based on its traditional character, so that its confirmation is to be found only in processes of individuation. What we have said so far authorizes our excluding (for the purposes of this chapter) mere formulae, whether conceptual or metaphorical, in order to concentrate instead on those *topoi* which constitute relatively autonomous discourse structures. It is the very fact that they owe their (Greek and Latin and medieval Latin) origin to books which explains why such structures are relatively rigid in their constituent elements, though they remain open to various ideological interferences. A *topos* is thus a structure endowed with strong internal coherence and with valences which allow it to be linked to external argumentation. Furthermore, precisely because they are arguments to be instrumentalized, *topoi* cannot constitute the subject matter of a text; they are not themes. We may say, then, that *topoi* are motifs: a *topos* is a motif which has been codified by the cultural tradition so that it can be employed as an argument.

5. The term *motif* has recurred over and over in these pages, and there has been an attempt at theoretical definition on the part of Panofsky, who identifies motifs with primary or natural meanings (as opposed to themes, which are secondary or conventional meanings). We shall return to this definition. It is, in any case, remarkable, because it is an attempt to pin down a semantic value of the most elusive kind. It is no accident that the very history of the word *motif*— as distinct from *theme*, which undergoes only minimal semantic shifts and extensions in uninterrupted continuity—registers movements in space and in value and shows a dangerous tendency to synonymic collision with *theme* (as can be seen even in the definitions quoted under §1). *Motivo* (in English, *figure*) is attested for the first time in Italian (at the beginning of the seventeenth century) in its musical meaning. It is a "musical phrase which reproduces itself with modifications in a piece, and which gives it its character" (Wartburg 1967, p. 162); "it is the shortest complete idea in music" (Parry 1954, p. 90). From this it passes to the other languages of culture and takes on values that are literary, figurative, etc. It is attested in French, with these latter values—a "theme, main subject of a work of art, which dominates it and endows with sense its accessory elements" (Wartburg 1967, p. 162)—from 1824, thanks to the influence of the German *Motiv*. Also derived from the German are such twentieth-century meanings as "ornament, linear and often repeated," or "traditional theme, which appears in a certain series of legends, of tales, etc." (p. 162). With *Leitmotiv*, it remains German in the very form of the word. This is the "main motif of a musical score or one which reappears many times" (Wartburg 1959, p. 455), and its diffusion is due to Wagner's theory and practice.

Given that *motif* originally arises out of the practice of music, it might seem legitimate to turn to the musicologists for illumination as to how it relates to *theme*. Are we dealing with synonyms, perhaps with different shades of meaning, or with complementary terms, clearly distinguishable from one another?

In any case, it is quite clear that a motif, which may be made up of a mere four or five notes, is the minimal unit that can be meaningful musically: "subdividing musical works into their constituent portions, as separate movements, sections, periods, phrases, the units are the *figures* [in Italian, *motivi*], and any sub-division below them will leave only expressionless single notes, as unmeaning as the separate letters of a word" (Parry 1954, p. 90). Between theme and motif, therefore, the relation would seem to be that of complex to simple, of articulated to unitary. The theme "is even more extended than a motive, which is too brief to have a formally developed shape of its own" (Borrel 1954, p. 409). But the relation is also that of idea to nucleus, of organism to cell, given that theme, subject, and *Leitmotiv* "are not already nuclei, as motifs are, but complex and differentiated organisms, of which the motif . . . is the original germ or cell" (Rossi-Doria 1934, p. 942.)

Lastly, a motif tends to repeat itself inside a single text: one of its characteristics is recursiveness (cf. the term *Leitmotif*); and it is also on the basis of recursiveness that the motif can be delimited within the musical continuum.

The extension to literature of the term *motif* has thrown into relief, as a whole and one by one, these basic elements of its definition: (1) the motif is the minimal meaningful unit of the text (or, prior to that, of the theme); (2) the motif is a germinal element; (3) the motif is a recurring element. For example, the definition of motif given by Frenzel (1963, p. 27) brings to the fore the first of these properties: "The word *motif* designates a small thematic unit which is not capable of embracing the whole of a plot or of a fabula but which already represents an element of content and of situation. In poems where the content is not particularly complex, it may be rendered in concise form by the nuclear motif, but, as a rule, the content, in pragmatic literary genres, is made up of more than one motif. For lyric poetry, since it has no argument as such and thus has no theme, . . . the only thematic substance is made up of one or more motifs." Frenzel thus uses fabula as her touchstone: while theme is coextensive with fabula, motif is one of its elements. On the other hand, compositions without fabula (lyrics, for example) develop round motifs—sometimes around one single motif. In short, motifs are to themes as words are to the sentence. This would lend support to the attempt of Polti (1895) to list dramatic situations exhaustively (in his view, they are twenty-six in number). Since themes are combinations of motifs, their number ought to be correspondingly greater.

Usually the term *motif* remains much vaguer—closer, if anything, to the second sense, the germinal element which is developed in a work. Trousson is an example we might quote. In his work on thematology, he expresses himself as follows: "What is a motif? We chose to describe in this way a backdrop [une toile de fond], a broad concept, which will stand both for a certain attitude—e.g., revolt—and for a basic, impersonal, situation whose actors have not as yet been individualized—e.g., the situation of a man between two women, the opposition between two brothers, between father and son, that of a woman betrayed, etc." (1965, p. 12).

When these indications are related to a narrative action, it becomes evident that motifs must be either generalizations (revolt consists of single acts of rebellion) or situations which exist prior to the development of actions (a man between two women, the opposition between two brothers, etc.). Motion is not that of linearized events; we move against a backdrop. Trousson himself comes even closer to a conception of motif as thematic germinal element when he tells us that there exist motifs which do not achieve concrete form as characters. "Certain motifs are never decanted to the point of becoming themes. They stop short at a stage of evolution which might be called that of the type: thus the motif, avarice, leads to the type of the miser which one finds in Plautus or in Molière, in Balzac or in Ghelderode, but which has not established a literary tradition based on one unique character" (p. 14). This time, the motif is the background not of the action but of the characters.

It seems as if, on any given occasion, the motif is capable of making its appearance in distinct areas of the literary operation, a fact which Thompson is courageously empirical enough to state explicitly in the introduction to his *Motif-Index of Folk-Literature*. "Sometimes the interest of a student of traditional narrative may be centered on a certain type of character in a tale, sometimes on an action, sometimes on the attendant circumstances of the action" (1932, p. 4; 1955, p. 11). Thompson, who theorizes the point of view of the researcher, brings this constitutional variety of motifs under a single heading, that of characterization, and this is something which the whole range of his book serves to confirm. "Most of the items [of the *Motif-Index*] are found worthy of note because of something out of the ordinary, something of sufficiently striking character to become a part of tradition, oral or literary. Commonplace experiences, such as eating and sleeping, are not traditional in this sense. But they may become so by having attached to them something remarkable or worthy of remembering" (1932, p. 9; 1955, p. 19). Motifs are, therefore, elements characteristic of characters, of action, or of the circumstances of action; they are, at any rate, such as to characterize a text.

The third definition of motif, based on recursiveness, is the one which refers most directly to its etymon (*movere* as motion) and to the ordinary use in music of *Leitmotiv*. It highlights the function which arises from repetition, as part of the verbal texture, of statements, considerations, descriptions, allusions, etc. (At first sight merely ornamental, such repetitions serve in substance to underline, to reinforce, and to convince as well as to act as suggestion). It is a subtle way of orienting, and of influencing, the reader's (or listener's) attention, akin to the recurring image as a technique in films. At the most deplorable level, its goal may be hidden persuasion. This sense of motif is the least remarked upon and the least studied, perhaps because research of this kind has been dominated by ethnologists. It is, on the contrary, of fundamental importance for the study of poetry (and of artistic prose as well), and it finds its confirmation and reinforcement in research into word frequency (into key words and theme words).

6. It is, then, the ethnologists who have discussed the concept of motif at greatest length. As against empirical definitions like the one we have quoted from Thompson or that of Volkov (1924), who by motif means the quality and

number of heroes, their actions, the objects in play, etc., there exists a doctrinaire approach which attempts to link motif to narrative action. The main representative of this line of thought is the great Veselovsky.

> (a) By motif I mean the simplest narrative unit, one which corresponds figuratively to the different requirements of the primitive intellect or of everyday observation. Given the resemblance, or identity, of the conditions of everyday life, and of psychological conditions, to the early stages of human development, such motifs might well have been established autonomously, while at the same time presenting features which resemble one another. The following may serve as exemplifications: (1) the so-called *légendes des origines,* the representation of the sun as an eye, of the sun and the moon as brother and sister or as husband and wife; myths of the sun's rising and setting, of the marks on the moon, of eclipses, etc.; (2) real-life situations—the kidnapping of the bride (a traditional marriage custom), the leave-taking banquet (in folk tales), and other customs of the same kind. (b) With the term *sjužet* (plot), I refer to a theme inside which various situations or motifs are interlaced: e.g., (1) folk tales about the sun (and his mother; Greek and Malayan legends of a cannibal sun); (2) folk tales about kidnapping (1897–1906, Ital. trans., p. 290).

A marked difference exists, however, between the two series Veselovsky indicates: the first embraces situations and their interpretations; the second, episodes which form part of a larger plot. It was by concentrating on the second of these two series that the Russian formalists (Tomashevsky first among them) were able to arrive at the minimal units for the plot, which they saw as a succession of motifs, and for the fabula as well. Then came Propp, and he replaced the term *motif* with the well-chosen *function*. In general, however, the ethnologists continue to use the word *motif* for the minimal element of an action, though they do occasionally prefer the newer derivative *motifeme* (from Pike). (Dundes does so, and so does Doležel, who broadens its scope to include narratology.)

While a functional definition of motif undoubtedly constitutes a gain on a theoretical level, it involves a corresponding loss terminologically speaking. A word like *motif,* with its rewarding interplay of values, has become specialized and has been confined to a meaning for which the term *function* is far more suitable or for which, if the level required is to be more general, we might better employ *action*. We are left with no term to stand for the various conceptual and structural applications of *motif*—applications which, as we have seen, highlight parallelisms with its original use in music.

The difficulties involved in a satisfactory definition of the term *motif* are, though, an invitation to investigate the matter further. Not that things are made any easier by positional or content-centered orientations, the ingenuousness and immaturity of whose attempts are at once obvious. This applies to Sperber, who distinguishes primary motifs (in a central or adjacent position) from accessory motifs (in a marginal position); to Petsch, who lists nuclear motifs (in a central position), frame-motifs (in an adjacent position and in support of nuclear motifs), and filler motifs; to Frenzel, who distinguishes motifs of situation, of type, of landscape and locality, and, lastly, psychological motifs (apprehensions and aspirations). What is important is that we should be aware of the nature of the concepts in terms of which any whole made up of motifs is constituted.

7. Research on motifs can go forward once more, our term of comparison now being not the fabula but the theme. It is a suggestion which one is led to make thanks to the recent vogue for "thematic criticism" (Poulet, Richard, Starobinski), an approach which, without overmuch distinction, moves in an area between motifs and themes. Richard, for example, in his most important work, adopts a phrase of Mallarmée to say that what he has been looking for in his author is "ces motifs qui composent une logique, avec nos fibres" (1961, p. 19). These motifs—individualized in the materials the poet prefers (mirrors, fire, veils, etc.), in the forms he selects (hills, jets of water, peninsulas, etc.), in his mental movements and essential attitudes—come together to form a museum of the poet's imagination, a repertory of his expressive formulae, the repertoire of his metaphors. The contents of such lists have come to light as a result of the frequency of their appearance (recurrence) or because of their presence in privileged areas or at privileged moments. So true is this that we are in a position to perceive the principles which impose order upon them. These principles are hierarchical (load-bearing themes are developed with more insistence) or articulated as oppositions—closed and open, clear-cut and elusive, mediated and unmediated (with possible interlacing). Thus, "the theme appears . . . as a transitive element which allows us to move in various directions through the whole internal extension of the work or, rather, as the 'hinge-element,' thanks to which it is articulated as a meaningful 'volume'" (p. 26).

Prominence is given to themes and motifs at the level of lexis, but they go beyond words toward the very existence of things, toward subtle vibrations of feelings. They do refer conceptually, but they are not cut off from the experience which produced the ideas. "Thus, the idea is not cut off from its oneiric foundation [de son soubassement revé . . .]; it remains musical [suave, rieuse, altière], at once transparent and appetizing" (Richard 1961, p. 22). What the theme highlights is "the movement by which flesh, blood, reverie give rise to creations of the intelligence" (pp. 21–22). Elsewhere, Richard expresses himself even more clearly (1967, p. 309): "The contexts are two, but as a rule only one of them is spoken of. There exists the work's successive, or metonymic, context and its metaphoric context, which is that of the work as a whole. A theme assumes no value outside an organized network of relations, and these are at once relations of language and of experience; they unfold within that kind of language complex which is the totality of the work."

Richard gives due weight to the play of rhythm, and he points out that it is possible to replace a succession of different elements to be integrated into a unity of substance or essence with a serial arrangement of analogous elements which have been made to undergo a process of variation. Hence, "a single element (of sense, ideology, or an actantial, phantasmatical element) will be repeated at a distance and be recognized as being like itself to the point of tracing out an explicitly meaningful line; it will, though, be modified at the same time, in terms of the variety of code or context in terms of which on each occasion it has been taken up anew, accommodated anew" (1974, p. 219). Richard distinguishes most opportunely between Proust's treatment of themes (e.g., that which links the motif of the kiss to Combray, those of jealousy, the church, the madeleine, asparagus) and the way these same themes are dealt with by the literary critic. He will base himself on "a fluctuating attention to the implicit, to the throbbing, the obsessive, to the iteratively involuntary," and reach the point of being able to "show forth, in their ever-shifting, never-obstructed relations, the vast, often barely conscious categories of a personal landscape" (p. 220).

Within a framework of this kind, it is difficult not to surrender to the temptation of psychoanalysis, and Mauron, though his findings are rigorously formalized and he is by no means insensible "to the musical analysis of themes and variations," abandons himself to it completely in his psychocriticism. He is committed to searching out, from inside a writer's work, associations or patterns of its images which are obsessive and probably unintentional. The aim is to discover how it happens that, in the work, "networks are repeated and modified, as are the patterns or, to use a more generic term, the structures which the first operation reveals, since in practice these structures rapidly embody dramatic figures and situations." Combining "analysis of the themes varied with analysis of dreams and their metamorphoses," it is possible to observe "shifts between associations of ideas and the imaginative fantasy." The point is reached of representing the "personal myth" of any given poet (1963, p. 33).

For his part, Weber goes so far as to link to the unconscious a single theme, seeing it as "an event or a situation which is (in the widest sense of the word) infantile, capable of manifesting itself—in general unconsciously—in a work or in a group of works of art . . . either symbolically or *in chiaro*" (1960, p. 13)—hence, the need to go back from one's findings on the modulations of a theme (or from its symptomatically obsessive lexical recurrence) in the poetic work, in order to investigate childhood traumas which were perhaps determinant for the author. In this way, an author's characteristic motifs, his images, his patterns will stand revealed as concomitant reflexes of a single memory, traces of an experience secretly conditioned by a trauma.

Naturally, any real attempt to account historically for this thematic and psychoanalytical literary criticism would have to take stock of the prehistory of its connections: from Bachelard, preoccupied with the poetical concretization of the archetypes of the imagination (the four elements of Empedoclean cosmology and their philogenetic realizations) to the symbolic literary criticism of the English and American schools. Here as an example is Knights, who, in *Some Shakespearean Themes*, individuates themes of time and mutability, of seeming and being, of the fear of death and of life, of the meanings of nature, of relational meanings. He then goes on to specify that "our talk of themes . . . is simply a way of pointing to the centers of consciousness that exert a kind of gravitational pull, to the dominant tones and emphases of a living mode of experience" (1959, p. 66); "Shakespeare used the analysis of character and personality in the exploration of ideas: the ideas in question being not 'abstract ideas' but themes and preoccupations of great personal urgency, which demanded to be worked out not logically and in abstraction but in terms of the greatest possible exposure to life and the imaginative apprehension of it" (p. 157). Our aim in the present section, though, is not historical but theoretical; thus, such indications as have already been given will suffice.

8. It might seem that our excursus into thematic criticism has merely made the confusion worse, but this is not the case. The multiplication of meanings for the terms under discussion now allows us to have some sense of a movement that is sufficiently uniform to be dealt with rationally. Let us return to function, fabula, and plot. In texts of narrative content, the linking together of actions—and even more of functions—exactly represents the chronological and logical succession of human events. These events fit into a logic of action identical with the logic which can be deduced from real behavior. As a result, it has no importance, from an epistemological point of view, that, in fact, the events in question are merely invented.

The scope of the unfolding narrative is not, however (except in the case of certain mass-produced literature), the exposition of a series of likely actions. It is, rather, to offer an experience or a conception of a world which such actions and their outcome will serve to verify. The discourse of events and actions thus implicitly carries on another discourse, one of ideas. It is between these two discourses, between these two sequences, that the narration as a whole complex unfolds.

Now, although discourse of events and actions can be formalized because it can be referred, not to reality but to the logic of reality (or to the possible reality of a possible world), discourse of ideas is not subject to formalization, both because it is not univocal and because it is not logical (it is perfectly prepared to violate the Aristotelian principles of identity, of contradiction, and of excluded middle). Nor is this all. Discourse of events and actions is a synthesis, to be effected through use of specific techniques, made up of facts which are described or uttered by the text, and it is, in some measure, homologous to the text. Discourse of ideas is deduction from these facts, a deduction which, for the most part, is not expressed inside the text (moralizing, when present, belittles). It is formulated mentally and tentatively by the user of the text, on the basis of the facts or of the way in which they are put forward.

Discourse of ideas, unless the literature is defending a thesis, aims not so much to demonstrate as to show. It individuates those conceptual areas which are determinant in delimiting the meaningfulness of events, and that of their motives or causes, and also in clarifying the types of contact, of tension, of development, of neutralization which may perhaps involve a number of areas. Hence, what we are dealing with are abstractions from reality, with conceptualizations of acting and of feeling. We are also dealing with ideas whose importance is that they have been deduced from living experience. A discourse of ideas is of value only insofar as it can be referred to a discourse of feelings and ways of behaving, just as a discourse of actions is of value because it can be referred to the discourse of their general interpretability. It is for this reason that the actions are endowed with sense and that they arouse our interest.

Deciphering a text integrates two vastly different operations. The first consists of individuating, on the basis of text data, determinant semantic areas, within which the generalization of real or pseudoreal data is developed. The second consists in formulating hypotheses for interpreting the tensions which exist among these areas or between one group and another. These tensions are not just semantic in character but existential and such that they may well not be prefigured by the denotative elements of the text, but only by its connotative elements (or they may even contradict both groups by way of eloquent antiphrasis and unconscious intuitions).

Fortunately, the second of these operations can be neglected here, for it threatens any illusion of rationalism. Motifs and themes are, on the contrary, basic material for the first operation. An embarrassing statement of Czerny-Krakau is worth recording: "The motif is essentially a structural and expressive unit-limit; it is a meaningful 'idea-force' (in the widest sense: notions, representations, sensible images, emotions, volitions); it is the indissoluble unity of thinking and acting. . . . Awareness of this indivisible duality, fundamental for the definition of motif, makes impossible *ipso facto* any exclusively formalistic aesthetic. . . . But at the same time, it sounds condemnation for any exclusively ideological aesthetic" (1957, p.41).

In speaking of "indissoluble unity of thinking and acting," Czerny-Krakau seems to sense that motifs (and themes) might occupy the ample terrain between discourse of events and actions and discourse of ideas. The various scholars already referred to have provided definitions of motifs or themes for situations, characters, feelings, objects, concepts: entities which are more abstract or more concrete as they are closer to, or farther away from, one or another discourse. An attempt has recently been made to formalize the operations by means of which the reader moves from the system of expressive techniques (here called motifs) to the system of semantic oppositions (here called dianoetic theme), to the point of individuating thereby the author's "poetic world" (cf. Ščeglov and Žolkovskij 1975).

Theme and motif are, therefore, stereotype meaning units which recur in a text or in a group of texts and which are capable of individuating determinant semantic areas. They are meaning units: we may, in fact, have to deal with the words, sentences, and groups of sentences of a text or with paraphrases of parts of the text which institute an autonomous meaning. They are stereotypes: the stereotype may be brought about by mere repetition, and inside a single text, but for the most part it is the product of continual cultural reemployment (repetition in a succession of texts which are regarded as one all-embracing text). Such stereotyping is all the more evident when the meaning is symbolic and is communicated immediately, thanks to its conventional nature. Stereotypes individuate determinant semantic areas. Whether it is the environment of the action or its conceptual fields, themes and motifs rest upon key points; they constitute a kind of thorough bass for more or less broad (narrative and illustrative) sectors of the text.

Themes and motifs thus effect the task of formalization—less strict and less easily circumscribed than that relative to the actions, because the reality they stand for is deeper and more stratified—and do so section by section in varied measure and at various levels. It is this formalization, however, which simplifies and accelerates our grasp of the discourse of ideas. It provides small, compact blocks of existential reality or of conceptual reality semiotically structured, and it is in the connecting areas between these blocks that the text can develop proposals of its own, integrating the new with the less new and interpreting the one by employing the other, in exactly the same way in which the known terms of a context point the way to an understanding of its innovations.

We shall call themes those stereotype elements which underpin a whole text or substantial areas of it; motifs, on the contrary, are lesser elements which may be present in considerable numbers. A theme is quite frequently the result of insistence on a number of motifs. Motifs are much more apt to declare themselves on the plane of language discourse, so much so that, when they are repeated, they act rather like refrains. Themes, though, are for the most part metadiscoursive in character. Motifs usually constitute discoursive resonances with respect to the metadiscoursive character of the theme.

Since the term *theme* is employed as much for the argument as for *dianoia*, we may find ourselves dealing both with dianoetic and with content themes, and this is no less true of motifs. Thus, Frenzel's statement, which we quoted earlier, that poetry makes use of motifs and not of themes is valid only where subject-matter themes are concerned (cf., too, the concept of "athematic tale" in Christensen 1929, p. 9). What Frenzel says serves, if at all, to underline the preeminence in poetry of dianoetic discourse over narrative discourse, or even lack of the latter. It is, however, beyond question that dianoetic discourse can remain wholly implicit, as against the frequent presence of the motifs which may serve to suggest it.

The distinction here proposed between theme and motif remains close to the musical distinction already discussed. It is the opposition of complex to simple, of articulated to unified, and of idea to nucleus, of organism to cell. It is a distinction which even non-Proppian folklorists observe when they distinguish type from motif, where type constitutes the immanent schema of a series of narrations and motif a single characteristic element. The motif is, in short, the characterizing term of reference for what, when it is looked at in relation to the logic of the action (and only when it is determinant for the action), is generalized and decharacterized as a function. For example, the four motifs "the tzar gives an eagle to a hero," "the old man gives Sučenko a horse," "a sorcerer gives Ivan a little boat," "the princess gives Ivan a ring" represent one single function for Propp: "the hero acquires the use of a magical agent." This is all the more true because they are invariably followed by the function, "transference of the hero" (1928, Eng. trans., pp. 44ff.). In a characterizing analysis, on the contrary, no relation exists between a journey in the talons of an eagle, the power of an enchanted ring, and the action of remote-controlled steeds or boats. What remains fundamental is our interest in the traditional continuity of each of these types of event—linked as they are to various (it may be mythical) conceptions of the world—in their diffusion over time and space, in their productivity at the level of fantasy. It should be added that such motifs may present themselves at different points in different narrations, and that their outcome may be different. When this is the case, they would, for Propp, constitute different functions, or they would simply not be functions at all—having lost their identity. The same discourse holds good for themes with respect to narrative models. Themes, which may be identical with the subject or may constitute large areas of it, maintain the semantic content of the fabula, content which the narrative model replaces with a syntagmatic of functions (cf. §1). It might be suggested that motif : function = theme : narrative model. The individuation of persistent themes, which are also realized by means of a change of functions, is no less important for the description and history of narratological schemata by individuation of identical functions within seemingly diverse vicissitudes. Themes are anthropological, and even gnoseological, concretizations. Propp's functional perspective and the historical-empirical perspective of field researchers imply two different (and complementary) approaches to stereotyping activity: one is a formalistic approach which sets its sights on the logic of an immanent succession within stereotypes; the other is realistic and deals with the constitution and the external cohesion of the stereotypes themselves.

It is even more difficult to maintain Panofsky's identification of motifs with primary, natural meanings and themes with secondary, cultural ones. The idea has, however, been taken over and transformed, in the literary sphere, by Scholes and Kellogg, who broadened the concept of *topos* so as to include the "traditional image." They then write:

> Insofar as a *topos* refers to the external world, its meaning is a *motif*; insofar as it refers to the world of disembodied ideas and concepts, its meaning is a *theme*. Traditional *topoi*, then, will consist of two elements: a traditional motif, such as the hero's descent into the underworld, which may be extremely durable historically; and a traditional theme, such as the search for wisdom or the harrowing of hell, which may prove much more subject to gradual change or replacement in the course of time. The *topoi* of oral narratives are identifiable on the basis of their consistent association of a given motif with a given theme. In written narrative, on the other hand, the relation of motif and theme, even with a conventional *topos*, is subject to the poet's manipulation (1966, p. 27).

The two authors have effectively grasped the difference, and the phase-differences, between a thematics based on content and one that is dianoetic. It is true that their terminology loses sight of the difference in extension between theme and motif, but its descriptive and theoretical advantages are nevertheless considerable. The fact is that traditional terminology (which we have here attempted to define and perfect) does not provide us with distinctions between content and dianoetic motifs and themes. But, as we have seen, we are dealing with oscillations which are constitutional for the sphere, and for the perspectives, of research. If need be, the addition of attributes might help to avoid a further confusion, that between verbal motifs and content motifs.

9. The discourse of facts thus provides the framework for the all-embracing literary discourse. What remains is material taken from life, which is made to conform in linguistic and literary terms; here "material taken from life" is to be understood as the totality of experiences, mental experiences included. Even without taking things back to the psychological presuppositions of our perceptions, we may regard it as self-evident that the operation by which experience is verbalized is a semiotic operation. It can be broken down into two stages: in the first, lived experience is referred to schemata of representability; the second is the linguistic realization of these schemata (Segre 1977, chap. 2). Rules for the linguistic representability of schemata have not as yet been formulated. Information is, however, available with regard to schemata of representability relative to a repertory of possible actions and situations; they coincide in part with themes and motifs. The study of thematics thus brings us into contact with the erratic material of experience, and this mankind has elaborated over time in terms of schemata. To such elaboration, writers have made a special contribution of their own, though it is merely a matter of consecration and formalization. Themes and motifs, as one can easily verify, are far from being the exclusive domain of literature.

This semiotic operation has been attributed by Jung to the unconscious (however collective his unconscious). The sum total of his findings, defined as "the psychic residue of innumerable experiences of the same type" (1931, Eng. trans, p. 320), constitutes an "unconscious mythology" (p. 319). The schemata, which Jung calls "archetypes," are referred to every time a human being finds himself in a typical situation. "In such moments we are no longer individuals, but the race; the voice of mankind resounds in us" (p. 320). The process of creation can readily enough be brought down to this, because it "consists in the unconscious activation of an archetypal image, and in elaborating and shaping this image into the finished work" (p. 321). However we decide to take Jung's proposals, it is well worth meditating in all seriousness on his description of the way archetypes exist in the unconscious. "There are no inborn ideas, but there are inborn possibilities of ideas that set bounds to even the boldest fantasy and keep our fantasy activity within certain categories: *a priori* ideas, as it were, the existence of which cannot be ascertained except from their effects. *They appear only in the shaped material of art as the regulative principles that shape it;* that is to say, only by inferences drawn from the finished work can we reconstruct the age-old original of the primordial image. The primordial image, or archetype, is a figure—be it a daemon, a human being, or a process—that constantly recurs in the course of history and appears wherever creative fantasy is freely expressed" (p. 319).

Frye takes up this theory of archetypes and applies it to literary activity (but see also Bodkin 1948). If we regard poetry as a social activity, as "the focus of a community," as a fact of communication, then the symbol will appear to us as "the communicable unit, to which [we will] give the name archetype: that is, a typical or recurring image." Thus, we will mean by archetype "a symbol which connects one poem with another and thereby helps to unify and integrate our literary experience" (1957, p. 99). Frye exemplifies with images from the physical world (the sea, the forest), with metaphors (the biblical metaphors of the shepherd and his flock), but with more complex themes as well. "To give a random example, one very common convention of the nineteenth-century novel is the use of two heroines, one dark and one light. The dark one is as a rule passionate, haughty, plain, foreign or Jewish, and in some way associated with some kind of forbidden fruit like incest. When the two are involved with the same hero, the plot usually has to get rid of the dark one or make her into a sister if the story is to end happily" (p. 101).

We need not follow Frye in his delimitations (justifiable as they are) with regard to the meaningful potentiality of the archetypes, the varied degrees of innovation with which they appear in the different genres of poetic production, and their progressive decadence. We might well take note, though, of the way, all too immediate, in which he links these archetypes of his to the primordial conflict between desire and reality, to such a point that the study of archetypes comes to be identified with the study of civilization, seen not merely as imitation of nature but also as "the process of making a total human form out of nature . . . impelled by the force that we have just called desire" (p. 105). Once placed on this metahistorical level, the investigation ends up by individuating two rhythms, one of them cyclical, the other dialectical. The former is that of the rite, a recurrent act linked to the natural cycles of the planets, of the seasons, of human life. The latter is that of a dialectic between desire and repulsion, whose fullest expression is to be found in dreams.

Dream and ritual converge in myth. "Myth . . . not only gives meaning to ritual and narrative to dream: it is the identification of ritual and dream, in which the former is seen to be the latter in movement" (Frye 1957, p. 107). Naturally Frye uses "myth" in a sense which is more figurative than literal, and he is led to do so by his propensity toward an autonomous study of literature. He thus builds out of desire and dream, rite and myth, nature and civilization an enchanting castle, though it is a somewhat fragile one.

It seems beyond doubt that, even if literature does indeed constitute the richest and most varied repertoire of themes, any investigation of the schemata of representability has to be carried beyond literature: it will have to involve all the symbolical expressions of the imagination. Investigations, on the part of ethnologists and historians of religion, of those symbols which have been conceived and modified over the course of thousands of years and those investigations which the folklorists have dedicated to the nuclei of situations and actions which recur in narrations—widely distanced and diversified narrations—must be compared with the symbolical activities of the unconscious and with their mutations when they can be seized upon. Our findings will then need to be analyzed in terms of a psychology of the schemata of experience.

It is advisable, on the other hand, to avoid clear-cut distinctions between the representability schemata to be met with in ethnopsychological research and those to be found in folk literature or in sophisticated literature. Our way of reducing reality to schemata is determined by literary clichés as well, and these enjoy currency at all levels of culture. If mankind confers upon characters, situations, and events the value of more or less universal themes, this is because they recognize in them those stereotypes on the basis of which, in their everyday experience, they tend to interpret characters, situations, and events. Themes are not just sublimation but heuristic models as well. This is also why the themes and motifs present in folk and literary texts constitute a fairly well-defined whole, with interchange between popular and literary. If, on the one hand, we find the *topoi* as an extreme example of stereotyping, we encounter, on the other, schemata which have not as yet been consecrated at a literary level, even though they may already be identified as patterns of collective experience.

It is here that the dialectic between theme and motif comes into its own. For themes, since they are more articulated and more easily recognized, are already able to act as *"types-cadre,"* as frame-types, in Zumthor's sense; motifs, however, may constitute an individuality of their own by virtue of the fact that they repeat themselves inside the text. This is one way of activating a self-selection from the otherwise infinite symbolic values which might be gathered on the basis of all of the elements of which the text is constituted. Selection by recursiveness can subsequently be integrated with the selection effected by the convergence of the motifs as they set up fields of meaning which may then be related to the theme. In this way, the theme/motif dialectic makes its contribution to the setting up of the sense.

The fact is that theoretical definition in this field is always less dangerous than the practice of interpretation. This is the case because the measure of literary stereotyping activity is something that can only be verified in cultural terms. The listener or the reader may well know nothing of the pedigree of a given theme, in the same way as, before Curtius, one might easily have regarded a great many *topoi* as the inventions of individual authors. We may presume that the person who makes use of the text will recognize universal themes more easily than historically determined themes, dianoetic themes rather than content themes (a fact which explains why people are driven to seek the moral of the tale, the thesis of the text). It is from phase differences such as these that it is possible to deduce an overlapping of the cultural, the rational, and the unconscious, as themes are handled and grasped.

10. Thematics is unquestionably an important element in text segmentation. Where descriptive themes are concerned, individuation of content units that are capable of synthesis in memory serve to bring clearly to the fore the series of events and situations which, upon further selection, will provide a more limited series, more consistent with those actions upon which a model of plot and fabula will be based. But whereas plot and fabula are already oriented toward the logic of the action, descriptive themes embrace situational elements as well and may even favor them. If analysis of the tale tends to separate actions from situations,

analysis of themes directly involves both actions and situations, and it does so without seeking for a distributional model, because in themes (as in motifs) the grouping of situations and actions was determined historically and culturally even before the text itself was composed.

Three extreme limits can be set for any content analysis. One is thematic, and it singles out actions and situations in accord with schemata of representability which have been elaborated and linked together historically prior to the text. Another is prefunctional and functional; it marks off actions and defines their logical and chronological relations inside the text. Yet another, which still awaits theoretical definition, furnishes descriptive models for situations, actions, and their links, the characters. Here it must be stressed yet again that actions, situations, characters, etc., still maintain, on the thematic level, part of their vibrant character as lived experience. It is this very characterization of theirs which rejects the functionalistic grids which would reduce them to nothing.

But it is from the historical, the strongly characterized, nature of themes and motifs that another consequence may be deduced, one which is no less important for text segmentation: there exists no preconstituted thematic level upon which thematic units can be based. Thus, it is possible to have, in different cases, thematic units of fairly limited extension (which are thus compact) and more extensive thematic units, perhaps constituted by breaking discourse down into non-contiguous segments. Motifs and themes form subsets in the text; sometimes they form a number of subsets on different levels. They lay down epistemological guidelines, which make it easier to move through the less conventional parts of the text.

What is typical of thematics (and this can be verified over and over) is the fact that it never breaks away unequivocally from lived experience. Any diminution of experience is compensated for by a closer connection with the experience itself and by reinforcement of its expressions. Two antithetical statements are equally correct from this point of view: (1) the writer imitates reality; characters and events, even if they have no objective reference, constitute an analogon of the human world in which we live; (2) the writer gives life to a possible world, where what is primary is not any homology with the real world but internal coherence. The relation of invention to reality is a symbolic relation. Symbolic is the descriptive capacity of the discourse, and no less symbolic is the representativeness conferred upon imaginary individuals, objects, places, and behavior. In the first case, this symbolical character is immediate; in the second, it does not refer to real referents but to a reality deduced from a generalization of referents (and of interreferential relations) akin to it. Yet it is not a question of first and second degree symbolizing: even when the referent is real, it is perceived and named thanks to schemata which are themselves the outcome of earlier generalizations from sets of related referents (and of referent relations). Literature, in other words, works with schemata of reality which precede the specific reality the writer himself observes. Obviously, literature will then compare such schemata with its own observations of reality. Just as the schemata will always, to some extent, conserve vibrations of the inaugural experience, new experiences will, as a consequence, easily transmit vibrations of their own through the schemata adopted for their description. This serves to explain why it is that art can be "larger than life." When it is, it is so because it embraces the mental conditions of our way of knowing. The coherence of possible literary worlds also adapts itself (and its degrees are clearly codified in accord with literary genres) to types of motivation and to causal relations which are proper not to reality but to our mode of representing ourselves and of representing reality. Yet this coherence is a matter of signs; it is symbolic. In short, motifs and themes are the language (the words, as it were, the sentences, the syntactic schemata) of our cognitive contact with the world of man. It is thanks to them, too, that literature continues to be one of the most comprehensive representations of our existence.

References

Beller, M.
    1970. Von der Stoffgeschichte zur Thematologie: Ein Beitrag zur komparatistischen Methodenlehre. *Arcadia: Zeitschrift für vergleichende Literaturwissenschaft*, 5, no. 1, pp. 1–38.
    1981. Thematologie. In M. Schmeling, ed. *Vergleichende Literaturwissenschaft: Theorie und Praxis*. Wiesbaden: Athenaion. Pp. 73–97.
Bodkin, M.
    1948. *Archetypal Patterns in Poetry: Psychological Studies of Imagination*. New York: Oxford University Press.
Borrel, E.
    1954. Theme. In E. Blom, ed. *Grove's Dictionary of Music and Musicians*. Vol. 8. London: Macmillan. Pp. 409–10.
Christensen, A.
    1929. Motif et thème: Plan d'un dictionnaire des motifs de contes populaires, de légendes et de fables. *FF Communications*, 18, p. 59.
Courtés, J., ed.
    1980. Le motif en ethno-littérature. *Bulletin du Groupe de Recherches sémio-linguistiques*, 16.
Curtius, E. R.
    1948. *Europäische Literatur und lateinisches Mittelalter.* 3d ed. 1961. Bern: Franke. (English translation. 1953 *European Literature and the Latin Middle Ages*. New York: Harper and Row.)
Czerny-Krakau, Z.
    1957. Contribution à une théorie comparée du motif dans les arts. In P. von Böckmann, ed. *Stil- und Formprobleme in der Literatur: International Federation of Modern Languages and Literatures, 7th Congress, Heidelberg 1957*. 1959. Heidelberg: Winter. Pp. 38–50.
Frenzel, E.
    1963. *Stoff-, Motiv- und Symbolforschung*. Stuttgart: Metzler.
Frye, N.
    1957. *Anatomy of Criticism: Four Essays*. Princeton: Princeton University Press.
Greimas, A.-J.
    1970. *Du sens: Essais sémiotiques*. Paris: Seuil.
Jung, C. G.
    1931. *Seelenprobleme der Gegenwart*. Zurich: Rascher.
Knights, L. Ch.
    1959. *Some Shakespearean Themes*. London: Chatto and Windus.

Levin, H.
    1968. Thematics and Criticism. In P. Demetz, Th. Greene, and L. Nelson, eds. *The Disciplines of Criticism: Essays in Literary Theory, Interpretation, and History in Honor of René Wellek.* New Haven: Yale University Press. Pp. 125–45.
Mauron, Ch.
    1963. *Des métaphores obsédantes au mythe personnel: Introduction à la psychocritique.* Paris: Corti.
Orlando, F.
    1975. Propositions pour une sémantique du leitmotiv dans L'Anneau des Nibelungen. *Musique en jeu,* January, pp. 73–86.
Panofsky, E.
    1939. *Studies in Iconology: Humanistic Themes in the Art of the Renaissance.* New York: Oxford University Press.
Parry, H. H.
    1954. Figure. In E. Bloom, ed. *Grove's Dictionary of Music and Musicians,* vol. 3. London: Macmillan. Pp. 90–91.
Polti, G.
    1895. *Les trente-six situations dramatiques.* 3d ed. 1924. Paris: Mercure de France.
Propp, V. Ja.
    1928. *Morfologija skazki.* Leningrad: Academia. (English translation. 1968. *Morphology of the Folk Tale.* Austin: University of Texas Press.)
Richard, J.-P.
    1961. *L'univers imaginaire de Mallarmé.* Paris: Seuil.
    1967. *Les chemins actuels de la critique.* Paris: Seuil.
    1974. *Proust et le monde sensible.* Paris: Seuil.
Rossi-Doria, G.
    1934. Motivo. In *Enciclopedia italiana di scienze, lettere ed arti,* vol. 23. Milan: Istituto Giovanni Treccani. Pp. 941–42.
Ščeglov, J. K., and Žolkovskij, A. K.
    1975. K ponjatii‹tema› i ‹poetičeskij mir›. *Trudy po znakovym sistemam,* 7, pp. 143–167.
Scholes, R., and Kellogg, R.
    1966. *The Nature of Narrative.* New York: Oxford University Press.
Segre, C.
    1977. *Semiotica, storia e cultura.* Padua: Liviana.
Šklovskij, V. B.
    1925. *O teorii prozy.* Moscow: Federacija.
Thompson, S.
    1932. *Motif-Index of Folk-Literature: A Classification of Narrative Elements in Folk-Tales, Ballads, Myths, Fables, Mediaeval Romances, Exempla, Fabliaux, Jest-Books, and Local Legends,* vol. 1. Bloomington: Indiana University Press.
Trousson, R.
    1965. *Un problème de littérature comparée: Les études de thèmes; essai de méthodologie.* 2d rev. ed. 1981. Brussels: Editions de l'Université de Bruxelles.
Veit, W.
    1963. Toposforschung–Ein Vorschungsbericht. *Deutsche Vierteljahrsschrift für Literaturwissenschaft und Geistesgeschichte,* 37, pp. 120–63.
Veselovskij, A.
    1897–1906. Poetika sjužetov. In *Istoričeskaja poetika.* 1940. Leningrad. Pp. 493–

596. (Italian translation. Poetica degli intrecci. In *Poetica Storica*. 1981. Rome: Edizioni e/o. Pp. 282–97).

Volkov, R. M.
    1924. *Skazka. Rozyskanija po sjužetosloženiju narodnoj skazki, I. Skazka velikorusskaja, ukrainskaja, belorusskaja*. Odessa: Gosudarstvennoe Izdatel'stvo Ukrainj.

Wartburg, W. von
    1959. Leitmotiv. In *Französisches Etymologisches Wörterbuch: Eine Darstellung des galloromanischen Sprachschatzes*, vol. 16. Basel: Zbinden. P. 455.
    1966. *Thema*, ibid., vol. 13, book 1, pp. 303–04.
    1967. *Motivus*, ibid., vol. 6, book 3, pp. 161–62.

Weber, J.-P.
    1960. *Genèse de l'oeuvre poétique*. Paris: Gallimard.

Weisstein, U.
    1975. *Einführung in die vergleichende Literaturwissenschaft*. Stuttgart: Kohlhammer.

Ziolkowski, Th.
    1977. *Disenchanted Images: A Literary Iconology*. Princeton: Princeton University Press.
    1983. *Varieties of Literary Thematics*. Princeton: Princeton University Press.

Zumthor, P.
    1971. Topique et tradition. *Poétique*, 2, pp. 354–65.
    1972. *Essai de poétique médiévale*. Paris: Seuil.

8.
Text

1. The word *textus* is found for the first time fairly late in Latin (in Quintilian *Istitutio oratoria*, IX. 4, 13) as a figurative use of the past participle of *texere*. It is a metaphor which sees the overall language complex of the text's discourse as a woven tissue, and the metaphor was renewed many times, once the term *text* had been codified. Thus, *testura*, in Italian, and *texture*, in French and English, from Plautine Latin *textura*, stand for the connection of the different parts of a work, of a poem, etc. This use, documented from 1540, has recently been revived by Ransom and by Zumthor. In like manner, *trama*, or *ordito*, is used for the thread of a narration and *tela* for the web of an argument or of a tale: "A dire come fu temuto sarebbe gran tela," i.e., "to tell how he was feared would need a wide web" (*Novellino*, LXXXIV). (The expression is a commonplace, and many authors make use of it.) *Tela* and *trama* are found, both together, in Dante: "Poi che, tacendo, si mostrò spedita / l'anima santa di metter la trama / in quella tela ch'io le porsi ordita," i.e., "when, falling silent, the blest spirit showed he had done weaving the warp of that cloth which I had set him" (*Paradiso*, XVII, vv. 100–02), And here all the metaphorical implications are followed out in Benvenuto's commentary: "Est enim trama illum filum quod deducitur in telam per ordituram; immo auctor noster dederat unum thema orditum, idest inchoatum tantum; et ille Cacciaguida texuit illum iterum interserendo multa verba, exponendo et declarando" ("The woof is the thread which is set in the cloth in its weaving; indeed, our author set a theme to be woven, i.e., one merely sketched out; Cacciaguida then worked it anew inserting many words, expounding and making manifest"). For *tela*, we may also turn to Petrarch: "S'amore o morte non dà qualche stroppio / a la tela novella ch'ora ordisco," i.e., "If love and death do not interrupt this new fabric I now weave" (*Rime*, XL, vv. 1–2); "Poi con gran subbio e con mirabil fuso / vidi tela sottil ordir Crisippo," i.e., "then with mighty beam and wondrous shuttle I saw Chrysippus weaving a fine cloth" (*Trionfo della Fama*, III, vv. 113–14). Equally well known is Ariosto's metaphor: "Ma perché varie fila a varie tele / uopo mi son, che tutte ordire intendo, / lascio Rinaldo e l'agitata prua, / e torno a dir di Bradamante sua," i.e., "but, because I need different threads for different tissues, and intend to weave them all, I leave Rinaldo and his tossing prow, and go back and tell of his lover, Bradamante" (*Orlando furioso*, II, 30, vv. 5–8); "Di molte fila esser bisogno parme / a condur la gran tela ch'io lavoro," i.e., "Much

thread is, I think, needed to carry forward the great tapestry on which I work" (XIII, 81, vv. 1–2).

The attention that is paid to the texture of a discourse is all the greater the more the text is endowed with its own special authority (cf., the Italian expression *far testo*). This is the case when the author we have to deal with is a classical author or a legal authority, and it holds good, of course, for the Bible, the book (the text) par excellence (and, in Christian liturgy, the Gospel). Here a distinction arises (an opposition) between the *textus* and its gloss or comment: an opposition which serves to emphasize, with the meticulousness of the accompanying elucidations, the importance of the text which requires and sustains them. If it is true that Plato's contempt for writing and for the book (*Phaedrus*, 274c–276a) was shared by Greece as a whole—writing being held to be a mere expedient for conserving oral discourse, "the discourse which is written by knowledge on the mind of the learner" (276a)—it is easy to understand why the word *textus* received its elaboration in the Christian world—indeed, under this aspect, in the Judeo-Christian world as a whole. For here it was thought that the tables of the Law had been "written with the finger of God" (*Exodus*, 31, 18), and that it was God himself who had made the act of writing sacred (Rabanus Maurus, *Carmina*, XXI; *Ad Eigilium de libro quem scripsit*, v. 11), God being the "dictator" under whom holy men wrote (Alcuin, *Carmina*, LXVI, v. 4 and LXIX, v. 15). Christianity spoke, too, of a book wherein the damnation or salvation of each and every man was contained in writing (For the whole question, see Curtius 1948, ed. 1961, chap. 16).

A text is, then, the linguistic texture of a discourse. In the meaning most current down to this century, what is meant is written discourse (for its voiced realization can no longer be called text). When one refers to the text of a work, it is the linguistic texture of the discourse that constitutes it which is being referred to; if, on the other hand, one alludes to content, work and text are practically synonymous.

This linguistic material is realized in written texts by means of signs. These signs are successions of letters and accents, and they constitute the words, successions of words, and the punctuation marks which, in parallel lines or in lines of poetry, make up the discourse as a whole. Its nature as sign is the precondition of its repeatability: the text can be transcribed many times over with different writing materials and different scripts without ceasing to be that particular text. Indeed, the concepts of archetype and original induce us to see in every written realization a more or less veiled reflection of a text whose consistency is purely mental. We shall have further occasion to speak of this; it is worth stressing from the outset, though, that the nature of the text is conditioned by the modes of its production and reproduction, that, indeed, the text is not a physical reality at all but a concept-limit.

From the Middle Ages, the concept of text has oscillated between the sign level (what is there, written in a given work) and the level of its material effectuation. Thus, *textus* has come to stand for the codex as well, the manuscript wherein the text has been transcribed, or even for the script (*textus quadratus, semiquadratus,* etc.; text on parchment, paper; manuscript or printed text). This oscillation was kept alive by both humanistic and by modern philology: both refer to the exemplars of a work as its *texts* (see, for this whole section, Rizzo 1973, pp. 9–11).

The various uses of the word *text* can be referred to the signifier/signified antinomy. We shall take into account the fact that the signifier may be considered in its sign function (which can be repeated) or in the material character of each of its transcriptions (which are not susceptible of repetition), while meaning may be literal (linguistic) or total (semiotic).

2. With one of his bold terminological innovations, Hjelmslev replaced Saussure's opposition of *langue* to *parole* with another, an opposition of system (or the language) to process (or the text). The language cannot be individuated and defined other than by starting out from processes, i.e., from texts. "The existence of a system is a necessary premise for the existence of a process: the process comes into existence by virtue of the system's being present behind it, a system which governs and determines it in its possible development" (1943, p. 39). To put it succinctly, "The objects of interest to linguistic theory are texts" (p. 16). There is no need to insist on the drawbacks of a terminology which alludes to all discourses with a denomination previously reserved exclusively for written discourses (for these latter will now require specifying attributes). There are advantages, though, in this use of the word *text*, for it draws attention to the substantial constitutional identity of discourses in relation to the linguistic system they objectify.

This identity will be found wanting, however, once the conditions and the agents of communication are taken into consideration. Oral discourse is pronounced in a common context, evident for the most part to both addresser and addressee. It is a discourse which makes sense only in its context, and to elements of this context it can refer in implicit form or by means of deictics. And this is not all. Such discourse is interwoven with its context. Though its effects may persist once the context has changed, only with difficulty can it be repeated just as it is.

It would be ingenuous to affirm that writing, the invention of a recent historical phase of mankind, allows discourses to be reproduced and fixed. Indeed, discourses themselves, when they no longer limited themselves to their immediate pragmatic contexts, created a need for their transcription. Whether it was recording a pact between contracting parties or with a divine agent, invocation of supernatural forces, archives for posterity, or celebrating events which were to outlast chronicles, writing was regarded as something sacred (hieroglyph means sacred writing) because it expressed an impulse toward eternity. Indeed, many of the characteristics of written texts depend upon their situation in time:

(a) The addresser may have a privileged addressee, but he is well aware that his text may be, or even will be, read by others as well. In the case of literary texts, the number of future readers is not unrelated to their value. The temporal project may involve various degrees of measurement: it will be limited for a human contract (which may subsequently be read, though with different intentions, by the legal historian or the student of language) but will be virtually infinite in the case of a divine covenant (for the faithful, that the gods should die is out of the question).

(b) With a few exceptions, like that of letters, a written text does not become part of a feedback mechanism; it is already formulated in view of what we might call this absoluteness. If it formulates questions or requests, they will be too weighty to be answered lightly, and, except for the privileged addressee, no person will be authorized to do so. Indeed, the addresser waits for no reply. Consequently, what is achieved is a diversification of the addresser's status, for "he confines himself to the meaning space traced out and inscribed by the writing: the text itself is the place wherein the author 'takes place' (Ricoeur 1970, p. 185).

(c) The written text can, in whole or in part, be read over and over again. The itinerary to be followed, and the time to take, are left to the discretion of the reader (the real or occasional addressee): a reading can be effected in silence or aloud, and, when it is aloud, it may take place in private or in public. The text's every detail may and must be dwelt upon, unlike an oral discourse. The written text might be held to be more accurate. It is less redundant and has fewer phatic elements, but what is most important is awareness of its different conformation in relation to its different reception.

(d) The written text is destined to be received in quite different contexts. As a result, it must embrace references to the context of its emission, when they are necessary, or, vice versa, it must organize an autonomy of its own which will limit contextual references. In any event, it must be enabled to pass through the most varied contexts without damage to its cohesion. Use of deictics, of moods, of tenses will be conditioned by an awareness, on the addresser's part, of this extracontextuality. Though brought to birth at a moment in time, the text will continue to introduce itself into the development of time.

The different position of the addresser with respect to his addressees and of the addressees with respect to the message, the different scope of the textual message, variation in the relation of text to context—all of these might well form the basis for a typology of texts. Genres, too, constitute a typology of texts, one, though, that is, in general, limited by the fairly uniform modes of literary communication. A typology of texts, indeed, might be able to assess the quantity of pragmatic involvement and the reciprocal proportions of the functions (referential, expressive, conative, poetic, phatic, metalinguistic). Such discourse is akin to that of Jakobson. His discourse, though, turns it upside down, for it starts not from the functions but from the message itself, indeed from its communication program. The use of functions conforms to a scale which is related to the type and scope of the message.

Whereas, for oral discourse, any realization will be no more than *una tantum*, repetition being impossible when an identical context is unthinkable, any realization in written discourse, in the text, will remain indefinitely, as Bachtin says, a "givenness," something given. Realization of the text is thus in a state of continual potentiality. The text will continue to exist as written material, rows of writing back and forth, inert until read. The text will begin to mean something, will begin to communicate, only when a reader intervenes. Its meaningfulness is retained meaningfulness. Its intersubjectivity is a long-distance matter. On each occasion, a subjectivity will exist ready to assume the message or, in its turn, to communicate it to other subjectivities. It is in this way that the material nature of the text, thanks to the "meaninglessness" which precedes and follows any reading of it, acts as its greatest safeguard against subjective distortions which might otherwise move away out of both sight and mind. The care taken to guarantee the text's conservation, or to recover its diction when time has defaced it, is really an attempt at defense against the encroachment of the subjective. The alternative is uncompromising: objectivity is possible only in the absence of any reading at all and, hence, of any meaningfulness. Every reading will involve some measure of subjectivity. It is only within the limits of such subjectivity that it is possible to set, as one's objective, a maximum degree of faithfulness in interpretation, and this will be dependent on one's mastery of the codes the text employs. The repeated readings to which a text lends itself make it possible to confront (though not to eliminate) errors and distortions.

3. The new conception of text advocated by Hjemslev, together with the way Bloomfield, Harris, and others have drawn attention to "structures beyond the sentence," has represented one of the authorities upon which text linguistic theory has been based. It would, in fact, seem evident (and proof is today being provided) that well-defined links must exist so that the sentences of a text can be linked together, and not be simply semantic. On this point, traditional syntax says not a word. But it is easy to verify not only that a random series of sentences does not constitute a text but even that a series of sentences linked on the level of content do not make sense (and do not make a text) if they are not formulated in the way required by what might be termed textual competence.

The trend which is coming to the fore in text linguistics, rightly so I believe, aims to investigate, together with the text, the pragmatic context within which it was produced. The need is evident, particularly when oral texts are in question, since in oral texts there can be no doubt whatever that codes (verbal, gestual, etc.) are mixed and that objects and real situations are here interwoven with their representation in words (think of deictics). There is also evidence of implications, which for texts of any other type would need at least to be suggested. In written texts, the pragmatic context is present in more subtle fashion, for, while a legal text, a business contract, etc., will start with a clear-cut initial situation, and set themselves an immediate perlocutive goal, the literary text may reflect, from the reality which surrounds the addresser, conditionings rather than data (for it envisages a much wider reality as well). And, as a rule, the illocutionary scale in which it will operate can neither be defined nor foreseen. I would suggest, therefore, that definition of text types should be made to depend upon the types of relations which exist for texts and contexts.

What constitutes a text? (Cf. Petöfi, 1979, 1981). When faced with this question, our reply, in light of what has been said so far, should not be a definition ("the text is constituted of . . ."); it should rather be a progressive series of restrictions on a more general definition of utterance. Account must be taken (a) of the type of pragmatic context within which a given type of text is produced; (b) of the type of illocutionary function that the text may perform in its specific context, irrespective of whether it was intended that it should perform it or not; (c) of the modalities of the text's communication (improvisation and nonimprovisation, with or without recourse to nonverbal codes and to direct actions, as monologue or as dialogue, oral or written, etc.); (d) of the existence of specific norms for the constitution of texts (norms which are especially strict for written texts); and (e) of its measure of repeatability. Only in terms of such a scale will it prove possible to formulate cohesion rules with any degree of success, whether their character is to be grammatical or thematic. This, quite simply, is because such rules will vary in accord with different types of text.

It is possible to affirm the individuality of a text when, on any one of its levels, it lends itself to unified paraphrase. In effect, and taking as exemplification the two opposite extremes, paraphrase either allows us to integrate contextual elements and implied connections of a fragmentary text, and thus to integrate the context into the text, or it will allow us to eliminate redundancies and fringe elements and thus bring to light the text's thematically unitary line. The verification here envisaged is semiotic in character, not linguistic. Summary paraphrase and integrating paraphrase formulate, in the form of language utterances, the "content" of a text, but this is no more than the translation of a semiotic substance. If ever these paraphrases were to be accepted in their linguistic aspect, we would merely be putting another text in place of the earlier one.

Arriving at the unity of a text by means of paraphrase is inevitably an interpretive operation. If a text is considered in its immediate aspect—as a succession of utterances which are elusive (given the constant use of ellipsis), ambiguous (hence, a constant need for clarification), and dispersive (its itineraries are not logically linear)—then what an integrating paraphrase will do will be to reconstruct the elements which are taken as understood. It will render univocal what was put forward as polyvalent, and it will reconstruct the succession and the consequentiality—thus the temporal and logical regularity—of the content of the utterance.

An integrating paraphrase cannot avoid including the system of the motivations. Motivations are often not expressed, because they are in some sense present in the pragmatic context, implied in the text itself, or suggested by intertextual relations. Such an extension will not distort the character of the text's deep structure, which certainly does not inherit from the text its (seeming) inadequacies and inconsistencies; it will, however, confirm the heterogeneous nature of such a structure with respect to the surface of the text. As for summary paraphrase, it is not enough to say that it is the synthesis of an integrating paraphrase. What a summary paraphrase does specifically is to seize upon the essential elements of content, those which cannot be ignored, together with their precise links. Its interpretive character is thus quite beyond discussion. Indeed, it might be added that essentiality corresponds to pertinence in a given pragmatic situation. It implies that one's grasp of context is well founded and that it is all-embracing. In this way, paraphrases will, in their turn, bring us back yet again to the axiom of the complementary character of text and of context.

Interpretive paraphrase and summary paraphrase are of necessity approximate terms. It is a fact, though, that our way of understanding, and even more of reformulating, the content of a text consists in drawing upon its semiotic constitution and at once "translating" it into words. The infinite number of possible paraphrases, the formulations which have been attempted, always pass through this semiotic stage, and they emerge from it in the form of verbal expressions. One text is defined with the help of another text, in a process which knows no end.

Perhaps the concept of text structure requires more careful consideration. It may be accepted that the structure is the sum of the immanent relations among all the semantic elements of the text. Any effort to define this structure imposes choices: it is a matter of individuating, from among all of the relations, those which are the most meaningful and, if possible, the laws which sustain them. It is within the area of these choices that "measures" will be fixed, preference being accorded in terms of exigency to simple or multiple, to concision or detail. A typical example is analysis of the tale, which chooses as privileged relations those which belong to the sphere of action and then decides case by case whether to remain at the level of explicit actions or to move to the more abstract level of the nature of the actions as they relate to the development of the plot.

It might prove illuminating to consider the various possible representations of the "content" of a text along a line which moves from a maximum of abstraction to a maximum of detail and articulation. Deep structure and surface structure are the terms used, and these would be innocent enough if this generative terminology did not suggest a type of statute which is certainly not that of our semiotic structures.

First and foremost, any genetic vision of this bundle of structures must be rejected. Our so-called deep structure (a) does not coincide with the project for the text which the person who produced it had in his mind; his project in fact was continually brought into line with the external, but also internal, shifting situation (with other motivations intervening); (b) it cannot be shown to be identical with the system of forces by which the addresser was conditioned or which he wished to explicate.

Even more decisively must we reject any idea that the text is the end result of a series of transformations from a deep structure (which is not preexistent) to surface structures and finally to realized discourse. It is not possible to speak of laws for a unique, unrepeatable event, such as the constituent operations of that particular text in that particular context at that particular moment. (Naturally enough, a great many codes and rules come into play, but they do not extend their action to include processes which precede the utterance.)

It is important to realize that structures individuated at different levels in the text exist only from the moment at which the text exists: they find their support in the totality of the text's immanent structure. If we free ourselves from temporal and genetic idola, it will become evident that a regressive procedure (from the text to its deep structures) is no less productive heuristically than a progressive procedure (from the deep structures to the text). What is important is that, as these structurings are individuated and classified, we should be able to grasp the connections between the text's semiotic structures and their manifestation.

If we turn now to those scholars who have attempted to define the grammatical rules of the text (anaphora, pronominalization, renominalization, etc.), we will have the impression that such rules involve only some elements of sentences: those which effect the welding together of sentences as text. On the other hand, scholars who have most strongly stressed the content and thematic plane (topic/comment, presuppositions, implications, etc.) embrace a wider portion of content substance but do not include grammatical articulations. I would maintain that it is constitutionally impossible for these two types of analysis to arrive at full integration. Fictitious examples apart, any sentence belongs to a text or constitutes a text. Hence, its elaboration has already taken place, and account has already been taken of content relations, of grammatical rules, and of the "rules of connection."

If we simplify a little, we might say that those who study texts either adopt a horizontal perspective (which links together elements of the text's surface) or a vertical one (which links the text's surface to its supposed deep structure). The incompatibility of these two points of view can be circumvented only if due consideration is given to the processes by which the text is produced.

The text is an utterance. It is the result of a series of connections, of content and of grammar, which do not achieve their final state in the order in which we find it useful to distinguish them a posteriori (content form and content substance, expression form and expression substance) but which are, thanks to a progressive series of refocusings, at once a matter of content and a matter of grammar. The two perspectives—"from the utterance to the text," "from the text to the utterance"—thus constitute two possible orders of investigation, but they do not correspond in the least to the utterance act process, when utterances are elaborated simultaneously with their text. The individuation of textual rules comes down to grasping traces of the utterance act within the utterance.

Of course, it is utterances we find ourselves having to deal with, not utterance acts. The connections that can be established (a) between a sentence and the grammar of a given language and (b) between one sentence and the others of the text to which it belongs fall within two perspectives, and they are as antinomical as are diachrony and synchrony. The moment I set a sentence against the paradigm to which it may be referred, I detextualize it; the moment

I compare it with others of the same text, I am accepting not only its grammatical structure but its semantic values and the implications which indissolubly link it to all of the other sentences of the text.

And this is not all. When a sentence is analyzed, due weight must be given to implied semantic valences, though this must be done within the range of values which the *langue* confers on them. On the contrary, an ordinary text (a nonliterary text) constitutes a single block with its pragmatic situation, given that the text is immersed in the pragmatic situation, conditioning and being conditioned. Thus, while grammar indicates norms or, at the outside, possible uses, any future text grammar will have to see use of the language as inseparable from the pragmatic situation.

When a text is examined, the alternatives to be taken into consideration for each sentence are not all possible alternatives but only those which are possible for that particular text. This is why textual rules appear primarily as lists of compatibilities and incompatibilities with respect to elements of successive sentences (here one may, or must, use a noun, here a pronoun; here the indefinite article must be used, here the definite, etc.).

It is along these lines, however, that research may most profitably be carried forward. The most ambitious program that can be formulated is perhaps this: given the sentences a, b, c, d, etc., show which forms are permissible for a sentence n to express content x. Any findings will be complicated by the fact that sentence n will be further conditioned by the form, and by the content, of sentence $n+1$ which will follow it, and so on. There is a constant play back and forth, from one utterance act to another, even though the progressive analysis just proposed will allow simulation of utterance processes.

What must be underlined is the one-to-one link between linguistic competence and textual competence: the latter can be realized only by means of the former; the former by itself does not allow sentences to be linked together as utterances. Text linguistics should study the combination of these two competences. Until now, it has, perhaps rightly, judged it more opportune to consider the one in terms of the perspective provided by the other. If the perspective was that of the sentence, it has attempted to individuate rules which might eventually govern the linking together of the sentences that establish the text; if the perspective was that of the text, it has attempted to grasp the trans-sentential connections which override the limits of sentences, considered as data.

More thorough, and it has already been attempted, is a representation of all of the elements in play, both linguistic and pragmatic. The end result would provide a model of the production of communication units. It would be a model of discourse situations. If this model also managed to represent the presence, absence, and quantity of the elements in play, it would further function as a model of utterance types. It would, of course, tell us nothing about single utterances, because for these only a posteriori explanations can be formulated. It is not possible, in fact, to make forecasts until the utterance process is under way; before that, the possibilities for ordering and for formulation are infinite.

The only mediation between words and types is that of genres and of *écritures*. But here we are touching upon a phenomenology which takes on consistency only in the case of literary texts or of texts that are in some way conventional (legal texts, etc.).

4. One of the fundamental tasks which philology sets itself is care of texts. Whenever a text was particularly venerable for intrinsic or extrinsic reasons, the effort to defend its genuineness has been made with fuller awareness. One will recall the Alexandrians faced with the Homeric poems or the Protestant biblical scholars of the eighteenth century. And it would be worth reviewing the history of text editing in relation to different concepts of truth and, hence, of the authority to be attributed to the texts themselves. Here this is impossible. It is, however, indispensable to note that textual criticism has been applied mainly to manuscript texts. This holds good even after the fifteenth century, for most of the texts that were held in the highest veneration went back to periods which predated the invention of printing. This has produced a certain bias in research, because the phenomenology of printed texts, in part different from that of manuscripts, has not been in any sense so systematically investigated. It might be noted that the possibilities for the corruption of an original are, in printing, concentrated at the moment the type is set. Misreadings, apart, interventions may also be made in the interests of linguistic coherence, and, at times, we find veritable rewriting at the hands of editors and editorial staff, to say nothing of political and religious censorship. On the other hand, printing guarantees uniformity in the copies, and they may run to hundreds or even thousands—whence a psychological presumption of genuineness. This, too, is the reason why reprints and reeditions (legitimate or not) usually leave the text intact, except for misprints. We should also bear in mind that printing, given its rapidity of execution and diffusion, allows the author to effect corrections while the edition of the text is still going forward; it may even allow him to undertake further, improved or changed, editions. Both possibilities are presented by the *Orlando furioso*, by Vasari's *Vite*, and by the *Promessi sposi*. And though the second possibility poses no problems, the first leaves us with ever-differing exemplars of a single edition, when for each "signature" various "types" will exist, the result of interventions while the impression was under way. The desirability of broadening textual criticism to include the tradition of printed texts, and to go beyond reconstruction of the originals, led Russian philologists to introduce the term *textology*—which was attributed to Tomashevsky but was already current in 1927 and which has also been accepted in France (Laufer 1972). It can be applied not just to textual criticism but to the study of the life of the text throughout the whole of its history.

The first expedients adopted by textual criticism (collation and conjecture) already indicate the two main avenues of possible research: the one is documentary and centrifugal; the other interpretive and centripetal. Hence, it has often seemed that, in philology, hard work and intuition, the systematic and the genial, stood opposed. The terms of the dilemma will change, though, when one takes into account the fact that an aptitude for conjecture—and even for uncovering corruption in a text—can only be developed thanks to experience of texts and thus to systematic work (of assimilation of language). A difference does, however, exist between comparison of diversified witnesses (which, through contrast, highlights genuine readings and bad readings) and an internal analysis of the text, of the laws of its stylistic and linguistic coherence.

This difference finds its verification historically. Conjectural activity has remained substantially unaltered over the course of time (with qualitative differences which relate exclusively to the culture and combinatorial felicity of operators), whereas study of the manuscript tradition has been conditioned by potentialities and constraints which can be represented as development. Thus, the search for the exemplars of a single work was, at the outset, an undertaking both adventurous and pioneering, the work of isolated enthusiasts, and it was not without considerable economic implications given the commercial value of codexes (copies were often made of them, always in manuscript). Later, when the majority of manuscripts had been brought together in public libraries, for the most part furnished with catalogues, it became fairly easy to dominate the whole tradition of a text, and in more recent times microfilms have offered faithful copies (even though, from a codical point of view, they are not exhaustive). These can be consulted and collated at leisure.

5. It is, then, above all in *recensio* (analysis of the tradition of a text and interpretation of the relations of codexes) that the greatest methodological transformations have been effected. At first, the simplest solution seemed to be that of the *codex optimus*. As one's basic text, one took the codex which, because of its age or the excellence of its readings, seemed to be the most trustworthy and then intervened if necessary by collation or conjecture at doubtful points. Later (and here the first printed books play some part), the *textus receptus* became usual. In other words, one accepted that phase of elaboration (itself the outcome of initial choices and successive interventions) which was authenticated by cultural or, in the case of sacred texts, by religious authorities. This *vulgata* of a text established a status quo, and it was unwise, or even outright dangerous, to throw doubt on it, in an attempt perhaps to illustrate its genesis.

Modern textual criticism originates in another method, that of *codices plurimi:* the readings which are supported by the greatest number of manuscripts are regarded as genuine. Such a method, though, gave no weight to any reconstruction of the genetic relations of the manuscripts, and it ran the risk of giving its approval to the evidence of groups, albeit large groups, of manuscripts which, since they derive from a single intermediary, do no more than multiply the witness of one.

Although its techniques had been applied and illustrated singly by earlier philologists, the method which goes under the name of Lachmann, its chief advocate, is founded upon reconstruction of a text's lines of development (the starting point being the original) and upon a logical probabilistic reconstruction of readings. It is a reconstruction which is based not on any mere majority of manuscripts but on how representative they are with respect to the whole.

Assume, for example, that manuscripts A, B, C, D, and E of a text can be traced back to an original in a way illustrated by the following figure.

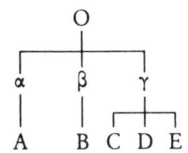

```
          O
    ┌─────┼─────┐
    α     β     γ
    │     │    ┌┴┐
    A     B   C D E
```

It is clear that the testimony of C, D, and E is no more valid than is that of A and B. Indeed, it is of less weight, since A and B are two independent witnesses, while C, D, and E represent one single witness, γ.

The two main stages of *recensio* are, for Lachmann's method, individuation of a genealogical tree, or *stemma*, and choice of genuine readings *(emendatio)* on the basis of the stemma itself. Logical and probabilistic considerations underpin both these operations. In the first (individuation of the stemma), the starting point is the principle that it is improbable that two or more codices should have made the same (not banal) mistakes in the same places. If, therefore, two or more codices show a series of significant errors in common, they must necessarily be linked genetically (though they may be contaminated, a not infrequent occurrence which we need not go into here).

The graphic repesentation which follows is based on this situation: A and B show a series of significant errors in common as against the correct readings of C, D, and E; C, D, and E present a series of significant errors in common as against the correct readings of A and B; D and E present a series of significant errors in common as against the correct readings of A, B, and C. (Here, no account is taken of *codices descripti*, those which have been copied from another manuscript which still survives, for it is obvious that their testimony is worthless).

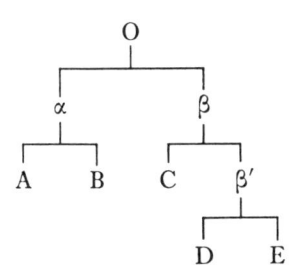

```
              O
         ┌────┴────┐
         α         β
       ┌─┴─┐     ┌─┴─┐
       A   B     C   β'
                    ┌┴┐
                    D E
```

In the second operation, *emendatio*, one starts from the principle that it is improbable that codices belonging to different groups should change their readings in the same way (unless such change is banal). The following figure illustrates this stemma.

```
        O
    ┌───┼───┐
    A   B   C
```

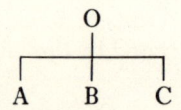

Thus, in the stemma, if a reading a is encountered in A and B and a reading b in C, the genuine reading will probably be a, since it is unlikely that manuscripts A and B could have changed an original reading b in exactly the same way: b, then, is the innovation. A similar argument is used when A and C agree against B, or B and C against A. The criterion is an almost mechanical one, and it is easy enough to apply it in cases when the branches of a stemma are three or more.

If the branches are two, the results the method can give are quantitatively reduced. Here is a straightforward case:

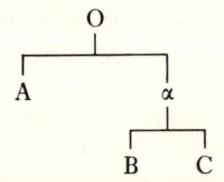

```
        O
    ┌───┴───┐
    A       α
         ┌──┴──┐
         B     C
```

A reading (not a banal one) common to A and B is to be considered genuine, since it is unlikely that A and B could have changed the text in the same way and at the same point; the change has been made by C. Analogously, agreement between A and C will indicate a genuine reading as against B's innovation. When, though, B and C agree against A, no logical criteria exist which would lead one to prefer the reading of B and C (for they represent an interposed α) to that of A, or vice versa. If the rival readings are equipollent, choice of one or the other of them can be no more than conventional.

Stemmata with three or more branches provide a mechanism for the choice of genuine readings. With two-branched stemmata, the mechanism will work only when there is agreement of part of the codices of one branch with the other branch. Unfortunately, the vast majority of stemmata have two branches. Joseph Bédier (1928) used this observation (together with a whole series of considerations regarding Lachmann's methods) to reinforce his almost total skepticism concerning the techniques of textual criticism and to launch anew the criterion of the *codex optimus*. He believed that the outcome of any *recensio* would almost always be a two-branched stemma, because the philologist unconsciously tended to rid himself of any mechanism which would limit his freedom of choice in the face of readings. There have been various replies to Bédier—historical, statistical, and technical. And it is now accepted with less marked amazement that twin-branched trees dominate the garden of critical editions.

6. Deductions as to the reliability of texts reconstructed critically are what interest us here. On the one hand, it can be affirmed that the philologist's work

of restoration eliminates a whole series of disfigurements introduced into the text by its scribes (and it should be noted that, between the original and the copies of it that have come down to us, many intermediate transcriptions, as a rule, exist, and each has errors of its own). On the other hand, it can be affirmed that such restoration has its limits, that no critical edition—however rigorous—can ever equal an original. The tradition does indeed link us to the text, but barriers exist which we may circumvent but cannot eliminate. These barriers are diasystems (Segre 1979, p. 58).

A text is a linguistic structure which realizes a system. Each scribe has a linguistic system of his own, and this comes into contact with that of his text in the course of transcription. If he is very careful indeed, the scribe will endeavor to leave the system of his text intact, but it is impossible for the scribe's own system not to impose itself to some extent. This happens because the systems in competition are historical participations, and it is as impossible to silence one's own system as it is to cancel one's own historicity. At best, the reverence felt for texts of considerable religious, legal, and literary prestige will increase scrupulousness. There do, though, exist texts which seem, in order to sustain their continued relevance, to invite transfusion from systems in force. The unfaithfulness of their scribes is the price texts pay for their survival: a text can continue to live only by being deformed.

Compromise between the system of the text and that of the scribe results in a diasystem. *Emendatio* is a kind of dialysis which separates elements of mediation systems from the basic system. And the possibility of a confrontation between diasystems should not be excluded, even when the diasystems in competition are reduced to two. What is important, though, is that those who will make use of a critical edition should be aware that it is an approximation, as close an approximation as is possible, to a structure whose system has been contaminated with other systems. It is an approximation in part realized in textual restorations, though in part it will remain potential, as a series of suggestions on the part of the editor when the original aspect of the text can only be a matter for hypothesis.

Bédier's positivistic solution (which accords credit to one particular manuscript, preferring its undeniably concrete character as product to the abstraction of any reconstructed text) is an attempt to conceal the ineluctably problematical character of the text, which, as it is handed on in a successive series of transcriptions (and interpretations), is rewritten mentally and interpreted anew by each and every reader. The reader, too, as he takes possession of a text, is unaware that he is setting up yet another diasystem. In the individuation of earlier diasystems, we move within a triangle with the text at one apex, now remote, and it is only when we move toward the side which joins the other two apexes (the sum of prior transcriptions, contemporary reading) that we will find ourselves in a position to glimpse more clearly some semblance of the text (Segre 1979, chap. 5).

Even if the modern concept of diasystem is ignored, it must be admitted that twentieth-century philology—the examples of Pasquali (1934) and of Lichačev

(1962) will suffice—has shown itself well able to appreciate textual transmission with all of its historical implications. What seem, in relation to the original text, to be deformations and corruptions are really fundamental documents of the life of the text and of the life of culture through time. Deformations and corruptions derive from reading perspectives opened up by different contexts. If they are, in part, the result of mechanical accident, more often they are the inevitable condition of assimilation and reactivation. For the same reason, the "bad" readings, which editors banish to the apparatus, enjoy a dignified status of their own in the history of the language (Corti 1960; Nencioni 1960).

7. There is no point in drawing up here all the obstacles which lie between us and any, even literal, contact with the text. Awareness of these obstacles does, though, help us understand what, at first sight, is a seemingly simple concept, the text. Even those who have theorized textual reconstruction have taken its limitations into account. They tell us that what they wish to do is "to produce a text as close as possible to the original" (Maas 1927, Eng. trans., p. 1), to "restore the texts as closely as possible to the form they originally had" (Reynolds and Wilson 1968, p. 281). Indeed, Avalle, after listing the objective limits of any reconstruction, concludes that "the critical edition is the result of this operation, and, as such, it must be understood as an extreme homage to a hidden truth, to an autograph which has disappeared" (1972, p. 20). Almost more important for any edition is that its reader must be alerted to the process of textual criticism in all of its phases: the editor "will put forward his own reconstruction in such a way that the reader can check what he has done" (Pasquali 1932, p. 477). "The business of textual criticism is in a sense to reverse this process [that of the work's diffusion], to follow back the threads of transmission" (Reynolds and Wilson 1968, p. 186).

More confident philologists speak of reconstructing the original. In reality, it is not so much the original one reaches as the archetype—the copy, already partially defective, from which as a rule the whole tribe of the transcriptions will have descended. In the routine of textual criticism, this name is given to the lost exemplar which offered the text in the form in which we reconstruct it on the basis of our *recensio* and which already contained a series of errors, at times even lacunae, and in certain cases gave alternative variants. The concept is undoubtedly an aleatory one, for it may designate, for Greek and Latin classics, a copy made directly from the original or a medieval intermediary, and it presupposes the technique of diffusion in manuscript. (The original, probable corrections apart, will have been composed with writing materials of inferior quality, and from it a professional scribe will have made a clean copy, thereafter employed for all further transcriptions). It may also presuppose the history of text transmission. (When marked changes in script occur, a copy of an ancient exemplar will have been made adopting the new way of writing.)

The concept of archetype renders concrete the necessity of mediation. The text has been able to survive only because it has been handed down. It is no accident that the whole concept of archetype is challenged not only because of the arguments which sustain it but also because the presence of errors is not its prerogative. Even autographs which by some happy chance have been preserved contain numerous errors. The author himself, when he makes a final draft of his own text, is no more than a scribe (though admittedly he will have the advantage of his own peculiar characteristics, and there will be no question of diasystemic combinations). All the same, he may well leave things out, substitute things unconsciously, fall victim to mental associations, trivialize, run into *quid pro quo*. During transcription a "mental dictation" exists, and it sets a distance between reading and writing. It is a space for silent articulation and verbalization, where the most astonishing errors can come into their own. It is this space which shuts us irreparably off from the text.

Or rather the nature of the text is not material: it exists before its writing (still untouched by the damage which this will produce) and after its writing (if it is possible to eliminate ideally the damage itself). This fact is well known to editors when they work on autographs, though they may not fully realize its implications, for they take it upon themselves to intervene, and rightly so, with regard to graphic peculiarities, introducing coherence and clarity should these be lacking. The text is, therefore, only an image: a virtual one if it is located at the end of stemmatic reconstruction; a real one if it results from a reading of its simulacrum, the autograph. It is always an image—an image of discourse. This discourse is the algorithm of a linguistic utterance act, but it can be seized upon only as an utterance, subject as such to the interference factors referred to above. There are two possible ways of working: to purify the utterance as far as possible or to take into account the rules of the algorithm. The two resulting images, virtual and real, can be brought to a maximum of correspondence, but they cannot be superimposed, given their heteronomy.

Avalle writes as follows: "The concept of original, in the sense of an authentic text which expresses the intention of the author, is one of the most elusive and ambiguous concepts in textual criticism. This explains . . . why a critical text often presents so problematic an aspect and is in some cases frankly random. What is more, not even autographs are immune from this condition, especially those which give the author's variants . . . every time an attempt is made to fix them in a form less temporary than that in which they have been transmitted by the author's copy. One is left with the impression that the original, in the sense in which we generally understand it, in other words as a text perfect in its every part, has never existed" (1972, p. 33).

Avalle is thinking particularly of cases for which the existence of variants multiples the images of the text. When, for example, a writer like Ariosto, Vasari, or Manzoni goes on intervening in his text even in the course of its printing (similar cases are known in the manuscript tradition: Cicero, among others)—even if we do manage to determine in every case, and to accept, his final intention—the text will still not be homogeneous, because the parts reproduced last constitute a "recentior" phase.

As for originals, we may possess more than one of them (Petrarch, for example, always prepared two exemplars of his letters; one to be sent, the *transmissiva;* the other to be kept, the *transcriptio in ordine*). Or a text may have been put together from separate parts (and perhaps retouched directly), as is the case for many theater texts, published, even during their author's lifetime, from papers which gave the lines for the single actors (or, more conveniently, from the prompter's copy).

We are not interested here in the repercussions of cases of this kind on the manuscript tradition (it is clear that copies from two or more autographs—with corrections which are at times concomitant, at times divergent—might well have been subsequently collated and contaminated, thereby multiplying the number of possible combinations). What is more important is that to the one attribute of nonmateriality we must add another—pulsations within time.

Take the case of an autograph which is full of corrections (there are many of them in existence, from Ariosto to Leopardi to Eliot). It constitutes a copresence of structures—separable, discernible, when copies have been made from the autograph during its successive phases of elaboration (but discernible, too, with graphic, or indeed structural, criteria). In a case of this kind, the text is not constituted from the materiality of the autograph but from a series of textual images which the autograph contemporaneously entertains. Of these texts, the modern consumer will usually, but not always, adopt the most recent. But, if the motivations for the passage from phase 1 to phase 2, from phase 2 to phase 3, are evident, and they usually are, we cannot be forbidden to contemplate a phase n, when the logic of the corrections should achieve its fullest realization. (The most straightforward case is that of corrections at the level of language, not fully carried through). Such an example is naturally theoretical, but it does serve to show how a text can be looked at from a temporal standpoint, along the line of its "drives."

Possible case histories for originals know virtually no limits. After the introduction of printing, any edition supervised by the author has been held to be the equivalent of an original, but it may still contain not just errors but editorial interference at the language level. In this case the image of the text is to be found in the space between autograph and print, for each of them contains errors and distortions that cancel each other out (when the printing has remedied defects in the autograph and when the autograph, with its correct readings, unmasks misprints). But they may also repeat and reinforce one another. And the writer may even have "authorized" adjustments, e.g., to the language, though he may not have effected them personally, or have "accepted" replacements suggested by censorship, by the Inquisition, etc. These are the "compulsory authorial corrections" dealt with by Firpo (1960). The situation is not made any simpler when the autographs are more than one in number, because the author often transcribes even earlier errors of his own, inopportunely endorsing them, or he may make inappropriate corrections, etc.

The fact remains that an autograph which represents the definitive intention of the writer constitutes a medium from which the text in its abstraction may not unreasonably be deduced. The scribe's system is, in fact, the same as that of the writer, and no compromise formations are produced. In the absence of the autograph, the media are diasystemic transcriptions, and the virtual image of the text will, to a greater or lesser degree, be evidently out of focus. There exists an additional phase difference in the images when transcriptions hide the traces of a plurality of transcriptions. A model for the transcription and the comprehension of a text, even should we wish to simplify it to the utmost, might be represented as follows (Segre 1979, p. 65): "Image of text 1 → draft /of the autograph/ → apperception of partial (word for word) meanings and of total meanings (syntagms) → comprehension → transmission of the same meanings → transcription by means of graphic signifiers → copy → apperception, etc. → comprehension → image of text 2." The image of text 1, that transcribed by the author (leaving aside phases of elaboration), only in part tallies with the image of text 2, that of the reader of the copy, because in each of the intermediate phases distortion phenomena may appear. The images of the texts 2, 3, 4, and n are virtual images. What can only be glimpsed, even in the presence of draft variants, is the dynamics which existed between the text as it was mentally elaborated by the writer and its graphic realization, because often the image is perfected by the very act of its writing. Writing takes the place of the text. Philology is an undertaking which aims to ensure that the image of text 2 (when lack of focus and doubling of images have been reduced to a minimum) will not so much coincide with the unattainable image of text 1 as replace it convincingly, as an image of the text or as text *tout court*. Any responsibility for texts once they have been produced is entirely our own.

We might stop for a moment and consider the image of text 1. Not even in its author's mind is the text present in its entirety, but rather in a synthesis, which only in part involves its verbal texture (when this is so vast as not to be easily memorized). Thus, we might define the image of text 1 as the succession of content-form units which the author has progressively, and sometimes at different stages, put into words, perhaps bringing them to perfection as he retouched his draft. Our image of text 1 is a theoretical construction as well. And it would be fascinating to map out the phases of the elaboration of this image.

It can be done, but only imperfectly. For many works we possess sketches and first drafts. Sketches are first attempts to put order into the material; they do not show a really serious, or at least determinant, engagement in terms of form. Instead, with early drafts, the material is already "formed," and it is possible to evaluate the poetic or narrative systems brought into being and to compare them with those of the definitive texts. All the intermediate stages, because they are not confined to the page, escape us. The overall complex of drafts, manuscripts, variants, and proofs can be viewed as a unity and called the avant-texte (Bellemin-Noël 1972), though it should always be borne in mind that (1) many phases remain at a merely mental stage and (2) elaboration is hardly ever coherent and linear but is almost always a network of retracings, of developments abandoned, of abrupt deviations. The definitive text does not represent the outcome of an unyieldingly rigorous initial program, even though it may prove profitable to settle upon such and see it as the conclusion of an inventive activity, using it as a touchstone.

Sketches and rough drafts may nonetheless be grouped together and related, though in a subordinate position, to the definitive text, but only if one confers on the latter the prestigious status of a work which, in literary terms at least, is exemplary and which commands respect and veneration. Otherwise, each version is a text in its own right, with internal, autonomous semantic relations of its own. The various texts which make up the avant-text are stratified as synchronic cross-sections of a diachronic elaboration which eludes our grasp in the course of its developments.

A diachronic and a synchronic perspective may strive toward mutual integration. The latter individuates structural links among all the elements of the text in a given phase (and, hence, ideally allows us to sort out, even from the unity of a manuscript which has been corrected at different times, the copresence of a number of texts); the former reconstructs the operations on the basis of shifts which, within one given phase of the text's structure, have led to the elaboration of a successive phase as a new structure. But since, in the elaboration of the text, structural forces act through the artistic consciousness of its author, any diachronic perspective must take into account the rejected alternatives, and even those which, though not documented and thus not definable, can hardly not have been experienced. What escapes variant criticism, and inevitably so, is not merely prelinguistic stages but the entropic margins of linguistic creation as well. This is far from denying that it still remains one of our most reliable tools for seizing upon the functioning, and the functionality, of textual elaboration, for it moves back far beyond the "definitive" form of the texts and allows us to grasp part of the dynamism which sustains and prepares their static character.

8. If the text is regarded as an image, two risks are avoided: that of identifying it with its material vehicle and that of locating it inescapably at the origin of the tradition's iter. It is only when thus cautioned that we can begin to deal with oral texts. In principle, the case of oral tradition ought not to fall outside the phenomenology outlined above; it is merely a matter of replacing transcriptions with memorizations, readings with recitations (or musical executions) and relative public reception. The minstrel, bard, singer, etc., has the same mediating function as a manuscript, and, just as scribes often allow themselves the liberty of reelaborating a text, so the singer may change it in terms of (presumed) appropriateness. The singer may also have knowledge of a number of versions of a text and mix them together; it is a mental *contaminatio* which then takes place.

Some modern scholars (Parry, Bowra, Lord, etc.), on the basis of investigation of oral epic still surviving in some traditional areas (for example in Yugoslavia), believed they could determine certain peculiarities of the oral tradition. These were the result of an incomplete memorization of a text and of the singers' aptitude for improvisation. Singers, in effect, would retain in memory the content and the fundamental parts of a narration, but on each occasion they would improvise the details and make full use of clichés (epic attributes, formulae, etc.). Hence, formulaic style and a multiplicity of variants would represent the constituent signs of oral tradition.

These field observations are of great interest, and they are incontrovertible. What was unwise, though, was their extension to other fields (from the Homeric poems to the *chansons de geste*), where the only documentation we possess is written documentation and where the tradition, as far back as we can go, tallies perfectly with the standards of textual traditions. As for the two principal peculiarities of oral style, one can confidently object that space for reelaboration is found no less frequently in other genres which are certainly not oral (which corresponds to a desire to render constantly new, and thus attractive, texts which might otherwise seem old-fashioned and out of date) and that formulaic style has been used, from classical times, even by the most literary of authors. Indeed, it is one of the constants of medieval "writing."

It must be recognized that specific formal properties for oral poetry do not exist, because the borderline between the facility which memorization would allow and the difficulty which a written transmission might require may well shift, for much will depend upon the abilities of a singer, the expectations of his public, etc. The only valid definition is a tautological one: it is possible to speak of the poetry of an oral tradition only when an oral tradition can be shown to be effectively at work. Now, for both the Homeric poems and the *chansons de geste*, we are (with but few exceptions) faced solely with a written tradition, and one which falls completely within the phenomenology of the written tradition. Whether these texts had a previous oral existence is not possible to determine, nor would our stating that they had serve to explain anything at all.

The situation is quite different for Spanish romances, for folk songs, and for other related productions which are epic or lyrical in character—for folk tales, etc. The tradition of these groups of works is undoubtedly an oral one; any transcriptions, whether ancient or modern, serve to fix only one of the many phases of a composition; they hardly ever affect its subsequent fortune. (They do not create, and still less do they consolidate, a tradition.) Folk tales may be neglected here, for they are independent of verbal or rhythmical structurings, and in consequence they are ecumenical. We are left with the romances, confined to Spanish-speaking areas, and with folk songs, whose linguistic transpositions, when they occur, set up new and autonomous structurings.

It is possible to collect numerous versions of these compositions (indeed, hundreds and hundreds of them), and their documentation may embrace many centuries. In general, one knows that, in the case of romances, the most productive period was the fifteenth century, and, for the Italian folk songs which can still be heard, it is possible to go back to the fifteenth century *(rispetti)* and to the sixteenth century (narrative and iterative songs). Obviously every text has its own story, long or short though it may be, and it is one that can be reconstructed sometimes more, sometimes less, easily. But it is the type of tradition involved (not the tonality or the content) which characterizes texts of this kind; it is the continual reelaboration to which they are subjected, thanks to usually anonymous interventions, in texts whose authors are not infrequently anonymous themselves.

With written literature, the tradition is the intermediary which links an initial phase (production of the text) and a final phase (its utilization). This mediation is subject to historical interferences, and these call for investigation. One will attempt to strip them away in the hope of arriving at the genuine product, i.e., the text. With oral literature, on the contrary, the tradition has the upper hand with respect both to the initial and to the final phase. Each innovating performance (which, of course, may be followed by passive, faithful performances) has an institutionalizing function. It outmaneuvers previous phases into nonbeing. Even when a single person did indeed compose the initial version of the text, the means were not available to keep alive his memory or that of his initial text, nor was there any desire to do so. The life of the text is to be found in its variations, says Menéndez Pidal, or, to put it perhaps better, every variation is a text. Production and utilization are practically synchronic.

Thus, from the point of view of oral or traditional communication as well, poetry is marked off from any other kind of textual transmission. Written texts contain a message, a semiotic structuring, which will be decodified within the framework of a particular semiotic system by anyone who makes use of it. The (unattainable) ideal for such decodification is the correct enucleation of its initial structuring, albeit within the new semiotic structure, for this new structure will be consubstantial with the interpretation. The tradition is an element of disturbance, though clearly it can be used historiographically because it is the outcome of intermediate systems. On the contrary, in oral poetry the new semiotic system is inserted into, and becomes part and parcel of, the basic structures; any distance between message and addressee is continually eliminated.

Certainly, modern philologists (first of all, Menéndez Pidal) have elaborated methods for determining the region and the epoch in which a composition was produced, with the aim of finding the most conservative of the surviving versions or, variant against variant, those which have the greatest probability of approaching the initial stage. But any reconstruction of an original is simply not possible. The reason does not lie, as might be thought, in the number and weight of the variants, i.e., in any entropic dispersion of the originating text. It is to be found instead in cohesion elements, because they are surreptitious. In short, it is due to every text's self-structuring and thus to its autonomy. Against the forces of dispersion (casual or locally motivated changes in the text), a reaction will exist within each new text in the form of a cohesion force, and this will bring the structuring elements to the fore or insert them *ex novo*.

This explains why every version has its own coherence, while internal references, motifs, and climaxes may belong to the first inventor or, equally, to any one of the reelaborators. The effects of the systolic-diastolic cycle (abbrevation-expansion) are manifold, for it contrasts, with no regularity of sequence, versions that concentrate on some dramatic or lyrical moment with others that expound premises and consequences.

Faced with cases like this, we may regard each version as an autonomous text (this is the perspective of the singer or singers and of their listeners) or embrace the totality of the versions in a single whole whose law is its variability.

The model for text perception is represented by the following figure.

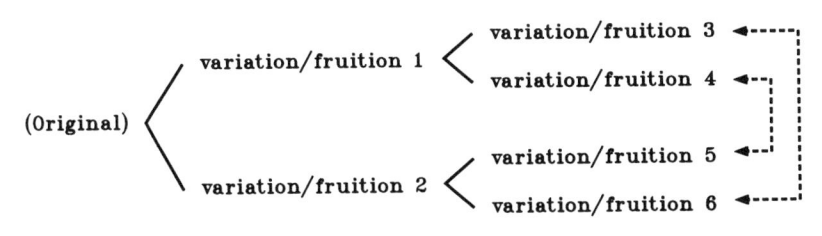

```
                          ┌─ variation/fruition 3 ◄─────┐
        ┌─ variation/fruition 1 ─┤                       │
        │                 └─ variation/fruition 4 ◄──┐   │
(Original) ┤                                          │   │
        │                 ┌─ variation/fruition 5 ◄──┘   │
        └─ variation/fruition 2 ─┤                       │
                          └─ variation/fruition 6 ◄─────┘
```

Dotted lines stand here for possible contaminations. Each performance constitutes an autonomous phenomenon, a text, in the consciousness of the participants (although they may well be able to recognize a theme and its variability). The position of the scholar is totally different, for he is engaged in collecting and comparing the largest possible number of the realizations effected. He will therefore see single executions as elements of a whole. The structural self-sufficiency of the single texts will, though, prevent him from reconstructing earlier evolutionary phases in any detail and will make it even more impossible for him to arrive at the original: the original is the immanent form which sustains the variants in their proliferation.

9. "In the most widely different cultures, there periodically arises the tendency to see the world as a text, while, as a consequence, knowledge of the world is made to equal the philological analysis of this text: its reading, understanding, and interpretation" (Lotman and Uspensky 1973, p. xiv). The climax of this descriptive invention was perhaps reached with Russian symbolism, for which the world presented itself as a hierarchy of texts dominated by one universal text, the reflection of a mythological conception of the world itself. This universal text finds its realization in "life texts" and "art texts": unity against plurality, where unity and plurality can be seen to be dominated by a general isomorphism or else as being in a generative relation (Minc 1976).

This metaphor of the world (of culture) as text has been revived recently, and the arguments are now more satisfactory. Research on the coherence of written texts authorizes us to describe as texts other products which call for similar coherence: a painting, for example. More broadly, any kind of communication registered within a given sign system may be called a text. "From this point of view we may speak of a ballet, of a play, of a military parade, and of all of the other sign systems for behavior as texts, in the same measure in which we apply this term to a text written in a natural language, to a poem or to a picture" (Lotman 1973, p. 61, n. 1).

If culture, according to modern perspectives, functions as a system of signs, it will be legitimate to consider as a text the complex of a given culture's expressions (whether they are literary or not). This, at least, holds good for those cultures which are primarily concerned with expression (like nineteenth-century realism), given that, for those more prevalently concerned with content (like European classicism), culture is regarded more as a collection of rules on the basis of which the single texts are produced. Thus, Lotman and Uspensky write: "To a culture directed toward expression that is founded on the notion of correct designation and, in particular, correct naming, the entire world can appear as a sort of text consisting of various kinds of signs, where content is predetermined and it is only necessary to know the language, that is, to know the relation between the elements of expression and content. In other words, cognition of the world is equivalent to philological analysis" (1971, Eng. trans., p. 217).

Foucault (1969) also inclines toward agreement with this vision of the world as text when he describes a historical-cultural block, or episteme, as a sum, almost an enormous archive, of utterances which can be referred to formation systems and linked by discourse relations. These relations, in a given episteme, afford discourse "the objects of which it can speak, or, rather, (since the image of an offer presupposes that objects are formed on the one hand and discourse on the other) they determine the bundle of relations which discourse must effect in order to be able to speak of these objects and of those, to be able to deal with them, name them, analyze them, classify them, explain them, etc." (p. 63).

This is an infinite overlaying of discourses which each person experiences in a different way and for which no one would be capable of fixing a "corpus" that would be in any way reliable. It is an overlapping, however, of which literary texts and the language itself provide concrete examples. With literary texts we find continual cross-reference from one to another, not merely by means of quotations, allusions, revivals, parodies but also through absorption of connotations. For each word, these will derive from the fact that it has been forged or diffused inside a particular genre of texts, always characterized ideologically. For the language, the tonal and ideological labeling of every word, normal syntagm, and expression is implicit, so much so that the language may be regarded as a "pluridiscoursive opinion of the world" (Bachtin 1934–35, p. 101).

Lotman is clearly well aware of the system/process dialectic, as is Foucault. But we should not lose sight of the fact that the close connection—the free and easy, to-and-fro movement—between system and process in a circumscribed activity like language, is light years away from any system-process relation that might be hypothesized for the totality of the culture, where processes are infinite and heterogeneous and the coherence of the system is more readily postulated than demonstrated.

And this is not all. Though it is true that the linguistic text refers us to a system, the *langue*, it does so thanks to the mediation of the use an addresser has made of it: the text is located between an addresser and an addressee, between two competences which recognize one another by means of textual performance of this kind. When, on the contrary, it is the world which is being regarded as a text, no communication process exists to which appeal can be made. We are obliged to refer back directly to the system for an indefinable number of processes. These do indeed communicate, but they only do so through yet other texts.

For this reason, and much more profitably, Lotman and Uspensky, as a rule, prefer the opposite perspective: from a representative historical text (called, in consequence, a "text of the culture"), it is possible to derive the cultural models of an epoch, and credence is accorded to the effort of the single text as it organizes the cultural elements it derives from reality in terms of relations presumed to be not improbably homologous with those of the world. In like manner, Bachtin saw the text as a "monad *sui generis,* which reflects in itself all of the texts (within the limits) of a given semantic sphere" (1959–61, p. 199). It is a perspective which lends itself more immediately to analysis, because it brings to the fore what is already known—the laws of whose coherence are at hand for analysis—and it removes the system which generates to the horizon (toward which one will always look but will never reach).

It is, however, worth the effort of meditating on the metaphor of the world as text. If the text is a virtuality by means of which we are able to glimpse aspects of the world, or of possible worlds, we may well find attractive the idea of organizing our knowledge of the world in such a way that it will form one large text (no longer a virtual text but an imaginative one). In like manner, our experience of the world—which is effected at least in part through the mediation of texts, whether written or oral—tends to transform knowledge of whatever kind into text, for only by way of verbalization does knowledge of any kind attain rationality. Full rationality, though, must be capable of measuring, and of controlling, the fact that it finds itself condemned to such logocentrism, and it must also be able to dominate the difference between objects or conditions whose nature is verbal and objects and conditions which have merely been expressed in words. Otherwise, what will escape us will be those very forces which are acting directly on reality, on the economy, on praxis, while we are contemplating in the texts, or as total textuality, the sublime interplay of the word.

References

Avalle, D'A. S.
    1972. *Principi di critica testuale.* Padua: Antenore.
Bachtin, M. M.
    1934–35. Slovo v romane. In *Voprosy literatury i estetiki.* Moscow: Chudožestvennaja literatura.
    1959–61. Problema teksta. *Voprosy literatury,* no. 10 (1976): pp. 122–51.
Bédier, J.
    1928. La tradition manuscrite du ‹Lai de l'Ombre›: Réflections sur l'art d'éditer les anciens textes. *Romania,* 54, pp. 161–96 and 321–56.
Bellemin-Noël, J.
    1972. *Le texte et l'avant-texte: Les brouillons d'un poème de Milosz.* Paris: Larousse.
Conte, M. E., ed.
    1977. *La linguistica testuale.* Milan: Feltrinelli.
Corti, M.
    1960. Note sui rapporti fra localizzazione dei manoscritti e ‹recensio›. In *Studi e problemi di critica testuale: Convegno di studi di filologia italiana nel centenario della Commissione per i testi di lingua (7–9 aprile 1960).* 1961. Bologna: Commissione per i testi di lingua. Pp. 85–91.

Curtius, E. R.
    1948. *Europäische Literatur und lateinisches Mittelalter*. 3d ed. 1961. Bern: Francke. (English translation. 1953. *European Literature and the Latin Middle Ages*. New York: Harper and Row.)

Dijk, T. A. van
    1977. *Text and Context: Explorations in the Semantics and Pragmatics of Discourse*. London: Longman.

Firpo, L.
    1960. Correzioni d'autore coatte. In *Studi e problemi di critica testuale: Convegno di studi di filologia italiana nel centenario della commissione per i testi di lingua (7–9 aprile 1960)*. 1961. Bologna: Commissione per i testi di lingua. Pp. 143–57.

Foucault, M.
    1969. *L'archéologie du savoir*. Paris: Gallimard.

Hjelmslev, L.
    1943. *Omkring sprogteoriens grundlaeggelse*. Copenhagen: Munksgaard. (English translation. 1962. *Prolegomena to a Theory of Language*. Madison: University of Wisconsin Press.)

Laufer, R.
    1972. *Introduction à la textologie: Vérification, établissement, édition des textes*. Paris: Larousse.

Lichačëv, D. S.
    1962. *Tekstologija: Na materiale russkoj literatury X–XVII vv*. Moscow: Akademija Nauk.

Lotman, Ju. M.
    1973. *Il problema del segno e del sistema segnico nella tipologia della cultura russa prima del XX secolo*, in Lotman and Uspenskij 1973, pp. 40–63.

Lotman, Ju. M., and Uspenskij, B. A.
    1971. O semiotičeskom mechanizme kul'tury. *Trudy po znakovym sisteman*, 5, pp. 144–76.
    1973. *Ricerche semiotiche: Nuove tendenze delle scienze umane nell'Urss*. Turin: Einaudi.

Maas, P.
    1927. *Textkritik*. Leipzig: Teubner.

Menéndez Pidal, R.
    1920–54. *Como vive un romance*. Madrid: Consejo Superior de Investigaciones Científicas.

Minc, Z. G.
    1976. Le concept de texte et l'esthétique symboliste. In Ju. M. Lotman and B. A. Uspenskij, eds., *Travaux sur les systèmes de signes: Ecole de Tartu. 1976*. Paris: PUF. Pp. 222–29.

Mortara Garavelli, B.
    1979. *Il filo del discorso*. Turin: Giappichelli.

Nencioni, G.
    1960. Filologia e lessicografia: A proposito della ‹variante›. In *Studi e problemi di critica testuale: Convegno di studi di filologia italiana nel centenario della Commissione per i testi di lingua (7–9 aprile 1960)*. 1961. Bologna: Commissione per i testi di lingua. Pp. 183–92.

Pasquali, G.
    1932. Edizione. In *Enciclopedia italiana di scienze, lettere ed arti*, vol. 13. Milan: Istituto Giovanni Treccani. Pp. 477–80.
    1934. *Storia della tradizione e critica del testo*. 2d ed. 1952. Florence: Le Monnier.

Petöfi, J. S., ed.
    1979. *Text vs. Sentence: Basic Questions of Text Linguistics*, 2 vols. Hamburg: Buske.
    1981. *Text vs. Sentence: Continued*. Hamburg: Buske.

Reynolds, L. D., and Wilson, N. G.
    1968. *Scribes and Scholars: A Guide to the Transmission of Greek and Latin Literature*. Oxford: Clarendon Press.

Ricoeur, P.
    1970. Qu'est-ce qu'un texte? In R. Bubner, K. Cramer, and R. Wiehl, eds., *Hermeneutik und Dialektik*. Tübingen: Mohr. Vol. 2, pp. 181–200.

Rizzo, S.
    1973. *Il lessico filologico degli Umanisti*. Rome: Edizioni di Storia e Letteratura.

Scherner, M.
    1984. *Sprache als Text: Ansätze zu einer sprachwissenschaftlich begrundeten Theorie des Textverstehens*. Tubingen: Niemeyer.

Schmidt, S. J.
    1973. *Texttheorie: Probleme einer Linguistik der sprachlichen Kommunikation*. Munich: Fink.

Segre, C.
    1979. *Semiotica filologica: Testo e modelli culturali*. Turin: Einaudi.
    1982. Strutturazione e destrutturazione nei Romances. In *Ecdotica e testi ispanici: Atti del Convegno Nazionale della Associazione Ispanisti Italiani; Verona 18, 19, 20 giugno 1981*. Verona. Pp. 9–24.

Timpanaro, S.
    1963. *La genesi del metodo del Lachmann*. Florence: Le Monnier.

Subject Index*

acoustic phenomena, see substance
acrostics, *45*, 75n, 165
actant, *171*, 229–30
action, see event; plan of a, 103
addressee, 3–4, 7, 9, 20n; see also reader
addresser, 3–4, 9, 20n, 119
alliteration, 50
anagram, 47–49, 165–67
analexis, 90, 112n
analysis of tale, see narratology
anaphore, 25
angle, dialogic, 105
anonymity, 6
antidiscourse, see hypodiscourse
antimodel, 135–36, 250, 252–54
archetype, 293–94; in textual criticism, *314–15*
argument, see theme
articulation, double, *47*, 75n
associative relations, see syntagm/paradigm
attribute, 169
auktoriale Erzählsituation, 14
authentication authority, 104
author, 5–6, 108–9; implied, 8–10, 20n–21n
autodiegetic narrator, see narrator
autograph, 314–18
avant-texte, 61–67, 317

behavioreme, *159*, 173
bilingualism of culture, 122

calligrams, 44–45
canzoniere, 73n
cardinal functions, see functions
carmina figurata, 44–46
catalisis, 92
cataphore, 25
character, 97–98, 102, 108–09, 120, *171–73*, 229–30
choice, stylistic, see style, stylistics
classeme, *26*
cliché, see *topoi*
clue, 91–92
coda, *95*, *113*n
code, 3–4, 72n, 116–17
coherence, discoursive and semantic, 30–31;

long term and short term, *30–31*; textual, 25, 27, 30–33, 71n, 175–76, 227–29, 304–05
combination, see selection/combination
commentative tense, see tense
communication, 143–44, 178–79; and history, 116–17; literary, 3–5, 8–9, 10–16, 27–28, 143–44, 217–19, 231–32, 302–05, 320; schema of, 3–4, 9, 20n; communication / information, 3–4
competence, linguistic, 21n, 308; narrative, 10; textual, 25, 308
complication, *95*, 113n
conative function, see function
connotation/denotation, 40–41, 80–81, 142–43, 274
constative, see utterance
contact, 3–4
content, invested, *102*; textual, 80–110, 121–22, 277–80, 304–07; see also expression / content
context, 3–4, 119–20, 173–78, 304–05, 307–08
coreference, 25–26, 161
co-text, *68*, 79n, 85
couplings, *271*
criticism, 194–98, 273–74; textual, 309–23; thematic, 287–89; variant, 62–67, 318; see also bilingualism of culture, text, typology of culture
culture and models, 122–25, 249–51; and history, 117–19; and texts, 125–30; see also bilingualism of culture, level, model, text, typology of culture

deictics, 10, 38, 174
denotation, see connotation / denotation
description, 102
deviation, stylistic, see style, stylistics
diagram, 44
dialogue, see angle, discourse, many-voicedness
dianoetic, meaning, 80, *110*n; nucleus, *81–82*; theme, 290–91
diasystem, *313–14*, 316–17
diegesis, 10, 223–25, 231
discourse, 142–43, 151–80, 302–03; direct / indirect, 10, 12–16, 18, 22n, 151–52; free indi-

---

*Numbers in italics refer to the pages where the terms are defined.

327

rect, 22n, *151–52;* of the Other, 178–79; narrativized, 18; alternative, see hypodiscourse; d. pattern, see pattern
dissemination, 47–48, 165
distance, 18
dynamic motifs, see motifs

écriture, 59, 121, 268
emendatio, 310–13
emotive function, see function
encyclopaedia, 4, 103, 118
enjambement, 53, 76n
*entrelacement, 112*n
episteme, 322
erzählte Zeit, 90
Erzählzeit, 90
etymon, spiritual, *56,* 273–74
evaluation, 95, 113n
event or action, 84, 88–101, *103,* 111n, 128, 170, 172–73, 226, 279, 289–90
expression / content, 39–40, 80; in literature 41–46
extradiegetic narrator, see narrator

fabula, 89–90, 167–73, 227–31, 279, 284, 292, 295–96
fantasy, 190
feedback, 4, 20n
fiction, 183–98
figure, rhetorical, 46, 159–60, 259–60; of the word 164; see also rhetoric
focalisation, 19, 108
folk songs, 319–21
form / substance, 39–40; in literature 41–46; simple f. *212*–13, 248
frame, 15, 31–32, 73n
free indirect discourse, see discourse
function, cardinal, 92; conative, *29, 157*–59; emotive or expressive, *29, 157*–59; ideative, *158;* interpersonal, *158;* linguistic, 29, 303; metalinguistic, 72, *157*–59; narrative, 90–101, 111n, 120, 168–73, 226–29, 286, 291–92; phatic, 15, 21n, 72n, *157*–59; poetic, 16, *29,* 61, *157*–59, 246–47, 271; representative, 157; referential, 72n, 157; textual, *158*

generalization, see scale of generalization
genotext, *111*n
genre, literary, 120–21, 136n, 146–47, 187, 199–221, 236–45, 247–49, 260–63, 309; see also system; text, types of
gesture, verbal, *212*
grapheme, 35, *74*n

hermeneutics, 7–8, 20n
heterodiegetic narrator, see narrator
hexagon of Blanché, 83–84
history, the text in, 116–36; see also communication
homodiegetic, narrator, see narrator

hypodiscourse, 142, 166, 171–72
hypostasis, *51–53*

Ich-Erzählsituation, 14
icon, 43, 75n
iconism, 43–49, 50, 53, 164
ideologeme, 59, 78n, *104–05, 119*
idiolect, 80, *110*n, 267
illocutive, see speech act
information, see communication
intertextuality, 67–71, 272
intonation, see supersegmental features
intradiegetic narrator, see narrator
isotopy, 26–27

langue / parole, 55–56, 77n, 152–57, 263–64, 302
*Leitmotiv, 111*n, 283–84, 285
levels of the text, 35–41, 93, 119–22, 167–73, 273; of meaning, 80–84; cultural, 119–22
linearity of language, 51, 162–63
linguistic, textual, *25–26,* 71n, 160–62, 304–09
literariness, 118, *136*n
locutive, see speech act

macrostructure, *110–11*n
macrotext, 31–33
manifestos, 251–52
many-voicedness, 67–68, 104–08, 271–72
memory, see synthesis in memory
mesostic, *165*
message, 3–4
metalanguage, 125, 129–30, *137*n, 162, 168–69; see also function
metalinguistic function, see function
metrics, 51–54
mimesis, *10,* 183–86, 224, 231, 238
mode of invention, 248–49
model, actantial or constitutional, 229–30, 278; cultural, 122–36, 322–23; narrative, 119–20, 171, 226–29, 279; of the world, 125–32, 134–35, 145, 188, 242, 248–56; see also system
moneme, 35, 79n, 54–55
mood, 17–18, 108–09
motif, 88–101, *111*n, 167–73, 212, 226, 277–97; dynamic, *91;* free, *91,* 169; static, *91,* 169; tied, *91,* 226
motifeme, *111*n, 286
motivation, 101–02, 169, 305
move, movement, 92–93
multivoiced, discourse, see many-voicedness

narratee, 21n
narration, 10–20, 84–110, 120–21, 223–34
narrative tense, see tense
narrativity, 223–34
narrativized discourse, see discourse
narratology, 94–104, 167–73, 225–34, 278–79, 306
narrator, 9–10, 14–16, 18–19, 104–09, 231–32,

SUBJECT INDEX

272; autodiegetic, 232–33; extradiegetic, 17, 233; heterodiegetic, 17, 232; homodiegetic, 17, 233; intradiegetic, 17, 233
narreme, 112n
nucleus, 92; narrative n. or nuclear sentence, 172, 226

onomatopoeia, 50-51, 164–65
orientation, 95, 113n

paradigm, paradigmatic, see syntagm / paradigm
paragram, see anagram
parallelism, 53–54
paraphrase or summary, 84–88, 91–92, 110–11n, 142–43, 163–64, 171–72, 225–26, 278–79, 305–06
parody, 79n, 106
parole, see *langue / parole*
pattern, discourse, 59, 177, 179; ideological, 59, 177
performative, utterance, see utterance
perlocutive, see speech act
person, 10–16, 109–10, 210–11
perspective, narrative, 17–20
phatic, function, see function
phenotext, 111n
philology, 309–23
phoneme, 75n
phonosymbolism, 49–50
plot, 88–101, 167–73, 230–31, 278–79, 286, 295–96
poetic, function, see function
poetics, 121, 136n, 148, 236–56
point of view, 16–20, 104, 106–09, 232–33
position, semantic, 105
pragmatics, 22n, 173–78
prolexis, 112n
psychocriticism, 288
punto distinto, 57, 270
purport, 40, 42

reader, 6–10, 119–20, 163–64, 313; implied, 8–10
reading, see reader
recensio, 310, 312, 314
recurrence, 25
referent, see context
referential, function, see function
register, linguistic, 58–59, 60, 266
reinforcement sign, 52
representability schemata, 88–89, 293–97
resolution, 95, 113n
reticence, 85–86
rhetoric, 236–37, 258–63, 282; see also figure
rhyme, 54
romances, 319–21

scale of generalization, 86–88, 93–94, 95–101, 169–70

selection / combination, 61, 271; see also syntagm / paradigm
selfcommunication, 16, 22n, 132–33
selfmodel, 122–25, 131
selfstructuring, 230
sema, semic, 37, 74n
semiological square, 83–84
semiology of communication, 74n; of signification, 74n
sender, see addresser
sense, 42
signification, 42
signifier / signified, 8, 24, 35–37, 39–40, 157, 162–67, 302; see also dianoetic meaning; levels of meaning
situation, see context
situationeme, 159
sociolect, 58–59, 266–67
sociolinguistic model, 78n
sociosphere, 121, 123
sonnet, 33–34, 52, 73n
speech act, 174–75; illocutive, 175; locutive, 175; perlocutive 175–77
Sprachstil, 264–65
static, motif, see motif
stemma, 310–12
stereotyping, 118, 148–49, 189, 281–83, 290–91, 295
Stilsprache, 264–65
stream of consciousness, 30, 72n
structure of the text, 33–35, 60; deep s. of the text, 87–88, 111n, 143, 305–07
style, stylistics, 54–61, 104–09, 145–46, 248, 258–74; style markers, 59, 266, 273; direct, free indirect, see discourse; stylistic choice, 57–58, 266, 269–71; deviation, 56–58, 265–66, 269–71; vector, 82, 110n
stylization, 106
stylometrics, 57–58, 269–70
subject, primary, 279–80; secondary, 279–80; of narration, 93–169
substance, acoustic, 49–51, 164–65; see also form / substance, phonosymbolism
summary, see paraphrase
suprasegmental features, 4, 20n
syntagm / paradigm, 60–61, 94, 133–35, 153–57, 227–28; see also selection / combination; syntagmatic relations, 77n; paradigmatic or associative relations, 77n, 263
synthesis in memory, 163
system, linguistic, 57–60, 145–46; modelling, 121, 126, 255–56; of literary genres, 209–10; system / structure, 34–35, 80

telestic, 165
tense, 10, 19–20, 210–11; close up and background, 19, 112n; narrative and commentative, 19; of narration and of discourse, 151–52
text, 24–71, 141–49, 300–23; types of, 12–20,

29–30, 120, 303–04; beginning and end of text, 30; literary, 10, 24–71; model of t. transcription and comprehension, 316–17; model of perception for oral texts, 321; t. of the culture, 126–30, 323; oral t., 318–21; see also coherence, competence, content, culture, levels of the text
Textlinguistik, see linguistic, textual
textology, 309
theater, 11–12, 30–31
theme, 144, 277–97; see also motif; theme / rheme, 25, 160
time, 90, 210
title, 72n
topic / comment, 25, 160
topoi, 281–83, 292–93, 295
tradition, oral, see text
trifunctionalism, 138n

tropoi, 259–61
true / false, 104
typology of culture, 131–36

universe, imaginary, 117
utterance, performative, 30, 72n, 174–76; constative, 174; utterance / utterance act, 9–10, 174, 268–69, 307–08, 315

variant criticism, see criticism
vectors, stylistic, see style, stylistics
verisimilitude, 185–86
voice, see person

word, key, 58, 164, 269; theme, 58, 164
worlds, possible, 103–04, 127, 188–90, 296

Zirkel im Verstehen, 265

Name Index

Acutis, C., 138 n
Afanasief, A. N., 227
Agosti, S., 73 n, 75 n, 166, 180
Agricola, E., 111 n
Alan of Lille, 135
Albert the Great, 190
Alberti, G., 242
Alcuin of York, 301
Alfieri, V., 66
Anceschi, L., 245
Antinucci, F., 175
Apollinaire, G., 44, 45, 164
Apuleius, 83
Ariosto, L., 12, 15, 65, 71, 76 n, 79 n, 98, 229, 241, 242, 300, 315, 316
Ariosto, O., 241
Aristophanes, 200, 260
Aristotle, 10, 21 n, 147, 184, 186, 187, 189, 199, 200, 201, 202, 203, 204, 211, 223, 224, 225, 228, 236, 237, 238, 239, 240, 241, 242, 243, 244, 247, 249, 256, 258, 261, 277
Asor Rosa, A., IX n
Auerbach, E., 253, 262, 274
Augustine (St.), 262
Austin, J. L., 174, 175, 180
Avalle, D'A. S., 78 n, 110 n, 113 n, 314, 315, 323
Averroes, 239

Bachelard, G., 288
Bachtin, M. M., 59, 67, 71 n, 28 n, 104, 105, 106, 108, 109, 114 n, 115 n, 119, 135, 138 n, 149, 271, 272, 274, 303, 322, 323
Bal, M., 22 n
Bally, Ch., 55, 57, 77 n, 151, 174, 180, 263, 264, 266, 274
Balzac, H. de, 285
Banfi, A.', 245
Banfield, A., 22 n
Barbusse, H., 56, 265
Barthes, R., 59, 74 n, 78 n, 91, 92, 100, 112 n, 136 n, 196, 197, 198, 268, 274
Basile, B., 78 n
Baudelaire, Ch., 47, 73 n, 114 n, 166
Baumgarten, A. G., 244
Beaugrande, R.-A. de, 71 n, 149
Beccaria, G. L., 76 n, 77 n, 165, 180
Becker, H., 213

Beckett, S., 12, 192
Bédier, J., 312, 313, 323
Behrens, I., 221
Bellemin-Noël, J., 78 n, 317, 323
Beller, M., 297
Belli, G. G., 13
Beltrami, P. G., 76 n
Ben Porat, Z., 79 n
Benveniste, E., VIII, 9, 21 n, 23 n, 151, 156, 157, 180
Benvenuto da Imola, 300
Bergson, H., 190
Bertinetto, P. M., 76 n, 77 n
Bierwisch, M., 110 n
Bigi, E., 79 n
Binni, W., 245
Biondi, G. P., 112 n
Blanchard, J. M., 114 n
Blanché, R., 83
Blanchot, M., 178, 197
Blankenburg, F. von, 245
Bloomfield, L., 74 n, 162, 304
Boccaccio, G., 23 n, 33, 75 n, 82, 96, 97, 98, 165
Bodkin, M., 293, 297
Boetius, 33
Boiardo, M. M., 241
Boileau, N., 199, 203, 243
Boklund, K. M., 138 n
Bono Giamboni, 5
Booth, W. C., 14, 20 n, 21 n, 234
Borges, J. L., 192, 193
Borghini, R., 241
Borrel, E., 277, 284, 297
Bourneuf, R., 21 n
Bowra, C. M., 318
Bray, R., 243, 256
Bremond, C., 95, 97, 98, 101, 112 n, 113 n, 225, 228, 234
Brik, O., 76 n
Bronzwaer, W. J. M., 23 n
Brooks, C., 19, 22 n
Browning, R., 12, 19
Brunetière, F., 208, 221
Bruni, F., 138 n
Bruno, G., 216
Brusoni, G., 112 n
Buffon, G.-L., 264, 274

331

Bühler, K., 157, 158, 180
Bulgarini, B., 241
Bunyan, J., 82
Burke, K., 88, 111 n, 172, 180
Buyssens, E., 74 n, 154, 155, 180
Buzzati, D., 23 n

Calderón de le Barca, P., 243
Callimachus, 201
Calvino, I., 71, 73 n
Camerana, G., 76 n
Camporesi, P., 138 n
Canziani, A., 73 n
Capponi, O., 241
Capriano, G. P., 240
Caretti, L., 79 n
Casadei, E., 72 n
Cascales, F., 240
Cassirer, E., 280
Castelvetro, L., 187, 198, 235, 240
Castravilla, A., 241
Cecco Angiolieri, 13
Cervantes Saavedra, M. de, 13, 16, 90, 98, 136, 196
Champigny, R., 234
Chapelain, J., 243
Charles d'Orléans, 41
Chateaux, D., 114 n
Chatman, S., 21 n, 74 n, 76 n, 112 n, 234, 274
Chomsky, N., 111 n, 143, 149
Christensen, A., 280, 291, 297
Christie, A., 17
Cicero, M. T., 32, 237, 240, 260, 315
Codax, M., 73 n
Cohn, D., 22 n
Coleridge, S. T., 26, 37, 49, 72 n
Coletti, V., 72 n
Collins, W., 19
Collodi, 71
Colonna, F., 44
Compagnon, A., 79 n
Conan Doyle, A., 17
Constant, B., 17
Conte, M. E., 71 n, 323
Contini, G., 77 n, 78 n, 79 n
Corbière, T., 49
Corneille, P., 243
Corti, M., 72 n, 73 n, 78 n, 135, 136 n, 138 n, 219, 221, 314, 323
Coulthard, R. M., 181
Courtés, J., 72 n, 79 n, 110 n, 152, 297
Cóveri, L., 71 n
Cremante, R., 76 n
Croce, B., 216, 217, 221, 244, 245, 256, 264
Croce, G. C., 136, 138 n
Crosman, I., 21 n
Culler, J., 100, 114 n
Cummings, E. E., IX, 43, 75 n
Curtius, E. R., 282, 283, 295, 297, 301, 324
Czerny-Krakau, Z., 290, 297

Dallas, E. S., 11, 210, 221
Daneš, F., 111 n, 180
Daniello, B., 203, 239, 241
D'Annunzio, G., 14, 67
Dante Alighieri, 5, 6, 32, 33, 51, 68, 73 n, 99, 185, 202, 203, 238, 240, 241, 262, 300
Darmesteter A., 260, 264, 274
Darwin, Ch. R., 208
Debenedetti, S., 79 n
Deimier, P. de, 241
Della Casa, G., 53, 73 n
Denores, G., 240, 242
De Robertis, G., 78 n
Devoto, G., 58, 77 n, 267, 275
Didymus the Alexandrian, 260
Di Fazio Alberti, M., 72 n
Di Francia, L., 20 n
Di Girolamo, C., 76 n
Dijk, T. A. van, 22 n, 71 n, 110 n, 111 n, 114 n, 228, 229, 234, 324
Diogenes Laertius, 6
Dionysius (pseudo), 135
Dionysius of Halicarnassus, 238, 240
Dionysius of Thrace, 201
Doležel, L., 22 n, 31, 73 n, 104, 111 n, 112 n, 114 n, 226, 228, 234, 271, 275, 286
Dombi Erzsébet, P., 75 n
Donatus, E., 261
Donne, J., IX, 38
Dorfman, E., 112 n
Dostoevsky, F., 105
Dressler, W. U., 71 n, 149 n, 161, 172, 180
Dryden, J., 203, 243
Du Bellay, J., 73 n
Dubois, J., 152
Duby, G., 138 n
Ducrot, O., 21 n, 110 n
Dufrenne, M., 20 n
Dumezil, 138 n
Dundes, A., 111 n, 225, 286

Easthope. A., 75 n
Eco, U., 20 n, 21 n, 74 n, 114 n
Eisenstein, S. M., 89
Eliot, Th. S., IX, 12, 13, 45, 48, 49, 64, 69, 78 n, 316
Eliot, V., 64, 78 n
Enkvist, N. E., 77 n, 275
Ennius, Q., 45, 183
Erlich, V., 136 n
Escarpit, R., 20 n
Euripides, 279
Even-Zohar, I., 138 n, 210, 221

Faccani, R., 21 n
Fantuzzi, M., 112 n
Faral, E., 237, 256
Faulkner, W., IX, 85
Ferrari Bravo, D., 137
Fetterley, J., 20 n

NAME INDEX

Fichte, J. G., 190
Fillmore, Ch., 88, 172
Firpo, L., 316, 324
Flaubert, G., 19, 77 n
Folena, G., 77 n
Folengo, T., 78 n
Folli, R., 79 n
Fónagy, I., 166, 180
Fontanier, P., 260
Formaggio, D., 20 n
Fornari, V., 241
Forster, E. M., IX, 85, 110 n
Foscolo, U., 34, 73 n
Foucault, M., 128, 179, 180, 322, 324
Frappier, J., 281
Freeman, D. C., 110 n
Frenzel, E., 284, 287, 291, 297
Freud, S., 178, 265
Friedman, N., 14, 21 n, 22 n
Frye, N., 110 n, 211, 212, 221, 248, 249, 256, 277, 278, 293, 294, 297
Fubini, M., 217, 221

Gadamer, H. G., 20 n
Gadda, C. E., 78 n
Galanter, E., 114 n
Gallavotti, C., 236, 256
Garavelli Mortara, B., 22 n, 324
García Berrio, A., 113 n
Gardin, J.-C., 162, 180
Garvey, J., 114 n
Garza-Cuarón, B., 74 n
Gautier d'Arras, 98
Gautier de Châtillon, 98
Genette, G., 17, 18, 19, 22 n, 75 n, 79 n, 109, 112 n, 231, 232, 234, 260
Geninasca, J., 73 n
Genot, G., 71 n, 73 n, 76 n, 113 n
Geoffroi de Vinsauf, 261, 262
Ghelderode, M. de, 285
Giacalone Ramat, A., 137 n
Giacomo, M., 152
Gilbert, A. H., 79 n
Giraldi Cintio, 241, 242
Goethe, J. W. von, 147, 190, 204, 205, 207, 221, 264, 275, 277
Golding, A., 70
Goldmann, L., 117, 136 n
Góngora, L. de, 243
Gorni, G., 71 n
Gottsched, J. Ch., 243
Granger, G. G., 275
Gravina, G. V., 216
Gregory, M. J., 275
Greimas, A. J., 26, 41, 72 n, 74 n, 79 n, 83, 94, 102, 103, 110 n, 152, 171, 180, 228, 230, 234, 278, 297
Grimm, J., 213
Guarini, B., 203, 242
Guastavini, G., 242

333

Gühlich, E., 20 n, 221
Guiraud, P., 57, 76 n, 77 n, 269, 275
Gullí Pugliatti, P., see Pugliatti, P.
Gutenberg, J., 218

Halle, M., 136 n
Halliday, M. A. K., 158, 181
Hambuechen Potter, J., 73 n
Hammett, D., 19
Hamon, Ph., 72 n, 114 n
Harris, Z. S., 25, 71 n, 161, 162, 181, 304
Hatzfeld, H., 275
Hegel, G. W. F., 204, 205, 206, 221, 244
Heidegger, M., 178
Heinsius, D., 240, 243
Heintz, J., 114 n
Helbo, A., 78 n
Helm, J., 113 n
Hemingway, H., 19
Hempfer, K. W., 72 n, 136 n, 149, 221
Hendricks, W. O., 111 n, 169, 181, 225, 235
Herbert, G., 44
Hermannus Alemannus, 239
Hernadi, P., 214, 215, 221
Herrnstein Smith, B., 72 n
Hintikka, J. K., 114 n
Hirsch, E. D., 20 n
Hiz, H., 162
Hjelmslev, L., VIII, 25, 37, 39, 40, 41, 42, 54, 74 n, 80, 85, 160, 219, 273, 302, 304, 324
Hoek, L. H., 72 n
Holenstein, E., 20 n
Homer, 186, 200, 223, 233, 237
Honorius of Autun, 135
Honzl, J., 73 n
Hopkins, G. M., 53
Horace, 183, 185, 201, 202, 203, 228, 236, 237, 239, 240, 243, 260
Hudson, R. A., 78 n
Hugo, V., 216, 239
Humbert de Romans, 135
Humboldt, W. von, 150, 264
Husserl, E., 36

Ingarden, R., 36, 72 n, 74 n, 273
Ingegneri, A., 242
Iser, W., 21 n
Ivanov, V. V., 71 n, 136 n, 137 n, 138 n, 250, 256

Jacques de Vitry, 135
Jakobson, R., VIII, 3, 11, 20 n, 21 n, 44, 60, 61, 72 n, 73 n, 75 n, 77 n, 78 n, 137 n, 157, 158, 181, 210, 221, 247, 256, 271, 275
James, H., 16, 17, 19, 22 n
Jauss, H. R., 20 n, 218, 222
Jean Paul (J. P. F. Richter) 210, 222
Johansen, S., 74 n
Johnson, A. L., 75 n
Jolles, A., 138 n, 212, 213, 214, 222, 248, 257

Joyce, J., IX, 66, 71, 72 n, 79 n
Jung, C. G., 293, 297

Kafka, F., 191, 192
Kant, I., 125, 244
Keats, J., IX, 50, 81
Kellogg, R., 22 n, 292, 298
Kemeny, T., IX, 137
Kerbrat-Orecchioni, C., 74 n
Kinneavy, J. L., 158, 181
Kittay, J., 114 n
Klinkenberg, J. M., 74 n
Knights, L. Ch., 288, 297
Koch, W. A., 159
Koselleck, R., 235
Kristeva, J., 75 n, 78 n, 79 n, 111 n
Krysinski, W., 21 n
Kuentz, P., 275

Labov, W., 95, 113 n, 228, 235
Lacan, J., 178, 181, 197
Lachmann, K., 311, 312
La Harpe, J.-F. de, 262
La Mesnardière, J. de, 243
Lämmert, E., 22 n
Laufer, R., 309, 324
Leech, G. N., 75 n
Leeman, D., 111 n
Le Hir, Y., 275
Leibniz, G. W., 244
Leopardi, G., 78 n, 216, 266, 316
Leskov, N. S., 105
Lévi-Strauss, C., 94, 103, 112 n, 225, 227
Levin, H., 280, 298
Levin, J. I., 21 n
Levin, S. R., 76 n, 271, 275
Levy, J., 78 n
Lewis, M. J., 16
Liborio, M., 114 n
Lichačëv, D. S., 313, 324
Lintvelt, J., 22 n
Lippi (fra Filippo), 47, 166
Livy, T., 33
Lombardelli, O., 242
Lombardi, B., 239
London, J., 14
Longhi, S., 73 n
Lord, A. B., 318
Lotman, Ju.-M., 16, 21 n, 73 n, 77 n, 78 n, 99, 114 n, 112, 124, 128, 130, 133, 135, 137 n, 138 n, 150, 173, 226, 235, 253, 255, 257, 321, 322, 324
Lucianus of Samosata, 71
Lucretius, 166
Luzán, I. de, 203, 243

Maas, P., 314, 324
Machado, A., 88
Macrobius, 259

Magalaner, M., 79 n
Maggi, V., 239
Malatesta, G., 242
Mallarmé, S., 78 n, 287
Manuel, don Juan, 6
Manuzio, A., 239
Manzoni, A., 65, 78 n, 79 n, 98, 315
Maranda, P., 225
Marco Polo, 71
Marghescou, M., 136 n
Marie de France, 98
Marino, G. B., 243
Marouzeau, J., 55, 56, 77 n, 264
Martin, R., 111 n
Martinet, A., 20 n, 75 n, 76 n
Marzaduri, M., 21 n
Matejka, L., 73 n, 114 n
Mathesius, V., 25, 72 n, 160, 181
Matthew Prior, 13
Maud, R., 78 n
Maupassant, G. de, 83
Mauron, Ch., 288, 298
Mauss, M., 118
Mauvillon, E. de, 262, 275
Mazzoni, J., 241
McCawley, J. D., 175
McHale, B., 22 n
Meddemmen, J., IX
Medvedev, P. N., 78 n
Meletinsky, E. M., 88, 102, 111 n, 114 n, 137 n, 225, 235
Menander, 260
Meneghetti, M. L., 138 n
Menéndez Pidal, R., 320, 324
Mengaldo, P. V., 237, 257
Meredith, G., 32
Meyer, H., 79 n
Miceli, S., 136 n
Mignolo, W., 21 n, 72 n
Milic, L. T., 275
Miller, G. A., 114 n
Miller, N., 72 n
Milton, J., IX, 12, 68, 278
Minc, Z. G., 73 n, 321, 324
Minturno, A., 203, 240
Molière, 203, 285
Montale, E., 80, 166
Morris, Ch. W., 173, 181
Mounin, G., 74 n
Mukařovský, J., 212
Müller, G., 22 n
Muzio, G., 240

Nelson, L., 282
Nencioni, G., 314, 324
Neubert, A., 22 n
Nietzsche, F., 178
Novalis, 263
Novellino, 98, 300

NAME INDEX 335

Opitz, M., 243
Orelli, G., 34
Orlando, F., 73 n, 298
O'Toole, L. M., 112 n
Ouellet, R., 21 n
Ovid, 69, 70, 99

Pagnini, M., 21 n, 72 n, 73 n, 74 n, 76 n, 136 n
Pajano, R., 245, 257
Panofsky, E., 279, 280, 281, 283, 292, 298
Papini, G. A., 78 n
Parisi, D., 175
Parodi, E. G., 54, 77 n
Parret, H., 181
Parry, H., 283, 284, 298
Parry, M., 318
Pascoli, G., 51, 67, 76 n, 165
Pasquali, G., 313, 314, 324
Patrizi, F., 240, 242
Pavel, Th. G., 114 n
Pazzaglia, M., 76 n
Pêcheux, M., 78 n, 177, 181
Péguy, Ch., 56, 265
Peirce, Ch. S., 44, 75 n, 149, 150
Pellegrino, C., 242
Pelletier, J., 241
Perloff, M., 79 n
Pessoa, F., 73 n
Petersen, J., 204, 222
Petöfi, J. S., 71 n, 79 n, 304, 325
Petrarch, F., 32, 73 n, 78 n, 300, 315
Petsch, R., 286
Phaedrus, 301
Philippe, Ch. L., 56, 265
Piaget, J., 35, 73 n
Picchio Simonelli, M., 76 n
Piccolomini, A., 239
Pigna, G. B., 241
Pike, K. L., 89, 111 n, 159, 160, 172, 173, 181, 286
Pinciano, A., 240
Pindar, 201, 203, 213
Pioletti, A., 138 n
Pirandello, L., 23 n, 67
Plato, 49, 184, 189, 199, 202, 223, 238, 240, 301
Plautus, M. A., 260, 285
Poe, E. A., 50
Politianus, 166
Polti, G., 284, 298
Pope, K., IX, 69–70
Popovič, A., 79 n
Portis Winner, I., 136 n
Pouillon, J., 235
Poulet, G., 287
Pound, E., 64
Pozzi, G., 75 n, 136 n
Pratt, M. L., 110 n
Prevignano, C., 22 n, 79 n, 136 n, 137 n
Pribram, K. H., 114 n

Prieto, L. J., 74 n
Prince, G., 21 n, 113 n, 235
Priscian, 185, 260
Prodicus of Ceo, 183
Propp, V. Ja., 92, 93, 94, 95, 96, 98, 101, 112 n, 113 n, 114 n, 168, 169, 170, 171, 181, 225, 226, 227, 228, 230, 235, 286, 291, 292, 298
Proust, M., 78 n, 226, 288
Psellus, 83
Pugliatti, P., 72 n, 79 n
Puškin, A. S., 129

Quilis, A., 76 n
Quintilian, 183, 185, 198, 237, 240, 282, 300

Rabanus Maurus, 45, 301
Rabelais, F., 44, 269
Racine, J., 265
Raible, W., 20 n, 221
Ransom, D. C., 300
Rapin, R., 243
Rastier, F., 72 n, 102, 114 n
Reformatskij, A. A., 112 n
Reynolds, L. D., 314, 324
Rhetorica ad Herennium, 185
Riccoboni, A., 239
Richard, J. P., 287, 288, 298
Ricoeur, P., 20 n, 325
Riffaterre, M., 77 n, 114 n, 271, 275
Rizzo, S., 302, 325
Robortello, F., 239
Romano, M., 112 n
Romberg, B., 21 n
Ronsard, P. de, 240
Rosiello, L., 77 n
Ross, J. R., 175
Rossi, A., 113 n
Rossi, L. E., 222
Rossi, P., 136 n
Rossi-Doria, G., 284, 298
Rostagni, A., 237, 257
Rousset, J., 21 n
Rüdiger, H., 222
Ruffinatto, A., 98, 113 n
Rustico di Filippo, 13
Ruttkowski, W. V., 222
Ruzzante, 12

Sacchetti, F., 6
Sade, D.-A.-F. de, 99
Said, E. W., 72 n
Salvestroni, S., 137 n
Salviati, L., 239, 242
Sannazzaro, J., 33
Santagata, M., 73 n
Sassetti, F., 241
Sasso, G., 75 n
Saussure, F. de, VIII, 35, 37, 39, 47, 55, 60,

74 n, 77 n, 145, 152, 153, 154, 155, 156, 162, 165, 166, 181, 219, 263, 266, 275, 302
Scaliger, G. C., 240, 241, 243
Ščeglov, J. K., 110 n, 290, 298
Schelling, F. W. J. von, 204, 216, 244
Scherner, M., 325
Schiller, F., 204, 221
Schlegel, A. W. von, 204
Schlegel, F. von, 244, 245
Schleiermacher, F. E. D., 187
Schmidt, S. J., 20 n, 325
Scholes, R., 32 n, 235, 292, 298
Schossig, A., 213
Schuchardt, H., 264
Scudéry, M. de, 208
Searle, J. R., 175, 181
Sebeok, T. A., IX, 20 n, 72 n, 136 n, 275
Segal, D. M., 227
Segre, C., 20 n, 21 n, 22 n, 71 n, 73 n, 76 n, 78 n, 79 n, 110 n, 112 n, 113 n, 136 n, 150, 163, 181, 227, 235, 255, 256, 257, 273, 276, 293, 298, 313, 317, 325
Serpieri, A., 73 n
Shakespeare, W., IX, 45, 46, 69, 70, 71, 73 n, 74 n, 289
Shelley, P. B., 12
Sibilet, T., 241
Sidney, P., 32, 240
Simonin-Grumbach, J., 181
Sinclair, J. McH., 181
Sinicropi, G., 110 n
Šklovsky, V. B., 73 n, 87, 89, 90, 110 n, 298
Smollet, T., 19
Sophocles, 200
Sørensen, H., 41, 74 n
Souriau, E., 230, 235
Spencer, J., 49, 275
Spenser, E., 49
Sperber, D., 265, 286
Speroni, S., 242
Spitzer, L., 55, 56, 57, 60, 77 n, 265, 266, 269, 270, 276
Staiger, E., 207, 257
Stammerjohann, H., 22
Stanzel, F. K., 14, 21 n
Starobinski, J., 75 n, 155, 165, 181, 287
Stegagno Picchio, L., 138 n
Stempel, W. D., 235 n
Stender-Petersen, A., 214, 222
Stendhal, 17
Sterne, L., 90
Stevenson, R. L., IX, 90–91
Stoppard, T., 71
Strada-Janovič, C., 73 n
Suleiman, S. R., 21 n
Svevo, I., 226
Szondi, P., 20 n

Tamir, N., 21 n
Tasso, T., 33, 65, 203, 240, 241, 242
Tavani, G., 76 n
Tennyson, A. L., 46
Terracini, B., 57, 58, 77 n, 150, 270, 275
Thackeray, W. M., 82
Theophrastus, 258
Thomas, D., IX, 47, 62, 63, 64, 75 n, 78 n
Thompson, S., 79 n, 285, 298
Timpanaro, S., 325
Tindall, W. Y., 63, 78 n
Titunik, I. R., 73 n
Todorov, T., 19, 22 n, 76 n, 78 n, 96, 97, 101, 111 n, 112 n, 113 n, 169, 225, 232, 235, 246, 257
Tolstoy, L., 87, 105
Tomashevsky, B. V., 76 n, 89, 91, 92, 93, 111 n, 112 n, 167, 168, 169, 181, 226, 235, 286, 309
Trabant, J., 42, 74 n
Trissino, G. G., 239, 240, 241
Trousson, R., 280, 284, 285, 298
Turolla, E., 79 n
Tynjanov, Ju. N., 76 n, 119, 136 n, 209, 210, 220, 222, 245, 250

Uguccione da Pisa, 5
Ullmann, S., 75 n, 276
Ungaretti, G., 32, 76 n
Uspensky, B. A., 21 n, 73 n, 108, 115 n, 116, 122, 130, 136 n, 137 n, 138 n, 150, 321, 322, 324

Vachek, J., 72 n
Vaihinger, H., 190
Vaina, L., 114 n
Valesio, P., 73 n, 76 n
Valla, L., 239
Vasari, G., 309, 315
Vauquelin de la Freshaye, J., 240
Vega Carpio, L. de, 98, 239, 241, 243
Veit, W., 298
Verga, G., 14
Veselouvskij, A. N., 88, 111 n, 113 n, 225, 286, 298
Vettori, P., 186, 239
Vico, G. B., 203, 204, 222, 244
Vida, M. G., 239
Viehweger, D., 111 n
Viëtor, W., 207
Vinogradov, V. V., 245, 257
Viperano, G. A., 240
Virgil, 60, 67, 68, 99, 183, 202, 237, 248, 261
Volkov, R. M., 285, 299
Vološinov, V. N., 78 n
Volpe, S., 22 n
Vossius, G. J., 240
Vossler, K., 55, 56, 264, 265
Vygotskij, L. S., 16

Waletzky, J., 95, 113 n, 228, 235
Warren, A., 222
Warren, R. P., 19, 22 n

NAME INDEX

Wartburg, W. von, 277, 283, 299
Waugh, L. R., 75 n
Weber, J. P., 288, 299
Webster, J., 69
Weinberg, B., 242, 257
Weinrich, H., 19, 22 n, 23 n, 112 n
Weisstein, U., 278, 299
Wellek, R., 222
Wiegmann, H., 257
Wienold, G., 79 n
William of Moerbeke, 239
Wilson, N. G., 314, 325
Winner, T. G., 136 n
Winter, W., 266, 275
Wright, G. H. von, 102, 114 n, 228
Wunderli, P., 75 n

Wunderlich, D., 20 n, 174, 182

Xenophon, 183

Yeats, W. B., IX, 64

Zacchi, R., 72 n
Ziolkovski, Th., 299
Žirmunskij, V., 76 n
Zola, E., 213
Zólkiewsky, S., 136 n
Žolkovskij, A. K., 110 n, 290
Zoran, G., 112 n
Zumthor, P., 41, 74 n, 75 n, 78 n, 281, 295, 299, 300